Persons, Roles, and Minds

Persons, Roles, and Minds

IDENTITY IN *PEONY PAVILION*
AND *PEACH BLOSSOM FAN*

Tina Lu

STANFORD UNIVERSITY PRESS
STANFORD, CALIFORNIA 2001

Stanford University Press
Stanford, California

© 2001 by the Board of Trustees of the
Leland Stanford Junior University

Printed in the United States of America
On acid-free, archival-quality paper

Library of Congress Cataloging-in-Publication Data
Lu, Tina.
    Persons, roles, and minds : identity in peony pavilion and peach blossom fan / Tina Lu.
      p. cm.
    Includes bibliographical references and index.
    ISBN 0-8047-3711-8 (alk. paper)—
    ISBN 0-8047-4202-2 (pb : alk. paper)
      1. Tang, Xianzu, 1550–1616. Mu dan ting. 2. Kong, Shangren, 1648–1718. Tao hua shan. I. Title.
PL2695.M8 L83 2001
    895.1'24609—dc21   00-054778

Original Printing 2001

Last figure below indicates year of this printing:
10 09 08 07 06 05 04 03 02 01

Typeset by BookMatters in 11 point Adobe Garamond

To Stuart

Contents

Acknowledgments	ix
Prologue	1
PART ONE: *MUDAN TING*	
Introduction to Mudan ting	19
1. The Girl's Portrait	28
2. The Lover's Dream	63
3. The Emperor's Promise	97
PART TWO: *TAOHUA SHAN*	
Introduction to Taohua shan	145
4. The Prostitute's Fan	160
5. The Actor's Stage	199
6. The Emperor's Throne	239
Epilogue: The Spider and the Snake	289
Notes	319
Bibliography	339
Index	345

Acknowledgments

I owe my first thanks to Tang Xianzu and Kong Shangren. Spending a few years of my life thinking about these two plays has been an enormous pleasure and a great privilege.

For insightful questions asked at talks I gave at Columbia University and the University of Pennsylvania, I thank C. T. Hsia, David Wang, Paul Goldin, and Minmin Liang. Haun Saussy and Shang Wei have been unstinting in their encouragement. I have felt honored by the support of Cyril Birch and Stephen West, both of whom offered valuable commentary on the manuscript. Wai-yee Li has been a model of warmth and generosity, and I am grateful for her friendship. For hours of conversation and advice about a life in the academy, I thank David Schaberg and Michael Puett.

At the University of Pennsylvania, David Silverman most graciously offered me a year of leave before the beginning of my job, allowing me precious time to work in relative leisure. Nancy Steinhardt, Paul Goldin, and Victor Mair have been generous friends, colleagues, and teammates. I have also considered myself very privileged to count as colleagues the faculty and graduate students associated with the Center for East Asian Studies.

In my first year of graduate school, Judith Zeitlin introduced me to Ming and Qing literature and has continued to stimulate and challenge me ever since. Marc Shell has posed untold numbers of challenging questions and has always been an example to me of brilliant and exciting scholarship. I am grateful to Patrick Hanan for generously reading an early draft of the first half, for graciously answering last minute questions, and for gently trying to curb theoretical excesses. To Stephen Owen, my friend and my teacher for more than a decade, thanks hardly seem sufficient. But I will try to requite him by giving to my own students the same unconditional support and joy in literature he has given me.

I have written this book while in residence at two nurturing university communities. For six years, Sandra Naddaff and Leigh Hafrey, the Masters of Mather House at Harvard College, provided me with one of the most pleasant environments imaginable. And I thank David and Ann Brownlee, Faculty Masters of Harnwell College House at the University of Pennsylvania, for their friendship, support, and advice—and for giving me a sense of home at Penn.

Matthew Sommer went over the manuscript carefully, enriching it at many points with his mastery of Chinese legal history. At very short notice, Victor Mair read the manuscript and gave helpful critiques. At even shorter notice, Maris Boyd Gillette pored through the manuscript and offered a number of invaluable suggestions. At the last minute, Wai-yee Li combed through my translations, saving me from many an embarrassing error. I am enormously grateful to all of them for their help. All errors that remain are my own.

Finally, I thank my parents for all their help and support to me over the years. I regard my friendship with Eileen Chow as a great and rare blessing, and yet at the same time so central to my life it is impossible to imagine myself without her. Threads of conversations with her mark virtually every page that follows. Stuart Semmel has lived with this work at every stage of its development: from notes that were lost, to outlines that were thrown out, to countless messy drafts, to its state now. At every stage, he was my stay, as well as my best reader, sometime copy editor, and emergency computer paramedic. A book largely on marriage, and on the possibility of knowing another, ought to have as its ground Stuart, who with his calm and grace is truly more precious than rubies.

T.L.

Persons, Roles, and Minds

Prologue

One of the stories in Pu Songling's seventeenth-century collection of tales, *Liaozhai zhiyi*, tells of a humble fisherman named Xu. Each night, before he began fishing in the river, Xu had the habit of pouring a libation of wine into the earth to appease thirsty spirits who had drowned. One evening, he was joined by a young man, to whom he hospitably offered a drink. Even though Xu was normally a very successful fisherman, that night he had no luck until the young man went downstream to drive the fish back, whereupon Xu was able to catch his fill of big fish. Xu warmly thanked his new friend, who introduced himself as Wang Liulang and proposed that they make a habit of meeting in the evenings.

After half a year of this, one night Wang Liulang told him he would no longer be coming around. Xu asked him why. Wang Liulang hemmed and hawed and finally explained that he was the ghost of a man who had drunkenly fallen into the river and drowned. Tomorrow was destined to be his long-awaited day of rebirth. At first Xu was frightened to be in the company of a ghost, but the two had been such good friends for so long that Xu's fear was only fleeting, and instead he offered Wang Liulang a toast, recognizing that his friend's rebirth was an occasion both to be celebrated and mourned.

Wang Liulang then explained how he would come to be reincarnated: the next day at noon, a woman crossing the river would drown, and he would take her place among the living. When daylight came, the two friends parted in tears.

Of course, Xu spent the next morning watching the river vigilantly for any unusual signs. Sure enough, at noon, a woman holding a baby appeared. When she reached the river, she slipped. Thrown onto the riverbank, the baby kicked and cried. As Xu watched, the woman struggled in the water. He thought about trying to save her, but remembering that through her death his friend Liulang would be resurrected, he stopped himself, not wanting to stand in the way of his friend's rebirth. Eventually the woman was able to catch hold of the bank and heave herself up. She rested a moment on the bank, and then carrying her baby, continued on her way. Xu wondered why his friend's predictions had not come to pass.

That night Wang Liulang turned up again. Xu asked him what had happened. Wang Liulang explained that he had seen the woman carrying the baby and felt sorry for them. In taking her place, he had realized, he would have destroyed two lives, and so he left them alone. Liulang sighed, since he didn't know when his next chance to be reincarnated would be. Once again the two friends began their nightly get-togethers.

Some evenings later, Wang Liulang once again bid Xu goodbye. The Lord of Heaven had heard of his act of compassion and as reward was granting him an official position as a minor deity. The story goes on to describe how Xu makes a long journey to a distant village temple to see his friend one last time. After Xu's return, he and his family enjoyed what neighbors regarded as mysterious good fortune.

Wang Liulang's story makes direct allusion to one of the most famous passages from Mencius, where the Warring States philosopher most succinctly describes the compassion at the heart of human nature. Mencius explains his position: "When I say that all people cannot bear the sufferings of others, what I mean is this: now when people see a baby suddenly about to fall into a well, they all feel a sense of fear and pity."[1] In the Chinese tradition, a baby helpless on a riverbank, spared through someone's compassion, cannot help but invoke this passage from Mencius. And both Xu and Wang Liulang make the allusion explicit. In calling his friend a "person of fellow-feeling" (*renren*), Xu assigns him one of the central Confucian virtues. When Wang

Liulang describes his own compassion towards the baby, he uses the same unusual term, with its unmistakable provenance—*ceyin*—that Mencius does.

Mencius makes a point of defining this kind of compassion as having nothing whatsoever to do with self-interest: a person does not want to save the child crawling towards the well with the goal of becoming closer to his parents, or of winning repute, or even of stopping the unpleasant sound of the baby's crying. Instead, a person is motivated by a spontaneous sense of fellow-feeling. Our hero Wang Liulang seems to prove his own disinterestedness by going Mencius's imaginary spectator one better. To Mencius, it is enough that a person does not stand to gain from saving the child. But instead of standing to gain, Wang Liulang actually stands to lose his life as a human being.

Wang Liulang makes what some might consider the greatest possible sacrifice—giving up his own human life to save that of the child. As he makes the decision to spare mother and child, he has no idea he will be rewarded with something even better, a sinecure as a god (if he did, his action could not be considered *ceyin*). Instead, Wang Liulang thinks that by saving the baby's mother he has put off the day of his rebirth indefinitely.

Mencius's formulation of human nature appears to be a straightforward description, but in fact he makes the conscious decision to exclude some people from the category of human. He begins with what appears to be a categorical description of human nature. But then he must account for the obvious objection—that some people are so depraved that they actually could stand by and watch a baby drown.

In discussing this matter in English, I am contrasting two terms: the biological human and the moral person. Mencius uses the single word *ren*, human. Yet he makes it very clear that some distinction is to be made between those who are morally human and those who—even though they function in society and are regarded as people by others—are not really human in some fundamental, internal sense. Right after his description of a person's reaction on seeing a baby crawling towards a well, Mencius goes on to say: "From this perspective, lacking the feeling of pity, one is not human; lacking a sense of shame, one is not human; lacking a sense of deference, one is not human; lacking a sense of right and wrong, one is not human."[2] In other words, one can argue that all people feel compassion when they see a baby about to drown, because those who don't feel compassion by definition do not count as people.

Almost two millennia later, Pu Songling takes Mencius's version of human nature—part descriptive and part prescriptive—and stands it on its head. Mencius tells us that a person who does not feel compassion at the sight of a baby about to fall into a well should not be considered properly human. If there are people who are biologically human but not morally so, then it stands to reason that exact counterparts to those people might exist who are morally human but not biologically so. How ought those beings to be regarded? How are we to classify someone who isn't human but who feels and acts on compassion, saving that baby and its mother? How can we square Wang Liulang's claim to personhood with our knowledge of his ghostliness?

This book on personal identity begins with a very short story whose whole focus is our understanding of what it is to be a human being. What is the place of a moral subject like Wang Liulang, who is decidedly not a human mortal? Throughout this book, I am concerned with Mencius's original question—namely what it is to be a human being—and with its inevitable corollary—what it is to be any specific, individual human being.

If in fact we decide that Wang Liulang should be regarded as a person, then what should his relation be with regard to other people? Obviously, he can participate fully in the bonds of friendship—one of the most important of the bonds that tie together the human community; the whole story, after all, is told from the perspective of Xu, the humble fisherman who becomes his devoted friend. But imagine for a moment the story if Wang Liulang had befriended a young woman instead of Xu. Could Wang Liulang have married the woman? Could they have had children? Would those children be human like their father or non-human like their mother? These are questions Pu Songling—and other writers concerned with the marvelous and the strange—address at length elsewhere.

This book deals with the problem of personal identity, focusing on two of the most important texts in the Chinese dramatic tradition: the romantic comedy *Mudan ting* (*Peony Pavilion*) by Tang Xianzu and the historical drama *Taohua shan* (*Peach Blossom Fan*) by Kong Shangren. *Mudan ting*'s story of two lovers who stake their all on their relationship was a popular success that changed forever the Chinese romance. Every romantic novel and play in the tradition after it bears its touch. A century later, in relating the fall of the Ming dynasty and the collapse of a small community of actors and afficionados, *Taohua shan* responds to *Mudan ting*, moving the concerns of the earlier play to the political arena, speculating on how the forces that brought the loving couple together in *Mudan ting* might cause an entire polity to break apart.

The genre to which both plays belong, *chuanqi*, descends from forms of drama originating in the south and represents Chinese drama at its most complex and intricate. *Chuanqi* is at once bawdy and energetic—and yet unmistakably the product of two thousand years of a continuous literary tradition. Since at least the Song dynasty, Chinese writers have experimented with embedding and juxtaposing different registers of language to create different effects.

Nowhere is this practice more prevalent than in *chuanqi*, where an awareness and deliberate manipulation of linguistic register permeates practically every moment: a character might use a quotation from the classics in the service of a scatological joke, while in the same act another character might follow up an aria in almost opaquely allusive poetic language with a remark in late Ming slang. In Act 17 in *Mudan ting*, a single monologue takes up most of the act. In it, Daoist Shi relates her life as a hermaphrodite, with its sexual difficulties and marital troubles, but bases practically every phrase on the *Qianzi wen* (*Thousand Word Classic*), a primer text in classical Chinese used because no character is repeated.

Plots tend to be extremely intricate: to bring its lovers together, *Mudan ting* needs fifty-five acts. Its epigone, *Taohua shan*, relates the monumental process of dynastic fall in forty acts. A complete performance of each play required a cast of five to ten highly trained singers and might well have taken a week of eight-hour days; mostly they were texts for highly literate men and women to read for pleasure.

My readings of these two canonical plays are not meant to be exhaustive; no reading of such immensely rich texts could be. Instead I am primarily concerned with two related problems concerning personal identity that both plays take up (and that Wang Liulang and his friend Xu confront as well). The following six chapters explore how both plays address these two problems. First, what makes someone human (and not, for example, a ghost or a representation or someone who cannot be regarded as a moral being)? And, second, once a person's humanity has been established, what makes an individual a specific human with a unique position in the human community (and not an impostor or even a double)?

The bulk of this work centers on close readings of these two masterworks of the Chinese dramatic tradition. I go where the plays take me, drawing on other texts along the way, but for the most part staying with the two plays themselves. In the case of *Taohua shan*, for example, I will be drawing extensively on other accounts of the Ming dynasty's fall—not with the primary goal of placing *Taohua shan* in a specific historiographic context, but instead with the intent of getting a handle on how *Taohua shan* (along with other texts dealing with the same topic) wrestles with some epistemological problems central to the dynastic transition.

In this introduction, I will not attempt a general introduction of intellectual trends and political happenings of the period, of the sort that Andrew Plaks provides in his extremely useful introduction to *The Four Masterworks of the Ming Novel*. Nor does this introduction explain the theoretical underpinnings of my approach. Readers interested in the book's methodology may wish to turn to the epilogue, which scrutinizes the basis for a study of comparative literature. This book is at its heart both comparatist and historicist, and while this introduction sketches out a historical and cultural backdrop, the epilogue poses the theoretical question of how it is that we can consider works from historically distinct literary traditions alongside each other.

Most of the following book adheres closely to the plays, drawing only tangentially on the vast array of texts and cultural practices of obvious relevance to the problem of personal identity, whether they are historical, ritual, or religious. In the next few pages, I sketch with just a few lines the historical and literary context of some of these concerns about personal identity, suggesting the pervasiveness of these concerns in other cultural endeavors.

Personal identity in both senses—human nature and the nature of any human—has been a concern of the Chinese tradition since its very beginnings. Mencius is only one philosopher deeply concerned with human nature (arguably the central topic of Chinese philosophy). Many others have also taken up questions concerning the essence of human nature, whether it is malleable or fixed, innately good or evil, and whence it arises that there are good and evil people.

Concern about the second half of the problem—how a specific identity can be established—permeates Chinese political thought, where one of the central concerns is fixing the positions of both the sovereign and the patriarch. All political philosophers from Confucius on are interested in the precise nature of the father's relation to his son (and the lord's relation to his minister). Who is the father? Who is the master? And how can one know? Absolutely certain knowledge of their identities cannot be compromised.

On this knowledge hinges a great deal: perhaps, for example, fathers and superiors are owed deference simply as a function of their identity (although this was a matter for continuing debate). In other words, the problem of fixing identities borders others equally difficult and central to the tradition of political thought. For starters, there is the question of whether this identity—as father, or as lord and master—can ever be dissolved, or whether once established it is fixed, regardless of behavior. Is the father's relation to the son (or the lord's relation to the master) wholly indissoluble? Or to put it another way, under what conditions can rebellion and disobedience (or adoption) ever be justified?

These questions have always loomed large and perhaps never more so than in the period of the two plays. *Mudan ting* was written at the end of the sixteenth century; *Taohua shan*, about a century later. In the hands of a historian, social and economic changes in the century spanned by the plays might partly account for this widespread interest. As in the European encounter with the Americas, encounters with members of other cultures—which happened frequently as Han peoples ventured into the southern parts of China and Southeast Asia, and as others entered China—seem to have triggered musings about the source and nature of cultural difference and the extent to which others were fully human, with the same capacity for moral and intellectual growth.

The seventeenth century was also a period of tremendous economic change and increasing specialization. Bullion from the South American silver mines flooded China, introducing radical changes to the Chinese economy (such as the rise of complicated systems of banking and credit) and increasing the disparity between rich and poor regions. Chun-shu Chang and Shelley Hsueh-lun Chang describe one career that illustrates the economic circumstances of urban Jiangnan: a style of summer shoe invented by one Mr. Shi became extremely popular among the rich, until many hundreds of others flooded the market with cheap copies, causing prices to plummet.[3]

Some scholars have suggested that such economic changes played a direct role in how people defined themselves. Craig Clunas, for example, has described the late Ming's culture of connoisseurship, where the market and theories of identity converge. In a consumer society, the things one buys and collects—one's tastes—promise to reveal one's true identity, as one of the cognoscenti, setting a person apart from his vulgar peers. Even though they belong to what was essentially a pariah group, many of the professional entertainers in *Taohua shan*, for example, do not see themselves as any different fundamentally from their literati friends who share the same politics and tastes, as if it were aesthetics and politics that truly define and identify a person.

But of course intellectual and literary trends are not foreordained by social and economic conditions. Any reading that suggests such a position seems ultimately insufficient, reducing the richness and subtlety of a text—

the infinite choices in every line that confront writers like Tang Xianzu or Kong Shangren—to what was predestined to be.

In the story "Wang Liulang," Pu Songling explicitly takes up the question of what a person is, from the specific perspective of the supernatural. The story concerns itself not with the grounds on which one can differentiate in any single case between human and ghost, but on whether any difference can generally be sustained. The way Wang Liulang's experiences mirror those of Mencius's imaginary bystander makes the philosophical question clear: when a ghost passes such a venerable test for humanity, are there any moral grounds on which one can maintain the distinction?

Any version of the first question concerning personal identity—what being a person is—necessarily implies the second. Imagine what it would be like to be a person without being a specific one, possessing a unique place among other people. Since people identify themselves according to their relationships to others—daughter to Du Bao, say, or wife of Liu Mengmei, or friend of the fisherman Xu—it is hard to imagine personhood apart from a specific identity (although, as the anthropologist Arthur Wolf has suggested in his studies of northern Taiwan, the absence of such ties might be precisely what distinguishes a ghost from one's own deceased ancestor).

Dying does not seem to have wholly deprived Wang Liulang of the position he had in life. He introduces himself to Xu with a name that even more than most does nothing but to place him in the context of a family of other people (who might be living or dead). For the name Wang Liulang—"Wang the Sixth Lad," literally—is nothing but a cipher for membership in a family, suggesting his rank among at least five other brothers or agnate cousins.

Although at first Wang Liulang finds it difficult to tell Xu about his ghostly identity, he reassures himself by reminding himself of the depth of their friendship: "I feel more deeply towards you than to my own flesh and blood."[4] One can imagine a free-floating consciousness embarking on a close friendship—especially with someone like Xu, who in the little we know of him appears to be something of a loner, with no ties to the other fishermen, and whose wife, when she appears near the end of the story, surprises us by belatedly reminding us that Xu's life of solitude on the riverbank actually exists in the context of his own network of relationships. But such a free-floating consciousness would hardly be in a position to compare friendship to the bonds of blood.

We are led to think that Wang Liulang's specific identity—whatever makes him irreplaceable as the sixth among the Wang brothers, and the fisherman Xu's dearest friend—continues after his initial death from drowning. Nonetheless, we cannot be sure of this continuity; after all, as a ghost Wang Liulang's other ties to the human world seem to have dissolved, leaving only his friendship with Xu, forged after his death. And there is even the faintest hint of a suggestion that Wang Liulang's act of compassion reforms him and so represents a change in identity in the same way that a religious conversion would.

The hoped-for rebirth is what would have marked a decisive change. It would have placed him into a new family, given him a new name and a new identity, and from Xu's perspective, would have transformed a grown man who is a friend into an unknown baby. Paradoxically, the rebirth would have been the real death, marking a break in identity and ending the ties that bound Wang Liulang both in death and as a ghost.

But it never takes place. Instead of being reincarnated, Wang Liulang is promoted to a position as a functionary in the hierarchy of heaven. Consequently, he enjoys a rare continuity of identity: as the minor deity, he continues to remember his former life as a human, his death through drowning, and his decision to save the mother and child. His friendship with Xu can continue, as the last part of the story relates.

What is to stop us from regarding this subject—whose identity as it progresses from live man, ghost, and finally to deity is continuous—as human? Some of the story's specifics make it hard for us to apply Mencius's ideas to the situation. One is tempted of course simply to say: Wang Liulang is as human as his friend Xu—only more so, since Wang Liulang actually saved the mother and child, while Xu sat by, suffering only the merest twinge of conscience necessary to maintain his own humanity. When the fisherman calls his friend a "person of fellow-feeling" (*renren*), there is nothing ironic about such a designation at all. He is certainly a moral agent: should he consequently be considered a person, or the moral equivalent?

But there is a sense in which Wang Liulang's status as a ghost and the possibility of his promotion to minor deity complicates matters to the point that such a simple application of Mencius's idea does not seem to hold. To save the baby's life, Wang Liulang sacrifices his own life—or so it seems. In fact, things are not quite as simple as that. For, more specifically, Wang Liulang gives up his chance at rebirth.

Life as a ghost followed by rebirth makes it impossible for us simply to equate the two kinds of moral subjects, ghosts and mortals. Even by the standards of Chinese literature, where such behavior has long been valorized, Ming and Qing literature is filled with people who, like Wang Liulang, knowingly give up their lives for another: loyalist generals who go to their deaths rather than betray their lord by swearing allegiance to another, wives who choose suicide to remain chaste, men whose ultimate expression of friendship is to give up their own lives. Normally, when one gives up life for another it is the ultimate sacrifice, both in that it proves that what was done was not done in expectation of recompense and in that the sacrifice of one's own life can only be made once.

But when Wang Liulang gives up his human life to save that of another, even if we believe in his sincerity, even if his motives were pure and entirely unselfish, something much less—if only because less final—is at stake. Rather than having offered up the ultimate sacrifice, Wang Liulang has merely lost his place in line. As the result of his sacrifice, he expects, the cosmic bureaucracy will prolong his wait for reincarnation, but otherwise his situation has remained the same.

Of course, Mencius does not expect or demand any sacrifice from the observer of the baby; his only requirement is that the observer not act out of hope of any gain. But what he does assume is that action on the part of the observer would save the baby's life. From what evil precisely has Wang Liulang saved the baby and mother? If he had not intervened and instead allowed them simply to die, the mother of drowning and the child of exposure, they would presumably have become ghosts just as he himself is now, starting their wait at the back of the line for their own chances to be reincarnated. One cannot help but feel that Wang Liulang's sacrifice for them—even though it entails precisely the same price, human life—is of an entirely different order than that of the loyal general, chaste wife, or loving friend. The general who gives his life out of loyalty does so precisely with the knowledge of finality. That particular sacrifice can only be made once.

And it is not simply the idea of sacrificing one's life that changes if one believes in reincarnation. As "Wang Liulang" suggests, Buddhist beliefs in reincarnation tint any formulation of personal identity in the Chinese tradition after the Han dynasty. If Wang Liulang had not saved the woman's life and had gone through with his reincarnation as planned, he would have been reborn into a new family, with a new name, a new appearance, perhaps a new gender. Lacking continuity of memory and of physical appearance, what makes Wang Liulang and this new infant the same person? Do the karmic debts and credits shared by the two really constitute the sine qua non of identity? And if that is the case, how is rebirth any different from death from the perspective of all who knew Wang Liulang?

If Wang Liulang's good deed had escaped notice and his life with Xu had just continued as before, there would have been no stopping him from doing the same thing over and over again. For each time his rebirth would depend on another person's dying. Why would he not sacrifice his human life (his place in line, rather) time after time? I can easily imagine an alternative ending for this story, one touched with the wryness that characterizes so many other tales by Pu Songling: the ghost Wang Liulang gets in the habit of saving the lives of those whose space in the human community he is supposed to take, since anyway he would rather spend his days drinking and fishing with his friend, rather than be born again as a human being at someone else's expense.

In some ways, the two works explored in the following six chapters could not be more different from Pu Songling's "Wang Liulang." The story is very short; the plays are very long. *Chuanqi* are written in language I have already described briefly: dialogue in prose and arias in poetic language, with both prose and poetic passages delighting in shifts of register. Classical allusions and high-flown language are deliberately embedded in the most vernacular of contexts. In contrast, the language of *Liaozhai zhiyi* is often considered a model of concision and classical purity, in an age when many writers fretted about the possibility of vulgarity and colloquialisms creeping into classical prose.

But perhaps most pertinently, the theatre suggests by its very forms questions of identity in a way that a classical tale either does not or cannot. Where tales can gesture or seamlessly elide, plays must be explicit in their staging. For example, the tale simply omits any mention of Wang Liulang's presence on the riverbank. We assume that as a ghost he was able to assume some special form so that Xu (who was carefully scrutinizing the scene) could not see him. But where exactly was Wang Liulang at that crucial moment when the mother fell? Was he actively saving her life, or passively refraining from taking it? Such a distinction is an important ethical one but left here to the reader's discretion. How could Wang Liulang have been the creature whom Xu at first mistook for another mortal and yet invisible on the riverbank, as if on some other plane of existence? Some attempt to answer questions just like these is absolutely central to Chinese drama.

Like early modern Europe, late Ming China was colored by a concern with the theatre, fascinated by the possibilities of costume and disguise both on and offstage. Theatre, a space that legitimated disguise, informed ostensibly non-theatrical spaces with its concerns. For costume and design were central to late Ming culture, not least in the realm of fashion. Urbanites in the wealthy, cash-rich Jiangnan region spent exorbitant sums of money on clothing, just as they did on other expressions of taste. Fashions changed rapidly: on the one hand, fashion promises to reveal something about its wearer, whether wealth, class, or taste; but on the other hand, it blurs social distinctions, making everyday clothes like theatrical costumes, full of the possibility of disguise. For example, the entirely respectable wife of a successful merchant might very well be wearing the same style of outfit as a professional entertainer and demimondaine (and even more surprisingly, what the male scion of a wealthy family might have worn would not have differed too much, earrings and all).

Early Qing China had a distinctly political stake in the question of disguise. The Manchu conquerors mandated that all male subjects shave their pates, plait the hair at the back of their heads into a queue, and wear a style of clothing based on Manchu riding gear (fitted and buttoned at the neck, instead of loose and tied at the waist as clothing in the Ming was).

During the dynastic transition (the period of time *Taohua shan* relates), thousands of men died refusing to conform to the new laws. Because the body was considered a gift from one's parents, marring it—even by shaving the head—was an affront to filial piety. In a convergence, then, of filial piety and loyalty to the vanquished Ming, some men chose death over shaving. And in the generations following, the state of a man's scalp continued to promise insight into the depth of his loyalty towards the state: stubble (even if the result of simple carelessness) could sometimes appear the outward manifestation of sedition, as could a shaved head in a mandated period of mourning (when shaving was not permitted).

To the state, appearances matter and promise access to a person's state of mind. But what about the many who obediently shaved their pates while secretly harboring sentiments of Ming loyalism? They surely felt that appearances—even a shaved head and the clothes to be worn every single day—were nothing but a disguise; but, of course, a fascination with disguise is another way of expressing interest in what a person might truly be.

By their very forms, plays can suggest arguments about personhood: for example, what makes a dramatic character cohere as a single entity? In *chuanqi*, all characters both participate in prose dialogue and sing in verse arias. In contrast, in *zaju*, or Northern drama, only one character can sing, while the others play distinctly supportive roles, setting up the star's long arias with their prose contributions. Normally the star is either a lead female character (*dan*) or a lead male character (*mo*), but experimental plays were written with other parts in mind—a singing clown (*jing*), for example. In some plays, the same actor sings a single role throughout the same play; in others, perhaps to highlight a virtuoso, the same star sings a different part in each act (but the same role type). In both cases, we follow one figure through the play, whether it is main character or the leading actor.

In the *zaju Yu chanshi* (*Zen Master Yu*), however, the sixteenth-century playwright Xu Wei makes it impossible to follow either a single character or an actor through the play. The play begins with a Buddhist monk who offends an official named Liu. To punish the monk, Liu has a prostitute seduce him (through some not very clever trickery). When the monk discovers what Liu has done, he kills himself in a rage, vowing revenge against Liu. In the second half of the play, the monk has become reincarnated as the official Liu's daughter, Liu Cui. By leading a life of dissolution that leads to prostitution, Liu Cui succeeds in ruining her family, thus exacting the monk's revenge.

In bending and pushing the conventions of *zaju*, Xu Wei addresses some of the same questions we have seen at work in "Wang Liulang." I have already written of the difficulty of tracing a single continuous Wang Liulang; it is impossible for us to know the extent to which the ghost and the man he was before he drowned are the same person. The difficulties increase when we throw the possibility of reincarnation into the mix. At least the drowned man and the ghost seem to share memories; what can possibly tie together the ghost Wang Liulang and the baby he would have been reborn as? If we speak of these two as sharing some essential quality that makes them somehow the same person, surely in so doing we are defining what it is to be a person. The only thing the ghost and the baby do share is a continuity of responsibility, so that people must pay off debts incurred in previous lives.

Fiction of this period also wrestles playfully and imaginatively with some of these problems. The great novel *Xiyou ji* (*Journey to the West*) arises out of a tradition, many works in many genres all telling the story of the monk Tripitaka as he travels to India to gather sutras; many other works retold the same events or included additional adventures to the ones the novel describes. But Dong Yue's *Xiyou bu* (*Supplement to the Western Journey*) departs radically from conventional additions: even more fantastical than *Xiyou ji*, it takes place entirely within one character's dream.

In *Xiyou ji*, the Monkey King possesses the ability to transform both himself and his cudgel magically. In the blink of an eye, he can make himself either infinitely large or infinitely small, or disguise himself by perfectly assuming another form. His magical powers invite us to speculate on questions that by now seem familiar: who—or what—his true essence might be, what continuity he retains as he changes from one form to another, and why we should privilege the monkey form (and the normal monkey size) as real over the others.

Since he can take on any form, outside observers cannot identify the Monkey King based on appearances (such misunderstandings are central to the resolution of a number of adventures). The Monkey King himself, however, seems to have no trouble identifying himself, no matter what form his body may have taken. Or can he? By setting his entire novella within the Monkey King's dream, Dong Yue turns the question of the Monkey King's changeability inward. A chapter in the original novel ends with the Monkey King's falling asleep. Dong Yue's work, packed with wildly imaginative adventures, is meant to be read as an insert at that point. But the reader (and the Monkey King) does not find out until the very end of the novella that everything preceding has been nothing but a dream, all of it an act of mind.

The same questions are pursued in other genres and media, often by highlighting sincerity and self-consciousness. Portraits had long been painted, but now self-portraits—an expression of a person's self-perception—flourished, such as those by Chen Hongshou and of course by the fictional Du Liniang, heroine of *Mudan ting* (who in turn inspired a legion of real-life young women to paint or have painted their own portraits).

In many ways, certain developments in how the visual arts were marketed reveals most clearly the intimate and often paradoxical relationship between sincerity, authenticity, and concerns with identity. As James Cahill writes in *The Compelling Image*, late Ming painters tended to be valued not for the verisimilitude of their works; that was the purview of mere draftsmen. Instead, collectors prized the works of those painters who were able to achieve an individual style. Paradoxically, precisely these recognizable stylistic features—and the market that valued them—are directly associated with the rise both of widespread forgeries and of entire studios cooperating together to produce something "unmistakably" an authentic Dong Qichang.

At the same time that artists struggled to articulate through painting and literature the nature of a person and of the mind, other writers—among them, literary critics and ethicists—addressed these problems in other forms. A number of philosophers—to name some of the most famous, Li Zhi, the entire radical Taizhou School, and the Yuan brothers—were all concerned with authenticity in style, in spirit, among people. Li Zhi concluded that those were most authentic who had retained a child's heart. That conclusion in itself exemplifies the kind of reevaluation so central in this time of who counts as human and what legitimate human endeavors are in a Confucian framework.

What Li Zhi privileges directly contradicts many of the most persistent features of funerals and ancestral worship. According to those conventions, married women occupied a distinctly secondary position (they were phased out of worship after a few generations); even that secondary status was introduced only in the late imperial period. Children of either sex who died before marriage had no role at all, since they obviously had no offspring and were themselves never to be ancestors. According to ritual practice, women and children hardly count. Not coincidentally, Li Zhi also argued that the human relation upon which all the others are grounded was not that between father and son, but that between husband and wife.

In writing about the two plays, the first a comedy of remarriage and the second a historical drama, I will be examining one marriage that takes place and another that can never get off the ground—one Emperor who has the power to rule on all the other characters' identities and another who cannot even hold on to his own identity. But throughout, my concern is basically the predicament of Wang Liulang, the ghost who uneasily straddles the worlds of the human and non-human and yet who retains the fisherman Xu's friendship: how someone can ever prove himself thoroughly human and the grounds on which he can maintain his specific identity, the ties to other people that give someone a unique position within the human community.

PART ONE

Mudan ting

Introduction to *Mudan ting*

Tang Xianzu's own preface makes *Mudan ting* out to be an illustration of the redemptive power of passion, or *qing*. He begins with a plot summary: "Of all the women of feeling in the world, was there ever one like Du Liniang? Dreaming of a lover, she grew sick, and the sickness grew ever worse, until she painted her own self-portrait to leave to the world before she died. Three years after her death, out of the void she was able again to seek the one of whom she had dreamt and come back to life. Such a one as Liniang can truly be called a person of feeling."[1]

One might fill out the summary in the same spirit: before her death of lovesickness, Du Liniang, the sixteen-year-old only daughter of Du Bao and Lady Zhen, completes her self-portrait and entreats her maid Chunxiang and her parents to entomb her body and her portrait in the garden that inspires the dream leading to her sickness and death. There, her tutor Chen Zuiliang and the Daoist priestess Shi care for her shrine until the young scholar and sojourner Liu Mengmei finds her portrait and falls in love with it. Du Liniang's ghost returns from the underworld, and she and the young man begin a passionate affair; upon learning her story, Liu disinters her body and brings the girl back to life.

Because Liu must rush off to take the examinations, they marry in haste without awaiting the approval of her family. Hurrying off to save his father-in-law from siege, Liu is detained as a grave robber, since he has articles from Du Liniang's grave on his person. Eventually all parties congregate at the capital, where the Emperor pronounces a decision on the family and sends them off with his blessing.

One could add much more, since after all, the play's length—fifty-five acts—and complexity are impressive even by the standards of the *chuanqi*. But in skeleton form, this is the play with which Chinese readers are familiar; the themes highlighted in the preface and in my summary—love, feeling, and desire—are those that commentators and critics from the seventeenth-century Three Wives to Wai-yee Li of our own time have chosen to discuss. But is this really the plot of *Mudan ting*?

Throughout the play, different characters—ranging from the maidservant Chunxiang to the father Du Bao—voice doubts as to whether this supernatural narrative of death and resurrection could really have taken place. In its place, they suggest much more pedestrian alternative explanations. Many of these intimations take place in the prose dialogue (*binbai*), much of which welcomes the kind of critical pressure most critics have reserved for the verse arias. From its sixteenth-century beginnings, *Mudan ting* has been as much a text for readers as for theatregoers, and as a written text, the prose dialogue demands attention: it is the site of constant wordplay (almost as intricate as that in the arias), and it bears most of the brunt of plot exposition.

If there is an alternative to that conventional narrative, it is embodied by Du Bao's doubts, which are the primary focus of the final act. He enters the act convinced that this creature who so resembles his dead daughter is a ghost and that the young man claiming to be her husband is a grave robber. Let us take seriously Du Bao's objections. By the end of the play, does the father fully accept his daughter's resurrection from the dead, or her marriage to Liu Mengmei? The Emperor must adjudicate on the question of whether Du Liniang and Liu Mengmei are in fact human or demonic. How do we know they are who they claim to be?

Much of the play calls attention to these very questions. By the final act, the reader has experienced many scenes dramatizing and problematizing recognition and proof. Virtually every important character in the play, at some point, stands in the position of needing either to establish his or her own proper identity or to adjudicate someone else's claims to an identity.

Among many other scenes of identification and recognition, such scenes include Liu Mengmei's identification of his spectral visitor with the girl in the portrait, the moment of Du Liniang's own resurrection, Du Bao's reunion with his wife in the last act, and the moving reunion of mother and daughter, despite the mother's initial conviction that her daughter is a ghost.

By the end of the play, the reader feels quite confident that every character has returned to his or her rightful position in society and within the family. But initially each encounter carries with it the possibility of failure. For example, Liu Mengmei might well have refused to identify the ghost with the girl in the picture; he might have disbelieved that such an equivalence was possible. When she encounters the daughter she knows to have died three years ago, Lady Zhen has every right to refuse to believe that this could possibly be her daughter. Why shouldn't we all feel as Du Bao does? Why shouldn't all reunions be foiled by the refusal to recognize?

According to Du Bao's version of events, a young shyster has somehow pulled the wool over the Emperor's eyes and, claiming to be both son-in-law to a high official and the top examination graduate, has positioned himself at—indeed infiltrated—almost the very pinnacle of the Confucian patriarchy, armed now with the imprimatur of the Emperor. With a ghost in his own family and a grave robber (by his own admission guilty of a capital crime) at the Emperor's right hand, something, Du Bao would no doubt tell us, is terribly wrong. Of course, every public servant occasionally disagrees with his sovereign, but what lies at the root of Du Bao's unrest is not a simple difference of opinion. Instead, he seems motivated by a sense of collusion and conspiracy against him. All his life a faithful servant of the state, he is now being threatened with a charge of treason for refusing to admit a ghost and a grave robber into his family, and even his loyal and loving wife opposes him on this matter. Everyone—Emperor, wife, the sheer weight of public opinion—seeks to coerce a change of heart from him. Having failed to cajole him, they now prepare to force him to believe what he knows not to be the case.

In response, Du Bao offers a compromise, but one that makes his own position clear. He agrees to accept his daughter's identity conditionally, so long as she will break off relations with Liu Mengmei: "If you leave Liu Mengmei, then when we go back, I will recognize you as my daughter."[2] Outraged, she refuses his offer, declaring it impossible, and then she falls into a faint. And it is at this moment that Du Bao calls her his daughter: he cries out in surprise, "Liniang, my child."[3] These are his very last words in the play; she has successfully exacted the recognition she sought.

But even this climactic exclamation does not escape ambiguity. He calls her his daughter, yes, but does that necessarily imply that he also concedes that she is human? From the moment he lays eyes on her, the striking resemblance of this creature to his daughter has impressed him not as proof of her resurrection, but instead as evidence that she is a ghost of the dead girl. Perhaps in his last line he is simply articulating what he has suspected—that she is at once his daughter and yet a ghost—and not that she is his daughter and a human.

Whatever we make of his actions in this final scene, during the life of his child and at her deathbed, Du Bao was a loving father, no less distraught at the passing of their only child than his wife. And in a sense, his sorrow was more meaningful than his wife's—her childbearing years are over, and this is the only child she will ever have; but as a man, and a wealthy, powerful one, Du Bao could easily have decided to take a concubine in the effort to produce another heir. In other words, his grief at her deathbed suggests a love of her as an individual, not merely as the future of his bloodline.

Perhaps the fainting spell constitutes nothing more than an act of emotional blackmail. It bears a significant resemblance to her death earlier: it too arises out of her general susceptibility to emotional strain and out of a father's unwillingness to accept his daughter's maturity and sexuality. At any rate, a replay of that scene would naturally elicit a powerful, visceral reaction from Du Bao. And in recalling her death, the fainting spell strongly debunks the notion of proof. After all, it suggests the one and only incontrovertible test for determining whether a creature is mortal: kill it, and if it dies, then it was mortal. Under most circumstances, a ghost cannot be killed. If nothing else, the fainting spell forces Du Bao to concede that he cannot prove Du Liniang's human status, since the only truly satisfying proof would be to kill her once more.

Two narratives contend for our belief and for how we are to read the ending of the play. On one level, a happy reunion is taking place, in which even Du Bao from time to time participates (he is, for example, overjoyed to see his wife alive and well, when he thought the bandit had killed her). For many of the characters—not just Liu Mengmei and Du Liniang, but also the tutor Chen Zuiliang, Lady Zhen, and the maid Chunxiang—have been lost and now are found. Together they celebrate the marriage of Du Liniang and Liu Mengmei as well as the continuation of society and family that the marriage embodies.

In this aspect, *Mudan ting* resembles nothing so much as the archetypal comedy in the Western tradition extending from Greek Middle Comedy, ultimately conservative in its affirmation of the existing social order: its course is that of potentially transgressive desire reabsorbed into sanctioned marriage and society. The passionate boy and girl at the beginning of the play have been transformed into a new family—a husband and a wife, who will themselves one day have children—which is at the same time a continuation of the old. In this particular case, the reassimilation could hardly be more dramatic: that supremely deviant union of ghost and grave robber ultimately receives the blessing of the Emperor. The genre demands such closure; *chuanqi* are supposed to end this way—in a grand reunion (*tuanyuan*) scene where everybody finds his way back to his proper place.

But there is the hint of another narrative. Until the very end, Du Bao seems entirely alone, not only bereaved of his only child—a terrible fate for any Confucian gentleman—but also widowed. And he of all people ought to celebrate the play's felicitous end, for to him the miracle ought to seem greatest, surrounded as he is at the end by his family, wife, daughter, and son-in-law. Something stops him from recognizing and participating in the happy occasion. Du Bao's evident reluctance leaves its mark on this happy resolution: the promise of a comedy is the future, the "happily ever after," and, if Du Bao indeed feels coerced into recognizing his child, then no fifty-sixth act immediately presents itself to the imagination. Would it be possible for Du Bao to graciously recant his earlier accusations and warmly embrace his resurrected daughter and new son-in-law?

The position he states in his penultimate line is clear: he agrees to accept Du Liniang as his daughter, but only under the condition that she give up Liu Mengmei. However, giving up Liu Mengmei would concede her case. From her perspective, a legitimized union with Liu Mengmei is precisely what proves her story. According to her version of events, her love for Liu Mengmei has brought her back to life, and hence, on it hinges both her human status and her status as a human, the rightful daughter of Du Bao and Lady Zhen, now the legal wife of the top examination candidate. Since it denies her story, the very offer implies disbelief in our heroine's humanity.

And yet, it does seem possible that a grave robber could concoct such a scheme, so that Du Bao's version of events and his lingering doubts do possess a certain intellectual rigor, in contrast to the tests imposed by the Emperor. The Emperor says: "We have heard that a person leaves a shadow when walking and that the form of a ghost resists the mirror."[4] After Du Liniang successfully leaves a reflection in a mirror and footprints where she passes, the Emperor decrees her human. We can better understand why Du Bao might think her a ghost than why the Emperor might think her human.

Du Bao's fears at least make sense: he saw his child die, and an outsider might well find in the wealthy, childless Du Bao a worthy target of blackmail.

All of this leaves the viewer or the reader in a bit of a bind. We agree with Du Liniang that Du Bao is wrong to bargain on this matter: identity must be absolute and not conditional. But we also identify with Du Bao's doubts. In the last act, both Du Liniang and Liu Mengmei lay claims to their specific identities: Du Liniang, as daughter of Du Bao, and Liu Mengmei, as the top examination candidate tested by Miao Shunbin, an official who has befriended the young man. But are these identities secure? Are any proofs of human identity adequate? And finally, what makes any of the characters human (especially Du Liniang and Liu Mengmei, who are accused of being ghosts)?

A great deal of weight rests on Du Bao's enigmatic last words—"Liniang, my child." Only if they are entirely voluntary—what a Kantian would call "free," representing a true and sincere change of heart—do these words represent the culmination of a romantic comedy, the final reunion and reconciliation of a family. And if they are coerced, then this final exclamation represents something else entirely. Does Du Bao think the ending represents the culmination of a romantic comedy or of a frightening conspiracy? He has suggested the latter possibility when he airs the theory that perhaps Liu Mengmei too is a ghost, and thus more than simply a confederate to Du Liniang's plan to infiltrate human society.

The conjunction of these two genres of narrative—comedy and conspiracy—is no coincidence. In the case of *Mudan ting*, as elsewhere, both are, as Stanley Cavell has suggested in the case of Western literature, related dramas of knowledge and its limits. In many tragedies and comedies, one of the two genres plants the seeds of the other.

Let us consider examples from two other dramatic genres. In the case of Hollywood movies, romantic comedy often seems to contain the seeds of something much darker, invisibly transforming itself into film noir, and vice versa; the same phenomenon appears in some of the best known of Shakespearean dramas, in which comedy seems at the very end to have implied tragedy. To cite just two complementary examples of this phenomenon: the 1946 *Postman Always Rings Twice* begins with the plotting of a murder, but after the two young lovers kill the woman's much older husband, they are pitted against each other by the law, each told of the other's supposed betrayal. Eventually, they are married and bound to each other not by ties of love, but of distrust, since as a married couple, neither can testify against the other in court. Even so, their marriage retains the potential of becoming a real one based on trust and communication, so that five minutes before the end of the movie, the couple drive off finally reconciled, happily expecting the birth of their first child. This might very well be the ending, and if it had been, the film would have been a version (albeit dark indeed) of the remarriage comedy. But such an ending is not ours: in the last moments, the wife dies in a car accident, and the husband is (this time wrongfully) tried for murder and sentenced to die.

Conversely, that sunniest of Shakespearean comedies, *A Midsummer Night's Dream*, ends with more than a hint of darkness. Oberon closes the play with a benediction, which can be read as bitterly ironic: "To the best bride bed will we,/Which by us shall blessèd be,/And the issue there create /Ever shall be fortunate" (V.ii.33–36). Readers familiar with Greek mythology or Racine's *Phèdre* know quite well the fate of this union between Theseus and Hippolyta and of the baby whose conception Oberon so blesses. He will grow up to be Hippolytus, and after his stepmother conceives a guilty passion for him, he will flee and be devoured by a monster. Even *A Midsummer Night's Dream*, where moonlight and romance are magically transformed into marriage and family, has at its end an ominous promise of incest and tragedy to come.

But the elements of both genres are mixed together most explicitly in Shakespeare's late romances, especially in *The Winter's Tale*. And there, too, is most explicit the shared obsession of comedy and tragedy with knowledge and its limits. Misreading innocent expressions of friendship, Leontes, the King of Sicilia, suspects adultery between his wife and his best friend, and the first three acts play out his fears in a truncated, but even more vicious, version of *Othello*. Since they are a married couple of long standing, with children, Leontes' mistrust of his wife targets not only her, but their children as well. Leontes' suspicions blossom into a full-scale conspiracy theory: if his wife is faithless, his children are not his own, and if his subjects refuse to share in and act on his beliefs, then their loyalties have been purchased, and they too are complicit in the perfidy. By the end of the third act, so far as Leontes knows, his son and his wife have died of grief, and his infant daughter has been abandoned and left to die. And if the play ended there, it would have been the tragedy of a king who, out of uncontrollable jealousy, tears apart his family and his kingdom.

In the last two acts, husband, wife, and daughter are magically reunited in an ending that highlights epistemology just as much as the beginning: the reunion is grounded in the transformation of suspicion into recognition and belief. Leontes had been told that his wife has died, and now, sixteen years after her supposed death, he is shown a statue of her. It comes alive, and what was an object, first of his suspicion and then of his abject contrition, is transformed into a human being—his wife, lost and now found. Earlier, Leontes had become convinced that the child born to his wife in prison was not his own, but fathered instead by his wife's adulterous lover. At the end, he comes to believe that the sixteen-year-old Perdita is his own daughter, based on the most tenuous and easily forged of markers—her name and her possession of the objects left with the lost baby. Shakespeare refuses to gratify us even with the reassurance of an identifying birthmark. Instead, Leontes takes her identity on faith, or on the testimony of a simple shepherd (and her own sterling qualities, which even in Shakespeare's day never did identify the highborn from the baseborn).

And so perhaps it is not that comedy and tragedy are alternate possibilities, but instead that each implies the other, or perhaps even that they coexist, and we must decide between them. In that way, comedy resembles the lawsuit with which *Mudan ting* concludes. Northrop Frye has commented on the similarity between comedy and lawsuit: "The action of comedy in moving from one social center to another is not unlike the action of a lawsuit, in which plaintiff and defendant construct different versions of the same situation, one finally being judged as real and the other as illusory."[5] Adjudicating, then, seems to be at the heart of what is going on. And this returns us to Du Bao: we know the Emperor's verdict on Du Liniang's identity, but where does Du Bao ultimately stand? And on what bases are proper judgments made?

By validating the marriage of Liu Mengmei and Du Liniang, the Emperor takes the place of their parents. Liu Mengmei's, we have been told, are long dead, but it is peculiar for a marriage to be declared valid by the Emperor when her parents are right there. The Emperor issues this verdict: "We have listened carefully to the testimony of Du Liniang, and there is no doubt that she has been resurrected. After the eunuchs have escorted them past the Meridian Gate, father and daughter, husband and wife will all recognize each other, and returning to their home, they will all form one family."[6] *Taohua shan* will ask more explicitly what sorts of beliefs can be coerced, but for now it is enough to observe that the Emperor decrees not just an action, but an act of mind—to look at this being and to see, not a ghost or impersonator, but his daughter. In fact, *chengqin*, which I have translated as to "form one family," usually simply means to marry. In other words, the marriage of Liu Mengmei and Du Liniang is really not so unusual. The process of recognition—so protracted and problematized in *Mudan ting*—actually takes place in all marriages.

For marriage dramatizes the very recognition Du Bao finds it so difficult to grant. The act of recognition (*ren*) is built into the very language of patriarchy in Chinese. There are in Chinese, as in English, two distinct ways to understand the notion of recognizing one's lord and master. Only by knowing who one's master is, as distinct from all other people, can one serve him or treat him as someone in his position deserves; there is no way to separate these two acts of recognition. As we will see in the case of *Taohua shan*, political dramas often turn on such a moment—when a monarch is either granted or denied recognition. And dramas of recognition recur in ritual; for example, in some of the more elaborate hymeneal rites, marriage culminated in a ceremony of recognition, *renqin*, in which the bride's family paid a visit to the groom's a month after the bride's own move, in a mutual recognition that from now on the two families were one, forever bound by ties of kinship.

Recognition—along with its attendant uncertainty—is built into a drama about marriage and family, and it permeates the particulars of *Mudan ting*. Is the final reunion performative utterance—simply effected by the Emperor's decree—or are there in fact any grounds by which one person can truly recognize another? At any rate, the command makes no difference to Du Bao, who continues to protest, desiring proof and not simply a command from his liege lord. By the end of the play, the powers of proof have become grossly attenuated; what kinds of proof of humanity still hold? Why is Du Liniang's mother, Lady Zhen, so persuaded of her daughter's humanity? Or alternatively, why is Du Bao so willing to believe his wife's story and so reluctant to believe his daughter's?

The first half of this book focuses, then, on the play's conclusion and on the extent to which Du Bao's final exclamation—"Liniang, my child"—attests to his belief in her identity. To celebrate the play's ending, we too must believe, first in Du Liniang's veracity and then in Du Bao's sincerity.

CHAPTER 1

The Girl's Portrait

Up until the very end of the play, Du Bao seems convinced that the creature resembling his deceased daughter is a simulacrum, approximating with frightening accuracy his child's appearance, but nonetheless a false version. This is one version of authenticity in the play—the authentic as contrasted to the counterfeit. That model pervades much of the play: rarely have the hero and heroine of a play devoted so much of their energy to proving that each is in fact the real version of him or herself among a range of hypothetical impostors. Nor do their efforts stop there: they must also prove their relationship real—a legitimate marriage—and neither illicit liaison nor figment of the imagination.

Not surprisingly, then, the words real (*zhen*) and false (*jia*), summoned in too many contexts, become warped out of shape with the burden of maintaining the distinction. Allusions to one of *Mudan ting*'s source texts serve only to complicate matters. During his own entreaties to the painting, Liu Mengmei compares himself to the hero of *Zhenzhen gushi* ("The Story of Zhenzhen"), another young man in love with a woman in a picture, who summons her by calling her name out for a hundred days.¹ That intertextual echo—Zhenzhen, Zhenzhen, unceasingly—helps to turn *zhen*, real, into nothing more than a nonsense syllable.

This chapter focuses on the play's central artifact—Du Liniang's self-portrait, itself a pun, since it is yet another appearance of *zhen*, meaning "likeness" and not "real" here: Act 14, in which it is painted, is called *Xiezhen*, "Inscribing a Likeness." One is compelled to ask whether this likeness is real—or how *zhen* this particular *zhen* is.

All portraits make assertions about identity, emphasizing what is perceived to be important about a person and eliding what is perceived to be unimportant. And a self-portrait seems to have even more convincing claims to privileged insight into a person. Du Liniang paints her portrait when lovesickness has already begun to take its toll on her looks, as a response to her knowledge of her own mortality. Through the painting, she hopes to preserve what is essential about herself; and since Liu Mengmei falls in love with the portrait and it sets off a chain of events that lead to her resurrection, the portrait's success on that count is unqualified (at least for the period of time that the play represents between Du Liniang's two deaths—the one conquered and the one we assume is to come).

Du Liniang paints precisely because she is so keenly aware of her own mortality. This painter has every intention of being replaced by her portrait, so that the painting, having taken on some of its painter's identity, cannot comfortably coexist with its painter. A reader might very well conclude that the painting kills her. However you look at it, the picture is implicated in her death and substitutes itself for the live girl. In language colored by Buddhism, she suggests one motivation for painting as she commands Chunxiang to bring her painting supplies: "Extinguish the three burning fires of desire in that temporary residence from which the soul will depart."² If the painting does nothing to extinguish the flames of desire, it does end up facilitating the soul's departure (Du Liniang uses the term *lihun*, which in romantic fiction and drama, at least, refers to the spirit's traveling away from the body and not to death). A portrait invested with this power—to speak for its painter beyond the grave, to be what she herself can be no longer, to represent the painter's true essence more than her current state—cannot simply be stored away in a closet until need for it arises.

This chapter addresses the questions suggested by the painting and the unique kind of representation it is. What special claims to authenticity does this painting (*zhen*) make? At places, one might almost surmise that it is the true version of Du Liniang—or rather, that more of Du Liniang's identity has been invested in it than in any other form. Are these suggestions of authenticity made in such a way as to diminish the claims of other versions of Du Liniang (her ghost and her corpse, for example), which are in turn implied to be counterfeit? These miniature acts of adjudication on our parts foreshadow Du Liniang's trial of identity in the conclusion of the play.

Every bit as much as his wife, Liu Mengmei spends the final acts of the play laying claim to both his human identity and his specific identity (unlike her, he even suffers a vicious beating in the process). In other words, Du Liniang's self-portrait, that central *zhen*, occupies the most important role in the debate over whether the authentic differs from the counterfeit (and if so, how), but it is hardly alone.

Other objects are also subjected to such questions as what it is to be real, in what sense representations can be real, and what value we attach to the real. For example, Liu Mengmei first introduces himself to his patron Miao Shunbin as the older man is busy appraising jewels. The younger man asserts that of all the jewels around only he himself is the true treasure. And later on, the Underworld Magistrate, who allows Du Liniang free passage into the world of the living, is clearly at once a minor deity invested with considerable powers and dingy three-foot-tall statues to be found in every city temple.

Only after one knows what category something fits into can one determine whether it is real or false. After all, a counterfeit dollar bill is at once fake currency and an authentic fake. In *Art and Money*, Marc Shell describes the work of American artist Otis Kaye, who specialized in trompe l'œil paintings of money: "'life-size meticulous reproductions of specific bills which, if they had not been signed and dated by the artist might easily be mistaken for counterfeit notes.'"[3] An authentic Kaye, then, is a counterfeit dollar (and the value of that authentic Kaye far exceeds that of the bills it represents). A painting might be a false version of a girl but be a very real painting indeed, while a girl might be a false painting.

Laitou Yuan makes Otis Kaye's point in his joking account of what has happened in the yamen. Farcical hanger-on at the yamen and sometime assistant to Daoist Shi, he explains Liu Mengmei's actions to the old family retainer Guo Tuo: "The young scholar took the real as the false, broke open the tomb, and stole the contents."[4] According to Laitou Yuan's version of events, Liu Mengmei finds the portrait, and, musing on it day and night and increasingly in the grips of an obsessive delusion, he brings himself to the point of committing the crime of grave robbery. Laitou Yuan reverses a standard formulation of representational confusion so that the picture is the real version, but such rhetoric is common in the play, as when the ghostly Du Liniang asserts her likeness to the portrait. In confusing an original with a representation, it is usually said that one has taken the false for the real, and not, as Liu Mengmei has done, taken the real for the false. The picture is a Ming version of an Otis Kaye original, which makes it impossible for us to rely on pat formulations of the real.

Laitou Yuan not only witnessed but even participated in Du Liniang's disinterment. He rather deliberately misleads Guo Tuo into thinking that his young master has been involved in a terrible crime. Of course, to someone who was there at the disinterment, Laitou Yuan is speaking in puns, because he might also be saying: "The young scholar took the portrait as the false, broke open the tomb, and stole the contents." When Liu Mengmei opens the grave, he proves that he loves the girl. For though to him the portrait came first and was the standard by which initially he measured his lover, he recognizes that the girl is antecedent to it. Once the girl has been disinterred, the portrait, except for one other brief appearance in the play, can then fade away, unimportant and secondary. Or, as Laitou Yuan says, the creature in the grave was *zhen*, and the portrait (the *zhen*) was false all along.

Before Laitou Yuan can explain what has happened, Guo Tuo and Laitou Yuan first must ascertain that they are speaking of the same person by comparing descriptions of Liu Mengmei. Here the two problems—of Liu Mengmei's identity, as well as Du Liniang's—are linked for the first time. Liu Mengmei's identity too is subject to a frightening degree of fragmentation. Later on, armed with suspicions of his master's wrongdoings and a physical description, Guo Tuo will try and fail to find him in the capital. And all of this confusion is supposed to somehow connect us by the end of the play to a bedrock version of the real Liu Mengmei and the real Du Liniang.

For everyone concerned, in some sense at least, the picture is, if not the authentic version, at least the prior version: the picture indeed comes before the girl, whether she be ghost or simply a wishful figment projected onto a corpse. Necrophilia and obsessive fixation with a portrait are literary neuroses; debased versions of a relationship with another human being both confuse—or deny—the limitations of a metaphor.

The painting and the girl are both *zhen*, real, and whether symbolically or psychologically, representational priority has become terribly confused. At the very least, the portrait has a sophistical claim, not only to being real, as all the characters seem to agree, but also to being the "real" Du Liniang. If there is indeed an authentic version and then a counterfeit, it is not clear in this case which is which—the girl (or ghost) or the portrait.

All the equivalences rest on the portrait: it is the girl in the portrait with whom Liu Mengmei falls in love, and many acts later, when she emerges from the grave, Liu Mengmei can only identify the woman who will be his wife through her resemblance to the ghost, who in turn is identified as the object of Liu's obsession only through her resemblance to the figure in the painting. In other words, what the figure in the portrait looks like is very important indeed; but for all that, the painting is explicitly neither a drawing from life nor a record of Du Liniang's current appearance. Instead, from the onset, the painting is marked by difference and absence.

It depicts not what Du Liniang looks like at the moment of painting, but what she does not look like; although both versions—the wasted painter and the lovely painting—lay claim to being what Du Liniang *is*:

> Let me take a look at myself in the mirror and see how things really are. (Making gestures of looking and of sadness) Oh dear! Before I was so enchanting and shapely—how could I have gotten so gaunt as this? If I don't take this time to make a drawing of myself to leave in the world of mortals, if I were suddenly to die, who will know that Du Liniang of Western Shu had such a beautiful face?[5]

What is to be preserved is not simply a quantity of beauty but the lineaments of an individual face, different from all others, but not her current visage, worn and thin from sadness.

Mirrors grant people two possibilities otherwise always denied: to look on oneself as others might, but also to look at oneself as if one were another—to be estranged from oneself. In an article on the painter Jacques-Louis David's self-portrait, T. J. Clark writes of the self-portraitist's gaze into the mirror: "the mirror naturalizes the movement, so to speak, making it seem to take place in space, between a self here where I am and another out there in the glass; it is only an obvious gloss on this to have the two selves be strangers to one another."[6]

In Act 10, four acts earlier, Du Liniang casually looks into a mirror before she and Chunxiang set off for their walk in the garden. But that gaze serves simply to confirm the perfect fit between who she is inside and how she appears. It provokes no thoughts on the nature of consciousness or identity. Instead, as she carries the mirror out, Chunxiang describes her mistress's elaborate coiffure and toilet for the day. Du Liniang's glance into the mirror allows her to confirm that inside and outside match up; the gazer claims the reflection.

In contrast, in Act 14, when Du Liniang gazes at her reflection in the mirror as she prepares to paint herself, something portentous takes place. This look into the mirror marks something significant, precisely a moment of estrangement: either the fragmenting of her identity or the realization that it has been fragmented all along. She is at this moment both the reflection and the gazer, as she will shortly be both the painter and the image in the painting. Later on, her identity will continue to be split among the corpse, the ghost, and the figure in the painting. Do these separate identities add up? Perhaps these different parts, referring back to a prior unity, constitute a single, unitary individual. But perhaps they resist reassembly—or even cannot be reassembled.

At the end of the play, Du Bao finds the task of properly identifying his daughter a dauntingly difficult one, since he cannot be sure whether she is who she claims to be, and if she is indeed Du Liniang, that she is human and not ghostly. But by that point, the problem of picking out the one true Du Liniang is already one of very long standing, and it is no easier to resolve here near the beginning of the play than it will be at its end.

Liu Mengmei's sense of authenticity involves priority, which can be relative. According to his own experience, the painting comes before the ghost, since he finds the painting before he meets the ghost. In what certainly parodies a conventional attitude towards portraiture, the apparitional Du Liniang finally asks him: "How do my looks compare to hers?"[7] Initially, at least, it is paradoxically not the portrait but the ghost who is so "like."

When she first appears to him, after his many entreaties to her portrait, he disbelievingly asks her: "Miss, you have come to me in the dead of night—is this a dream?" He ought to know better than to pose such a question. If he can dream up a beautiful woman, he can just as easily dream up a beautiful woman who will deny that she is a dream.

We can read her response just as we will Laitou Yuan's playful lie to Chen Zuiliang several acts in the future—as a pun on *zhen* and as playful inversions on what the real and the false are. She is a strange creature, a ghost with a peculiar relationship to a painting, both prior to it (in that some might argue that she was the painting's model) and secondary to it (in that if she differed from the painting, Liu would later consider her to be false and the painting to be real). So it is hard to tell whether she is the model for the painting or whether the painting is the model for her. But we know from Liu

Mengmei that the ghost looks like the girl in the painting, whereas she never makes any claims to looking like the girl who painted the portrait.

Such a creature faces quite a dilemma when she goes about claiming to be real. Best then to respond with a joke as she does, toying with any complacent distinction between what is real and what is not real: "It's not a dream. Take it for real [or a portrait]. My only fear is that you won't countenance me."[8] The answer satisfies Liu Mengmei at least enough so that he can make love to her in good conscience.

But the answer doesn't quell his doubts so much as underscore them, suggesting again the possibility that this entire exchange between Liu Mengmei and Du Liniang takes place within his mind either in dream or in fantasy. In a play that concludes with a trial, where both lead characters are confronted with the possibility that they might lose their identities, identity is no joking matter. The only daughter of a high official might be cast adrift, uprooted from her family and status; and the orphan, who by dint of struggle and hard work has managed to become the top examination candidate, might instead be executed as a nameless felon.

Nonetheless, he accepts the weakest of self-identifications. Liu Mengmei has been longing for the girl in the picture and has been disappointed and frustrated that he cannot have sex with a painting. To this, she says: "Take me as you would the picture" (but cannot since it is merely a picture).

This problem—that there are multiple versions of Du Liniang, each with its own claim to being the real and unique one—recurs throughout the play. Du Liniang has shown herself subject to such experiences. Her dream near the beginning of the play suggests some connection to shamanistic experience; her soul leaves her body, but then returns eventually to report what it has seen and done. As with the shamans of the *Chuci* (the ancient anthology that David Hawkes renders *The Songs of the South*), her soul leaves on a journey (and like those *Chuci* excursions, this one too is dense with flora and mysterious experience). During that dream, it is difficult to judge which—traveling soul or momentarily abandoned body—is the locus of identity or of experience. The soul's falling in love leads to her bodily decline. And even though her body remains in the yamen and has never been left alone with any man, her dream experiences already compromise her chastity.

The question of whether there is an economy of identity reaches from the beginning of the play to its end. Do the journeying soul and the sleeping body add up to the same quantity as the painter and the painting or, to choose another moment in the play, the corpse, the ghost, the painting, and the sacred tablet? Is that sum something constant and fixed that we can call Du Liniang (and which by the end of the play is invested entirely in the creature who appears in court)? According to Du Bao's way of envisioning identity, the creature claiming to be Du Liniang either is his daughter or she isn't, but the painting suggests a more complicated answer, since unitary identity itself is the question.

These issues are brought up explicitly in Act 10, in which Du Liniang paints herself. Returning to that act, we count three distinct versions of Du Liniang: the girl gazing into the mirror, her reflection in the mirror, and finally the still unfinished portrait. Mine seems to be an unexceptional accounting of this scene. A 1617 woodblock illustration depicts three faces of Du Liniang, each looking recognizably similar to the others but significantly different. I have suggested some of the reasons why the portrait and the portraitist look different, but the reflection and the person reflected are also different in appearance. Even under the best of conditions and the clearest of mirrors, reflections look different from a view of a person head-on (since everyone is asymmetrical, especially someone with a brush in her hand). Here these differences are precisely the object of observation. She takes up the project of self-portraiture, because the image in the mirror is not herself.

The painted self is enough of an other that she can address it as if it were somebody else:

> Oh, shadow. I will carefully gauge myself against you. Your cheeks so cheerful, just awaiting the mark of a cherry mouth, the stain of a willow brow, and the wash of cloud hair of floating mist. The ends of your brows fade into your hair, and you are in the felicity of the eyes. And the small kingfisher-colored filigreed pale autumn ornaments are so fitting.[9]

The image in the mirror looks quite different from its painter, but both are Du Liniang. The cheeks of a girl who has been pining away for weeks are decidedly not cheerful. Two different viewers suggest that this self-portrait, painted by a bitter, pining girl, bears an expression of serenity. Entirely independently from each other, both Liu Mengmei and the prison guard mistake it for a picture of the bodhisattva Guanyin.

The portrait aims first to capture the individual essence of Du Liniang—whatever makes her unique—but also how it differs from her current state, saddened and emaciated. Du Liniang gazes into the mirror and then speaks to herself, or rather to her self-portrait in progress. The binome I have translated as "gauge" (*pingduo*) reveals something of the problematic. *Ping* refers to a criticism on a scale of merit (here the scale is obviously aesthetic), while *duo* in contrast, alludes to a measure of accuracy. Does the portrait aim to be like or to be beautiful? Does Du Liniang the gazer consider how beautiful the portrait is, or does she gauge how closely she and the portrait resemble each other? The two acts of comparison might easily contradict, and in fact, both are gestured towards: her eyes—which like her mouth seem not yet to be painted—aim for felicity and to capture her individuality, while her ornaments are chosen for their fitness and charm.[10]

But there are manifest limits to how much we can know of Du Liniang's perception of herself. Ultimately, it is not given us to know whether there is any correspondence between how we see her and how she sees herself. After all, whatever Liu Mengmei and the prison guard might make of the girl in the portrait, she might truly be painting herself according to her own notions of incipient decline. What looks to them in the painting to be serene beauty might be to the painter subtle traces of pain and sadness. Or conversely, her decline might not even be visible to others; Chunxiang provokes Du Liniang's extreme anxieties (which are then directed toward the project of self-portraiture), not by pointing out some evidence of illness, but instead by simply mentioning as one item in a long chain of helpful bits of advice: "If you keep on worrying, then your ten-parts visage will get nine-parts worn."[11]

In other words, the painting reflects something ultimately private—a person's contemplation of her own appearance, which observers, both within the play and without, can never entirely share. And in this respect, it is not dissimilar from the dream itself, which also highlights what by now is a familiar problematic in the play—that relation between a body's surface and what lies inside.

For the moment, though, let us forget what lies inside; we will return to that later. Any time we aspire to a transparent matchup of the girl, the ghost, the figure in the portrait, and the resurrected girl, we do so only futilely. We cannot establish that the appearances of all four correspond perfectly—only that through some kind of transitive property of resemblance, they roughly approximate each other. The girl in the portrait looks something like the painter; the ghost looks something like the girl in the portrait; and finally, the resurrected girl looks something like both the ghost (according to the groom) and the painter (according to her parents, Lady Zhen and Du Bao).

But any notion that one might be a perfect copy—incapable of being distinguished from the others—is scrupulously withheld from the reader. After completing her self-portrait, Du Liniang asks her maidservant Chunxiang for her opinion. At this point, Chunxiang could compliment either the painted figure's beauty or its verisimilitude, but Chunxiang avoids either option: "The girl in colors and lines is easy to trace, but the real essence of a person is hard to copy."[12] Chunxiang, the only witness in a position to compare the portrait and the painter, leaves the question unresolved, whether in fact the real nature of a person has been successfully copied.

Nor does Liu Mengmei himself, intimately familiar with both, connect the girl in the picture with his nocturnal visitor, even though we might expect him to. After several acts of gazing fixedly and obsessively at the portrait, he still fails to identify his ghostly lover with the girl in the portrait. Only when the ghost (losing patience, I presume) finally prompts him does it occur to him to connect the two. Liu Mengmei does not automatically equate the ghost with the girl in the portrait, but once the ghost suggests the connection to him, at least he does not protest.

We have hardly any evidence that the ghost perfectly resembles the painter of the self-portrait; none of the people who knew Du Liniang well in life—her parents, her maidservant, her tutor—ever has the chance to see the ghost. Daoist Shi does catch a fleeting glimpse of the ghost, but she met Du Liniang only once in life, and that as an invalid on her deathbed, not the blooming beauty. If the ghost captures Du Liniang's likeness at all, it is at the moment of her greatest allure, recapturing the first encounter of the young lovers in Du Liniang's dream.

Skepticism, as I have maintained, is built into the play; we are denied perfect, or even adequate, equivalences between the versions of Du Liniang. Du Liniang paints herself as she appeared in her dream. But this is the very self she could not possibly have seen; the dreamed self, as Zhuangzi would argue, can appear as anything—even as a butterfly. The mutability of the dreamed self emphasizes the unbridgeable gap between what we think we look like and how we might appear to others. Of all five versions of her face, the portrait's appearance is the only one important, not in relative terms, to confirm that one face resembles one or more of the others, but in absolute terms. Du Liniang paints it to be singular, and Liu Mengmei falls in love with the individual lineaments of this particular, presumably unique face. However, this is precisely the face to which we are most denied access.

After the disinterment, Liu Mengmei must confront the difficulty of matching these various faces to each other and to a single identity. He treats it as a reunion (after all, this is supposedly his lover of many nights, to whom he has pledged his troth and for whom he risks the capital crime of grave robbery). But it is also a first meeting—no less a blind date than any orthodox late imperial wedding, no matter what else sets it apart. Anyone could have emerged, and he has already made his promise, just as anyone might really be lurking beneath a veil, regardless of what devious efforts might have been made to figure out what the bride really looks like.[13] Gazing for the first time upon the creature in the tomb, he describes her: "The young mistress is right here. An unusual fragrance draws one in, and her beautiful visage is just as it was before."[14]

Partly, he means to explain elegantly that the entombed body has undergone no rot or vermiculation, but when he tells us that she looks just as she did before, he incidentally reminds us that he is actually in no position to tell. Never having seen her before her death, he cannot judge whether the resurrected Du Liniang *does* look just as she did in life. Daoist Shi, who attended the girl at her deathbed, comes the closest, but none of them really can tell whether the girl in the tomb looks like the girl who died. Du Liniang's moving reunion with her mother and Chunxiang offers us our first authoritative proof that an equivalence can be drawn between the resurrected girl and the dead girl. Up until that point, for all we know, the three might even have broken into the wrong grave, have resurrected that girl, and treated her as if she were Du Liniang (a far-fetched possibility, but in keeping with the end of the play, where Liu Mengmei is accused of usurping another's identity—or rather, the constituent elements of his bureaucratic identity, his name and his registration on a list of successful examination candidates).

At the end of the play, no character has seen Du Liniang in all of her alleged appearances (girl, portrait, ghost, and then, after resurrection, girl again), so no individual is in a position to claim authoritatively that all four of them look alike. Perhaps when Liu Mengmei says she looks just as she did before, *rugu*, he means to say she looks just like his ghostly inamorata and that the appearance of this girl does not surprise him. Liu Mengmei can make this claim with authority, but needless to say, drawing an equivalence between the ghost and the resurrected girl doesn't remove us from this loop. We still cannot establish that all four versions of Du Liniang's face are identical (much less that they all represent the same person).

The tendency of the painting to stand in for its painter places it squarely within the constellation of issues addressed by traditional Chinese portraiture. According to Richard Vinograd, Chinese portraiture was seen as a less rigorously imaginative form of painting, whose attenuated demands on the imagination were often compared to copying. Effigy portraits in particular stood in for the deceased; Vinograd suggests that what the effigy generated was an "intimate linkage to a subject, possibly to the point of confusion."[15] Du Liniang's portrait can take her place, but so too can her sacred tablet. If the portrait has claims to being a "real" Du Liniang (claims notably strengthened by the girl's death), so too does the sacred tablet (*shenwei*), cared for and fed as the girl was in life, by order of her parents as her emanation on earth now that she is dead.

Moreover, the portrait, the tablet, and the corpse form a peculiar trio, each providing something the others don't, as if splitting up different functions of Du Liniang's identity now that the girl in whom those functions were united has died. The corpse, a repository of physical particularity, does not even figure until the scene of resurrection. Meanwhile, the sacred tablet takes on official, public duties—a version of her known to all, sanctioned by her family—while the portrait remains private, hidden, and devoted solely to her secret passion.

Representations of the same girl and possessed of complementary functions, the tablet and the portrait seemingly cannot occupy the same space at the same time. When he first visits the garden, Liu Mengmei fails to see the presumably obvious location of the shrine where the tablet is, but manages without difficulty to find hidden, within rocks no less, the portrait. And later still, accompanied by Laitou Yuan and Daoist Shi as they set out to unearth the corpse, he can find neither the location of the shrine nor the erstwhile one of the portrait. At once infinitely capacious and yet embedded in a world of mortals and institutions, the garden behind the yamen is every bit as mythical and resistant to quotidian mapping as its epigone in *Honglou meng*.

After her death, Du Liniang's identity is split up, but on the other hand, as the circumstances of her self-portrait's inception suggest, it is by no means clear that her identity was singular even in life.[16] One might facilely dismiss the core of the problem and argue that the girl was singular before she painted the picture, but the play resists that kind of solution.

Her dreaming introduces us to these problems. The spirit goes forth to meet and make love with a young man, while the body remains at home. Dramas in which the body and the soul part usually highlight the separation of body and soul, but nothing so easy takes place here. Among northern dramas, the heroine of *Qiannü lihun* (*The Soul of Qiannü Leaves Her Body*) goes into a coma at the departure of her lover: the body remains at home with her family, while her spirit joins her lover. Two separate actresses—one playing body, the other spirit—come together in the end to represent her body's awakening. A similar scene takes place in *Changsheng dian* (*The Palace of Eternal Life*), another *chuanqi* dating from the early part of the Qing dynasty. There the merging of body and soul is fraught with violence, as the actress playing the soul knocks down the one playing the body in miming their reunion.

But the situation is different here. Du Liniang's parents are clearly wrong to believe in the separation of body and soul, since no such separation seems possible. They are both guilty of identifying their daughter solely with her body at least partially because, as an only child who is a daughter, she is only a provisional solution to the problem of their family's future. In the absence of a male heir, she will have to do—a womb waiting to have a son.

To keep her chaste until they arrange her marriage, her parents sequester her body within the yamen. When she dies of passion, even though she has never left their guard, their adequation of Du Liniang with her body is proven wrong, although only Lady Zhen recognizes her mistake. Du Bao refuses to accept that what transpires inside his daughter *matters*, or that she might be different from the body whose death he witnessed. The separation of body and soul simply does not work: not only is their precious only daughter's chastity put into question, but the body sickens and dies because the soul falls in love. Later the soul needs the body; it cannot marry Liu Mengmei without the body.

Observing the girl as she paints her own portrait, there is no easy way to assign a referent to the portrait; if it is a copy, it is one that might have usurped all the qualities of the original. It represents the imagined self of the dream; and while Du Liniang is prior to her portrait in that she creates it (and nominally at least, it represents her), the portrait ends up setting off the chain of events that summons her back from the dead. The girl at the end who is married to Liu Mengmei, acknowledged to be Du Bao and Lady Zhen's daughter, judged to be human by the Emperor, and who claims continuous identity with the painter of the portrait, owes her very existence and cedes priority to the portrait found in the rocks.

Discussions of identity in contemporary Anglo-American philosophy are frequently grounded on examples like the case of Du Liniang, narratives whose like we do not expect ever really to encounter in our daily lives. To test the limits of different models of personal identity, Sydney Shoemaker, for example, proposes the case of two men—Brown and Robinson—who undergo a peculiar surgical procedure. If Brown's brain is put into Robinson's body (after Robinson's own brain has been removed) so that the resulting person seems to share all of Brown's interests, to be convinced that Brown's wife is his own, and to remember Brown's experiences, who *is* this amalgam—Brown, Robinson, or neither?

In a similar vein, Derek Parfit speculates about individuals whose bodies have been destroyed, but not before every imaginable item of information about them has been recorded and transported. He discusses one example (which resembles in some respects Du Liniang's life story):

> the Scanner destroys my brain and body. My blueprint is beamed to Mars, where another machine makes an organic *Replica* of me. My Replica thinks that he is me, and he seems to remember living my life up to the moment when I pressed the green button. In every other way, both physically and psychologically, we are exactly similar. If he returned to Earth, everyone would think that he was me.[17]

Narrative and identity are closely related problems in Western philosophy. From Plato to John Locke to Derek Parfit, philosophers seem forced to rely on story to discuss identity, and many of their conclusions seem demonstrable only through narrative.[18] Scholars of non-philosophical bents also tie together narrative and identity. For example, some psychologists argue that with Multiple Personality Disorder (MPD), more than one personality can reside within a single person. They illustrate such arguments with case studies whose plots would not seem out of place in Shoemaker's work or in Chinese tales of the supernatural.

This conflation of arguments about identity with stories takes place partly because, according to one common strategy, personal identity can only be talked about as a contingent function, something which defies and resists discussion in absolute terms and which can only be suggested in contingent cases, such as story or court case.[19] According to this strategy, discussions about identity are indeed historically inseparable from legal issues (which naturally differ from polity to polity)—no discussion of identity can ever escape its real-life context in courts of law where blame and reward are determined.

Locke writes about identity, but what he says applies equally to narrative, memory, and personal culpability: "For as far as any intelligent being can repeat the idea of any past action with the same consciousness it had of it at first, and with the same consciousness it has of any present action; so far it is the same personal self."[20] One might easily imagine this as a definition of what sort of testimony counts in court, or whether such a testifier would be criminally culpable.

According to Locke's criterion, our main character would have trouble proving herself the same individual from beginning to end. Does the creature whom the Emperor pronounces human at the end of the play have the same consciousness of her death from lovesickness as the girl who actually dies? Is this subject actually the same from beginning to end? Until the end of the play, Du Liniang refuses to give a comprehensive narrative of her experiences. And even afterwards, one might argue that her consciousness of death has radically changed: on her deathbed she regards her own passing—as her parents' only child, an unfulfilled girl who never met her lover—as unmitigated tragedy, but from the perspective of the end of the play, that death is a means to her ultimate happiness. Death allows her to meet her true love, to test his feelings for her, and finally to marry him. Locke defines a continuous, unchanging subject, who experiences actions but is not herself changed by them—and this is precisely the sort of subject Du Liniang is not.

It is not even clear how the audience could come to know of the events described by the play. The literature of the supernatural has traditionally foregrounded each incident's provenance, since how it comes to be known and who knows it constitute its proof (David Hume, for example, similarly links authority and proof). In *zhiguai* (short accounts of marvelous happenings) and *chuanqi* (not the dramatic genre but the classical short stories, often with supernatural themes), narratives are frequently structured around how the author purportedly learned of the events. Historical narratives can work the same way; unofficial histories always record how the writer has come by his information. *Taohua shan*, *Mudan ting*'s great epigone, is entirely framed by a minor figure who personally witnesses the great events of the time, and the play scrupulously accounts for those occurrences he could not have personally observed, both within the plot and in a bibliography of historical sources. *Mudan ting* is very different indeed. No single individual is granted the authority or the experience to relate the entire story, perhaps least of all its central figure Du Liniang.

In fact, more generally, the play itself defies sequential retelling. On one level, the play is simply very hard to explain: different subplots are elaborately interwoven, and the temptation is to explain each separately and the connections only later. I still have found no simple way of integrating certain important subplots to my own retelling: for example, it is entirely vital to the plot first that Lady Zhen and Chunxiang escape from the siege and then that

Chen Zuiliang is duped into thinking that the two have died. Both of these events set up the other, lesser-known resurrection at the end of the play, for from Du Bao's perspective, his dead wife also returns to life.

But something more than mere complexity of narrative stands in the way of telling the story straight from beginning to end. Both of the lead characters, Du Liniang and Liu Mengmei, challenge that Lockean sense of identity as a continuous, straightforward narrative, with a subject whose experiences change but who herself remains unchanging and constant.

Our first encounter with the garden comes in the second act. We are introduced to it not by Du Liniang, with whom the garden is so associated later, but by Liu Mengmei. The second act in *chuanqi* introduces the hero, and after telling the audience about his family background, his poverty, and his hopes for examination success, Liu Mengmei explains the source of his name: "I dreamt of a garden, where under a plum tree stood a beauty, neither tall nor short, perhaps shying off, or perhaps beckoning me. She said, 'Young Master Liu, Young Master Liu, only when you meet me will you find your destiny in marriage and your hope of worldly success.' Therefore I changed my name to Mengmei, 'Dreaming of Plums' and my style to Chunqing, 'Spring Lord.'"[21]

Much later, when Liu Mengmei espies the poem inscribed on the painting, he is surprised because it refers to his name:

> If you look closely, I am clearly standing.
> Seen from a distance, I am as free as a flying immortal.
> In some later year, I will accompany some retainer of the Lunar Palace,
> If not by the side of a plum, then by a willow.[22]

His next comment then reminds us that if the poem does suggest his name, it is also implicated in the very creation of his name. What is suggested here is no simple relationship between an object and a subject, no independent portent, randomly arising, foretelling what is to come. Cyril Birch translates Liu's response: "Wondering, pondering,/can it be true that what will come to pass/was already perceived in dream?"[23] But punning again on *zhen*, the lines just as easily read: "Is this a portrait of that which my dreaming spirit saw?" It depicts the dream with which he introduced himself in the second act, although this time it appears reinforced by an additional detail: "With that half sprig of green plum in her hand, as if embracing my very self!"[24]

The girl and the plum tree originally suggested his name, but the painting depicts not Liu Mengmei's but Du Liniang's dream. There is a circularity in identifying Liu Mengmei by his name, since the girl in the dream gave him the very name by which he later identifies himself as her destined lover. Are the dreams of the girl and the young man actually the same dream but told from different perspectives? The narrative and their relationship are circular, so that there is seemingly no point that we can choose as the beginning of the relationship of Du Liniang and Liu Mengmei, and there is no way to construct a linear timeline for it.

People are unrooted from their distinguishing marks throughout this play. Liu Mengmei is wrong to read the painting as referring to him; instead it refers to the source of his name. The mystery of his name's origin again disrupts any assignment of relative importance to Du Liniang's different manifestations. One suspects that to everyone at the end of the play, the ghost and the girl in the picture existed only to facilitate the resurrection of the girl who is the painter. The ghost and the picture give way to the official Du Liniang, the daughter of Du Bao and now the wife of Liu Mengmei. But when the ghost appears to Liu Mengmei, she appears as the girl in the picture, who represents the girl in the dream, who gives Liu Mengmei his name, as if the painter—the girl born to Du Bao and Lady Zhen—had lived only so that she could dream and paint and inspire dreams.

The portrait is a mystery when Liu Mengmei finds it. First, he thinks it depicts the bodhisattva Guanyin or the moon goddess Chang E; only after closer examination does he realize it is the self-portrait of a human girl. But Liu Mengmei's notion of self-portraiture is notably less complicated than that of Du Liniang. He doesn't read it as expressing any deep thoughts on identity or consciousness; instead, it simply contrasts with the real girl it presumably represents. Accordingly, repeated comparisons between the painting and that imagined girl accompany his first solitary, rapturous handlings of the painting.

Even if the painting's content seems magical, depicting what we think it cannot possibly, it is made simply of silk and of pigment, vulnerable to the elements. From the scene of its creation onward, the play's treatment of the portrait highlights its physicality. Du Liniang caps off the portrait's magical creation by letting this most precious of possessions out of her hands, when she sends it off with detailed instructions as to its mounting.[25] At the same time that the painting has claims to being the true version of her, its substance—fragile silk and paint—is also on our minds.

Liu Mengmei repeatedly takes up the problem of the painting's physicality. For him, this problem takes the form of concern over the painting's fragility and its vulnerability to damage.[26] However, he reassures himself that, unlike a human, if it should be damaged, the painting can always be copied: "Lest that biting wind scrape this lingering immortal, I will inlay a brocade-edged ivory to protect it. Lest it be damaged by scraping, I will seek an expert to copy it."[27]

The proposed act of copying highlights the ways in which the painting is not and cannot be a girl: unlike most people, a painting can be copied. Vinograd suggests that all portraits are at their essence copies. At any rate, in the painting of her portrait, Du Liniang explicitly aspires to make a backup where one copy still has priority. As Chunxiang suggests, it aims to copy its painter's "true essence": "The real essence of a person is hard to copy."[28]

In the hands of another artist, whatever claims it has to being Du Liniang might be lessened, but we have no particular reason to think this to be the case. The ghost of Du Liniang responds by emerging when she comes upon the young man beseeching the portrait; but what calls forth the spirit of Du Liniang is not some singular essence emanating from the painting—no exclusive tie between an artist and her work, nothing unique to the original that the copy could not share. One suspects that the result would be no different had Liu Mengmei been kneeling before a copy of her portrait. If instead Liu Mengmei had made many copies of the painting, one suspects that something about the paintings' importance would be diminished, even presuming that each copy resembled perfectly all the others.

The proposed copy presents us again with the problem of an economy of Du Liniang's identity. Previously, the question was whether all the forms of Du Liniang added up to one constant sum; this time, we ask what would happen if the paintings were copied infinitely, all exactly the same. Would all of them cease to have her identity invested in them? Would the final sum of all of the paintings be diminished, increased, or the same? When he contemplates making a copy, he has in mind perfect reproduction: like us, Liu Mengmei lives in an age of mechanical reproduction, insofar as the issue is not accuracy, but proliferation.

Copying the painting eases Liu Mengmei's worries, because he would then have an extra copy and would not have to worry so about the original's being destroyed by chance. It does not address Liu Mengmei's anxiety that the painting is a two-dimensional version of a girl and not a three-dimensional one. The copy would simply produce another painting, equally inhuman and equally susceptible to damage: "I almost accidentally ruined the painting when the wind blew embers from the lamp."[29] But if the portrait is a pornographic object whose purpose is to excite desire, then copying it would be an entirely practical idea.

As icon to be adored, as emblem of Du Liniang's identity, a copy might not retain some singular essence—Liu Mengmei does indeed fall in love with the girl in the picture, but of course he directs his affections not to the picture itself but to the imagined girl in it. He prays that the girl in the painting might emerge and be, if only for a moment, flesh and blood. To Liu Mengmei, there is only one axis along which the painting is adequate—he makes it clear that in terms of how much desire each can excite, there is no difference between a painting and a girl: "I will draw a cake to sate my hunger; you gaze to the plum as if to appease your thirst."[30] He considers taking the painting into his bed with him. What stops him is not any understanding that the painting isn't real, or recognition of its difference from a love woman, but instead recollection of its inhuman fragility: "If it were not that lifting it up I would fear besmirching the paint, I would embrace your image and lie with it."[31]

All of this behavior should strike the reader as highly suspicious, especially in a young man who just before he finds the painting complains of an excess of sexual desire: "The weather today clear and pleasant, I air out my blanket with its cloudy residue."[32] What was going through Liu Mengmei's mind on that occasion of blanket staining? And how, if at all, do those thoughts differ from these on the occasion of his longing for the girl in the picture?

He himself sows the seeds of doubt: we have every right to mistrust those intensely private early scenes between the ghost who claims to be the spirit of Du Liniang and Liu Mengmei. He asks the nocturnal visitor whether she is part of his dream, and once that possibility is suggested, it can never quite be quelled. No denial ever quite suffices to silence it entirely, since the very denial might constitute part of the dream. Later, since the resurrected girl either refuses to speak of or fails to remember what has happened, those experiences are rendered as private and unverifiable as any dream and equally unverifiable with only one witness who can or will speak of them.

I think we are meant to ask whether anything has really happened. Perhaps a ghost appears in the room who then requests that Liu disinter her body, or perhaps everything that happens takes place in Liu Mengmei's imagination. What would a witness peeking into his room have seen? The trysting couple? Or Liu Mengmei masturbating before the portrait (or dreaming and experiencing a nocturnal emission)? The scene begs these questions, especially since two of the witnesses give competing versions of events.

Laitou Yuan gives one alternative explanation in a conversation with Chen Zuiliang, suggesting that having become obsessed with her portrait, Liu Mengmei, in a bout of necrophiliac confusion, is led to unearth her corpse. When Daoist Shi barges in looking for evidence of sexual misconduct, she finds nothing, even though Liu Mengmei challenges her to look. At this point, Liu Mengmei has no clue as to his night visitor's ghostly status. Supposedly he accepts her explanation that she is a neighbor's daughter. Not knowing of her special powers, how could he so rashly place confidence in her ability to hide? He challenges Daoist Shi: "Go ahead and look: will you find some trick here? Is it hidden in the bed? In the trunk? Or stuck in my sleeve?"[33] One wonders whether he challenges Daoist Shi precisely because he knows that he is alone, except for an imagined or dreamed companion.

The characters themselves suggest this kind of forensic reading; legal action is near the surface both of this scene and of many others and explicitly fuels the two climactic scenes—both Du Liniang's trial in the underworld and the conclusion at the imperial court. In this portion of the play, characters threaten a move to court at the slightest threat of conflict. In reassuring her lover, the apparition tells him (falsely, as it turns out) that her family can take Daoist Shi to court should she start any trouble: "Don't worry—I am the daughter of a neighbor. If Daoist Shi refuses to give this matter up, then we shall accuse her of procuring."[34] And after Daoist Shi fails to find anything suspicious in Liu's room, her assistant asks sarcastically: "Are you going to willy-nilly take this matter to court, or resolve it privately?"[35]

Psychologically and symbolically, an obsession with a painting and with privately sequestering himself within his room obviously implies a measure of narcissism. However, whatever solipsistic existence is being suggested also has sexual implications beyond the psychological.

If Liu Mengmei's yearning explicitly recalls the figure of Zhenzhen's lover in the Tang tale, it also closely foreshadows the figure of the pathological masturbator in *Honglou meng*. In Chapter 12 of that canonical novel, the mysterious Daoist (whose appearances thread their way through the novel and always hearken to the novel's religious and cosmological themes) turns up once more. He gives to Jia Rui, a cousin from a poor branch of the clan, a two-faced mirror and the warning that he never look at its obverse. With such a warning, Jia Rui, who the reader has been told earlier has a history of chronic masturbation, naturally enough cannot refrain from looking and sees therein the object of his incestuous lusts, Wang Xifeng, beckoning him in to engage in sexual activity. Compulsively repeating this activity and each time losing another quantity of precious semen, Jia Rui soon dies of exhaustion: "Still in his heart he was not satisfied, and once again, he turned the mirror to its obverse. There he saw Xifeng beckoning him with her hand and calling to him, whereupon he went in again. This happened three or four times."[36]

The fact that through this entire experience Jia Rui is gazing at himself in a mirror makes the narcissism underlying this expression of sexuality explicit. The novel sets up a contrast between what is publicly visible and the private experience, highlighting the exclusivity and inaccessibility of the private: we are given two versions of his death scene, one from his perspective and one from the bystanders'. To everyone but Jia Rui, the reason for his physical decline is anything but supernatural. What the world sees simply is a man masturbating to death in his sickbed while looking into a mirror.

The same elements constitute the scene in *Mudan ting*: privacy, obsession, helplessness in the face of temptation, and a desire to pierce through a membrane of image to join the beloved in a picture. In fact, Liu Mengmei's relationship with the picture can better be compared to masturbation rather than to a nocturnal emission precisely for those qualities—a suggestion of self-aware compulsion that he might be able to resist but can't. Before the appearance of the ghost, Liu Mengmei sighs: "Alas, alone here, I cannot help myself from addressing her portrait, morning and night fondling it, adoring it, calling to it, praising it. First having her person, let me exult. I daresay the willow and the plum will have some entanglements? Oh, Miss, Miss, I am done to death looking at your form without substance."[37]

Despite his claim, of course, it is the very person he doesn't have. The picture may be many things and lay quite solid claims to Du Liniang's identity, but what it fails to be is her person in this sense, and any relationship Liu Mengmei can have with it must sadly pale before a sexual relationship with someone three-dimensional. So, much as Jia Rui—after gazing longingly at the beloved—enters the mirror, Liu Mengmei attributes thought and motivation to the girl in the painting, suggesting an equally solipsistic sexual activity. Liu also longs to enter the painting, not only comparing himself to the willow branch in the portrait, but also sighing: "I hate that this narrow spindle of a painting suffers not our two spirits to change, so that I might become a jade-leaning reed in the painting."[38]

However, the similarity between Jia Rui's demise in *Honglou meng* and Liu Mengmei's admiration of the painting in *Mudan ting* runs even deeper. Here too a perfectly prosaic and unsupernatural explanation of events is set against an internal, private—and perhaps fundamentally unknowable—experience. Even if we are led to question what happened in the room, we can never come to a truly adequate answer (just as there is no single way to articulate the cause of Jia Rui's death).

Nor is it coincidental that the two scenes in *Honglou meng* and *Mudan ting* involve masturbation and fantasy. Articulating exactly what subjectivity is through fiction and drama may in fact necessarily refer back to the circumstances of private pleasure reading, associated as they are with leisure and license in the early modern reading habits not only of Europe but also of China.[39] In *Honglou meng*, two plays seduce Lin Daiyu—seduction is indeed the operative word—and one is *Mudan ting*. At any rate, by comparing the experience of an audience (even Daoist Shi's audience of one) with that of Liu Mengmei, the scene forces us to question what witnessing is, what seeing itself is, and how the notion of the private is implicated in any formulation of both of those.[40]

Can we make the same diagnosis of Du Liniang's painting of her portrait? The very painting of the portrait—as she looks at herself and speaks to herself—bespeaks a certain measure of self-absorption. Nonetheless, the scene resists the kind of reduction Liu Mengmei's encounter with the ghost invites.

One might contrast Du Liniang's experience to that of Liu Mengmei but also to that of one of her most famous admirers. Of the many readers deeply moved by *Mudan ting*, one was Xiaoqing, an unhappy young woman who deeply identified with Du Liniang. Like her heroine, Xiaoqing became a figure in popular culture (and might have been just as fictional). Sold into concubinage, she incurred the jealousy of the primary wife, who saw to casting her into exile. A few years later, she died like Du Liniang, a frustrated teenager. Dorothy Ko describes the cult that grew up around Xiaoqing's death, complete with tourists who visited places she had lived and bought souvenirs of her brief life.

Even though Xiaoqing bases her experiences on Du Liniang, Xiaoqing's is a much more conventional form of self-expression, tinged with narcissism. Like Du Liniang, Xiaoqing speaks to her own reflection, but in contrast to Du Liniang, this is clearly a staged interiority put on for the benefit of the maidservants. One suspects that in the absence of witnesses, Xiaoqing simply would not have bothered:

> She loved speaking to her own reflection. Sometimes when the sunlight at dusk was speckled, and the mist was high and the water clear, then she would gaze down at the pool and look at herself, and chatter at her reflection as if

in conversation. When maidservants saw this, then she would stop, but then you could still see traces of sadness around her brows, as if she meant to cry.[41]

There is nothing private about Xiaoqing's actions. Instead, only ostensibly private, these actions actually constitute her public persona—that of a delicate aesthete offended and violated by the cruel buffets of fate.

But here is the real contrast with Du Liniang's talking to herself: in Xiaoqing's case, we have no real sense that this exchange with the self is a real conversation, that the reflection has any grounds to be considered another version of her, which, in another moment, could itself become an agent. Instead of representing a real fragmentation of identity—or in other words, a person's relationship with herself—the scene is meant to be read as simply the symptom of a melancholia which must be reported, lest it go unpitied.

One place these problems have converged in Western philosophical traditions is in discussions of perspective in the visual arts.[42] There are a number of passages in Shakespeare's plays that refer explicitly not only to perspectivist representations, but also to their limitations (one recalls especially the mentions of perspective in *Richard II*[43]). Literature of the Renaissance also concerns itself with this problem in art theory in less obvious ways: for example, Renaissance uses of perspective in painting resemble more than coincidentally Shakespeare's models of interiority and the unique texture of Shakespearean mimeses of reality. Both written and visual representations—in some ways more highly artificed than any that came before—have paradoxically been exorbitantly praised for being true to life, an effect dependent in both cases on a hypersensitive awareness of the relation between the spectator and the spectated, of partial relativism, and of a gap between surface and depth.

Even as Renaissance artists amazed the public with feats of verisimilitude, those same artists were keenly aware of the limitations of scientific perspective and that in some ways, at least, it was based on a fiction. As Leonardo da Vinci wrote: "If many eyes are brought together at the same time to see a single work produced by this art [scientific perspective], only one will see the function of the said perspective clearly."[44] Later on, Leonardo expressed concern that even that one set of eyes is a fiction, the picture having been created for one eye or a single point within that eye. And yet it is precisely binocular vision which leads to the effect of dimension.

To stress this paradox, artists including Leonardo and Hans Holbein in *The Ambassadors*[45] used anamorphosis first to demonstrate their own facility with scientific perspective and then to emphasize its fundamental artificiality. A perspectival representation comprehensible only from a single skewed angle, anamorphosis makes clear the fictiveness of scientific perspective: the picture that claims to represent a three-dimensional object can only be seen from one specific angle and is utterly illegible otherwise—the viewer is compressed to one point. But such a compression is always fictive and hypothetical for any viewer; it is an impossible visual cogito, since the average viewer is blessed with two eyes. Related to the Cartesian ego, it is also accordingly plagued by Cartesian anxieties and concerns: interiority, subjectivity, and how a viewer can determine what is seen simply by being present.

I have already touched upon some of the ways in which the same set of problems seems to meet in the self-portrait in *Mudan ting*. James Cahill has accounted for the rise of portraiture in the late Ming by pointing out two cultural phenomena: an increased interest in the individual and an influx of European pictures.[46] In *The Compelling Image*, Cahill argues convincingly that European pictures brought into China by Matteo Ricci and others were profoundly influential—even to those painters and members of the viewing public who made no explicit mention of them, and especially in the Jiangnan urban culture of which *Mudan ting* was a product and where it found its greatest following. Even a conservative painter like Dong Qichang, who seemed utterly uninfluenced by Western techniques, in some ways was indeed articulating a negative response to those very techniques.[47] So the fact that our portrait wrestles with these perspectival questions might even be a direct response to Western art, since Matteo Ricci, along with his woodblock prints and drawings, arrived about ten years before *Mudan ting* was written (although no direct historical connection is necessary to this argument).

It goes without saying that contemporary Chinese observers probably knew nothing about the specifics of the intellectual debates regarding perspective in Europe, but their comments are remarkably evocative—both of the problems of perspective and of *Mudan ting*. Cahill cites a contemporary's marveling at the verisimilitude of Western portraits and the work of a contemporary Chinese portraitist: "He painted portraits that looked like reflections of the models in a mirror," and "[t]heir eyebrows, eyes, and the folds of the garments were as clear as images in a mirror."[48] Jiang Shaoshu was referring to portraits in general and not exclusively to self-portraits; why then use a mirror image as a figure for resemblance rather than simply praising these paintings, for example, for being lifelike? On the one hand, scientific perspective empiricizes vision; on the other hand, the same methodology points out the limits of empiricism. Perspective concedes that there is no single, absolute way anything looks, no view that is not in some way limited, and no sight that does not implicate a particular viewer, occupying a single and fixed location in space.

Mirrors make similar demands, also producing images that seemingly occupy three-dimensional space, but in fact do not. We can tell because unlike three-dimensional objects, the images in a mirror can be seen only from certain angles. Mirrors dramatize the role of viewers in seeing, first, because the viewer often is the substance of the image, and also, because the image always reflects the position of the viewer. Any look into a mirror highlights both privacy and the way in which a particular viewer is implicated in any vision: one can never share perfectly the image one sees with another viewer, since he cannot occupy the same space as the gazer. And the image is ephemeral too—unlike a hand scroll, a mirror cannot simply be passed to a companion to show him what you yourself have just seen. In fact, in our own age, filmmakers often use mirrors to express subjectivity—for example, revealing by means of the image in a mirror how the viewer sees himself. Usually this shot is used to indicate a terrible delusion on the part of the subject, who wrongly sees herself perhaps as deformed or as beautiful or as young. In such cases, the camera then pans back to the viewer to establish what an objective witness would see, implicitly comparing the two.[49]

A handheld Chinese mirror, then, too small to contain the images of two viewers at once, becomes an apt figure for a kind of privacy, in its own way as appropriate and evocative a figure for subjectivity as dream. For there can be no perfect communication to someone else of how one's own reflection appears, and that indeed is how these problems introduced themselves to us initially in the play—with Du Liniang's gazing into the mirror and expressing dismay at her own appearance, an experience as private and as unverifiable as her erotic dream and one that introduces to us some of the epistemological problems so central to the play. In staging that scene, I envision a moment in which we cannot see the image in the mirror and perhaps not even the face of the actress, seeing instead only the face of the mirror back, dramatizing the opacity of how she sees herself. And indeed, in that scene, since what she ends up drawing is a remembered self, a dreamt self, one layer of interiority upon another—aptly embodied by the reverse of a mirror—separates us from Du Liniang's own experience.

Not only the mirror but the self-portrait itself foregrounds some of these concerns. The self-portrait seems of no constant size with regard to the girl (or to the apparition): drawn by a weak and sick young girl from life, easily carried and hidden, we assume it must be smaller than her, yet improbably she is able later to hide behind it. After the resurrection and elopement, Daoist Shi puts the question to Du Liniang directly: "How could a painting allow a person to hide? Such a thing would deceive gods and frighten ghosts."[50] This painting, changeable in size, has other magical properties as well, allowing Du Liniang to transform from one emanation of herself to another. One can readily imagine how beautiful these transformations might be when staged; when she paints the portrait, it emerges out of her, and later on as a ghost, Du Liniang can return back to it.

But in addition to being beautiful and generating a sense of uncanny, the painting also has another effect: inconsistencies in relative size identify perspectival representations. When in a picture we see a person looming taller than a house, we assume that is because the person stands much closer to us than the house. Such a picture also serves to focus attention on the viewer, since there is only one place *we* can stand where the person and the building assume those proportions. In other words, the inconsistency of relative size among girl, portrait, and ghost can also be an indication of relative distance, so long as we know that we—as the audience or the viewing public—must take account of our own presences as onlookers. Just as before, in observing Liu Mengmei's private contemplation of the portrait, all of this dramatizes what it is to witness something. Where are we the audience that we see this? And is what we are observing someone else's internal experiences?

Nor is this the only picture in the play to exhibit these characteristics. As if to underscore these points, the act directly following our heroine's painting of her self-portrait features another picture that shares some of these characteristics; the Barbarian Prince commissions a landscape painting of Hangzhou and West Lake that turns out to be similarly subject to size distortion (if only in its interpretation). For Su Shi of the Song dynasty and for poets ever after, Hangzhou's West Lake—one of the great scenic spots in China—stands in for Xi Shi, a famous beauty from the period of the Warring States. Su Shi writes: "I wish to compare West Lake to Xi Shi;/ Whatever she is, lightly made up or in heavy cosmetics, it always suits her."[51] So closely following on the heels of Du Liniang's own portrait, this painting of West Lake—metaphorically yet another portrait of a beautiful girl—is a ridiculous echo.

From the picture, the Barbarian Prince estimates the size of West Lake (actually a delicate jewel of a large pond) at ten times its size in life. He obviously has no sense of scale (or propriety as a barbarian threatening the Empire) and, not surprisingly for a barbarian, not much of an eye for looking at paintings. We cannot but mock his unsophisticated failure to understand the very nature of paintings, namely, that the size of a picture has nothing at all to do with the size of what it represents.

But he only fails to realize this essential truth about representations, because he has a notion of viewing in which the viewer is not implicated, in which there is no viewer supplying his own sense of scale and sense of relative location to interpret a picture. Even in much earlier landscape painting, figures of different sizes people the scene—not to indicate a height differential between those at the foot of a mountain and those on the top, but to indicate where the viewer was in relation to the scene. In late Ming landscape, as opposed to portraiture, one is on safer ground asserting the influence of perspectival perception, especially in a picture whose composition, like those Cahill discusses, implies a view from above (a technique unknown before the sixteenth century). This view is precisely what the Barbarian Prince describes in his imagined painting: "The tallest peak above that lake is Mount Wu, and I'm on a horse on it. Don't I look fierce! Mount Wu is the tallest, and I on my horse atop Mount Wu am the tallest still."[52]

Du Liniang, pining away for the lover encountered in the dream garden, realizes her own mortality and paints a self-portrait to preserve something of herself. But what exactly does she paint? In describing the portrait, Du Liniang uses some of the most opaque language in the play (and this in a play widely regarded by its contemporaries as stretching the envelope of opacity and allusiveness).

As some indication of how opaque and difficult the language of this act is, reputable scholars can gloss Du Liniang's aria on the completion of the portrait in wildly differing ways. The following translation is based on Xu Shuofang and Yang Xiaomei's usually excellent notes (which I have relied on extensively, but which are in this case incorrect): "I am not the equal of a petty girl of the countryside, from a little peasant household, who might meet a talented young man, and from childhood play together, playing and teasing each other with a sprig of green plum."[53] One can hardly tell that Cyril Birch is translating the same passage: "A hint of hill and stream, a gate, a door and my own self captured in likeness, bearing in hand a 'green sprig of apricot.'"[54] So the opacity of the language is one additional obstacle preventing us from getting a clear, head-on look at the painting. We have no idea what it looks like and what it really depicts. All the description—verses and verses on what she is painting and on the process of painting—ends up obscuring as much as it illuminates.

We cannot know what it looks like nor even what its subject is, because it depicts two ultimately interior scenes whose sight we cannot share—the reflection in the mirror or her memories of what she looked like during her dream jaunt in the garden. We would like to know what the girl in the painting looks like first in absolute terms, since it is she with whom Liu Mengmei falls in love, and also in relative terms, since it is against the portrait that Du Liniang the ghost compares herself. The ghost's resemblance to the painting proves to Liu Mengmei her identity as the ghost of the girl in the painting. Only through that resemblance does she become not just any ghost but that of Du Liniang.

Knowing what the portrait looks like is important for another reason as well. Like the practice of physiognomy, also popular in late imperial China, portraits promise both that people look different and that what a person looks like matters. But this portrait promises something else as well. In *Taohua shan*, what a prostitute looks like matters too, but not because anyone cares about what lies inside. A portrait like that of Du Liniang matters not merely because it depicts a beauty, but because it reveals internal truths about her, what she is. Somehow Du Liniang hopes that by leaving a portrait of herself, someone will be able to read from details of her appearance, the set of her mouth, the expression in her eyes, what her life has been about. That she ultimately succeeds must be counted as a miracle.

But that ultimate success cannot quell our questions about the very enterprise. For on a general, theoretical level, portraits—especially self-portraits—problematize the relationship between what lies inside a person and what that person looks like. Who, in looking at a photographic portrait of himself, has not felt a twinge of alienation? This portrait dramatizes that disjunction; born out of the painter's surprise at her own appearance in a mirror, there is nothing easy about the relation between how one looks and who one is.

The self-portrait opens the way to a more wide-ranging skepticism. For if we cannot know for certain that all the versions of Du Liniang look exactly like one another, we have even less guarantee that what a person looks like corresponds to who that person is. We cannot know if all four—girl, ghost, portrait, and resurrected girl—look perfectly alike. Nothing close to a perfect equivalence can be drawn, although we can tell that they do approximate each other. But even if they were perfect facsimiles, indistinguishable from each other to someone judging by external appearances, would that prove anything about whether they share a single identity?

The girl who emerges from the grave looks as Liu Mengmei expects her to—*rugu*, "as she did before"—but at first she refuses to talk and seems to remember nothing of those actions chalked up to her as a ghost, no encounter in the yamen, no nighttime trysts, no plighted troth. Even later her memories remain vague, and mostly they pertain to what she experiences not as a ghost, but as a corpse. Perhaps out of decorum, she carefully maintains distance from her memories of ghostly days, and her retelling of them is carefully drained of all the passion that marks her ghostly self. She begins her explanation to Daoist Shi of how events have appeared to her: "Events from my earlier life, I once recall[ed]."[55] It is possible to have once recalled events—in the case of amnesiacs, for example—but one might argue that the person who remembered and the person who does not might well share the same body but in some sense are different individuals.

But because she looks *rugu*, "as she did before," everyone seems to assume that she is the same creature as the ghost and hence responsible for actions she initiated then. What if the converse were the case? Suppose someone emerged from the grave looking entirely different—of unmistakably different facial features and body—but who remembered all her experiences with Liu Mengmei in detail and could speak of experiences no one else could possibly know about. Could that person be considered the resurrected Du Liniang, and would her claims to that identity be stronger or weaker than those of the creature who ends up as Liu Mengmei's wife? That possibility lies there latent in her resurrection, particularly because we never can place full faith in the physiognomic promise embodied by the portrait—that Du Liniang is who she is because of how she looks.

It is a venerable trope in Chinese literature to express shock at a change in physical appearance one has been too distracted or too depressed to notice before: white hair, gaunt and faded cheeks, loosely hanging clothing. As she prepares to paint herself, Du Liniang fits squarely in this tradition, but a much more radical disjunction between the external and the internal is in play here.

On television, we see many people whose experiences superficially resemble those of our heroine; the airwaves are filled with people who claim to have died and want to communicate their experience of the afterlife. A few attempt to prove their claims by describing a scene in which, dissociated from their bodies, they glide upwards and, looking down, see their bodies; this rather cinematic shot implicitly argues for a continuous subject. But most never touch on the problem Du Liniang repeatedly grapples with: how can a subject articulate its own birth or death? Once dead, who is left to talk about what has happened? No one is left, which makes quite appropriate Du Liniang's inarticulateness (or perhaps blindness) with regard to her own death and her rebirth.

T. J. Clark writes of David's self-portrait as a response to a traumatic encounter with a mirror, which fragments identity in just such a way. Clark reads some self-portraiture as the reassembly of identity, even as it admits the possibility of that project's failure:

> And sure enough, the face of loss stares out from scores of painters' pictures of themselves; of loss or doubt or distance or fascination with one's own unfamiliarity; the face being given back its unity—reappropriated as a totality—precisely by its look of having encountered the possibility that no such unity existed. Skepticism about the self, in other words, is one of self-portraiture's deepest and most ordinary conventions.[56]

In fact, Du Liniang decides to paint her self-portrait precisely after she senses a fragmentation in her own identity. She depicts herself out of a fear that she might not be what she looks like, or more exactly, that she has already ceased to be what she really is.

I have said that the self-portrait claims to represent uniquely privileged insight into Du Liniang's being. However, it is born as an idea, not because its painter is especially privileged in knowing how she looks, but instead because she (like all of us) is uniquely in the dark as to how she looks. After Chunxiang warns her, Du Liniang knows to look for her own decline, and only then does she make an extra effort to look in a mirror: "Oh dear, from what Chunxiang says, I Liniang must have become nine parts wasted away! Let me examine my reflection in the mirror and see what I look like."[57] And then the reflection surprises and saddens her: she is not how she looks.

She begins, as self-portraitists are wont to do, by gazing in the mirror. But one of the few things we do know for certain about the portrait is that no mirror figures in it: unlike Parmagianino, in his famous self-portrait, she elides the mirror, even though it is central to the painting's creation. When Du Liniang sits down to paint herself, she has at least two options, one of which she pursues—painting herself at the mysterious moment of the dream, clutching a sprig of plum.

But she has another option as well, not to paint a smiling girl in a garden but a closer approximation of what she sees in the mirror—a girl sadly gazing into a mirror—as an invitation to a truly understanding viewer. Such a person might look and understand what she is—a beautiful girl formerly in the bloom of health and youth, now not only worn away by lovesickness, but confronting death as she looks into a mirror. Du Liniang makes the decision not to paint that more literal portrait.

Let me contrast Du Liniang once again with Xiaoqing, the girl who may or may not have existed, who was so deeply influenced by Du Liniang. According to one version, before Xiaoqing died, she had three portraits of herself painted by a professional artist. For different reasons, the first two dissatisfy her. The first doesn't quite get her spirit; the second lacks fluidity; and so she prepares the artist to paint the third:

> She ordered him to put his pen to the side. Then, with an old serving woman, she pointed and looked, laughed and talked. At one point, she fanned the tea warmer; at another point, she picked out some books and pictures; at another point, she straightened out her own clothes; at another point, she mixed paints for him, in red and blue and many colors—all of this to set free his imaginings. After a long while, she ordered him again to start the portrait. Soon, the painting was done; and sure enough, it reached a height of eerie precision. She laughed and said, "It will do." After the artist left, she took the portrait and placed it before her couch, lit incense, and poured a libation of pear wine to it, saying, "Xiaoqing! Xiaoqing! Could your fate possibly be in this?" Clutching the table, she wept. With tears falling down continuously like rain, she cried out and died.[58]

According to the author of the prose piece, the two inadequate pictures survived, but this last painting disappeared after her death.

Xiaoqing rejects the second painting precisely because it is too accurate a depiction of her current state, which in light of her decline and impending death is understandably somber (she expresses concern that a viewer might interpret that somberness as arrogance). To prepare the artist to paint her again for the third and final time, she puts on what is explicitly a forced performance of naturalness. Even though she will die of heartbreak later in the same day, she forces herself to laugh and to perform little tasks so that he can imagine her in better days. Xiaoqing decides, as Du Liniang does, that her current ailing, grieving state is not truly herself; instead, affecting attitudes of naturalness, she must perform that true self for the painter's benefit.

As Du Liniang paints herself, the other person in the room, the ubiquitous maidservant Chunxiang, speaks to her constantly, asking her questions and commenting on the painting. But most of Du Liniang's comments during the act have been directed mostly to her half-drawn likeness and to her reflection. At that moment, if Du Bao were brought in to adjudicate (or the Emperor, or anyone else involved in that final scene), which Du Liniang would he consider to be the real one—the speaker, the reflection, or the painting? Du Bao would choose the speaker, but Du Liniang herself might not.

And anyway, the reflection cannot be separated from the speaker, even in appearance; the reflection too is an image of someone looking. Du Liniang gazes at herself gazing at herself gazing at herself, and so on—in an infinite chain, as T. J. Clark writes, broken only by fiat. The look into the mirror figures not only privacy and subjectivity, but consciousness as well: the self who is aware of a self (who is aware of a self, and so on). There is no innocent glance at one's own face in a mirror, no possible looking at oneself in a mirror in which the reflection does not also gaze back.

In the Buddhistic tradition as well, mirrors stand in for the mind. Before Du Liniang begins her painting, she takes a cloth and wipes off the mirror. One can hardly wipe off a mirror without its evoking a layer of textual memory. In the classic of the Chan tradition, the *Platform Sutra*, poetry provides the stage for an ideological battle. One monk writes a *gatha* (a poem to inspire meditation):

> The body is the tree of Perfect Wisdom (*bodhi*).
> And the mind is a bright mirror.
>
> At all times diligently wipe them
> So that they will be free from dust.[59]

His rival responds with two poems. The first reads:

> The tree of Perfect Wisdom is originally no tree.
> Nor has the bright mirror any frame.
> Buddha-nature is forever clear and pure.
> Where is there any dust?[60]

As she prepares to paint who she is, as a statement to a future in which she will have died, the gaze into the mirror is portentous indeed, a look into the mind.

Of course, this glance as she prepares to paint herself is only one of three times she looks into a mirror. The first time there seems to be no strain at all between the reflection and the girl. How can she return to that naturalized relationship between viewer and viewed?

The girl who gazes in the mirror at this moment has not yet painted herself, has not yet died, has not yet been resurrected; but after all those things happen, she will look into a mirror again, in one of *Mudan ting*'s mysterious repetitions, to prove to the Emperor and to her father that she is human. As incontrovertible proof of humanity, this test is inadequate, and it will be discussed in greater detail in the next chapter. For right now, though, imagine what it would be like for someone to hold a mirror and not leave a reflection. It strains—even defies—the imagination: what would the hand holding the mirror look like? And of course such a possibility would present obvious difficulties in the staging.

But as a gesture, it is powerfully evocative. Du Bao's difficulties in recognizing and accepting his daughter do not surprise us, partly because he has many reasons not to believe that the creature at court is really his daughter (to name just one, he did watch her die). But his reluctance is also foreshadowed by the constellation of questions surrounding the portrait and its creation. As readers, we have already grown accustomed to asking who the real Du Liniang is and to wondering whether it makes sense to think that one version can ever be proven to be real and the others false.

The act of looking into the mirror this final time also enables her to do what has escaped her before. Ever since her resurrection, Du Liniang has been notably reluctant to provide a single narration of her personal history, one which traces all of its steps and incorporates all of her identity's various forms: the human girl, the dream lover, the figure in the self-portrait, the ghostly sweetheart, the corpse, and the resurrected wife. She resists all of her mother's and Chunxiang's requests that she tell the story from a single perspective—that of the human woman who has undergone all of these experiences and who is now reunited with her family and married to Liu Mengmei. In the end, it is only after she looks into the mirror for the final time that she gives a history of her experiences in a way that she could not—or would not—before. Perhaps, she can tell the full story only after staking a claim to a unitary identity, since that claim allows Du Liniang the resurrected woman to appropriate the experiences of the ghost.

After she passes both components of the test—leaving a reflection on a mirror and footsteps as she passes—the Emperor asks her to tell him the story of her death and resurrection: "Since Liniang is of human body, she should report to the throne the events of her earlier dying and later resurrection."[61] She responds to this command with precisely the kind of testimony Locke regards as the linchpin of identity—as if the subject at the beginning, the dreaming girl, were the same as the one here at the end, the resurrected girl. If she can tell the whole story from beginning to end, from a single viewpoint, she must have been the same person from beginning to end (although passing through some very disparate forms):

Myriad years! When your servant was sixteen years old, she painted a single self-portrait. I had before dreamt of this young man, "beyond some willows, by the side of some plum trees." Because of that I grew sick and died, and I was buried in the back garden beneath a plum tree. Later, it indeed came to pass that this young man, surnamed Liu ("Willow") and named Mengmei ("Dreaming of Plums"), took up my portrait and thought of it day and night. On account of this, I appeared, and we married.[62]

But this ability comes quite late to her. She eloquently describes her experiences, but just a little bit before, she told Lady Zhen she feared testifying in court because she had no idea what to say and carefully dodges all of Chunxiang's persistent questions about the specifics of her experiences.

And so perhaps this is the way to understand the Emperor's test—as a response to the skepticism about the self brought up by Du Liniang's first look into a mirror. When she gazes into the mirror earlier in preparation for painting the portrait, she introduces two related doubts: first, there might not be a single self (or any self at all). And second, there might not be a perfect correspondence (or any correspondence at all) between how one looks and who one is. Different characters identify her (whether ghost, portrait, or resurrected girl) as Du Liniang based on equivalences between one version of her and another, each precipitously premised on the equivalence before. And these equivalences dissatisfy: they at once do not stand up to careful scrutiny, but are also all we have to tie each version of Du Liniang to the others.

The final gaze into the mirror addresses both halves of this skepticism in that it attempts to reassure us that indeed everything called Du Liniang does pertain to a single identity and that the face reflected in the mirror is a part of that. The gaze reconstitutes what was divided, and this reconstitution is entirely necessary in light of what has taken place before. All the other different versions of her have disappeared, because all have converged to form the girl before us now. Both the portrait and the sacred tablet mysteriously disappear but only after they make the resurrected Du Liniang possible. The portrait brings together Liu Mengmei and Du Liniang but then vanishes after he is imprisoned. Laitou Yuan and Daoist Shi have long abandoned the sacred tablet, since they have seen the girl resurrected, and the Emperor will momentarily grant the official existence the tablet represented to the creature before him now. We can precisely account for the corpse and the ghost, since we witnessed the melding of the two together to form the physical frame before the Emperor now. In fact, the only manifestation of

Du Liniang's identity left totally unaccounted for is the reflection, and here Du Liniang claims it for herself.

Perhaps what the Emperor seeks from this test is precisely what takes place, an answer to the second half of that skepticism about the self—that she might not be what she looks like. He grants her the opportunity to claim her own reflection, to confirm what otherwise must always be left to question.

When she looks into the mirror the first time before venturing into the garden, the reflection and the viewer are unproblematically tied to each other. The second time she gazes at her reflection, as she prepares to begin her painting, she is shocked at her own decline and disavows her own reflection, because her fragility and her emaciation are not a part of what she considers herself to be, and that disavowal leads to all the other more radical fragmentations of her identity. In contrast, the final time, at the play's conclusion, she claims her reflection as her own. The alternative when she is handed the mirror and asked to prove herself is not that she might not leave any reflection at all (as it has been pointed out, it is difficult to conceive of how this might be so), but instead that she might look into the mirror and reject what she sees there, finding it ultimately alien and not herself.

I have speculated already on how we are to know that the ghost and the resurrected girl represent the same individual, on what would have happened if someone had emerged from the grave looking entirely different, but possessed of all of the ghost's memories. There is also another possibility: what if a creature had emerged looking like Du Liniang (even possessed of some portion of her memories, as Liu Mengmei's wife seems to be), but who, once shown her own reflection in a mirror, either claims to be somebody else or rejects the reflection as someone else's? That frightening possibility will always haunt us until the resurrected creature has an opportunity to gaze into the mirror and to assent that indeed she belongs to the face, and vice versa.

The last look into the mirror responds to that skepticism—does a face necessarily match a person?—since after all, only Du Liniang can compare all the different versions of herself and assent that indeed they, including the reflection before her now, are all herself. There is only one witness who can tell us whether all five faces belong to the same person, and that is Du Liniang herself. To look into the mirror, to see neither ghost nor human but simply oneself constitutes her true claim that she is Du Liniang.

CHAPTER 2

The Lover's Dream

Dreams serve as an integral element of *Mudan ting*'s plot, partly because they have a direct impact on how Du Liniang and Liu Mengmei make decisions when awake, and also because other than the dreams there is no reasonable way to account for their actions. Someone *not* privy to the dreams of these two characters would be at a loss to provide even a remotely satisfying plot summary of the kind with which Tang Xianzu begins his preface. But it is the very nature of dreams that others are not privy to them, and this ignorance characterizes the central characters in the play. Until the end of the play, when Du Liniang reveals to the Emperor and to those gathered around exactly why she fell sick and died, most of them would not have been able to explain at all what had happened: exactly how can a girl whose death was witnessed now appear at the imperial court?

Critics and readers have long regarded dream not just as a plot device, but also as a central theme in this play, the most famous of Tang Xianzu's four "dream" plays, which also include *Nanke ji* (*The Record of Southern Bough*), *Handan ji* (*The Record of Handan*), and *Zichai ji* (*The Record of the Purple*

Hairpin). Dream was a fascination of the age, and especially in the late Ming and early Qing, the word came to evoke a whole range of concepts, including imagination, memory, subjectivity, and sensibility. At its heart, dream represents what happens inside a person, but it only achieves meaning by being juxtaposed against what is happening outside. Whole worlds might be born and die within, while without, an observer might simply see a person sleeping (as takes place in *Nanke ji*, for example). The great belletrist Zhang Dai called his two collected reminiscences of life before the fall of the Ming dynasty *Taoan mengyi* (*Recollections of Taoan's Dreams*) and *Xihu mengxun* (*Dream Seekings of West Lake*).[1] In their contrast to the new world around him, those memories are like dreams, existing now only in his mind and highlighting how much the interior experience can differ from the exterior one.

Dream stands in for the internal even for those who do not seem to believe in it. The Commentary of the Three Wives—reflections on the play compiled by the wives of a single gentleman over the course of the latter half of the seventeenth century—takes the link between dream and waking very literally, but even as they regard Du Liniang and Liu Mengmei with admiration, they explicitly associate the waking with the real. According to the Three Wives, what is internal (or what takes place in a dream) can only become real when it is effected so that others can share in the experience.

The Commentary summarizes what takes place between the two lovers: "Du Liniang did not know of Liu's dream, and later Liu did not know of Liniang's dream. Each had passion, and each had a dream. Each did not regard it as a dream, and thus was able to make it real (*zhen*)."[2] Because Liu Mengmei and Du Liniang regard their dreams as real, they are able to make events from the dreams come to pass, but initially they labor under an illusion.

The critic Wai-yee Li summons the concept of subjectivity, partly to avoid giving priority to the external experience: "In a philosophy of radical subjectivity, the margin between dreaming and the wakeful state is immaterial, insofar as the affective power of dream images is no less than that of images from waking life."[3] She identifies dreaming with enchantment and waking with disenchantment, and from there she launches into a discussion of a number of late imperial literary texts, arguing that enchantment and disenchantment form a dialectic.

But it is not clear to me whether one can in fact always (or ever) distinguish between enchantment and disenchantment. It is the very nature of enchantment that one cannot recognize it as such. This chapter focuses precisely on that act of distinction, or on where some of the issues introduced by dream meet with those of adjudication, both when the problems are purely epistemological and when they are specifically legal. Dreams always seem to invite adjudication—did I dream that or did it actually happen?—so that adjudication on identity often invokes the conditions of dreaming.

In *Mudan ting*, dream and waking are contrasting narrative frames. Explicitly and implicitly, it is difficult to distinguish one from the other, just as it is to grant one frame priority over the other, as the Three Wives wish to do. They refer to waking as real, suggesting that dream is false and secondary, but *Mudan ting* constantly undermines any assignment of priority.

The girl who became a role model for generations of late imperial women is either the one who had the dream or the one in the dream—and definitely not the one who claims her proper place in society at the end of the play. Readers do not valorize the young matron who brags (perhaps a tad defensively) to her parents that even though wealthy families cannot find a son-in-law who is an official, she herself "from her dream and from her ghostly tomb picked out a top examination candidate. How's that for an appropriate match!"[4] To most readers over the last four centuries, the married woman at the end of Act 55 is not the real Du Liniang.

Dreams and trials are paired together in this chapter, because in this play the two can hardly be talked about separately. The reader is constantly in the position of adjudicating. Comparable affective power or not, the difference between dream and waking is of great importance indeed, at least for political and legal reasons (and those reasons are central in determining the questions of identity so important to the play).

The broad concept of judgment in Chinese is very closely associated with legal adjudication, whose literature is very ancient and rich. Legal themes appear in the histories from the *Zuozhuan* onward, many dramas in all forms, and fictional narratives as well. But they are foregrounded in *gongan*, which sometimes focus on the exploits of great magistrates of the past, like Lord Bao or Lord Di, and can take any of the narrative and dramatic forms common in the late imperial period: vernacular short fiction, vernacular novels, classical short fiction, and drama (both *zaju* and Southern forms). These narratives resemble detective fiction in that the hero discovers the perpetrator of a crime and brings him to justice—although the detective in question is also the magistrate who will try the case, and more often than not, the culprit is revealed to the reader at the beginning rather than at the end. What unfolds in the body of the narrative is the execution of justice. Sherlock Holmes might find out that the guilty party is Moriarty, and yet Moriarty might still elude justice. In a *gongan*, no discovery of wrongdoing escapes the law's reach.

Dreaming, identity, and culpability are tightly bound together. Dream stands in for a subject unbounded by bodily limitations, yet a person is not considered guilty of actions committed in dream, and this provides some of the substance of Du Liniang's defense at her underworld trial: as the Flower God argues in the spirit's defense, "In response to Your Honor, this young lady committed her crime in a dream, which makes it as ephemeral as a dawn breeze or a crescent moon."[5] Her reprieve hinges at least in part on her having committed her transgressions in dream; perhaps this turn of argument suggests that the dream Du Liniang and the spirit Du Liniang—at least forensically—do not share precisely the same identity.[6]

The dream subject is guilty of fornication, but the consequences of that illicit sex are notably different than if it had taken place in a waking state. She is in no danger of becoming pregnant from a dream liaison, and she experiences no loss either to her reputation or to her virginity (similarly, the resurrected Du Liniang will disown responsibility for the sex she had with Liu Mengmei as a ghost and also claim to be a virgin).

Dreams open up many of the possibilities explored in the preceding chapter; they are a natural companion to skepticism for two reasons. First, like Zhuangzi, who dreamt that he was a butterfly and then woke not knowing whether he was truly man or butterfly, the dreamer might have a difficult time identifying one frame as dreaming and the other as waking. And second, a dream represents a point of view that can never be shared with another; to anyone who is not the dreamer, experience is always secondhand.

Du Liniang's dream represents an exception where we are in a uniquely privileged position; we witness not just the frame of her dream—her falling asleep, her waking, and her realization that what had transpired was dream—but even the dream itself as it takes place, and not from her perspective, but from our own, confirming her version of events. We do not doubt the dream. Later on, she further legitimates our perspective by taking it for her own when she paints her self-portrait. She paints the dream not as she saw it (for of course she herself could not be included in such a picture) but as we and the dream lover did.

In the annals of dreaming, our witnessing of Du Liniang's dream makes it entirely anomalous, whereas our experience of Liu Mengmei's dream represents the norm, since it is known to us only through the testimony of the dreamer. With his name as proof of the dream, Liu Mengmei relates his dream to the audience as part of his self-introduction.

We cannot verify that the girl in the dream and the nighttime lover of later in the play represent the same person. After all, other than remembering that his dream lover is of middling height, "Neither tall nor short,"[7] Liu Mengmei gives no evidence of being able to describe her physical appearance. No one can help Liu Mengmei in his quest for the girl of the dream. Contrast this uncertainty to Du Liniang's dream, where we are in a position to identify the dream lover as Liu Mengmei—provisionally, at least, since the same actor plays them both. Between Liu Mengmei's dream and us lies a seemingly insurmountable gulf.

In the Western philosophical tradition, dream has been an important question at least since Descartes posed the question: "For from whence does one know that the thoughts that occur in dreams are any more false than the others, seeing that they are often not less vivid and express?"[8] Intellectual historians often date the birth of modern notions of identity, subjectivity, and agency from that question and its better-publicized declarative sibling *cogito ergo sum*. This question suggests a very disturbing possibility, to be refuted later: if indeed one might not be able to discern the difference between dream and waking, then any moment might be dreamt, and the link between one's thoughts and the material world might be entirely fictive.

As knowingly and as cannily as Descartes' *Discourse on the Method*, even as *Mudan ting* sets up a way of talking about subjectivity, the play also questions and fragments that idea, taking apart its companion, unitary identity. Wai-yee Li and others have read the dreams in *Mudan ting* as promising a kind of subjectivity where things exist only insofar as they affect the subject, so that a state of dreaming and one of waking might not really differ from each other. However, the same two dreams in *Mudan ting* that promise that kind of subjectivity—a world reduced to what takes place inside a person's mind, with every potential for Berkeleyan solipsism—paradoxically also allow each dreamer to give life to the other. One might presume that such subjectivity is predicated on a fixed, unchanging, and unitary subject, but instead, neither Du Liniang nor Liu Mengmei is at all such a subject. Any desire we have to reduce each dreamer to a Cartesian ego—a point able to reflect on itself but incapable of proving that anything else exists—is consequently thwarted. Through dreams, the two lovers are finally able to find each other in a set of scenes whose circularity similarly defeats our efforts to generate any kind of a sequential, unbranching narrative in which single causes and effects can be isolated and matched up.

When Liu Mengmei seeks the girl in the picture, he knows nothing about her except how she looks. Du Liniang's spirit embarks on the matching quest armed with knowledge not of her lover's face, but only with hints of his name. He will prove her identity by matching her face to the picture's; she, by matching his name to the poem. In short, when the two predestined lovers meet, each has been looking for a different element of a human identity.

If recognition is vital to the play's ending, it must also take place before the couple can truly fall in love. He must identify her as the girl from the portrait, and she must identify him as the lover with whom she trysted in dream. Both of these acts of recognition turn out to be fraught with difficulty.

After he finds the portrait, he beseeches the figure in it to come down and join him. The Three Wives describe the scene: "'Miss, Mistress, Beauty, Sister'—he calls her randomly, the names slipping out of his mouth. It certainly shows the condition of distraught lovesickness."[9] I interpret those random names haphazardly called out more literally; to me, the scene shows mostly that Liu Mengmei does not know how to refer to the girl in the portrait, since he does not know her name (the poem on the painting provides a clue to his name, but not to her own).

Seeking her lover and wandering through the yamen, Du Liniang comes across a young man calling desperately to a picture, whose plight at first glance seems wholly unrelated to her own. Until she reads his name, she has no idea that he is the lover of her dream:

> Who would have thought that as a spirit wandering through this temple on several nights, I should hear from within the eastern rooms a student whispering audibly, "My sister, my beauty." That sound was so piercingly sad that it moved my spirit. Silently I crossed into his room and saw a small painting hanging up. I examined it carefully, and discovered it was the portrait of myself I had left. On the back there was a poem, matched in meter to my own. I saw the name, and it was Liu Mengmei of Lin'an. "If not by the side of a plum, then by a willow"—could this not have been ordained earlier? And so, I got leave from the judge of the underworld, and taking advantage of this opportune evening, I have come to fulfill that earlier dream.[10]

He literally summons her, calling to the painting; but it is not to his impassioned calls that she responds, for since these summons are not addressed to any name, she cannot tell that they are directed towards her. And so she asks him rhetorically: "Why do you not sing out the personal name and surname of the one you love?"[11] Only after reading his poem—and recognizing the name of the author—does she recognize him: he is the lover of whom she dreamt and for whom she pined to death.

But what she does *not* realize is also important. The name to which she responds was given to him by some emanation of herself (although she does not recall her own presence in his dream). Liu Mengmei tells us in Act 2 that he renames himself *Mengmei*, "Dreams of Plum," to commemorate his dream of a beautiful woman standing next to a flowering plum tree.

Each lover gives rise to the other, which is an added confusion in a play that deals with the oldest of all of Confucian problems—the correcting and naming of family relationships. When Du Liniang gratefully thanks Liu Mengmei after she has come back to life, she draws on a trope about benefactors, but in this family drama that concludes with a father's attempt to disown his daughter, the trope has added significance: "By resurrecting me, you are more familiar to me than my own parents."[12] *Qin* implies both emotional intimacy and consanguinity. By summoning her spirit from the portrait and by overseeing the disinterment of her corpse (which suggests not grave robbery, but midwifery), he gives her being and life and takes the place of her parents.

Paradoxically, the physical resurrection deprives her of the social status with which she was born. As the sacred tablet attests, the dead Du Liniang is still her father's daughter. But without Liu Mengmei, the risen Du Liniang would be a rootless, nameless creature. The lover takes over her father's position both in deciding who she is to marry and in granting her a place in society. The first time she is born, she is Du Bao's daughter; the second time around, she starts as Liu Mengmei's wife.

She in her turn, inspires not only his *zi* or style—Chunqing, or "Spring Lord"—but also his *ming* Mengmei, usually given one by one's parents. We can find no indication at all of what his name was before or how friends like Han Zicai might have referred to him.

The play suggests repeatedly—and especially about Liu Mengmei—that a person and a name might not be equivalent. For one thing, far too much hinges on this name, while the circumstances of its creation suggest its arbitrariness. Character after character goes out to search for him, but of all of them, Du Liniang is unique. Only she successfully identifies him merely on the basis of his name, and that perhaps because she created the name herself, not because of any intrinsic tie between the name and the man who bears it. We are left with the deep suspicion that he could be anyone—or that who he was as an individual before she named him is unimportant. In that sense she gives rise to him.

Liu Mengmei tells us about his dream in the second act, and we see Du Liniang's in the tenth, but since the play never ties the two together, we cannot know the temporal sequence of Liu Mengmei's and Du Liniang's dreams. The two dreams are mysteriously connected, but whether one is cause and the other effect cannot be known. In poetry, flowering plum marks the end of winter; its presence in both dreams would usually suggest simultaneity, but one can *dream* of plum in any season. If Du Liniang's dream came first, it would not contain hints to a preexisting person who might be found by matching him to his name. Instead, she would have been responsible for creating the name Liu Mengmei, and then later on she would have sought her own creation. All of this makes tracing an individual, sequential history for each one of them as an independent subject virtually impossible.

Nor does either of the lovers know the extent to which the narratives of their lives have been entangled. After Du Liniang's resurrection, Liu Mengmei questions her:

> Wife, you have never told me—at first, you only said you were a neighbor's daughter; who would have known that we would have moved even the underworld to mercy and have hastily become husband and wife? But all this time, to this day you have not yet told me. Did you see me at the western end of the Daoist garden? How could your poem have had the line, "Whether by the side of a plum or willow," and pinpointed my very name? Wherein this mysterious connection?[13]

Her answer to this mystery is incomplete, relating the erotic dream that followed the walk in the garden and that eventually led to her longing, her wasting away, and her death. The other part, that other dream of his in which she names him, remains unmentioned, obviously unknown to her—who of us knows when we figure in another's dream?—and perhaps forgotten by him.

In a play that so foregrounds and explores the question of what it is to be a subject, there is a kind of difficulty implicit in expressing the birth and death of a consciousness, which is exemplified by Du Liniang's peculiar behavior at her resurrection and by her reluctance later on to answer specific questions both about her birth and her death.

Perhaps the lovers cannot know the extent to which they owe each other existence. In a waking state, they start off ignorant of each other's names, and each learns the other's only with difficulty. The apparitional Du Liniang's discovery of Liu Mengmei's name is fraught with difficulty. And Du Liniang herself will not divulge her name to Liu Mengmei until he extends a promise to her, despite much wheedling on his part. In contrast, in dream, each knows the other's name. Liu Mengmei's dream girl calls to him: "Master Liu, Master Liu!" And in her parallel dream, Du Liniang allows the young man to approach her partly because he knows who she is: "I was on my way to follow Miss Du home."[14] Inexplicably, they sing to each other: "Where have we seen each other before? Now we gaze at each other silently."[15] The intertwined dreams explain their foreknowledge but also render impossible any attempt to narrate their existences separately, suggesting again that their identities coexist like the two sides (or one side) of a Moebius strip, where no independent beginning can be found that does not also entangle the other.

"Startled Out of Dream" (*Jingmeng*, Act 10) is more frequently anthologized and performed than any other act in the play, while most retellings of *Mudan ting* (whether prose fiction or plot summary) elide Liu Mengmei's dream entirely. Act 10 is characterized by the verbal bravura and polish for which Tang Xianzu is famous: his writing delights in the virtuosic, in word play, in allusion, in density, and in difficulty. In contrast, Liu Mengmei tells of his dream in straightforward, unadorned prose.

The play would be a very different one without Liu Mengmei's dream; in its absence, we could sustain the fiction of an entirely autonomous subject. Du Liniang's dream would simply have been prophetic; having dreamt of someone with a certain name, she simply later found him. Or perhaps Du Liniang might simply be the beneficiary of a fortuitous coincidence; in the course of ghostly wanderings, she has been seeking a man who happens to have a plum and a willow in his name. Having found him, she is fortunate that by coincidence he is young, handsome, and promising—an entirely suitable mate. What Liu Mengmei's companion dream does is undermine any faith we might have in the separation between a subject and an object. First she names him, and then she looks for the name. When she finds him, it is because she has created the object of her search.

But some sort of proviso to this version of identity is needed: it might be true that Liu Mengmei gives Du Liniang life, but only if one equates Du Liniang with the ghost. If one equates Du Liniang with the portrait or the corpse, Liu Mengmei does no such thing.

Similarly Du Liniang's spirit might be said to have left the underworld for any number of reasons. None is privileged in the play over another, and their very abundance indicates just how fragmented her identity has become: the maid Chunxiang and Lady Zhen commemorate the third anniversary of her death and pray for her speedy reincarnation; Daoist Shi and her assistant celebrate a memorial service for her, also to hasten her rebirth; the judge of the underworld grants her a pass; and finally, Liu Mengmei has been calling to the girl in the picture. If we privilege any single cause of her ghostly emergence over another, we have implicitly ruled on the question of who or what we think Du Liniang "really" is at that moment. If we credit Liu Mengmei for the spirit's emergence, we decide in favor of the portrait as the locus of Du Liniang's real identity. Adjudication is quite literally what takes place; as we shall see more clearly later, being and a very literal version of jurisdiction are indeed intimately connected.

Consequently, by suggesting that each lover gives rise to the other, I have implicitly decided what I think each *is*. In making such an assertion, I am adequating Du Liniang with either her spirit or her body (but not, for example, her name, which as her spirit tablet has been doing just fine without Liu Mengmei's intercession) and Liu Mengmei with his name (but not, for example, his body or his spirit, both of which we presume do not need Du Liniang's help).

In fact, though, Tang Xianzu is quite careful to render both of these imperfect equivalences, so two distinct and separate fictions of unitary identity are being disrupted. The first is a unitary identity based on narrative or on causal integrity, which premises that we can trace a single Du Liniang through time who is causally consistent. This means, first, that what a later Du Liniang knows includes anything known by an earlier Du Liniang (except those things she has forgotten), and second, that given sufficient information, we can trace in any later Du Liniang an earlier Du Liniang. By itself causal integrity does not prove identity; after all, a corpse is not the same thing as a person—even though one follows from the other and could not arise without it—no more than an acorn and an oak tree are the same thing. But upon causal integrity, identity is sometimes premised, and without causal integrity, it is difficult to make even the weakest argument that two people, separated by time, actually share the same identity.[16]

The dreams defeat efforts to forge any such consistency. We cannot perfectly equate the girl in Liu Mengmei's dream with the girl who dreams of Liu Mengmei, for they do not share memories and knowledge. In Liu Mengmei's dream—our first encounter with the heroine—she recognizes him already, exhibiting knowledge about his present and his future she cannot possess. And in her dream, the two lovers sing in unison of having seen each other before—perhaps in elliptical reference to his dream, as if that had somehow been a shared experience, rather than solely his—but certainly nothing in the waking course of events accounts for this knowledge.

Over and over we are shown that the dream world is not secondary to the waking world. And this parallels the ways in which the portrait undermines notions of representational priority, so that relatively simple questions like who the model is for the portrait become virtually impossible to answer. These inversions of priority in turn make certain assumptions we have about identity untenable.

We cannot figure out whether Liu Mengmei's name change is caused by Du Liniang's dream—or if the name change in some ways causes the dream. Du Liniang might prophetically dream of a name already in existence, already attached to a young man, but that is only one possibility. If he had been named something else, not surnamed Willow, just to pose a possibility, would her dream consequently have been an entirely different one, gesturing towards another name? Or would she simply have been looking for another individual who happens to be of the same name, seeking the willow and the plum, but no longer the individual who is the hero of our play? It does seem that she is seeking a name and not the person per se, except insofar as he is attached to the name.

The play consistently thwarts two versions of unitary identity: first, that there might be a single Du Liniang (to choose our heroine as an example), and second, that critical features of her identity cannot be split up and divided. Du Liniang's identity is divided and apportioned out to the point that assuming that she is either the ghost, the corpse, the portrait, or the sacred tablet always leaves something unexplained.

The same fragmenting of identity occurs to Liu Mengmei as well. In Chinese dramas, characters mark their first entrance onstage by introducing themselves to the audience. Liu Mengmei tweaks that convention a little bit, since the name by which he introduces himself is one he has given himself. Who is the person identifying himself by his name if the name itself is something of only recent invention? When he describes his change of name, he expresses some anxiety, for even though he changes his name both to commemorate the dream and to make himself easier for the dream lover to find, he still worries that she will find it difficult: "Even though I have changed my name and replaced my *zi*, without prophesy, how will that charming spirit know it beforehand?" In fact, the plot unfolds exactly as Liu Mengmei predicts: in the tenth act, Du Liniang *does* seemingly prophesy his name in her own dream, so that the spirit Du Liniang comes to think that she knows it beforehand—as if the name were preexisting and as if the link between man and name were fixed and constant. But we know that neither of these presumptions is true and that instead the link between the man and his name is potentially arbitrary, the product of choice. Ultimately, Du Liniang's ghost can only find Liu Mengmei by referring to the name she herself has given him.

After the two lovers are united, we might assume that his name has seemingly fulfilled its purpose and whatever natural, easy relationship people have with their names might resume. Such an assumption is confounded—perhaps between name and person no such naturalized relationship exists. The fit between Liu Mengmei and his name continues to chafe. Towards the end of the play, two searches for the young man we call Liu Mengmei are conducted simultaneously—one by Guo Tuo, the old family retainer intimately familiar with the young man's appearance and name, but not with his new status as top examination candidate, and another by two bumbling deputies from the court, who know only the young man's name and status. After a fruitless search, one deputy suggests to the other that their efforts might be rewarded with a shortcut or that they might more easily find a Liu Mengmei simply by creating one: "Let's just take someone, put the scholarly turban on them, and go to the banquet. Then when the real guy turns up, we'll just return him the cost of the dinner."[17]

The shortcut the deputies propose sounds far too familiar to us; after all, creating a person one seeks by naming him is precisely what Du Liniang herself might have accomplished through the two dreams. We know the circumstances of his name's inception. Ever afterwards, some sense of arbitrariness continues to linger on connected to his name. Even near the play's end, Liu Mengmei's name has a tendency not to stick fast to him. As the two deputies suggest, it can be separated from him, dressed in a turban, and serve as an impostor for the real man.

In highlighting the nature of spectatorship and of witnessing, dreams bring a number of legal questions to the fore, but they also suggest questions about the theatre. In some ways, Du Liniang's dream written to be performed onstage refers to the circumstances of performance itself. For at first glance, dreaming and theatre would seem to be incompatible, premised on opposites and demanding contrary beliefs. Theatre is all outer show; dreaming, in contrast, is all inner reality. A play about a dream is a creature of paradox, wrestling at all points with the complex correspondence between the inner and the outer.

Our play poses questions that have equal relevance for performance, for dream, and for legal rulings: Does outer show in fact illuminate inner reality? What remains private and unknowable? Through careful attention to outward detail, can an alert observer—whether reader, audience member, or magistrate—come to a true understanding of what is really taking place? Or are some parts destined forever to elude him?

We observe Du Liniang's dream, but none of the other characters do—they must take her account on faith. In fact, our vantage point turns out in some respects to be superior even to hers. Since we actually see her in the dream, the scene depicted in the portrait to us represents a remembered scene. To her, what she paints is only imagined. The portrait's inclusion of Du Liniang herself in the dreamscape asserts that dreaming is not mere solipsism. The portrait argues elliptically that if she could see—the scene of love, the peony pavilion, and the handsome young lover—then she too could also be seen. The portrait depicts not what she saw, but what the dreamed lover would have seen, as if such a person possessed an independent perspective.

Scenes where one person is dreaming contrast what is taking place in a person's mind with what an outside observer might see. Recall again Jia Rui's death in *Honglou meng*. None of the observers by his bedside has any idea what is really taking place; the outer show—a dying man slipping in and out of consciousness—does not do justice to Jia Rui's colorful inner life. He looks into the mirror and sees a skeleton, but turning it to the other side, he sees his beautiful in-law Wang Xifeng beckoning him into the mirror, whereupon he enters to make love to her. Of its own accord, the mirror flips over again, revealing the skeleton. But Jia Rui, unable to resist, turns it over again and continues to have sex with Xifeng until he dies. This is what the bystanders see: "They only saw him take up the mirror and look into it, let it drop, and then with his eyes open and staring pick it up again; finally the mirror fell and he did not move anymore."[18] Any effort on the observers' part to know what is truly taking place can only be entirely futile: nothing in Jia Rui's appearance indicates the drama within. Imagine this scene as it might be staged, and one clearly perceives the conflict between theatre and dream: dream is usually one moment when theatre is defeated, for then outer show fails entirely to reveal what is taking place inside.

In *Mudan ting*, though, no conflict between dreaming and the theatre arises; after all, dreaming itself is staged. That people might have dreams unknown to others is conceived of as a kind of freedom, just as the theatre itself is—a place where people are not trapped by their identities, but can be anyone, anywhere. The historian and anthropologist Greg Dening characterizes the many different opponents of theatre, some of the most famous of whom include Plato, the Catholic Church, and the conservative reign of the Qianlong Emperor, more than a century after *Mudan ting*'s writing. Dening implicitly suggests some of the connections between dream and the theatre: "Any authority, really, that is disturbed by the possibility that there is some independence between outer show and inner reality; any authority that is convinced by religion, politics or philosophy that realism is not of their own making, any authority uneasy at an audience's freedom to interpret a drama is anti-theatre."[19]

One might hate the theatre on other grounds, too, but what Dening writes is suggestive: in *Mudan ting*, realism is indeed of the characters' own making—a situation created both by dreams and by performance. And this freedom marks even the level of language. For the difficulty of the play's language—its punning, its ambiguity—leaves an unusual degree of exegetical freedom for the reader. Even a cursory glance at different glosses and translations shows how clarity is sacrificed for readerly liberty: Birch's translation and Xu Shuofang and Yang Xiaomei's edition—both impressive, even monumental, works of scholarship—differ at too many points both great and small to detail. To be bystanders—or call it what you will, the audience, the readers, the witnesses—is a position of great freedom.

All plays are not like *Mudan ting*. All plays do not exult in the liberty of the theatre; many express deep discomfort with performance and its possibilities. *Taohua shan*, discussed at length in the second half of this book, has profound misgivings about the theatre and is deeply critical of the way in which *Mudan ting* resolves the problem of internality and performance. In *Taohua shan*, performance flirts with being mere dissimulation in a way it never does in *Mudan ting*.

Since dreams limit and exclude knowledge, the power to know what is really taking place is given to no single character in the play, not even Du Liniang. Other than the viewer, there are limitations on the knowledge of every character, but there always remains the hint of a problem. Different characters' versions of what has truly taken place ultimately might not accord; Du Bao's final protests begin to suggest the kind of Rashomonian chaos the collected, conflicting testimony of all the characters would generate. Just imagine the difficulties involved if one attempted to emerge with a single coherent account based on the testimony of any two of the characters, say, the retainer Guo Tuo and the tutor Chen Zuiliang. As with Descartes, a discussion of dreaming naturally leads into a discussion of knowledge, privacy, and of proof—all legal, forensic questions as well.

In foregrounding proof and evidence, the play also foregrounds what it is to be a witness. Does a witness by her very presence change what is seen? If tests of identity are performed, does it matter who the audience is? In that light, it seems especially significant that Liu Mengmei and Du Liniang's bond is formed initially under intensely private conditions, carefully hidden from the eyes of others, except those of the audience.

Or is Liu Mengmei alone the whole time? The play makes room for—and even forces us to confront—an alternative explanation to the ghostly trysts, one that the remainder of the play debunks, but one that makes sense at this point. Perhaps Liu Mengmei is alone; perhaps the girl who appears to him is indeed a figment of his imagination or a part of a dream; perhaps we the audience and the readers at this moment are simply participating in this imagined act watching something no other possible observer could. Perhaps what is onstage represents something taking place within Liu Mengmei's mind, with no correspondence in any shared world. We have seen Du Liniang's dream precisely as if it were a waking episode—why should we not also be able to witness fantasy? Those nighttime trysts represent moments that might well be dream—and only after scrutiny (and even then the question remains worth asking) are revealed to be waking.

At this point, a reader may protest. How can the nighttime visits be fantasy or erotic dreams and not the visits of a ghost? After all, the play does say Du Liniang is there, and since everything we the readers and audience know comes from the play, we have no choice but to believe what the play says. We must rely on its directions. Or more succinctly: if the play says she is there, then she is there.

In his comments on one of the most famous of Yuan *zaju*, *Zhaoshi guer* (*The Orphan of Zhao*), the seventeenth-century playwright, essayist, and short story writer Li Yu suggests one contemporary response to this objection. In the play, a loyal retainer saves the only survivor in the House of Zhao, an infant boy. Killing his own baby son, he brings the heir up as his own child. The retainer teaches the young orphan to avenge his slaughtered family and then finally kills himself.

The basic outlines of this play's plot do not seem to have troubled Yuan or early Ming readers, but they did arouse Li Yu's suspicions. He suggests that the retainer only kills himself at the end to prove that the baby he killed was in fact his own child and not the Zhao heir. For if the old man had survived, surely someone would have suggested that simply by claiming that his own child was the Zhao heir (and killing that infant and not his own), he had assured himself glory that could never be his otherwise. Killing himself, according to Li Yu, indicates that he was not pursuing gain and that everything from beginning to end had been an act of loyalty. But of course the old man's suicide doesn't actually prove anything. For if his son were passing as the orphan of Zhao, the old man would need to kill himself, to appear truly a loyal retainer, so that his son could be a perfect impostor. *Mudan ting* had skeptical contemporaries.[20]

That particular promise—that what is onstage, is—does not hold in Tang Xianzu's plays and is a problem tied explicitly to dreaming. According to the objection, the action in *Mudan ting*'s most famous scene, "Startled Out of a Dream," when Du Liniang meets and falls in love with Liu Mengmei, does not take place, since it occurs largely in a dream (although the audience, having seen the heroine fall asleep, is informed that the dream is not contiguous with normal experience). Those onstage events represent subjective experience that cannot ever be fully proven (and whose strongest evidence is Du Liniang's death and resurrection, as the Three Wives point out)—and that in the legal senses I have already outlined (the dream lover is under no obligation to Du Liniang or her family, and their lovemaking does not compromise her chastity) did not even occur. In other plays as well, onstage events represent occurrences taking place only in the protagonist's consciousness and unknown to others. For example, in *Handan ji*, based on the Tang tale "The Record of Inside the Pillow," most of the action takes place within a dream, where everything onstage is subjective and later shown not really to have existed at all (in that case, however, unlike the protagonist, we the audience do know it all to be a dream).

But these two cases do not precisely counter the primary objection. Since the events onstage in both cases are explicitly indicated to be dream, at no time could a careful viewer truly claim confusion. Instead, by seeing Du Liniang first fall asleep, then dream, and finally wake, the reader can properly categorize any moment within Act 10. But what if there is no explicit indication at all that something onstage is illusion? Is there any precedence for judging such an onstage occurrence to be the product simply of a character's dream or imagination? Of course, I would not expect to find such convention *within* a text (whether *Mudan ting* or any other), since precisely what I am seeking are markers of distrust about what the text says. Such a precedence—of readerly skepticism—would by definition be impossible to find explicitly within a text and would be reflected instead in a critical tradition.

In *Mudan ting*, the theme of privacy is exemplified by dreams but is also an element of the romantic comedy. In a play about history and politics, like

Taohua shan, the problem might center on plots and persecutions (which also imply a contrast onstage between the perceptions of one character and those of all the others, since there too, as in romantic comedy, disparities of knowledge are highlighted). Debates in the staging of Shakespeare's *Macbeth* recapitulate some of these problems: should the ghost of the murdered man appear onstage (as the stage directions instruct) so that the audience shares in Macbeth's perspective? Or instead should the ghost not appear, so that Macbeth might recoil in horror at and speak to nothingness while the audience shares in the confusion of the other guests at the banquet?

In the last half of the seventeenth century, Lü Zhongyu claimed to have identified the real-life event that inspired *Mudan ting*. According to Lü, a young man named Mu Maocai and a young woman named Du were betrothed. But because he failed at the civil service examinations, her father planned to marry her to somebody else, whereupon she killed herself—but not before leaving a self-portrait, which her father buried with her. Several years later, when Mr. Mu tried to sell the portrait to Mr. Du, he was taken into custody on suspicion of grave robbery but refused to confess.

Shortly before approaching Mr. Du with the portrait, Mu had taken the civil service examinations; when his name appeared on the Record of Successful Candidates as the first-place candidate, he had to be freed. A month after his release, Mu and his wife tried to pay a visit to Mr. Du, but still holding a grudge, the older man refused to see the young couple. When Mrs. Du heard about the aborted visit, she secretly sent a maidservant to sneak a peek at the young man and his wife. The servant reported that Mu's wife was the dead daughter—not that the girl had been miraculously resurrected, but that her death in the first place had been a fraud, specifically perpetrated so that the young couple could be together. Lü Zhongyu concludes: "Tang Xianzu's *Mudan ting* basically relates these events; if you correlate the play to this account, it accords."[21]

Lü Zhongyu's comments speculate as to the real-life origins of the play. By no means does this short narrative purport to be literary criticism, commenting directly on the play, only to relate the supposedly real-life events upon which the play was based. Nor do I assume that in watching or reading the play Lü Zhongyu would suspect (as I have) the *characters* Liu Mengmei and Du Liniang (as opposed to their real-life counterparts, Miss Du and Mr. Mu) of wrongdoing or dissimulation. His is not, as mine is, specifically a reading of the play.

Nonetheless, Lü Zhongyu's version, which follows *Mudan ting* closely, is tantalizing in its closeness to the kind of readerly skepticism I have proposed. Applied to the play, Lü Zhongyu's account expresses a distrust of the central narrative dovetailing neatly with what Du Bao suspects: nothing magical has taken place, only something both mundane and venial. The girl whose love defeats death itself turns out to be a fraud who just wants to be with her boyfriend.

What Lü leaves out of his account are precisely the dreams and the trysts in the yamen—the unverifiable, private experiences at the center of Du Liniang and Liu Mengmei's relationship. He explains them away by the verifiable—that the young couple had a preexisting relationship. Here quite explicitly, those subjective perceptions that can never quite be proven to observers are reduced to one person's version of events—a part of legal testimony that might be believed or disbelieved by a magistrate. What would happen if Mr. Du and his daughter were both brought before the magistrate? How would he decide between the father and his daughter, who might in such desperate straits cook up a fantastic story involving a magical resurrection? If only by omission here, the connection between dreams and trials is a close one. Underlying *Mudan ting* is in fact another story—hints either of a naturalistic explanation for the magical turn of events in the play, or perhaps simply of conflicting testimonies, as Lü Zhongyu has picked up.

Essentially, Lü reads *Mudan ting* as if it represented the first half of a conventional court case. In this case of licentiousness (*jian*), as in many others, the two perpetrators have gone to extraordinary lengths to hide their wrongdoing and throw the authorities off their track. Mr. Mu and Miss Du faked her death so that they could be together. According to this reading, Miss Du's poem (the same as that written by our own Du Liniang), in which she writes, "Whether by the side of a plum or a willow," is not evidence of the supernatural or of prophesy or of the nature of a subject, but instead simply of fornication. Because she already knows the young man in question, the poem alludes to a person she already knows and has in mind, the lover whose surname Mu means "tree." Only the fact that *Mudan ting*'s Du Liniang had never met her lover except in dream (in the skeptical spirit of things, I feel obliged to add—so far as we know) saves her from such an interpretation.

In Lü Zhongyu's version, the young couple plan and execute an elopement. They are involved in a sex crime. What they do is not dissimilar from, for example, the following account of a murder case in the Yongzheng reign in the early Qing: one night, during a thunderstorm, a man was hit by lightning and died. A few weeks later, the culprit was caught and brought into custody under suspicion of murder. Earlier he had bought a large quantity of explosives, ostensibly to hunt birds with, but when searched and interrogated, he was unable to produce the quantity of explosives that would have been left over from hunting. Upon investigation, the house where the dead man had been supposedly struck was discovered to have exploded upwards—consistent with explosives and not with lightning. Later, it was discovered that the murderer and the dead man's wife had been engaged in an adulterous affair and were simply waiting for a thunderstorm at night to effect their murderous plot.[22]

Such crimes were often motivated by the desire of an adulterous pair to get rid of an inconvenient spouse, and the annals of Chinese crime are filled with clever murders of men committed by their wives and their lovers. Or are they? Quite often the mere fact that the murdered man's wife was discovered to have a lover was enough to convict the adulterous pair. One suspects that many a murderer escaped scot-free, lucky enough to have killed someone who happened to have a cheating wife.

In Lü Zhongyu's version, the two lovers do not make the claim that Miss Du has been resurrected, partly because in Lü's very dry, mundane account, such a possibility would simply appear preposterous. But imagine for a moment that they had made such a claim. In that case, if the father believed his daughter guilty of premeditated wrongdoing, such a case would certainly have passed on to a higher authority. The play and the case would then accord on basically every single point, except for a very important one: in such an account, if we are to believe in Lü Zhongyu, the young man and woman would be lying, and in *Mudan ting*, if we believe Du Liniang, they are telling the truth.

But Lü says none of this explicitly, only that his narrative does follow *Mudan ting* closely. He leaves it to the reader to apply his reading to the play. At the very least, he does intimate a reading of *Mudan ting* where their dreams do not figure and where, in consequence, the hero and heroine of our romance are just two hucksters guilty of a sex crime.

Lü Zhongyu's implied reading of *Mudan ting* suggests competing testimonies. The one represented by the play itself is elided entirely but present in the reader's mind. However, the two testimonies do not just contradict each other; they also seem fundamentally of different categories, one relying on naturalistic explanation, the other on supernatural. While Du Liniang argues that she has been resurrected from the dead by the lover whom she met in a dream, Du Bao accounts for the presence of the two lovers with a grave robber and his moll's attempt to usurp the identities of the top examination candidate and his own daughter.

The two versions mutually exclude each other, as any two competing testimonies do; if a person believes Du Bao's claims, he cannot also believe Du Liniang's. But choosing between Du Bao's story and Du Liniang's is different from adjudicating in a murder mystery between the butler and the angry ex-wife. Instead, the two claims represent different epistemological modes: one version resembles a miracle, whose proof lies in the claims of observers; the other, a phenomenon whose virtues lie in our understanding of its mechanics and likelihood. In contrast to Du Bao's suspicions (which are born out of a piece of evidence, namely, Liu Mengmei's possession of items from Du Liniang's grave), the strength of Du Liniang's case lies in the fact that so many characters corroborate it and that they are people of good repute who have nothing to gain.

In suggesting a distinction between the supernatural and the natural, I am obviously invoking a distinction foreign to late imperial Chinese thought and with its own complicated past in the intellectual history of Western Europe during the early modern period.[23] I suspect that given the absence of Western science and the culture surrounding it, many sinologists will dispute any contemporary Chinese distinction made between the supernatural and the natural. Let supernatural and natural then stand in as shorthand for these two modes of explanation, where one frames the other. Relying on logic and verifiability, Du Bao's explanation attempts to subsume Du Liniang's version (she is either a criminal or a ghost; in both cases, she has ample reason to lie).

Ji Yun records an account of a mysterious multiple murder in *Yuewei caotang biji*, an eighteenth-century collection of notes. He concludes with a reflection on the nature of judgment. One evening, in a little village near Xiancheng, two Daoists sought shelter with two Buddhist monks. The next day, it was discovered that all four men of the cloth had disappeared, although their belongings (including the silver on the travelers' persons) remained untouched and the door shut from the inside. Soon thereafter, their dead bodies were discovered, many *li* away, piled on top of one another in a dry well but otherwise mysteriously undamaged.

The case confounds its observers. The magistrate examines the evidence and cannot come up with either how or why it might have been committed: "Since nothing is missing, it's not thieves; since they were all elderly, it's not some form of licentiousness; since the Daoists stayed with the monks entirely by chance, it's not revenge; since their bodies haven't suffered even an inch of injury, it's not murder." Moreover, not even the mechanics of the crime make sense to the magistrate: "How did these four men die together? How were the four bodies moved to this well? If the gate of the hut were locked, how were they able to leave? How were they able to get to so distant a well?" Finally he concludes that he can neither solve the case, nor just as importantly, can he administer justice. In the end, no wrongdoers can be punished: "This whole incident is outside of logic; while I can try a person, I cannot try a ghost. Since there is no person to try, I can only resolve it as an open case."[24] Ghosts stand in for whatever naturalistic explanation cannot account for and for whatever realm the law cannot reach.

I am not primarily interested in arriving at a definition of the supernatural or in speculating as to whether a distinction between the natural and the supernatural could be understood by, say, a Ming dynasty playwright. Instead, I have invoked the distinction between the natural and the supernatural as a way of conceiving of the relationship between two different modes of testimony. There is nothing intrinsically different per se between the phenomenon we categorize as supernatural and the one we categorize as natural, only a difference in how we perceive it and explain it. Du Bao and Liu Mengmei—or Lü Zhongyu and Tang Xianzu—might argue forever about how the girl's return came to pass and whether it was natural or supernatural. But there is ultimately no way to *prove* a supernatural explanation any more than a naturalistic one.

Within a naturalistic framework, one might be able to substantiate one possibility over another, for example, the guilt of one suspect and the innocence of another. But imagine a judge who investigates a crime and then determines that a ghost did it. Such a judge, like the magistrate in the *Yuewei caotang biji*, has decided on a different framework entirely. While some evidence might disprove a ghost as a possible murderer—a confession, for example, explaining how the monks were lured out and ended up in the well— nothing empirical can ever *prove* that ghosts committed the murders.

Defining the supernatural as that which resists and eludes naturalistic explanation still begs the point. Such a definition does not explain how the distinction between the two originates and instead merely assigns phenomena to one category or the other. Once introduced, the concepts of the supernatural and the natural define each other. In Western intellectual history, Lorraine Daston, for example, traces a period in which "evidence *of* miracles"—when miracles provided proof for Christian doctrine and when there was no distinction between the natural and the supernatural—became the problem of "the evidence *for* miracles"—after such a distinction was made, miracles themselves were doubted and needed proof, within the framework of naturalistic explanation.[25]

In other words, the question of whether something supernatural took place resembles the question of whether something took place in a dream or in waking. Arthur C. Danto asks the same question of the work of art: "What is to distinguish an object that happens to be discontinuous with reality as thus far defined by an audience from just a new piece of reality?"[26] Ask a Ming audience about whether two realities might be alike and yet somehow discontinuous with each other, and I suspect one would get a resounding agreement, illustrated by two obsessions of the age, both the focus of our play: dreaming and the theatre.

In pursuing the question of how we mark off art from what is not art, Danto begins by invoking the example of the theater: "For knowing that it is taking place in a theater is enough to assure us that 'it is not really happening.'"[27] But if onstage and offstage look so much alike, how can we distinguish them, and why should we consider one to have priority over the other? If dreaming, the supernatural, and the theatre are frames, we must wonder how they are sustained, and how we can distinguish what lies outside the frame from what lies within.

Some of *chuanqi*'s generic characteristics invite such questions. Not only are its themes frequently metatheatrical, but also the genre's monumentality, slowness, and elaborateness invite some speculation as to the nature of the theatrical frame. Performed in its entirety, *Mudan ting* might have taken five full days or so; whole chunks of the play seem to take place practically in real time. More chamber music than symphony, *chuanqi* were performed in fairly intimate settings, the stage—even to the audience—set apart not by architecture, but by convention. A viewer would be justified in feeling the distinction between the play and real life to be blurred.

The theatre and the supernatural are bound together at many points, not least because the stage is indeed the site of wonders the like of which we do not often see otherwise. Both demand a privileged space. How does one mark off a space for the supernatural within a naturalistic framework? And how does one set aside space for a stage?

The contrast between the uncanny and the mundane, or the natural and the supernatural, is also the source for much of the play's humor. In Act 33, after he has promised his lover that he will disinter her body, Liu Mengmei turns to Daoist Shi for help. In the course of so doing, he is forced to disclose his relationship with the girl's spirit. Naturally, having just personally checked out his quarters for any trace of impropriety and failing to find anything suspicious, Daoist Shi needs a little convincing. She expresses her concerns: "You, young scholar, possessed by a spirit—could it be? Could it be?"[28] Liu Mengmei's response to her is enigmatic to an extreme: "If you don't believe me, I'll manifest some preternatural powers for you to see. I'll put a dot on the *zhu* [a character], and it will move."[29] He then inscribes the dot, and to the amazement of Daoist Shi, indeed it moves. Liu Mengmei then explains that he plans to disinter his lover's body, to which Daoist Shi responds, "Such preternatural powers, you must be the King of the Underworld!"[30]

The savvy Daoist Shi doesn't really believe Liu Mengmei is King of the Underworld, but she would like him to be the one to admit it. And she succeeds. The situation is brought back to earth when he responds, "You'll be helping with the shoveling, too."[31]

This kind of humor—in which the uncanny is juxtaposed against the mundane—reappears throughout the acts featuring Du Liniang's resurrection. Her return to life seems the most magical and ethereal of events, a miracle brought about by true love. But it is surrounded by the comic and the utterly mundane. Daoist Shi goes out to buy medicine for the soon-to-be-resurrected Du Liniang. At Chen Zuiliang's medicine shop, she chooses restorative made out of the pants of a virile man—all, of course, to the accompaniment of a constant stream of bawdy jokes.

In *chuanqi*, the characters represent a cross section of society; *Mudan ting*'s characters range from the Emperor to a scabby-headed servant, and this diverse mix is reflected on the level of language. A self-consciousness about registers of language marks much of Chinese literature from the Song dynasty on, and that use of language, of multiple registers warring—or conversing—within the same work, reaches a height in *chuanqi*. Highly allusive language drawing on the many-thousand-year legacy of Chinese literature rests cheek to jowl with bawdy jokes on bathroom functions.

In *Mudan ting*, that *chuanqi* juxtaposition of the ridiculous and the sublime takes on a philosophical dimension. The language of the play mirrors the struggle to mark off one realm as mundane and the other as miraculous. In bandying back and forth about topics as disparate as the King of the Underworld and who will have to do the shoveling when the corpse is resurrected, Liu Mengmei and Daoist Shi also struggle to delineate the metes and bounds of Liu Mengmei's supernatural powers.

Du Liniang's disinterment and resurrection from the dead is explicitly a moment where the transcendent and the material meet. After digging for a while, Daoist Shi and Laitou Yuan finally reach the coffin. Once it is exposed, Daoist Shi observes: "So the heads of the nails have rusted through, and the joints of the wood opened. I suppose the young mistress must have been going elsewhere to send off the clouds and the rain."[32] Throughout the account in the preceding acts of the liaison between Liu Mengmei and the spirit of Du Liniang, we have been told that it is her disembodied spirit that wandered the underworld, found Liu Mengmei at the old yamen, and began an affair with him.

If we take Daoist Shi's comments seriously, the spirit's progress is decidedly not metaphorical, which suggests that under the right conditions, it could be empirically confirmed, since the ghost leaves material traces, as when she deliberately scatters the plum blossoms at her shrine. Do the blossoms scattered by a ghost appear different from ones scattered by the wind? No evidence can prove the uncanny. But what of the already opened coffin? How did the spirit break it open without disturbing the earth on top of it? Like the earlier conversation between Liu Mengmei and Daoist Shi, the coffin with its opened joints and rusted nails, is another necessarily comic renegotiation of the supernatural's boundaries.

In Act 48, Chunxiang and Lady Zhen encounter in an abandoned, darkened house a solitary creature who uncannily resembles the dead Du Liniang. They both suspect that this creature is a ghost partly because of her extraordinary resemblance to the dead girl but also because of the circumstances in which they find her: she is alone and she is in the dark. Then Daoist Shi turns up, back from buying oil for the lamps. For the attendant of a young woman newly risen from the dead, she greets her old acquaintances with remarkable sangfroid, as if nothing were different: "Ho! Madame and Chunxiang, where have you come from? Everybody making a mountain out of a molehill." But then Daoist Shi begins a most ambiguous aria: "Look at her hesitate, that Lady Zhen, scared of a dimmed tomb lamp, moving away. And our Miss Du, too, looking as if she wished the sepulchral chamber would give rise to light so that she could approach."[33]

All reading is to some extent an act of adjudication, of deciding for one meaning over another; but what neither Birch, nor I, nor any translator can capture are all the multiple miniature acts of adjudication any reading of this particular poem (and hundreds like it in the play) demands, all the turns the reader might ultimately not take but which at that moment of decision also present themselves. I take this poem as an example: Daoist Shi enters upon a scene of terrible confusion. Both Lady Zhen and Chunxiang desperately want to know who this mysterious creature is, and Daoist Shi has the power immediately to enlighten Lady Zhen and Chunxiang; she might, for example, quickly declare the girl's humanity (and her own, as well) in simple, clear prose.

Instead, however, everything Daoist Shi says sustains the moment of ambiguity, allowing for both possible alternatives. *Qideng*, which I have rendered "tomb lamp," literally means "lacquered lamp," which is indeed literally the object Daoist Shi is carrying. However, *qideng* also alludes to a story about a mysterious grave.[34] While I try to combine both meanings in "tomb lamp," Birch chooses simply "lacquerware lamp." Similarly, according to Daoist Shi, Du Liniang lurks in what I have translated as a "sepulchral chamber," *youshi*, and what Birch renders as "dim shades," and what might also simply be "a dark room." Which of these three is our *youshi*? We find out later that the darkness signifies nothing more than the absence of lamplight, but *you* connotes the mysterious darkness of the tomb, a suggestion we end up rejecting because it is simply not at work in this scene. The difficulty of the play's language demands that at the level of reading—even of making sense of the play—we participate in those judgments and recognitions around which the play's plot revolves.

If we can never prove the presence of the supernatural, can a test in fact be constructed to determine whether someone is a ghost? Chunxiang and Lady Zhen suggest that the conditions of being alone and of being a ghost might have something in common. As they flee from the siege, Lady Zhen and Chunxiang seek refuge on the road and encounter someone who closely resembles Du Liniang. Naturally, since Du Liniang is dead, the resemblance frightens them; for what else could it suggest but that this creature is Du Liniang's ghost? And so Lady Zhen orders Chunxiang: "Go look in the room, quickly, to see who else is there. If there is no one, I daresay she is a ghost."[35]

The reunion of mother and daughter formally resembles Liu Mengmei's supplications to the painting: there are two competing explanations for what is taking place—one which welcomes empirical proof and one not. In contrast to that earlier scene, in this case the naturalistic explanation frames the supernatural one. Anyone who has seen the first part of this act knows there is a perfectly mundane reason Du Liniang is sitting alone in the dark: oil for the lamps has run out, and Daoist Shi has gone out to buy some more.

Lady Zhen has said that if the creature is alone, then she is a ghost.

Chunxiang sees that she is by herself and comes to the conclusion agreed on before: "Just an empty room, without even a shadow of a person. She's a ghost! She's a ghost!"[36] Rather than accept Chunxiang's conclusions, Lady Zhen begins the testing process anew. She continues: "To show me you aren't a ghost, I'll call to you three times, and I want you to respond to me, each time louder than the last."[37] Once again, the subject fails a test of her humanity, this time her voice weakening with each response. And evidence further continues to accumulate that she is a spirit when the creature exhibits the icy limbs of a ghost: as Lady Zhen observes, "Child, your hand is so cold!"[38]

Of course, the audience knows more than any of the characters do, and so we interpret her failures of these tests in the context of Du Liniang's emotional experience. There is a simple, quotidian explanation for her solitude, and overwhelming emotion accounts for the failure of her voice as well as for the coldness of her hands. But we must recall that Lady Zhen has no evidence that her daughter is alive, only a preponderance of evidence to the contrary. Not only has this creature failed each of the tests, but Lady Zhen kept vigil at her deathbed and even watched her die. Yet in spite of failure upon failure and the evidence of her own experience, Lady Zhen still decides that this is a human and her daughter. Her reaction, in short, is exactly the opposite of her husband's: at the end of the play, he remains resistant to all proof and practically all coercion, while she, in the face of a creature who fails each of her tests, judges her not only human but her own beloved daughter. Or to respect the order of Lady Zhen's decisions—by recognizing the creature as her daughter, she cannot simply turn it away as a ghost.

Evidently, just like scenes on a stage or perspectival pictures, proofs cannot stand alone; they always imply a watcher. They cannot be divorced from their target audience, for ultimately proof and belief are too closely related. Observed scenes implicate their viewers, and these trials too implicate their experimenters. We know from her conversations with Chunxiang earlier in the play that even now, her reproductive years over, Lady Zhen is far from reconciled to her own childlessness. She still longs for a child of her own as distinct from one her husband might have with a concubine.

And what about Chunxiang? Even though it was Du Liniang's solitude that convinced Chunxiang of her ghostliness, Daoist Shi's return from her errand is not enough to change Chunxiang's mind. When the results of the test change, the conclusion she reads out of the result remains the same. Instead of changing her mind when she sees Daoist Shi, Chunxiang replicates Du Bao's move at the conclusion of the play. She suggests: "I daresay this auntie is a ghost, too!"[39] Once the idea is in place that someone is a ghost, anyone who vouches for her humanity is a ghost as well, also hoping to infiltrate into humanity. And Daoist Shi, an irrepressibly irreverent hermaphrodite, would make a peculiar ghost indeed.

To both Du Bao and Chunxiang, one naysayer is a ghost; two, a conspiracy. If those who defend Du Liniang might themselves be ghosts, then what if everyone defends her (as comes to pass at the end of the play)? Would they all be subject to the charge of being ghosts? Might they not all be ghosts? Descartes suggests something similar in his search for something he can truly trust: perhaps "some malicious demon of the utmost power and cunning has employed all his energies in order to deceive me. I shall think that the sky, the air, the earth, colours, shapes, sounds, and all external things are merely the delusions of dreams which he has devised to ensnare my judgement."[40] Sometimes skepticism seems almost imperceptibly to shade into a certain kind of paranoia, as we will see much more clearly in the darker *Taohua shan*.

Shining light on to the girl's face, Daoist Shi does not even bother addressing Chunxiang's and Lady Zhen's doubts, instead striking an emotional chord: "Cease your worrying: move the lamp or go into the moonlight and look her over closely. Is it not the human face of yesteryear?"[41] Daoist Shi sings of a "human face," when she has by no means proven that or even explained why anyone should consider it a human face—since after all, it is one defining characteristic of ghosts that they look like people even when they aren't. Her companion's resemblance to the dead Du Liniang might just as well reinforce rather than debunk the argument that she is a ghost. And, in fact, the reader familiar with the play knows that resemblance proves nothing. Several acts later, that same resemblance to the dead girl (which convinces the mother of her humanity) has the opposite effect on her father. His first look at her outrages him: "This ghost is the very spirit and image of her. What shamelessness!"[42]

Like Lady Zhen, we trust in Du Liniang's identity, but do the tests meant to confirm it—checking whether she is alone, asking her to respond more and more loudly—make any sense at all? After all, we know already that it is not her failure or her success at these tests that makes her mother and Chunxiang believe in Du Liniang's humanity and identity. Lady Zhen believes the girl is human even when she fails each test; and Chunxiang believes she is a ghost even when Daoist Shi shows up and vouches for her young mistress.

Perhaps such tests are in themselves flawed because they are simply incommensurate to the task at hand. This general critique of evidence and proof comes from within the play, where tests (though central to the play in some respects) do not seem to work very well, for mostly they are deployed to mark off the borders of the supernatural. As the magistrate in the *Yuewei caotang biji* discerns, the closest one can get to a proof of the supernatural is to concede that no naturalistic explanation can account for the phenomenon.

Back in Act 33, after revealing his relationship with Du Liniang, Liu Mengmei proves his account of events by making the character *zhu* move. If Liu Mengmei means to prove something specific to Daoist Shi, he has botched things up considerably: it is by no means clear what he seeks to prove by so doing. His proof—precisely because it invokes the supernatural—lacks any specificity. In its magic and defiance of expectation, Liu Mengmei's test might be proving anything. Making the dot move works equally well to prove that he is possessed, or a ghost, or even the King of the Underworld, as Daoist Shi suggests. A test in the context of the supernatural might prove just about anything. One surmises that demonstrating magical abilities is not the most effective or persuasive means of proving to Daoist Shi or to anyone else that one is not possessed by an evil spirit. In fact, of all ways, it may well be the worst.

The only consistent reading of this scene is as a threat. Indeed almost immediately after this demonstration of prowess, Daoist Shi becomes remarkably pliable, obsequiously agreeing with everything Liu Mengmei says and offering him all sorts of help. As befits someone coerced but unpersuaded, she only protests when faced with an unpleasant choice: opposing Liu Mengmei's wishes or those of an equally coercive and potentially punitive power—that of the state. When he tells her that the task he has in mind is the disinterment of Du Liniang's body, she fearfully cites the Ming Code's punishments for grave robbing.[43]

Interestingly, Liu Mengmei's demonstration fails to provoke a single question from her (even though everything we know about her inquisitive—someone less sympathetic might even say prying—nature leads us to think that inside she is bursting with questions). Later, the instant she is left alone with the risen Du Liniang and no longer threatened, all the repressed questions emerge—especially those concerning specific details of their relationship and her resurrection.

As the reader of the play knows, this relatively minor act is among the least important attempts at proof in the entire play, which, after all, builds up to those much more grandiose tests conducted by the Emperor himself. But does this exchange between Liu Mengmei and Daoist Shi serve as a model for how proof works in all cases in *Mudan ting*? Proofs here and elsewhere can be acts of violence. Perhaps the Emperor's tests—rather than Du Bao's suspicions—establish whether Du Liniang is a human not because of what the tests are, but because of who the examiner is—the most powerful individual in the Empire and Du Bao's superior.

There seems no separating proof from its human context, no promise of knowledge not limited to a specific individual. But knowledge and proof are not always so invidious as Daoist Shi's reactions to Liu Mengmei's demonstration. This kind of knowledge, inseparable from its context and the person who bears it, is also the stuff of which all human contact is built, at its highest ends, granting humanity and expressing love.

In Christian traditions, many of these discussions—about identity and what it is to be a person and about the exact demarcations of the spiritual realm—have their origins in theological debate. I have argued that the concept of the supernatural has the same relationship to the natural as dreaming does to waking. But the word "supernatural" has its own complicated history; it originates in the work of Thomas Aquinas and is itself a word heavy with debate. In a discussion on authority and knowledge that I have drawn on, Hume questions miracles, but his critique remains inextricably linked to his attack on the Church Fathers. Western philosophy and Christian theology share something of the same lineage, and many of the questions addressed by the one are inseparable from their versions in the other. When one asks how scattered parts of a body are to be gathered together at the Apocalypse and at what age and in what physical condition the body will enjoy eternal life, one is really not too far from asking what the true essence of a person is.

Christian theologians worried about the problems that cannibalism, for example, presented to resurrection: once the eaten part became integrated within the eater, how would resurrection of the two separate people take place? How could they be separated if one had become physically incorporated into the other? Twentieth-century counterparts to these theologians concern themselves with similar problems: who would result, for example, from a brain transplant, the person whose brain it was or the person whose body it was? The work of Caroline Walker Bynum, the European historian, focuses on the medieval part of this lineage of thought, and she at one point explicitly compares medieval thinkers on identity with their modern counterparts, comparing some of the modern thought experiments I have discussed to "medieval considerations of risen umbilical cords and fingernails."[44]

Mudan ting contains many of the elements of the Christian passion for a different reason: resurrection as a plot device can be a natural partner to questions about identity even in the absence of Christianity.[45] Exactly what part of Du Liniang experiences resurrection? If what lies inside the coffin is indeed her body, and if her spirit (a separate entity) has been the one to engage in the love affair with Liu Mengmei, then how are they to come together and form a single unit? And here too we encounter the belated ironic version of these debates: once there is a distinction between the natural and the supernatural, certain questions—the number of angels that can fit on the head of a pin or whether the nails in the coffin of a resurrected girl will show strain—become humorous.

Mudan ting deals with subjectivity and identity by wholeheartedly embracing complexity and contradiction. While there is a historical context for these ideas, there is certainly no consensus as to what such things as a subject, or identity, or the mind might be—even with cultural and historical limitations in place, if only in the Chinese case, say, or if in the sixteenth-century Chinese case, or if in the case of Western Europe. For to be sure, there is no such consensus, neither for any period nor for any intellectual tradition.

But it is tempting to project consensus on the past even when we do not expect it of the present. Focusing his attentions on pre-Buddhist texts, Yü Ying-shih has examined different terms in Chinese—*hun* and *po* (and to a lesser extent *ling*, *gui*, and *shen*)—which are all usually translated as "soul," attempting to fix exactly what constant relation each bears to the others.[46] In this context (and with obvious relevance for the reader of *Mudan ting*), Yü cites the Han thinker Zheng Xuan, who divides up the body and the mind: "the hun governs man's spirit (*shen* including *hsin*, mind or heart) and the *po* governs his body (including the senses.)"[47] Yü both seeks and posits "a common core of beliefs . . . shared by the elite and popular cultures"[48] and examines texts without very much concern for their particularity, but only as elucidating a single *mentalité* stretching over centuries and very disparate subcultures. This kind of effort rests on the assumption that such unified concepts exist and await a scholar to reassemble them out of their textual fragments. Naturally, he finds precisely what he is seeking—or rather, as Du Liniang might have done with her lover, he creates the unified tradition he seeks.

Some of the texts Yü Ying-shih chooses are actually engaged in precisely the same act as Yü himself, creating a single tradition where there were many. My sense is that Yü's project cuts off at the introduction of Buddhism precisely because he seeks an ideologically pure, entirely Han world (an intellectual move as old as the Tang dynasty).

Yü focuses his attentions on a period fifteen hundred years before *Mudan ting*'s time, but I am sure some of my readers are now wondering why I have not chosen a similar approach, by examining the use of the term *hun*, say, or *gui*, in contemporary sources. I hope I have shown clearly that *Mudan ting* consistently foils these unifying moves; any effort to find a single answer to what the *hun* is of *Huanhun ji* (*Mudan ting*'s other title, *The Record of the Soul's Return*) is as patently futile as the search for a single Du Liniang, a discrete body we might trace from the beginning of the play to its end. Instead, the play delights in paradox, in good humor, in a soul that bursts its coffin's nails in its eagerness to get out, but who at the same time has been arguing her case before an underworld magistrate, in a ghost who still delights in the most human of activities: physical passion with another person.

In other words, a play like *Mudan ting* practically mocks the efforts of scholars like Yü Ying-shih (and his late imperial counterparts) to define the different components of a soul, to analyze a word like *hun* in search of a single constant meaning (or even a set of meanings). Identity's paradoxes, Du Liniang's experience argues strongly, cannot be sorted out simply by proper categorization and diligent philology.

Yet despite the impossibility of ever pinning down a single vision of identity shared by a culture, the substance of this problem of comparison is one of the central philosophical concerns of our own time, appearing in many different forms throughout the academy. For example, where feminist scholars might ask whether in fact a male subject is the same as a female subject, a European historian might ask whether a sixteenth-century European subject is distinct from a twentieth-century one. An anthropologist might question whether the subject itself even exists in certain other cultures, and a political scientist might struggle with the political implications of these different histories of the subject.

My version of the question, though weaker, is more venerable and traces its lineage from some ways of accounting for cultural difference dating from the Enlightenment. I am not interested in characterizing a generic sixteenth-century Chinese subject or a generic twentieth-century American one, but—as befits a literary critic—in particularities, in whether, say, a conversation between Descartes and Tang Xianzu is possible. In researching and writing this book, I have drawn extensively on Western philosophical sources, so the problem seems particularly relevant to me on at least two levels: first, that I have inherited this problem from generations of Western thinkers, and second, that *Mudan ting* itself approaches the question of what it is to be a subject and what a soul is from an altogether knowing and sophisticated perspective.

I opened this chapter with Descartes, and an astute, historicist reader might well criticize me for taking his ideas about knowledge and subjectivity out of context. Later in *Discourse* and also in *Meditations*, there are passages not only less frequently read but much more difficult to understand, since they draw heavily on contemporary theological argument. To wit, Descartes resolves a potentially nihilistic skepticism by proving first that God exists and then that a benevolent God would not deceive his creatures.

The dreamer of whom Descartes speaks, who cannot tell whether he is dreaming or awake, who does not know whether in fact his senses inform him correctly or whether an evil demon controls them, is also profoundly informed by more than a thousand years of Christian thinking. Descartes' dreamer has very different concerns from our two dreamers, Liu Mengmei and Du Liniang. But is there any ground on which these dreamers can meet? I close this chapter, then, with another devoutly Catholic thinker, who also muses precisely on this question—what dreams imply about the soul and the subject—and defends his views to a contemporary Chinese intellectual.

Giulio Aleni, a Jesuit in the generation after Matteo Ricci, in his attempt to convert Ye Xianggao, a scholar-official, presented to him some of the main tenets of Catholicism, to which Ye Xianggao posed a number of interesting objections. Later, Aleni wrote up the dialogue (perhaps with some editorial help) in classical Chinese.

Aleni explained the Catholic religion, fielding questions on the nature of God and of the soul. When he reached the doctrine of eternal reward and punishment, Ye Xianggao presented an objection; he could not accept Aleni's concept of the hereafter. Reward and punishment are perceived by the senses, Ye argued; once the body has died, it will have lost the wherewithal to perceive either punishment or pain. How then can eternal reward or punishment be dispensed in the absence of the capacity to feel pain or pleasure? Ye maintained: "When a person dies, he can be seen immediately to have collapsed. His body will have lost that through which it experiences, and pain and pleasure will have lost that which they can affect. Even if the spirit were not extinguished, how could it see the body decaying and returning to dust? Much less able to receive pleasure or pain!"[49]

Aleni responded by emphasizing various points of Catholic doctrine, but making no headway in convincing Ye Xianggao, he switched tacks. To address Ye Xianggao's objections, he began an anecdote. Aleni told of an otherwise devout physician who shared Ye's exact doubts about the immortality of the soul. Although he was otherwise a faithful Christian, he could not swallow his doubts about the soul's fate after death. Like Ye Xianggao, he wondered how the soul could perceive eternal punishment and reward after the body's death.

The good doctor's doubts were resolved by a series of dreams in which a beautiful youth appeared to him and led him into a city full of delightful sights and sounds. After a few visits to this city, the beautiful youth challenged the physician by asking: "How were you able to see those heavenly things? Were you dreaming or waking?" The physician responded that he was dreaming, and after further inquiry, agreed that he could see even though his eyes were closed. The youth then responded triumphantly: "Therefore after you die, your spirit will itself have that which it can use; without ears, it can hear; without eyes, it can see; without a tongue, it can taste. So pain and pleasure will necessarily have receptors and will not float with nothing to which to attach themselves."[50]

There are several important points to note here. To Ye Xianggao, dream served to prove a subjectivity that can be separated from a body—as we have seen in *Mudan ting*. As in the play, dream represented to Ye and to Aleni a mode of reality and perception no less real than waking, though framed by it. But perhaps most importantly, in a conversation on subjectivity and the soul, on who a person is beyond simply bodily continuity, a seventeenth-century Jesuit and his contemporary, a Chinese literatus—each fully the master of his intellectual tradition—are able to communicate with each other, and in terms not at all alien to this work.

In *Mudan ting*, things strain at their frames. A representation strays out—literally from its frame—and becomes what it represents. Dream blurs with waking. Naturalistic explanation cannot keep the supernatural within its bounds. The miraculous is sought: the cries of a bereaved mother that she might once again have a child, the pleas of a lover that a girl in a picture might emerge. But then it will not stay where it is expected and instead keeps intruding into the mundane—those rusted nails that show the corpse straining its way out of the coffin.

And so ultimately, all this talk of frames, and of subjects, and of adjudication, of how one can tell dreaming from waking, comes to this—the point at which the play arrives as well: what is the difference between people and ghosts, and how can it be established? Clearly, no one can tell the difference through superficial observation (or even close scrutiny), since characters do not trust their abilities to tell at first glance, or at second or third.

There is some evidence that the difference between human and ghost is not a physical one. When the mother and the daughter are reunited, as if to discourage an adjudication on physical grounds, Du Liniang's cold hands turn out to be a red herring, and eventually Lady Zhen chooses to treat this creature as her daughter for entirely different reasons. Liu Mengmei makes it clear that while still in the old yamen, the lovers consummated their relationship with normal sexual intercourse, and he was unable to tell whether she was human or not—or instead, that not having any reason to think her anything but human, the question never even came up.

This conforms with what we know about ghosts: they are simulacra of people, whose very likeness to and ability to pass as humans is what makes them ghostly, so that it would be quite paradoxical if any immediately apparent physical characteristic could distinguish them. When each character is forced to make a judgment on Du Liniang's identity, each one makes an entirely different sort of ruling. I have already discussed the contrasting responses of Du Liniang's parents in their attempts to determine whether their daughter is a human or a ghost; Liu Mengmei can scarcely believe it when the apparitional Du Liniang tells him what she is but accepts what she says on faith; and the dénouement of the play hinges, as I have said, on the Emperor's judgment on this crucial question.

All the other acts of adjudication foreshadow this one: what is it to be a ghost? And how does answering that question also determine what it is to be a human? In concluding that he could not resolve the case, Ji Yun's magistrate from the *Yuewei* starts us off with as good a working definition as any: "I can bring a human to trial. I cannot bring a ghost to trial." But could he marry a ghost, as Liu Mengmei seems to do? That is the subject of the following chapter. Ultimately, in this play, although the question of what distinguishes ghost from human also implies positions on aesthetic, literary, and epistemological axes, the last scene makes it explicit that one functional answer is determined by the point at which politics and the family meet: after all, the final decision, by which everyone else will have to abide, remains the Emperor's.

CHAPTER 3

The Emperor's Promise

Like the last acts of the play, this last chapter on *Mudan ting* concerns Du Liniang's reintegration into human society. This particular focus lies well outside the mainstream both of scholarship on and popular interest in the play. For all one could tell from most readers' impressions of the play, one might think that Du Liniang really had died, even though there are thirty-five acts yet to go. Traditional readers seem to have been mostly interested in the heroine's excess of feeling for a lover encountered only in dream, her absolute refusal to accommodate herself to circumstances diminished in any way from those of the dream, and her willingness to die for love.

According to the priorities of such readers, it is her death that is real and the resurrection and reintegration in human society later on that seem somehow less real. Readers' responses hint that the dream existence is as real as the waking one. Nonetheless, in my view, *Mudan ting* firmly comes down on the side of marriage and wakefulness, arguing strongly that the Confucian polity is ultimately redeemable not just in dream, but in waking fact. What other romance spends so much of its energies describing the reunion between a lover and her parents? These reunions—first with her mother and then with her father—occupy the last twenty acts of the play, and fully as much care and art has been invested in their unfolding as in the conclusion of the relationship between the two young lovers.

This chapter focuses on the Emperor's command to Du Liniang and to her family, which essentially concludes the play. After she passes both tests—leaving a reflection in a mirror and footsteps where she passes—the Emperor proclaims: "We have listened carefully to the testimony of Du Liniang, and there is no doubt that she has been resurrected. After the eunuchs have escorted them past the Meridian Gate, father and daughter, husband and wife will all recognize each other, and returning to their home, they will all form one family."[1]

The Emperor's declaration of her humanity must be meaningful, since so much of our understanding of the play depends on how we read Du Liniang's resurrection. But hers is a peculiar passage from death to life. For one thing, it is by no means clear what differentiates her particular death from life. The problem of differentiating the living from the dead confronts Liu Mengmei, Lady Zhen, and Du Bao, and their criteria for making a judgment will be discussed at greater length in this chapter. But even to the reader, distinguishing between Du Liniang's life and death is no easy task. What makes the difference between life and death meaningful, when they seem so similar in Du Liniang's case? For her, death and life involve many of the same activities and preoccupations, central among them making love to Liu Mengmei.

The first half of this chapter mostly deals with Du Liniang's resurrection, which takes on a special importance, since any sense in the play of what ties together the living and the dead while keeping them different and separate must be grounded in the actual moment of her rebirth. We know that when she died, Du Liniang's body was placed in the tomb, but other objects were as well. Later, when she emerges from the grave, those objects also emerge. Traffic between the world of mortals and the netherworld takes on many forms and colors our understanding of both Du Liniang's life and her death.

In the second half of this chapter, the other part of the Emperor's twofold promise will be explored: "After the eunuchs have escorted them past the Meridian Gate, father and daughter, husband and wife will all recognize each other, and returning to their home, they will all form one family." *Chengqin*—which I have translated as "form one family"—usually refers simply to the act of marriage, through which two unrelated people become relatives. In legal sources, *chengqin* refers to the consummation of the marriage that takes place after the bride has *guomen*—"entered the house."

But this is a very special case. Here, *chengqin* does not refer simply to the young couple, but to all of those concerned: all four of these individuals (for recall that Du Liniang's mother and father have also been separated and are also reunited) must come together to form a family. The questions of her human identity and her position within a family are obviously tied together. After losing her human identity by being resurrected, she and Liu Mengmei get into trouble claiming to be related to Du Bao. This chapter will also examine what makes people members of the same family. Why would anyone, much less the Emperor, consider the young lovers to be a married couple when they have contracted their union without the permission of her parents or even recognition of her human status?

At her rebirth, Du Liniang risks becoming a person without an identity, whose parents refuse to recognize her as their daughter, while the state in turn refuses to recognize Liu Mengmei as her husband but instead as a possible grave robber (who has perhaps committed an unspeakable act with the girl's corpse)[2] or an illicit lover. The only records that corroborate her account are those of the underworld bureaucracy, impossible for her to gain access to in the world of the living. The possibility of that plight highlights a number of important questions not only about her specific identity, but about everyone's. If Du Liniang's hold on her identity seems so tenuous, what makes any individual who he or she claims to be? If she can be deprived of these roles, precisely what does being a daughter or a wife consist of? What makes anybody's identity more secure than Du Liniang's?

When the Emperor declares that she has been reborn, he is contributing to what is already a complicated debate. At every step, the play defies our efforts to reach fixed definitions of *ren* and *gui*. In this play, ghost (*gui*) and human (*ren*) form as fragile a binary as real (*zhen*) and fake (*jia*) do, or as dream and waking—an opposition always in danger of collapsing, sometimes in entirely playful ways, and other times, when the implications are dead serious.

Even on a syntactic level, the distinction between ghost and human is not always easy to maintain. To cite one example among hundreds, bidding goodbye to the yamen after her resurrection, Du Liniang laments: "I sigh that for three years I dwelt here; three years I was buried here. Dead, I cannot return. Only alive can I go back."[3] This sentiment strikes any Chinese reader as peculiarly familiar; if only the terms "alive" and "dead" are reversed, this becomes the standard, clichéd plaint of any bureaucrat or political exile stranded far from home, recognizing that the only way back is in a coffin. From the unique perspective of a girl resurrected from the dead, paradoxically, it is coming back to life that allows her to return.

With so much hanging on the line, Tang Xianzu takes playful delight in making a mockery of that distinction between human and ghost on the level of language, drawing on too many phrases which casually use either *ren* or *gui*. For example, the Ming colloquialism *woderen* or *anderen*, meaning simply "my beloved," also means literally "my person." Both Du Liniang and Liu Mengmei bandy about that term with great ease in referring to each other. The common phrase can only be disingenuous in this play, where the entire point is that the beloved is at first *not* a person. It is precisely the quality of being a beloved that makes her a person, but even then she must fight to claim that status. A conversation between Du Liniang and Liu Mengmei makes it clear that even casual uses of *ren* are not safe from rigorous questioning:

LIU: Then you are Miss Liniang. Oh, my love! (*anderen*)
DU: Sir, I am not yet human.
LIU: If not human, then you must be a ghost.[4]

Du Liniang responds to Liu Mengmei's affection with an *asteismus*, a reply that repeats the earlier word but uses it in a different sense. "My person," she points out, isn't one at all for much of the play. The wordplay poses in shorthand the question of whether someone who is not human can be "my person." Perhaps it is the act of love itself that renders such a being a person, so that "my person" is not so much a descriptive endearment as a performative one.

And these puns take place throughout the play. Like personhood, ghostliness is subject to constant tweaking. In a passage I have already discussed, Du Bao rejects Du Liniang's descriptions of the underworld by calling them "nonsense." I aimed for the colloquial in my translation; a literalist would have simply rendered *guihua* "ghost talk." *Guihua* is a pun here, both simply nonsense and spoken by a putative ghost about ghostly matters.

In this context, even the most casual use of *gui*, such as when one of Du Bao's guards offhandedly refers to Liu Mengmei as a "shameless, hungry ghost," inevitably takes on a certain weight. After all, that insult is directed toward a man who considers himself married to someone who once was a ghost and who very shortly will himself be accused of being one. Perhaps it is that Du Liniang's particular problem of proving herself human colors every other moment in the play. Or perhaps the play suggests that the problem is not particular to her at all, but instead central to all endeavors, permeating the whole of the language even.

There are times when this exuberant wordplay defies both logic and translation. Once again, Liu Mengmei is answered with an *asteismus*. When he asks Daoist Shi for workmen (*renfu*), she pointedly twists his words: "You serve as the husband (*fu*); she is your lover (*ren*); you can command the ghosts."[5] Once again, a conventional usage of the word *ren* cannot escape being turned into something more loaded.

In her response to Liu Mengmei, Daoist Shi makes this the object of humor, but the dead and the living can marry. Although one reason Du Liniang is eager to be resurrected is that she might marry Liu Mengmei; in fact, strictly speaking, being dead does not present a bar to her getting married. Marriages between the living and the dead were not uncommon during the premodern period (Arthur Wolf writes about such marriages taking place in Taiwan a mere generation ago, and probably in some remoter pockets of rural China they continue in some form to this day).[6]

When Liu Mengmei tells Du Bao of his marriage to Du Bao's daughter, Du Bao's initial response is not that such a marriage is impossible because she is dead, but that such a marriage is impossible because he has not granted permission. Living people are not the only ones who marry: "My daughter has been dead for three years. Let's not even talk of accepting presents and pouring tea—there wasn't even an informal betrothal of a fetus."[7] An engagement could be entered into before a bride or groom was even born, as Du Bao indicates, but it could also take place after one party had died. Du Liniang's own particular situation—as the only child of a prosperous family—would also have made her a prime candidate for posthumous betrothal, marriage, and even *de jure* motherhood. She could have been married after her death to a living man; when her husband later took a "secondary wife," their children would in all rites of ancestor worship regard the dead woman as their mother (and their own biological mother as their father's concubine). Lady Zhen contemplates a similar sort of motherhood for herself after the death of her only biological child when, in a conversation with Chunxiang, she speculates about how she will feel towards a child of Du Bao and a concubine.

Such marriages were particularly common among families like Du Liniang's: if a daughter passed away before marriage, some loving parents could not bear the thought that her spirit would have no place in ancestor worship. No one would ever worship her spirit: a daughter had no place within a clan's worship, since never having been a mother, no children would ever care for her. Such a woman was doomed to eternity as a hungry, lonely ghost. Parents of such a child might spend a considerable dowry to marry her to a poor man. What stands in the way of Du Liniang's marriage is not her death, but that her parents have not consented.

Threads of wish fulfillment lie behind the magical throughout this play. As an orphan lacking all family and connections, Liu Mengmei, prior to his examination successes, would have been a prime candidate for such a marriage. The girl who dies but finds happiness in marriage anyway consoles not only other young girls forced into marriage, but also heartbroken parents bereaved of young daughters.

The ghostly Du Liniang can do as she pleases, because she lacks the human Du Liniang's position within the polity—as wife of an official, as daughter of an official, perhaps someday as mother. In some ways, this provisional definition of a ghost—as someone dangerous precisely because she lacks official identity—fits the resurrected girl better than it does the ghost, who is after all dead. The dead girl is a daughter, and if her parents so wished, could be a wife; she possesses the sacred tablet marking her name and place of origin. The resurrected girl has nothing to tie her to who she claims to be. Du Liniang's encounter with the Underworld Magistrate in Act 23 demonstrates that a ghost decidedly has an official and legal identity even if worldly officials are in no position to access it. Only when the dead circulate in the world of the living are they frighteningly unrooted.

Some version of this definition of a ghost (as someone who isn't connected to living people) has a central position in the literature of the supernatural in Chinese. The anxiety that ghosts might infiltrate into human society runs through the history of this literature from its very beginnings to its present-day forms. Most often, of course, men succumb to the charms of ghostly lovers without knowing their identities. Sometimes people unknowingly fall in with a whole group of spirits. But there is more to the nature of ghosts than simply a displaced fear of outsiders infiltrating the human community.

If the possibility of impersonation were the only reason to fear a ghost, then a human stranger of no name, of no particular family, would present exactly the same threat to society, possessing the same potential to weasel his or her way into a particular position (some kind of sexual liaison or even marriage, as seems to be the goal for so many young ghost women). In fact, humans with less than secure ties to a community and family—a little bit like Liu Mengmei, but more like a number of characters in *Taohua shan*—do threaten the social fabric but not quite in the same way as a ghost. A human who, unbound by a specific identity, pretended to be another, for example, or married into a family even though she entirely lacked one of her own might be dealt with according to human law: first, properly categorized and identified (as a runaway slave from Sichuan, for example) and then punished according to the central principle of the law—reciprocity. At least the law promises it can deal with all the living, promising that if one person wrongs another, the original wrong can be redressed by punishing the first person.

Even if the particular wrongdoer somehow escapes punishment, whether by fleeing or by dying, the expectation is that recompense could still be exacted from his or her family. What happens when a person's family cannot be established presents serious problems to this way of thinking about justice, as we will see shortly. What then is to be done when the trespasser is a ghost? One might punish the body, exposing it to the elements (*lushi*). But what if, as is often the case, it is impossible to determine the identity of this particular ghost?

If one cannot find the material body, how is the ghost to be punished? A ghost cannot be imprisoned or executed or flogged, either with a light stick or a heavy one, or subjected to any of the many other punishments prescribed by the Ming or Qing legal codes, each particularly suited to the crime. Nor, under normal circumstances, can a ghost's family be brought in to endure punishment in his stead, though the literature does record rare exceptions. Or, conversely, what is to be done when a human has wronged a ghost? Outside of the confines of Pu Songling's *Liaozhai zhiyi*, ghosts generally are not in a position to take their enemies to court. They do not present their cases before a magistrate and do not expect the state to redress wrongs against them.

In one of *Mudan ting*'s most important acts, the ghostly Du Liniang and Liu Mengmei pledge their troth, swearing to each other that they will marry. Vows are made to establish what will take place if they are broken. What would have happened if *this* particular one had been? The ending of the play shows a tremendous faith in the power of the human order to redress wrongs. But the vow that seals their love, exchanged in isolation of all other people, lies outside of that power; had it been broken, neither Du Liniang nor Liu Mengmei would have had any particular hope for redress. We cannot imagine either taking the other to court for reneging on the promise given the difficulty they have when they pursue official channels to establish that they are living people. Even if they were human, this sort of vow—binding the two to marriage without the permission of their families—would not be binding to human authorities.

Properly painting the political relationship between ghosts and people requires exceedingly subtle shading. Even though a human and a ghost cannot precisely treat each other as members of the same polity, the worlds of the living and the dead are connected by complicated political bonds, based largely on the same reciprocity that ties together all living humans. Between earth and hell there is a complicated political economy—or perhaps I should say, several economies. There is an obvious economy of souls, which move constantly from the world of the living to that of the dead. The Underworld Magistrate requires Du Liniang to carry a chit establishing her identity as she navigates between the underworld and the world of mortals, as if these bureaucrats are sensitive to the tendency of Du Liniang's identity to proliferate. If there is a Du Liniang beneath, then there cannot also be one above—a fact bureaucratic records both above and beneath must reflect.

I have mentioned that marriage can be entered into as a living human, an unborn one, or a dead one, but other relations can be contracted between the living and dead as well. According to Valerie Hansen and Terry Kleeman, some of the earliest contracts discovered have been in tombs—unsurprising in itself, given the fact that so much of what we know of China's early material culture comes from tombs, since they are sites that had a good chance of remaining undisturbed for centuries. What is curious about these particular contracts, however, is that they are specifically concerned with mediating between the worlds of the dead and the living. Hansen describes the Tang grave of the moneylender Zuo Chongxi, who took to his grave fifteen contracts.[8] She supposes that perhaps Zuo Chongxi hoped to collect on these outstanding debts once he got to the underworld. Although Hansen does not speculate, one wonders how Zuo Chongxi thought he would have been able to collect: was he hoping for official intercession, or was he planning to take matters into his own hands by haunting the debtors?

Focusing on the Han dynasty, Kleeman writes about other contracts found in tombs, especially those concerned with establishing the rights of the person buried in the tomb to that specific plot of earth. Such contracts might have been directed towards living people who might have competing claims to the land, towards dead people, and towards gods (who were thought to have claim to all the land a certain number of feet underneath ground level). What fascinates me is that from the texts of the contracts, one simply cannot tell who is living and who is dead. Kleeman worries about this problem, too: if the buyer and the seller are living, then what is the contract doing in the tomb in the first place (where no living person could ever read it)? And if the buyer and the seller are both dead, then how are we to reconcile the fact of their death with our knowledge that an actual transfer of land has taken place, one which might be contested in court?[9] It might be of interest to Terry Kleeman and me whether those involved are living and dead, but to the writer of the contract—within the particular bounds of the contract—that aspect was obviously of no concern. According to this version, whether living or dead, a person's obligations—what he owes and is owed—continue.

Yet at the same time that certain reckonings continue past death, such as Zuo Chongxi's of how much money he is owed, others are only made for the living, and these are primarily bodily. For example, Du Liniang dies at the age of sixteen, and though she has been dead for three years, the ghost identifies herself not as a nineteen-year-old (nineteen years have elapsed since her birth, after all), but as a sixteen-year-old.

And it is as a sixteen-year-old that she is resurrected, just as she returns to being a virgin, apprehensive about her wedding night (even though by some accounts it will represent no less than the third occasion of her loss of virginity). But how do we square the state of her body with her memories? Chunxiang voices what any observer must be thinking when she asks Du Liniang how she could possibly be a virgin. In their first private conversation together after their reunion, Chunxiang asks her mistress all the uncomfortable details Du Liniang's own version of events has elided: "I ask you: when you trysted in his study, how did you cover the lamp? When you toasted him with lovers' wine, how did you buy the wine? When you took your pleasure, that breaking of your maidenhead must have taken some blood."[10]

Du Liniang refuses to answer: "Silly girl, that rendezvous in the shades, we were to each other as in a dream—so what's the use of asking all this?"[11] It is one thing for the body to stop aging at death, but how can an accounting of acts dependent on human agency stop? How can the virginity of the body matter if the spirit has already and on many occasions experienced sexual relations? On the one hand, Liu Mengmei holds her to the vows made as a ghost; on the other, she does not regard herself accountable for the sexual relations she initiated as a ghost.

Du Liniang claims continuity as a moral agent: first the girl who fell in love with the young man in her dream, then the ghost who visits Liu Mengmei, and finally the young woman who presents her case and is vindicated by the Emperor. I have questioned the consistency of this continuity, but the multiple occasions of her loss of virginity brings up yet other problems. Her identity has been continuous, but her body has not been. The body stopped aging, and it was not deflowered when the ghost took her pleasure with the young man. The vexed problem of Du Liniang's virginity points to a contradiction in which claims of continuity of identity as a moral agent conflict with claims of bodily discontinuity.

For even if she is reborn as a sixteen-year-old virgin (so that somehow the last three years and the episodes of lovemaking with Liu Mengmei do not count), she is clearly not precisely the same as the sixteen-year-old virgin who died of lovesickness three years ago (despite her occasional assertions to the contrary, which will be taken up later in the chapter). Acts and decisions she initiated as a ghost determine the quality of life the resurrected girl will enjoy; continuity of agency, after all, allows Du Liniang to take advantage of Liu Mengmei's promise that he would marry her. He fulfills his promise only because he is convinced that the woman he promises to marry—the ghost— and the woman he actually *does* marry—the resurrected girl—are one and the same.

For on many fronts, the resurrected girl and the ghost share the same running tally when it comes to legal and moral obligations. In the final act, Du Liniang needs to justify having married without first obtaining her parents' permission. Naturally, she argues that a debt incurred as a ghost carries over even after she has been resurrected. Weeping, she says: "Your Highness, your servant was indebted to Liu Mengmei for the favor of resurrection."[12]

Of course, everyone knows that responsibility and obligation continue after one dies; it is a truism that people must often pay for the consequences of actions initiated in life once they are dead. Reams and reams of popular literature attest to that fact, describing the poetically appropriate punishments exacted upon wrongdoers in the netherworld. Moreover, we observe in person the underworldly resolutions of worldly crimes; in Act 23, the Underworld Magistrate sentences a group of miscreants to reincarnation as various appropriate insects.

After encountering one version of the relationship between the worlds of the dead and the living in the person of Du Liniang, everyone at court (with the exception of Du Bao) is interested in knowing what kind of punishments await emperors and officials lacking in virtue. After the Emperor declares her to be human, Du Liniang describes the tortures performed on the evil Song minister Qin Gui and his wife in hell, much to the interest of those listening. Only Du Bao displays no curiosity about how the worlds of the living and of the dead are connected or, specifically, how unfairness in the world of the living is resolved in the underworld. Instead, he implies the separateness of these two worlds when he demands of Du Liniang that she return to the matter at hand: "That is nonsense! But let me ask you, evil ghostly spirit, when one elopes in the human worlds, there is naturally punishment. Is there with officials in the underworld?"

Du Bao is the only character at this moment to retain a Confucian distaste for discussion of the supernatural. When the Master was asked by a disciple how to serve ghosts and the spirits of the dead, he immediately reprimanded his student: "You do not understand even life. How can you understand death?"[13] Like Confucius, Du Bao refuses to make justice contingent on some understanding of the netherworld, and of all the characters, he alone refuses to invoke the underworld in discussing the question of ultimate recompense, returning instead to absolute rights and wrongs in each world.

The Emperor's eagerness to find out what has happened to bad officials should strike at least a little hesitation into the heart of any Confucian official. A belief that everything unresolved—all unpaid debts, all unpunished crimes—will simply be resolved in the hereafter might simply be a license for unfairness in the here and now. The Emperor and the bureaucrats who serve him manage the world of the living, making sure that good and ill are paid back in kind. If the Emperor had truly succeeded by becoming a sage of yore who managed to transform the morals of his subjects, then there would be nothing left for the underworld magistrates to do. Good and ill would be paid back in kind in our own world—that of the living. The Emperor should not greet Du Liniang's descriptions of the underworld's activities with glee.

In *Taohua shan*, the need for the living to imagine punishment for the dead is far from innocuous. Rather, it implies that injustice in our own world of the living cannot be resolved through the existing social order, which is so complicated that no distribution of punishment and reward in the here and now will ever even things out. In *Taohua shan*, the only solution is to throw everything out and begin anew.

As part of his contribution to this discussion of judgment in the world of the dead, Du Bao asks Du Liniang what her punishment should be for having eloped. Her response infuriates him. She refuses to fall for the bait and instead insists that underworld justice is a critical part of justice in the human world: "Yes, of course. Daddy went overboard in dispensing those seventy strokes to Liu Mengmei. But your daughter has already redeemed those with the underworld officials."[14] According to the reciprocity scrupulously built into the penal system, someone who was shown to have falsely accused another person for a crime was punished with the exact penalty merited for the original crime. In other words, for having falsely accused Liu Mengmei of grave robbery, Du Bao is now subject to being given the seventy strokes with the cane he gave the innocent man. Instead of being beaten, his punishment will be his daughter's elopement.

Valerie Hansen describes a number of popular religious texts that attempt to describe the legal codes of the underworld. Such codes tended to be harsher than their mortal counterparts, punishing not only crimes (murder, adultery, treason, and the like), but also what on earth are considered mere inequities and irritations, beyond the reach of the law. One concern of such legal codes was what was owed the dead. Ghosts required a few inviolables to maintain a minimal standard of well-being; lacking these basic requirements, a ghost was entitled to pursue legal action, to return to haunt those who had wronged them. Among many other reasons, ghosts could sue over improper burial, an absence of sons to serve them, and even over the circumstances of death.

According to the play, Du Bao has wronged Du Liniang by failing to marry her off in time and so rendering her particularly susceptible to the kind of illicit passion that ends up killing her. The list of obligations goes something like this. By beating him without justification, Du Bao wronged Liu Mengmei; by marrying without his permission, Du Liniang wronged Du Bao; by indirectly contributing to her early death through his failure to arrange her marriage, Du Bao wronged Du Liniang. It is far from clear why the tally is evened up now. Certainly no authority earmarks a specific punishment for Du Bao's delay or Du Liniang's disobedience.

In other words, the particular willing suspension of disbelief demanded by *Mudan ting* rests upon a reciprocity built in straight through, complete with the underworld. Ultimate justice rests not so much upon an absolutely just earthly government as on a faith that the worlds of the dead and the living can be mediated. Liu Mengmei suffers seventy strokes for a crime he did not commit—and not light taps either, but with a cane; but all is fair, since he deserved that punishment anyway for another crime (which remains unpunished by human powers), that of eloping with his wife. Things come out; every debt is paid and every obligation ultimately fulfilled, but not through the agency of the living.

As Du Liniang suggests, there is a direct causal relationship between Liu Mengmei's undeserved punishment at Du Bao's hands and his being allowed to marry Du Liniang. After having him beaten, Du Bao owes Liu Mengmei something; unwillingly and unwittingly, and negotiated through the dead, he ends up bequeathing his daughter to Liu Mengmei as recompense. Or perhaps the sequence is reversed: perhaps having taken his daughter from him without requesting permission or exchanging any gifts, Liu Mengmei owes Du Bao the beating he suffers. At any rate, by the end of the play, the score is evened.

But how can such reciprocity ever be ensured? Most mortals do not know what transpires in the world of the dead, which explains everyone's curiosity about what Du Liniang has seen. Direct communication with the underworld is one obvious method, but rare and unreliable. Some *gongan* narratives resemble Conan Doyle's stories of Sherlock Holmes, with a sleuth who deduces purely from evidence at hand the guilty party. Others, though, have a decidedly supernatural element. For example, in fiction and drama, Lord Bao, a historical magistrate of the eleventh century, sometimes exhibits the ability to range freely across both worlds, gathering incontrovertible (and sometimes unverifiable) testimony in the netherworld so as to execute justice in that of the living. Needless to say, Lord Bao's abilities set him apart from the common run of man (making him instead much closer to being a minor deity, which in fact he *is*, according to some traditions). And when everyone else in the world of the living lacks such abilities, why should we believe a Lord Bao?

Literal traffic between the netherworld and the world above, such as that achieved by Lord Bao or Du Liniang, can only be negotiated with great difficulty. Mostly, the traffic between the two worlds is not literal so much as symbolic. In Act 23, the Underworld Magistrate introduces himself and his jurisdiction. He and the clerk sing a humorous duet together. Finally, towards the end, the clerk tells the Magistrate that his pen has run dry. The Magistrate replies, in a parody of a corrupt official: "To moisten my pen, ten ingots of gold, banknotes worth ten strings of cash, a hundred sheets of paper lucre."[15] Money, as the Underworld Magistrate says, can make its way regularly from the world of the living to the one below.

What sort of money does the Underworld Magistrate have in mind—the very real treasures of gold often placed within tombs, or the paper facsimiles of gold ingots burned at funerals? My guess is that he means the latter: he doesn't demand items whose value lies in and of themselves, like the jewels appraised in an earlier act, but instead currency or even representations of that. Are all three kinds of money he suggests as possible bribes interchangeable—the equivalent of four quarters for a single dollar bill—or is attempting to pin a precise value on a piece of spirit money a vain endeavor?

If my translation reads awkwardly, it is partly because the Magistrate has summoned up virtually every kind of currency from a fiscally complicated society—ingots of precious metals, strings of cash, banknotes. *Ding*, which I have translated as "ingot," might either be a regularly shaped piece of a precious metal or a three-dimensional paper facsimile thereof used in funereal rites. Or like the other sums of money mentioned by the Underworld Magistrate, *ding* might refer not to actual quantities of gold or silver, or even a paper sculpture of them, but instead to pictures of ingots printed onto paper money. In sum, a *ding* might be an actual ingot, a paper version of an actual ingot, an ingot printed on a bill, or even simply a sum of money equal to an ingot.

If *shiding*, ten ingots, suggests the possibility that representation and value are related, the second figure for money, *shiguan chao*, allows for no other possibility. *Guan* refers to a string of a thousand copper coins, assigned the value of a tael of silver, each coin molded with the name of the reign it was made under and with a hole through the middle. Yet though a string, or *guan*, has the value of a thousand coins, in actuality it was always somewhat fewer than that—the difference being the sum of money gone to pay the moneystringer.[16] *Chao* are paper bills, but the character also means "to copy"; so *shiguan chao* is, in addition to notes worth *shiguan*, also a copy of ten strings of cash. Finally, he also asks for a hundred sheets of cash; but without mentioning the value of each sheet, he makes it impossible for us to know what sum he is even gesturing towards.

Even the moistening of the pen (*runbi*) is a close cousin to the various banknotes the Underworld Magistrate calls for, referring to what really speeds the pen along—bribes to accelerate official documents along their bureaucratic way. In other words, along with the strings of coins and different banknotes, *runbi*, too, in that it implies the specific exchange of commodity for a state-sanctioned document, suggests in some way money. And finally, the Underworld Magistrate himself bears an uncomfortably close resemblance to money. He, too, like the goods in the tomb, exists in two senses— both as the dusty clay sculpture found in city temples throughout the land and as the greedy judge who determines Du Liniang's fate.

The money has gotten devalued, as paper money tends to do. There is the intimation that ten ingots of value seem to have proliferated beyond control and become three when they are one: "ten ingots of gold, banknotes worth ten strings of cash, a hundred sheets of paper lucre." The list of monies is how paper money looks to those who distrust it, where a government prints out more money than it can back up and devalues what is already in circulation. Surely, the fiscal situation resembles that of the Underworld Magistrate himself, who is at once many clay versions of himself, all of which can be copied endlessly, all of them referring to the single individual who passes judgment on Du Liniang. Except that in the case of the money, it is not clear that a single referent exists at all (since we never see any actual ten ingots, and even if we did, there would be nothing to distinguish them from any other ten ingots of gold). But why am I trying to figure out if the money possessed by this clay deity is real? For of course all the money he refers to is really just an idea—at least by the time it reaches him—paper that has been burnt on its way to the spirit world.

The tomb contracts that Kleeman discusses establish ownership of the grave plot: many of them explicitly mark—even represent—a sale, but exactly what is being transacted and between whom remains unclear. The sums of money are frequently fantastically large (mostly consisting of sequences of the auspicious number nine), suggesting that the transaction is symbolic and that any appropriately impressive sum would do. Paper money, in its essence, is always a kind of spirit money, with the capacity of transformation into ingots but itself simply paper, subject to exchange and transformation. And paper money for graves seems to have predated paper money used outside of graves by several centuries. According to Tseun-hsuin Tsien, paper cut into a string of cash has been discovered in tombs from the early Tang, almost two centuries before real paper money was adopted.[17]

Like the Underworld Magistrate and like Du Liniang herself as a ghost, the money exists simultaneously in two realms. The money is worthless paper among the living but can grease the wheels of hell. The girl who pleads her case in hell is also a corpse in a coffin buried in the earth; the magistrate she petitions is at once judge and dusty statue. And yet the lines between these two worlds are constantly crossed and transgressed.

And what of the contents of Du Liniang's grave? Are they real? We know already how difficult it is to apply the word *zhen* to the girl, since she embodies the word in too many senses. She struggles to prove herself *zhen*—both really that particular individual and really alive—and has uneasy relations with other meanings of *zhen* as well, since the word also refers to the portrait where her identity is partially invested and to a Daoist immortal (which in some sense Du Liniang can be said to have become when she is resurrected from the grave). But what about her belongings? How are they real?

In fact, we are able quite precisely to follow the contents of Du Liniang's grave and to witness both sides of their double lives. The grave goods have been placed within the grave to support Du Liniang in the underworld. Once the girl returns to the world of the living, though, the grave goods are quickly discarded (Chen Zuiliang infers from their disarray that Du Liniang's grave has been robbed). Her ornaments continue to retain their value; they are sold to finance Liu Mengmei's journey to check up on Du Liniang's parents.

The lives of these trinkets outside of the grave are pretty straightforward; they either convert into objects that indubitably belong in the world of the living (food, drink, travel expenses), or they are discarded as waste. But before they are removed, while these objects still remain in the liminal space of the tomb, we see, with bifurcated vision, how these objects exist on two planes at once. The first thing Du Liniang does upon resurrection is to vomit the piece of metal placed in her mouth at burial (probably to prevent decomposition). Laitou Yuan desirously eyes it: "This chunk of loose silver must be heavier than twenty *fen*; come on and give it to this Laitou."[18] To Liu Mengmei, however, the silver remains what it was in the underworld, not the valuable commodity it is in the world of the living. He scolds Laitou Yuan: "Essence held in the dragon's mouth and spat out by a phoenix, I shall revere it as a heirloom. You will have some other form of recompense."[19]

His high-minded explanation seems a little hypocritical, for later on, in Act 49, Liu Mengmei himself, at the end of his rope after a journey which has exhausted his resources, will do exactly what he chided Laitou Yuan for thinking. Liu Mengmei tries to exchange that piece of silver for some food, only to discover that it defies being turned into currency among the living. He tries to give it to a bartender, but finds that it cannot be picked up, instead sliding away. Finally after some slapstick trying and failing, the bartender concludes that it is really *shuiyin*, "liquid silver," or mercury. And then Liu Mengmei says to himself, as if trying to convince himself, what he had earlier told Laitou Yuan with such certainty:

> That's right. When the young lady was buried, the mercury was in her mouth. When the soil in a dragon's mouth turns to a pearl, he ascends into heaven; when the mercury in a ghost's mouth turns to cinnabar, she appears on earth. That is as it ought to be. Once it encountered the winds, it changed in substance. Before when the young lady died, the mercury also died. And now that she is alive, it too has come to life. What a shame that people cannot understand this marvelous object.[20]

Liu Mengmei tries to work out the double nature of the *shuiyin*. He struggles to apply an empirically observed explanation to the transformation, invoking dragons and wind exposure to explain what happens. In short, it was mercury all along, both before in the grave and now.

The empirical explanation doesn't quite work: if it really had been just mercury the whole time, it would have "come alive" at the resurrection. And then how would Liu Mengmei have managed to get it out of Du Liniang's mouth in a single piece in the first place, much less tote it around on a journey of hundreds of miles afterwards? The silver in her mouth is like the spirit money—the ingots and notes desired by the Underworld Magistrate are nothing but paper in the mortal world. But how do these objects start as one thing and end up as another? The transformation cannot have been purely physical. What matters is that what stood for value in the grave cannot be exchanged for commodities outside of it. Liu Mengmei might just as well have tried to pay for his bite to eat with a bill from the Underworld Magistrate's cache of spirit money—worthless on earth, but of value to the dead in the netherworld.

Marc Shell has suggested that the traditional Christian anxiety with money has everything to do with Christ's fiduciary qualities. Like a coin and like the money the Underworld Magistrate desires, Christ is both "the manifestation of an idea *and* a real thing."[21] In some sense then, money—both idea and real thing—is at the heart of the barrier between the world of the living and the world of the dead, explaining how the dirty clay sculpture and the powerful deity can be one and the same or how the dragon's essence can be mercury. Money or notions of value profoundly related to money play a central role in commemorating the dead; traditional funereal practices include burning the representations of coins and ingots and burying the dead with representations of things necessary in the underworld, thus transferring intangible value to the world of the dead. These earthenware representations are so detailed they provide us with much of our knowledge of everyday life in premodern China: how pigs were kept, for example, or what a Yuan dynasty stage looked like.

The picture of an ingot that is burned is transformed into the idea of its value. But what about Du Liniang herself, who also passes between the world of the living and the dead? Unlike the ingot, she is somehow physically the same in both states. The three conspirators unearth her, and they discover her body undecomposed, perfectly intact. She is, as Liu Mengmei observes, just as she was before (*rugu*). But what of all those other dead people we know of in the play? What if other graves were opened—those, say, of the three malefactors whom the Underworld Magistrate sentences before he comes to Du Liniang's case? I assume that in contrast to hers, their bodies would be decayed, that they have somehow become two, like the Underworld Magistrate and his dusty statues—both the souls whose rebirths are being determined and their decomposing bodies. In contrast, Du Liniang is one—the spirit who obtained permission from the Underworld Magistrate to come to Liu Mengmei and the perfect and intact body in the coffin are the same.

And the fact that there is only one Du Liniang even after death is striking within the context of other literary resurrections as well. At least two other plays—the Yuan dynasty *zaju Qiannü lihun* (*The Soul of Qiannü Leaves Her Body*) and the early Qing *chuanqi Changsheng dian* (*The Palace of Everlasting Life*)—choose to stage similar scenes with two separate actresses, one to play the soul and the other to play the body. *Qiannü lihun* ends with the reunion of body and soul; Qiannü's soul has followed a departing lover, leaving her body at home in a coma. For much of the last scene, while Qiannü's soul walks around onstage, the body lies inert. Finally at the end, by some mysterious means, the two meld together. That body and soul are separate entities is even more overt in *Changsheng dian*, a play that tells of the love between the Tang emperor Xuanzong and Concubine Yang. For in this play, the merging of body and soul (which takes place when Concubine Yang's soul is granted status as an immortal) is only accomplished through violence (indeed something that looks uncomfortably close to a rape). The soul is told that this is her body, and then the stage directions read: "The corpse chases the soul around the stage for one full circuit; the soul hits the body and falls over it; the body slips offstage."[22]

In contrast, Du Liniang is played by a single actress, and we are not allowed to fall back on the presumption that underlies the resurrection scenes in *Changsheng dian* and *Qiannü lihun* in our play: the body and soul are not entirely separable entities, depriving us of a moment (present in the other plays) where one can look upon the other and comment on it. Consequently, Du Liniang's coffin, as a material object encasing what is both material and spiritual, also finds itself in a complicated position. No divine explanation is enough to account for the absence of vermiculation. To explain why the body has not been eaten by bugs, Liu Mengmei also looks at the coffin and says: "Look at the dirt on its lid, but at the joints there's not even half a worm."[23] Someone looking at Concubine Yang's coffin would not need to make such an argument; the body and the spirit, which meld together magically, were originally separate, so that the material conditions of the grave are not a subject of concern.

Discussions of the coffin continue—and continue to worry at the problem. Liu Mengmei goes on to describe her passage in the underworld in the coffin, as if it had joined her there like the girl herself—the same thing in two worlds (unlike the Underworld Magistrate and his money, or the *shuiyin* in her mouth, two very different things in both worlds). It serves as her vehicle: "Her warm dark fragrance enclosed within these four slabs of gorgeously speckled wood; her smooth sweet face half pillowed here on its way in the Yellow Springs."[24] Daoist Shi speaks of the coffin less respectfully but struggles equally with its particular role in Du Liniang's experiences of the last three years: did it go with her to the Underworld? Does it, like her, exist whole and entire in both worlds? Are there two coffins—one in this grave and one in the underworld—or only one? Recall her musings on the coffin: "So the hearts of the nails have rusted through, and the joints of the wood opened. I suppose the young mistress must have been going elsewhere to send off the clouds and rain."

Incidentally, some of the difficulties the characters here encounter when they talk about her coffin might shed a little light on the importance traditionally given to coffins. At least one story of filial piety relates how a child, at great personal risk to his life, manages to save a parent's empty coffin. The child is valorized as much as if he had saved his parent's life—and much more so than if he had rescued other possessions from the fire. Other grave goods are facsimiles, whose real existence is elsewhere in the world of spirits, (and which in the world of the living are mere paper and clay), but coffins, like the dead person herself, have a place in both worlds.

Even within the bounds of her actual person, certain negotiations must take place before she can wholly join the world of the living. Some parts of the body belong in the world above, while others do not. Upon being resurrected, Du Liniang promptly expels what was inside her body, vomiting twice: first the silver and then the other contents of her body. Partly, this double vomiting serves as the high point of the play's constant juxtapositions of the ethereal and the bawdy and emphasizes that the creature being resurrected is entirely bodily. As a figure for semen, the disgorged silver must be purged to restore Du Liniang's chastity.[25] The potion Du Liniang vomits up after the silver was meant to build up her strength after her magical resurrection but is composed of "the trousers of a strapping fellow" (*zhuang nanzi de kudang*).[26] No scene, no matter how elevated or concerned with matters of passion, escapes the comic touch. But partly, the double vomiting specifically highlights our concern with separating what is of her body from what is of the tomb and can be discarded. Even things within her body are not necessarily of her body.

And what of the trinkets, which, other than the person, are the only things saved from the grave? When she is first risen from the dead, Du Liniang cannot quite recognize her benefactor. Once Liu Mengmei is pointed out to her, she sings her gratitude. Immediately after her thanks, she issues an order about what is to be done with all of the grave goods: "Keep the trinkets (*baowan*) that were inside my coffin. As for everything else, throw them into the pond."[27] Grave goods find themselves in a peculiar position once their owner is resurrected—no longer possessed of their double life, but simply pathetic husks in our own world. The trinkets we know will be pawned so that Liu Mengmei can check up on his new parents-in-law. And the rest? Paper and clay manifestations of all those goods Du Liniang would need in the underworld, returned above ground and with no one to serve in the underworld, they are reduced to mere paper and clay husks, representations without referents. The silver in her mouth dribbles away uselessly in the world of the mortals, tempting, but still only a mirage of silver.

One by one, each one of the objects created for her death—the portrait, the goods in the tomb, the silver in her mouth, the trinkets exchanged for traveling expenses—disappears, as if erasing the fact that she has died. The erasure remains imperfect, or rather impossible; when Chen Zuiliang returns to the yamen, the very absence of a grave alerts him that something wayward has taken place (in one of the few accurate acts of detective work in the play, he supposes that a grave robbery has taken place).

In addition to discarding her grave goods, she also suggests a matchmaker twice—both times when the services of a matchmaker would have been entirely in vain. Du Liniang—a ghost who has taken advantage of the absence of her parents to choose her own lover—yearns for marriage. Simply loving Liu Mengmei in private will not do. What she wants is an orthodox marriage, so she herself invokes what at that point can only be an impossibility—asking for a matchmaker in Act 32, so that she can secure a promise from Liu Mengmei that she will be his primary wife: "If you feel this way, why don't you send a matchmaker to arrange matters? That would save me much anxiety and fear."[28] Most ghosts with human lovers are not so fearful that they will end up as concubines and not as proper wives.

Her request makes no sense, because there would be no place for such a matchmaker to go, no home she shares with her parents. Later, after her resurrection but before her human status is fully public and legitimate, she again requests a matchmaker, just as illogically. How would their two families compare horoscopes and exchange presents when he as an orphan lacks a family and her parents think she is dead? In putting off Liu Mengmei's advances, seemingly with no recognition of how far her own relationship has gone beyond the pale of conventional courtship, she invokes Mencius, "One must await the commands of the parents and the words of the matchmaker."[29] The kind of marriage Du Liniang seeks, both before and immediately after resurrection, is fundamentally impossible, isolated and unrooted as she is.

No more than a ghost, a newly resurrected woman whose parents think she is dead is in no position to engage the services of a matchmaker. Du Liniang expects her death to have been perfectly erased. Partly, for reasons discussed in earlier chapters, she regards herself not as resurrected from the dead, but instead as a girl who had never died at all.

But *is* she the same as a girl who had never died at all? Do these economies work out? At the end of the play, in arguing to her father that she has been allowed to marry Liu Mengmei with no penalty because the elopement evens what had been an unbalanced score, Du Liniang invokes a very powerful notion: the play ends when all the debts have been paid and all the credits have been redeemed. Everyone who owes pays up; everyone who is owed has been paid.

This contention brings up two related problems. First, are all the balances in fact even? Du Bao would argue not, and we might agree. Even if he does come eventually to accept her as his daughter returned to him, he has paid an enormous and seemingly excessive price for failing in the first place to recognize that his teenaged daughter was grown and ready to marry. And second, if the balances are even, is that actually sufficient to erase all the transactions that took place to achieve that balance, even when they involved life and death? These questions are central to *Taohua shan*'s response to its predecessor *Mudan ting*. *Taohua shan*, surely the greatest historical play in the Chinese tradition, explores the problem of recompense—and when, if ever, debts are repaid and the score returned to zero—from the perspective of historical change, the family drama here writ large to encompass the concerns of an entire empire: when, if ever, is the trauma of the Ming dynasty's fall over and erased?

Perhaps the theatre provides the only consistent way of thinking about how the dead and the living are separated. Some sinologists have explored the intersections between popular religion and popular theatre, noting some of the many ways in which dramas often became integrated into religious rites. Wolfram Eberhard, for example, discusses the slips drawn at Chinese temples used to tell a person's fortune; at first glance, opaque and heavily allusive, these slips turn out actually to refer to different dramas. Familiarity with an enormous number of plays could simply be assumed.[30] The theatre and religion are also tied together in other ways: plays were often performed during major religious festivals, and a large number of plays share themes and characters with popular religion (General Guan Yu of Three Kingdoms lore and Lord Bao, for example, were also worshiped as minor deities, in addition to being the lead characters in innumerable narratives and plays). By the Ming dynasty, the connections between popular religion and the theatre run much deeper and are much more complicated than simply a question of influence in one direction or the other. The ways in which the dead were conceived had been thoroughly colored by experiences with the theatre and vice versa.

Ghosts and actors are also morphologically similar. Both are members of two worlds at the same time: ghosts are denizens of the netherworld who appear to the living, while actors exist both onstage in roles they play and offstage. Moreover, both actors and ghosts are often in the position of impersonators, or more precisely perhaps, simulacra, lesser copies of originals. Ghosts try to pass as people, while actors pretend to be people they are not. It might even be argued that an actor, like a ghost, is not fully a person. In the Ming dynasty, actors were placed in the same category as hereditary chattel (*jianmin*) and not allowed to participate fully in the polity; they and their offspring were not allowed to take the civil service examinations, for example. They were not allowed to intermarry with the commoners who comprised most of the rest of the population (*liangmin*).

Perhaps these prohibitions, which attempt to keep actors separate as a group from most people, were established precisely to keep actors and their troubling lack of a fixed identity from polluting the population of respectable citizens—just as one would not want a ghost to marry into one's family. Who is an actor really? Is she the role she plays or the player of the role? *Mudan ting* wrestles with the symbolic problems injected by the theatre, suggesting parallels between its own relation to the world offstage and the way the living and the dead coexist. *Taohua shan* explicitly deals with the social effects that entertainers, and specifically prostitutes, can have on a patriarchy.

The theatre makes an ostensibly simple question like that of Shang Xiaoling's identity impossible to answer. Shang Xiaoling was a Ming dynasty actress famous for her performances of *Mudan ting*. During one of her performances, who was the person onstage—Shang Xiaoling or Du Liniang? Shang Xiaoling's name gives us one clue to the answer. *Xiaoling* 玲, "Little Chime," was also sometimes written *xiaoling* 伶,[31] which simply means "Little Actress"—referring to her profession, and so really not much of a name at all. Xiaoling, according to one reading of her name, is merely a capacity for taking on other roles, and nothing of an identity in and of herself.

The position of an actor onstage differs in fundamental ways from that of the many enthusiasts who participated in amateur theatricals. When the aria ended and the play was put away, a literatus returned to his real identity, his position in society secure and the same as it was before, defined in relation to his father and his family. In contrast, professional actors frequently sidelined as prostitutes, and prostitutes and their offspring are notoriously vague about who their husbands and fathers are. Such an ignorance poses profound problems in a patriarchy where one's identity is determined by who one's father is. In other words, even after the costumes have come off and the makeup washed off, it still is far from clear who the particular actor or actress is. If marriage is a union of two different families, a dead girl of good family can be integrated into the ancestral worship of another family far more easily than a live actress can.

Finally, the word *gui*, or "ghost," can be used to refer to actors. The usage probably began because actors so often play dead historical figures, but it then took on a life of its own. For example, Zhong Sicheng's *Lugui bu* (*Record of the Ghosts*) sounds as if it might contain tales of the supernatural, or perhaps be a Daoist text about recordkeeping in the underworld; instead, it documents members of the bygone theatre community of the Yuan dynasty. Incidentally, the official document the Underworld Magistrate rifles through has a name that sounds much like Zhong's book: *Diangui bu*, the Record of the Ghosts. Everyone in that underworld scene would be found listed in both sorts of records under two different names—both those of the dead characters and of the living actors. For at that moment, they are *gui* in both senses, actors playing the dead.

Both ghosts and actors are present and not present. They simultaneously belong to two different worlds. When offstage, the young actress Shang Xiaoling inhabits entirely the same world we do, but onstage she is separate from us. There she is the romantic heroine Du Liniang, into whose world we cannot penetrate. Similarly, when the character Du Liniang appears to Liu Mengmei as a ghost after having traveled back to the human world, she is part of his world—a companion and a lover—but also still part of another, wholly inaccessible one; unlike his new lover, Liu Mengmei is in no position to speak to underworld officials.

Tombs are a threshold between the dead and the living. A tomb's space is distinctive at least partially because of its symbolic similarity to the theatre. Both tombs and stages occupy two worlds at once—or rather they are where two separate worlds cross. The staged space, too, pretends to be a portal to another world: when Liu Mengmei and Du Liniang fret about events taking place in Huaiyang, where Du Bao is stationed, we may be sure that those events are not taking place in our own Huaiyang but in an imagined one. Instead, in this play and in many other *chuanqi*, even if the stage is the only place we can observe, it is a small window looking out onto a huge fictional space, parallel to and as large as our own world, across the whole of which action is simultaneously taking place. This sense of simultaneity is most pronounced in political and historical plays that involve the whole of the empire—like *Changsheng dian*, the *chuanqi* about Concubine Yang and her imperial lover, and *Taohua shan*—but seems an important feature in all *chuanqi* (in *Mudan ting*, action takes place simultaneously in Hangzhou, Huaian, and Nan'an).

Similarly, tombs open up to the netherworld even as they are contained and discrete parts of our own world. We know the position of Du Liniang's tomb within the world of the living: Daoist Shi performs mundane tasks to care for it, and it is small enough that Liu Mengmei can miss it in his first cursory explorations of the garden. But at the same time, it marks an entrance to a world parallel and equal in scope to our own. The tomb contracts studied by Kleeman, for example, negotiate the tomb's position in both worlds—some clearly dedicated to protecting the land on which the tomb rested from human claimants, others from ghostly or godly ones.

One implication of this double life is that tombs—or specifically, the funereal goods that fill them—are a place in the Chinese tradition where the full ramifications of symbol can be explored. The tricolored ceramic horses of the Tang dynasty are at once works of earth and glaze buried with a dead person, and stand-ins for something else (necessary means of transport for use once the deceased reaches the underworld). Issues basically unimportant in mainstream Chinese philosophy are of central importance in thinking about tombs as well as theatres.

The same word applies to both the passage between the tomb and the world of the dead and the door between the stage and the audience; both are referred to as the "ghost gate," or *guimen*. During the resurrection scene, the actress who plays Du Liniang begins the scene offstage. When in their digging they reach the grave, Liu Mengmei, Laitou Yuan, and Daoist Shi all hear Du Liniang's voice as she groans from offstage, still in the world of the dead. And then as they lift open the casket, the stage directions read: "They all squat facing the *guimen* and pantomime opening the coffin."[32] Finally, she leaves her place offstage to emerge onstage.

As she is resurrected, Du Liniang passes through two sorts of *guimen*—both the stage door and the ghost gate that connects to the underworld—and the passage occasions a magical transformation. Or, I should say, two simultaneous and equally magical transformations: first, she who was dead is now alive, and second, an ordinary woman of low status, got up in paint and costume, who had been on our side of the stage, is now suddenly Du Liniang, the romantic heroine whose passion was so great it was able to defeat death.

Hansen reproduces one illustration from the *Dili xinshu* (or *Earth Patterns*, as she translates) that shows the layout of a proper burial, including the respective locations of the tomb and the participants. The reader of the prayer and the chief mourner each reverentially gaze towards a central altar, where the dead is and the tomb contract soon will be. It looks nothing if not like a stage, complete with audience and a stage door, *guimen*.[33]

Actors and the dead stand on the other side of the ghost gate from the rest of us—the living and the audience. In *Mudan ting*, two characters stand on our own side of the divide. These two speak, but from offstage: Du Liniang, as she is about to be resurrected, and the Emperor, who delivers all of his judgments from offstage, never appearing onstage. He too stands apart from the rest of the staged reality, though he is not dead. *Taohua shan* takes up this issue—of whether the Emperor really is different from other people—exploring the relationship between theatrical roles and social ones. Both sorts of *guimen* allow for passage, but only selectively.

After establishing a reputation for her portrayal of Du Liniang, the young actress Shang Xiaoling collapsed and died onstage in the middle of one performance. In some sense, her identity onstage is more firmly noted than her identity offstage: onstage she is Du Liniang, daughter of one official, wife of another. Offstage, she hardly has a name. Her identity onstage seems more fixed, partly because she has achieved fame through a single role. And she achieves her fame not through any particular, learned skill in the performing arts, nothing that could be taught to somebody else, no ecial singing technique, for example, which might be applied to other roles nsmitted to others. Instead, Shang Xiaoling is famed precisely for mingling her own identity with that of the role, so that in the end, the two—Shang Xiaoling and Du Liniang—are indistinguishable and inseparable.

When she dies onstage, nobody watching initially can tell who has died, the actress Shang Xiaoling or the character Du Liniang:[34]

> Every time she acted out the role of Du Liniang, whether in the act "Seeking the Dream" (*Xunmeng*) or "Mourning the Dead" (*Naoshang*), or any others, it was really as if she had physically experienced those events, full of longing and melancholy, with the tracks of tears welling up. One day, while acting out "Seeking the Dream," she sang the lines: "I wait to exhaust this thin slice of sweet soul, and then when the dark rain falls from a plum sky, I'll hold fast at the root of the plum tree to see you again." Then gracefully inclining her head, she slumped to the ground according to the music. When Chunxiang went up to see her, she had already breathed her last.

From the perspective of the literary critic, it is too bad that Miss Shang wasn't able to hold out until performing "Mourning the Dead" in which the character Du Liniang actually dies, for then the question of determining who has died would be truly impossible to answer. Just imagine if she had actually expired at the moment of Du Liniang's death of sadness: which one can be said to have died?

Nonetheless, she does manage to find quite an appropriate point in the play to stage her own death—the moment when Du Liniang recognizes her own mortality and plans her future burial underneath the plum tree. Other than melancholy, we cannot tell what the cause of death might be—and whose melancholy would that be, Shang Xiaoling's or Du Liniang's? No easy answer presents itself. Perhaps particulars from Shang's life might have caused her sadness (certainly young prostitutes were vulnerable to terrible abuses), but Du Liniang also suffered, from the sense that her youth was passing her by. Nor is there any obvious way to distinguish their feelings, since Shang Xiaoling's fame arises precisely from her ability to share Du Liniang's sense of "longing and melancholy." Paradoxically, the young actress manages to achieve everlasting fame for herself by immersing herself in Du Liniang's identity. The melancholy that will cause Shang's death is Du's: during performances she acts "as if she had physically [literally, "in her own body"] experienced those events."

After the girl collapses onstage, someone rushes to attend to her, and this leads to another round of questioning by the audience, who must attempt to make another judgment of identity: who is it really who rushes onstage? Is it the supporting actress playing Chunxiang who spontaneously responds to a genuine medical emergency not written into the script, or is it Chunxiang herself, properly attending to her mistress? Is this an improvised addition to the scene, or an event contiguous with offstage reality? We cannot for the moment know, but surely we can see a similarity between the act of adjudication demanded at this moment and the many acts of adjudication demanded of the many characters throughout the last few acts of *Mudan ting*. Is she human or ghost? Is she the character in an inaccessible and independent world onstage or a person acting, who lives and has her being in our own world?

No physical test can ever answer this question: examining the actress who plays Chunxiang from head to foot, inside and out, will not clear up the question of whether she is onstage as Chunxiang attending to her mistress or as a person responding to the unforeseen death of a colleague. She seems a person by the measure of any physical condition, but that still does not help us to determine whether her reality is ours or that of the stage.[35]

Though they stake so much on their certainty that Du Liniang is human, her husband Liu Mengmei and her mother Lady Zhen also concede the futility of attempting to determine her humanity through physical criteria. Liu Mengmei has had the closest physical contact possible with the ghostly Du Liniang, and afterwards, he is left incredulous that his sexual partner could possibly have been a ghost: "But it clearly was a human union, with semen and blood."[36] There is no difference per se, only that fragile aesthetic frame that separates what is onstage from what is offstage.

Du Liniang herself suggests that humanity is performative. As a ghost, she had no compunctions about making love to Liu Mengmei. As a resurrected girl, however, she resists his approaches, insisting that they must marry first. She is questioned about this apparent inconsistency: why, when she claims narrative continuity with the ghost, should she have compunctions now about what she did so freely before? She answers: "Scholar, things are different from before. Yesterday I was a ghost; today I am human. Ghosts can be careless about passion, but humans must effect propriety."[37] She never so clearly and explicitly differentiates her ghostly existence from her human one again (the only runner-up would be her description to Chunxiang of her days as a shade, where she compares that experience to dreaming). Perhaps she is intimating in this explanation to Liu Mengmei that it is only abiding by a set of predetermined rules for behavior that makes one a human; disregarding those rules places one outside the human community, making one a ghost.

There is no perfect translation for the terms *xuqing* and *shili*; "to be careless about passion" and "to effect propriety" do not begin to exhaust their meanings in Chinese. Many riches lie here, and a sense that even if the division between human and ghost is simply a matter of behavior, the exact nature of the distinction is still complicated and perhaps even a little contradictory. *Xu* and *shi*, or "empty" and "solid," form one of the most important binaries in Chinese thought. In contrasting the terms, Stephen Owen writes, most suggestively for our case, that *xu* implies "'empty' or 'plastic,' referring to substances like air or water that conform to 'solid' shapes; it is extended to refer to the changing fluidity of the emotions and the way they may be 'invested' in solid things."[38] *Xu* might easily refer to Du Liniang's dream, where everything is imagined, not rooted to the "solid" things of the waking world.

The contrast between *xuqing* and *shili* also suggests that the resurrected Du Liniang has a vision of Confucian probity not too dissimilar from her father's. *Xu* implies not only what is imaginary and unrooted but also what is purposeless and in vain; sex for a ghost is indeed without consequence, demanding no responsibility, bearing no possibility of shame or pregnancy. In another syntactic setting and in the words of another speaker, *xuqing and shili* might not be parallel verbs, as they are here, but instead parallel nouns, categorical descriptions contrasting *qing* and *li* as two competing forces directing human behavior. Where *li* instructs a person in proper behavior, *qing* is selfish desire, which only *appears* imperative. In another context, one might translate the four characters something like: "empty [or fictive] passion and solid propriety."

Du Liniang implies that behavior and humanity are intimately related, that what made her a ghost was precisely her willingness to trifle with passion, just as her earnestness about propriety now makes her human. But suggesting that humanity is simply performative—the result of a series of prescribed actions rather than any preexisting phenomenon—doesn't come close to making the issue any easier, as any educated Chinese person of the late imperial period would have known. Instead, the relationship between being and action—whether true knowledge necessarily prompts action, as Zhu Xi would have put it—is one of the central problems in Neo-Confucian ethics, argued and debated over endlessly. Is it possible to understand without action? Does the ghost then not know of propriety? If the ghost knows everything the resurrected girl does but simply chooses not to act on it, then perhaps there is a difference in their quality of understanding, which in turn casts doubt on her subjectivity's continuity.

When Liu Mengmei muses over the act of love shared with Du Liniang, he characterizes it: "But it clearly was a human union, with semen and blood." I have translated *rendao jiaogan* as "a human union." In another instance of play on the word *ren*, *rendao*, literally "the way of people," means two very different things, both of which might apply here. Liu Mengmei calls what happened between the two of them *rendao*, which in addition to sexual congress, has an older meaning—literally, the normative way of humanity. According to the older usage, *rendao* is synonymous with *renlun*, those five essential relationships between people that are the basis of all social organization: father and son, lord and retainer, elder brother and younger brother, friend and friend, and finally, husband and wife.[39]

Both senses of *rendao* animate this play: can a person have *rendao* with someone who isn't human? If *rendao* is simply sexual intercourse, Chinese literature is filled with examples of men who aspire to or actually succeed in making love to non-humans. Some of the lovers are animals, like the fox fairy in the Tang tale *Renshi zhuan*, whose body upon dying morphs back into its true form—that of a fox. Others are divine, as in the *Loshen fu*; and finally, countless numbers of these non-human lovers are ghostly. But what makes Liu Mengmei stand out (though not uniquely) among these lovers is his desire to marry, to make his lover into his wife, to share *rendao* with her in both its meanings—of sexual intercourse and of a normative relationship. But how is a ghost to marry? We have arrived at the second half of the Emperor's promise, where having readmitted Du Liniang into the human community, the Emperor then grants her a place within that community, a position within a family: he commands "father and daughter, husband and wife will all recognize each other."

Perhaps the central question one should ask here is one of great interest in the late Ming: which human relation—paternity or marriage—has primacy in sorting out all the other human relations? Can someone like the resurrected Du Liniang first become a wife and only then achieve status as a daughter? The late Ming thinker Li Zhi (who was very much of the same school of thought as our playwright Tang Xianzu) argued that the bond between husband and wife was the one according to which all other human bonds became aligned:

> Only after there has been a husband-wife relation can there be a father-child relation; only after the father-child relation, can there be an elder-younger relation between brothers; and only after the elder-younger brothers' relation has been established, can there be a distinction between superior and subordinate. Should the relationship between husband and wife be proper, then all

the relations among the myriads of living things and nonliving matters will also be proper.[40]

Li Zhi makes it clear that in addition to being an ethical concern, deciding which bond has primacy is also an epistemological problem. Ultimately we only know who someone is by placing that person in the context of others, and in late imperial China, by knowing who that person's family is. Are people to identify themselves through the identity of their fathers or of their spouses? If it is the latter—and consequently the case that we are who we are because of who our spouses are—identity becomes far less fixed and predetermined and far more a matter of choice.

Li Zhi's reordering of the family relations might almost form an alternative preface for *Mudan ting*, retelling precisely the parts of the play's story that are elided from Tang Xianzu's preface, which focuses on dream and passion. Li Zhi's reordering provides Du Liniang the means for finding her place in society. The resurrected girl is a human and not a ghost only because she is Liu Mengmei's wife: only after that relationship is confirmed can she stake a claim to another identity, as daughter to Du Bao and Liu Mengmei. Or, to put it in Li Zhi's words, "Only after there has been a husband-wife relation can there be a father-child relation."

The legitimacy of Du Liniang's union with Liu Mengmei and its ultimate compatibility with the existing human order is the only reason that she is a human and not a ghost. But according to more conventional means of defining a person's identity, as long as her father refuses to recognize her, Liu Mengmei's wife cannot be Du Liniang. She cannot be filial to a father who does not see her as his daughter, and she certainly cannot marry according to his wishes. But on another level, so long as her father refuses to recognize her, she cannot even claim the name Du Liniang, something bestowed and now withdrawn.

In other words, Du Liniang establishes a position for herself in society in a highly unconventional manner: she becomes a daughter again because she is a wife, while all other women become wives only because they are daughters. Their husbands can only recognize them as wives because their fathers have first recognized them as daughters. Even the Emperor's command cannot sway Du Bao, who continues to resist it, although as a Confucian minister of state he must recognize the impropriety of his disobedience towards his sovereign. The deal Du Bao offers Du Liniang expresses his belief that paternity comes first in determining identity. He will recognize her as his daughter, but only if she in turn will reject Liu Mengmei as her husband: "If you leave Liu Mengmei, then when we go back, I will recognize you as my daughter." Fainting, she refuses, making her position clear. She must be Liu Mengmei's wife before she is Du Bao's daughter.

If Du Liniang manages to fix her own position within society only through marriage to him, how Liu Mengmei comes to fix her identity is of primary importance. After a number of nighttime visits, all Liu Mengmei really knows about his lover is that she is young and beautiful. She will not tell her name—until he promises to marry her. She insists that he take her not as his concubine, but as his official wife. We know from retrospect how important the distinction between being a wife and a concubine is, since later on the legitimacy of their liaison extends to legitimate Du Liniang's very presence within the human community. Still ignorant of her name, Liu Mengmei is coaxed into marriage. Together, the two lovers sing this vow:

> Gods of heaven, gods of heaven, I swear an oath on this burning incense. I, Liu Mengmei, Liu Mengmei, staying at Nan'an prefecture, met this beauty and do take her to be my wife. May we in life abide in the same room, in death rest in the same tomb. If my words and my heart not concur, may my life end just as the incense burns down.[41]

Like a character in a fairy tale, Liu Mengmei goes to enormous ends—promising marriage—to find out his beloved's name.

But even if Liu Mengmei may not know much about his bride, the knowledge he does possess about her is precisely what a traditional bridegroom would lack about his bride. As we know, Liu Mengmei has personal experience and knowledge of his fiancée. He knows—and this is of central importance in the play—what she looks like. Which is more important—knowledge of a person's individual traits or of a person's niche within society and within a specific family? Does one kind of knowledge necessarily follow the other? Liu Mengmei and Du Liniang's experience argues strongly for the primacy of knowledge of a person as an individual: stripped of her name and any position in society, Liu Mengmei nonetheless chooses her and in making her his wife, gives her a place in society.

One thing is for sure: the bride and the groom at their unusual ceremony can be replaced by impostors only in one sense—the bride is no living girl but a ghost. The moment at which a more conventional bride and groom recognize each other is just as fraught with a different sort of difficulty. For since neither knows what the other looks like, either one could be an impostor (a situation which arises with some frequency both in court cases, in *huaben* stories, and in drama). A statute of the Great Qing Code describes one fraud:

"This means such [circumstances] as when the woman has a defect or infirmity, and they take a sister and falsely let her be seen and afterwards use the woman with a defect or who is infirm to complete the marriage."[42]

In contrast, our two lovers are playing straight with each other. To fulfill her side of the bargain, Du Liniang divulges her name, her family, and finally that she is the ghost of a girl who has been dead for three years. To fulfill his end, Liu Mengmei promises to disinter her. That Liu Mengmei promises Du Liniang marriage precisely in order to find out her identity colors our understanding of the entire rest of the play. So much depends on this vow: their marriage is grounded on it, and on their marriage is grounded the Emperor's recognition of Du Liniang as a human woman. In other words, every specific attribute of her political identity—whose wife she is and then whose daughter—is paradoxically founded on a moment when her identity isn't known—not her name, not her family, not even whether she is human or ghost—when the most specific way Liu Mengmei can find to address her is as "this beauty."

When she emerges from her grave, Du Liniang fails to recognize Liu Mengmei, even though he is the lover with whom she has shared many nights and is by now her fiancé; Liu Mengmei must resort to confirming his identity with Daoist Shi. I have discussed some implications of this failure of recognition in the first chapter, namely, how it casts doubt on the resurrected girl's unity with the ghost. But in the context of the fifty-five-act play, it is actually not so extraordinary a moment. Throughout the play, people find themselves in the position of needing to prove to their loved ones that they are who they say they are. That act of recognition, so important in the Confucian tradition, is subject to mistake and confusion.

To treat people as they ought to be treated, one must first *zhengming*, "rectify names," or bring names into accord with reality. Within a family, that implies a knowledge of one's relations. In *Mudan ting*, people have an extraordinarily hard time properly identifying members of their own family: loving parents call their only child a ghost; defying the direct order of the Emperor, a father refuses to recognize his only child; a mother distraught with grief over her child's absence still has difficulty accepting her return; a wife who has come from the world of the dead cannot recognize her husband; a devoted husband cannot name his wife.

The second part of the Emperor's promise is as complicated as the first; if human identity seems difficult to establish, specific identity is as well. It is always defined against other individuals: if Du Liniang is Du Bao's daughter, then who is Du Bao? And can we be sure? Or to put the question explicitly into the context of the play: if Du Liniang is Liu Mengmei's wife, then who is Liu Mengmei?

Like his lover's, Liu Mengmei's identity can fragment. Since she is defined first and foremost as his wife, and her identity rests on his, no firm ground remains for us if his is also subject to confusion. And yet, pinning down his identity is a recurrent problem. Other than one friend and a family servant, he seems surprisingly lacking in family or connections. Unlike Du Liniang, he does not need to ask anyone for permission to marry, since there is no one to ask — not even an uncle, agnate or affine.

She becomes four: the painting, the corpse, the ghost, and the sacred tablet. When near the end of the play the two deputies and Guo Tuo seek Liu Mengmei, he has become three: the top examination candidate, the young master Guo Tuo remembers, and the accused grave robber. The last act simultaneously resolves both of their identities, since each claim depends on the other's success. Just as she lays claim to the identity of Du Liniang, daughter of Du Bao and Lady Zhen, he too must lay claim to the identity of Liu Mengmei, top examination candidate. Unless she is successful proving that she is human, he cannot prove that he is not a grave robber. In the few acts preceding, he has been the locus of two entirely separate identity squabbles: first, does his possession of Du Liniang's grave goods indicate that he is a legitimate son-in-law of Du Bao, or a grave robber? And second, is the man whom Du Bao detains and interrogates Liu Mengmei the top candidate, a fraud posing as Liu Mengmei, or someone who just coincidentally bears the same name?

Liu Mengmei himself bears partial responsibility for the confusion. When he goes to check up on his new father-in-law, he introduces himself to Du Bao not by name, but simply as his son-in-law; and since Du Bao has arranged no marriage for his deceased daughter and can consequently have no son-in-law, the young man on whose person Du Liniang's portrait is discovered is naturally presumed a grave robber. When he orders Liu Mengmei's beating, Du Bao seems hardly cognizant of the young man's name (in their extensive dealings constituting two acts, he has only been told it once, seemingly in passing). Consequently, when the young man later claims to be Liu Mengmei, it does look suspiciously as if he has simply seized upon the name of the top examination candidate at the last minute as a convenient way to get out of a fix.

Later, the two deputies and Guo Tuo separately search out Liu Mengmei. From the details each is armed with in his search, it is not clear at first that all these details actually constitute parts of a single person. The two deputies know what he is—the top examination candidate; but without knowing what he looks like, they have no idea how to find this individual and no way of distinguishing him from any other individual. Guo Tuo, from his long years of service, at least knows what he is looking for once he finds him, but he doesn't know his young master's new official identity as top examination candidate.

Du Bao refuses to believe that his prisoner is the top examination candidate in question: "Everyone who is a top candidate has an official register of the successful examinees to prove it. What evidence do you have?"[43] His demand is a peculiar one, since the only information such a register would provide would be a name; and the name, in isolation from any specific person, is precisely what Guo Tuo and the two deputies have both already given Du Bao. Corroborating the list with Guo Tuo and the deputies' testimony only proves that their stories were consistent; any crook wanting to perpetrate such a fraud would have first consulted the lists anyway and then given that name to Du Bao. Checking the list fails to do the only thing that counts at this moment, attaching the name Liu Mengmei to the man held in custody.

Here, near the end of the play, we are in the same position as we were at the very beginning, when Liu Mengmei told us about the dream that led to his name. Once again, a person stands curiously apart from his name; the glue that sticks a name to a person has come unstuck. A name guarantees and proves nothing; it can refer to anybody, and anybody could pose under it. Moments later, Miao Shunbin (who is also looking for his protégé Liu Mengmei) produces the register and shows Du Bao the name Liu Mengmei inside:

> "His is the name marked first by the vermilion Imperial Pen itself, Liu Mengmei as the support of the state."
> "I daresay it cannot be he."[44]

Du Bao's reaction is all too predictable. Rather than accepting the correlation between the name in the register and the young man, Du Bao suggests an alternative: that either this young man is not called Liu Mengmei, or that he is someone who coincidentally shares the name Liu Mengmei with the real top examination candidate. Curiously, Du Bao does not doubt the truthfulness of either the register or of Miao Shunbin. Liu Mengmei's success in the examinations has led to a fate similar to that of Du Liniang's upon her painting of the self-portrait; a seemingly unitary identity has split up. It seems possible that there might be a number of men, all named Liu Mengmei, each claiming to be that top examination candidate.

The two deputies suggest a similar possibility when their search for Liu Mengmei proves fruitless, and they jokingly propose simply detaching the name from the person. The result of the deputies' shortcut would be the creation of another Liu Mengmei, who could contend with our Liu Mengmei for the status of top examination candidate. With the deputies' suggestion still in our minds, Du Bao's suspicions are not unwarranted—that the Liu Mengmei recorded in the register is another one, and that there might be another Liu Mengmei out there, one with stronger claims to being the real one than this person here.

Many of the characters in this romance are bureaucrats, relying on records and registration of all kinds. In this context, Du Bao's suspicions represent a terrible skepticism, especially in someone who is himself a high government official, for if we follow his line of reasoning, no government records make any sense at all. Taken to their natural conclusions, Du Bao's beliefs are incompatible with any faith in government's abilities to order the human realm.

The problem of Liu Mengmei's identity appears beyond resolution: the deputies, who know that he is the top examination candidate, do not know that this man is Liu Mengmei, while Guo Tuo, who knows that this man is Liu Mengmei, does not know that he is the top examination candidate. Just then, by a stroke of good luck for Liu Mengmei, the only person in the world who can vouch for his identity *both* as Liu Mengmei and as the top examination candidate turns up. But we must remember that it takes a monumental series of coincidences to cement Liu Mengmei's identity and to save him from Du Bao's harsh and wrongheaded version of justice.

For Miao Shunbin is the only person in the world to know Liu Mengmei in both his capacities—and only because of coincidence after coincidence. In some sense, it all rests on a foreign policy disaster. Only because the Barbarian Prince invades are the examinations delayed, making it possible for Liu Mengmei—who was too late even for these postponed examinations—to petition Miao Shunbin for a private and oral examination. Surely if the examinations had been held in time, Liu Mengmei would have missed them entirely.

As it turns out, missing the regular examination was an immense stroke of luck. Taking the examination orally means that Liu's answers are associated with his physical person in a way unique among all the examinees: Miao Shunbin can vouch that this particular man—Liu Mengmei, whose specific appearance he can match against the man before him now—gave these particular answers. But for every other examinee who went through the institution of the examinations in the late imperial period, elaborate safeguards had been set up: the test papers were graded anonymously, after scribes had copied them, so that the handwriting would provide no hint as to authorship. All of this was done to protect from the possibility of favoritism or bribery, but its result was also to separate any answer from a specific respondent. If Liu Mengmei had arrived in time to take the examinations on paper, neither Miao Shunbin nor anybody else would be in a position to identify him later on as the top examination candidate.

Yet another coincidence has to take place beforehand to make Miao Shunbin's later identification of Liu Mengmei possible: the older man allows Liu Mengmei to take his examination in such a fortuitously unconventional manner only because he has met the young man before, in Act 23, when Liu just happens to stop at the temple where Miao Shunbin had been previously assigned. The possibility of properly adjudicating Liu Mengmei's identity hangs on a fragile thread of coincidences and contingencies; had not Miao Shunbin showed up at the right moment, he would have been dead and buried a nameless grave robber.

In *Mudan ting*, the connection between the family and the entire nation is largely implicit; in contrast, its epigone *Taohua shan* foregrounds this conjunction, as many histories of the end of the Ming do, associating moral decline with the fall of the state. How are we to understand the obsession of those historians with the relationship between behaviors having to do with the family—both sexual and otherwise—and the state of the land?

Wang Xiuchu, in recording the bloody fall of Yangzhou, observes some women who have become quite familiar with the invading Manchus. Wang immediately connects their behavior with the fall of the dynasty. He relates the comment of a Manchu soldier comparing the behavior of Chinese women with Korean ones:

> At one point a soldier said to the men, "When we were on the Korean campaign, we captured tens of thousands of women, and not one of them failed to keep her honor. How is it that glorious China has reached this level of shamelessness?" And this, alas, is how China came to these troubles.[45]

The connection that Wang Xiuchu sees as so transparent as not to need any further explication eludes us. Hoping to intimidate the rest of the China into submission, the Manchus were never crueler than in their butchery of the citizens of Yangzhou. What do some individual women forced to trade sex for their lives have to do with the fall of the nation? These poor women did not directly cause the fall of Yangzhou. If any individual is to blame, it is the general Shi Kefa, who leaves Yangzhou unprotected but whose very career embodied the value of loyalty.

It is difficult to conceive exactly how some licentious women *could* directly cause the fall of the dynasty, short of all the women in the country throwing up their Chinese husbands in favor of Manchu lovers. Perhaps it is that the same conditions that foster chastity also encourage loyalty and filiality. But that explanation does not account for Wang Xiuchu's tone of loathing.

Scholars of European history and literature have made a great deal over the intersection between family politics and the politics of the nation: Lynn Hunt, for example, has written about the ways in which propagandists during the French Revolution made use of the royal family, making statements about the institution of kingship through jibes at Queen Marie Antoinette's reputed promiscuity, for example. A number of works dealing with early modern Britain have explored the ways in which the complicated marital life of Henry VIII colored an entire political culture. No discussion of what a marriage is or what a legitimate family consists of could avoid touching on these other problems of immense dynastic and political significance.

In Ming China as well, a sovereign's family life represented an intersection between the realms of the private and public. For example, the Jiajing Emperor, who succeeded not his father but an uncle who died without male issue, precipitated an enormous uproar when after his succession he rejected the recommendation of the Ministry of Rites: to smooth over this heterodox succession, they suggested that he take his grandfather, the deceased Hongzhi Emperor, as father and his uncle, the previous Emperor, as older brother. The Jiajing Emperor refused saying, "Can a man change his father so easily?"[46] In protest, a number of officials offered up their lives.

The Emperor who was on the throne when *Mudan ting* was written had his own family problems. Favoring his concubine Lady Zheng, the Wanli Emperor spent over a decade trying to have their child take over the position of Crown Prince. The whole affair was well-known to literate urbanites, since during the last years of the sixteenth-century and the first years of the seventeenth, anonymous pamphlets widely circulated rumors about the intrigue. Some unofficial histories (*yeshi*) even circulated some of the more lurid of these rumors, magnifying intrigue into conspiracy: they told of Lady Zheng's affairs and her secret control of government. Eventually, after many years, the Emperor gave up and the ministers won; instead of the Empire, the prince was forced to accept from his father a fiefdom so magnificent it practically bankrupted the dynasty. Much of *Taohua shan* deals with the spoiled grandson of that prince, the Southern Ming Emperor Hongguang.

Many questions brought up by the Wanli Emperor's experience seem of some relevance to *Mudan ting*, even though the timing of the Emperor's troubles makes any direct influence unlikely. In some cases, these seem to be the concerns of an age. For example, like Du Liniang, every member of the court had to wrestle directly with the difference between a primary marriage (as between the Emperor and the Crown Prince's mother) and a secondary one (as between the Emperor and Lady Zheng). The Emperor's experiences suggest other questions with resonances in our play. The problem of choice, for example, appears again in this Emperor seeking to choose the mother of his heir. In the union between a man and a woman, what should be the proper relationship between private concerns (companionship and love, for example) and dynastic concerns?

Other issues cut right to the heart of *Mudan ting*: surely bystanders and the reading public must have understood the struggle between Emperor and bureaucrats as a conflict between two ways of conceiving of the parental bond. Perhaps parents love their children because they find them lovable individuals; or maybe a father loves his son because of his deep feelings of tenderness for the boy's mother. But such a love can prove dangerous for a number of reasons. When love of a child no longer depends simply on his being one's offspring, one might love a younger son more than his elder brother, as the Wanli Emperor did; or one might love a daughter and treat her as human without regard for whether she is a ghost, as Lady Zhen does. Or one might even, under extreme circumstances—and this is one of Du Bao's greatest fears—accept someone else as one's own child, since the fact of parenthood becomes secondary to more important individual qualities. Du Bao and the Wanli Emperor's ministers of state would argue for an alternative account of the parental bond: children are important first and foremost because of their position within a family—and only then cherished and their personal qualities prized.

The familial conflict is set in a greater political context, but the play neatly averts a truly radical statement about the relationship between the personal and the public. Uncertainty about personal identity plagues supporting characters as well as the leads; Chunxiang and Lady Zhen, for example, must also reclaim their identities after their deaths have been reported and falsely verified by Chen Zuiliang. Nonetheless, uncertainty fails to touch *Mudan ting*'s Emperor. It is impossible to pin down which Emperor he is, or even to imagine him a specific individual, with a personality, with the possibility of self-interest, with his own wives and family.

Mudan ting offers us a vision of the intersection between the familial and the political, where all of humanity lies connected together within a single organic web, a polity of the living governed by an Emperor, with complex ties to the world of the dead. When Du Liniang returns from the world of the dead, not only the individual members of her family, but also the polity itself must figure out how to reincorporate her.

With a single command, the Emperor ties together four people—a marriage, but one uniting not just a husband and a wife, but an entire nuclear family: parents to a child, to each other, and to a son-in-law. Each person is being reunited with—and married to—all three of the others. The beginning of the play's last act finds Du Bao just as convinced of his wife's death as his daughter's; Lady Zhen's return and reunion with him is from his perspective no less a return from the dead. The Emperor's final command focuses as much on the ties between parents and child as on the marriage between husband and wife.

Can we more reliably know a person's parents than his or her spouse? A Confucian political theorist who argues that personal identity should be defined by who one's father is would argue that one can, and that situations where that knowledge is blurred or absent (prostitutes, for example, and actors) are anomalous. *Mudan ting* suggests that this uncertainty lies at the center of all families. No one in Du Bao's family is guilty in any obvious way of sexual conduct that might disrupt knowledge of paternity. Nonetheless, even in the absence of any impropriety, such knowledge is shown to be imperfect, buckling under the lightest of critical pressures or alarmingly prone to becoming nothing but a metaphor.

Something of the fragility of the system shows as early as Du Liniang's dream. If even Du Liniang—a virgin so hermetically sequestered she has no knowledge of the garden behind her own home, so sheltered that the work of literature that sets her mind roaming is of all things a poem from the *Shijing*—can still manage to fall in love and begin an affair with a man of her own choosing, it seems impossible ever to perfectly guard a woman's chastity, which bodes ill for one of the central promises of patriarchy. Small wonder then that Du Bao directs such rage towards Liu Mengmei.

More specifically, though, family relationships simply can't be kept straight. Du Liniang praises her husband Liu Mengmei several times as someone who has given her life, explicitly equating his role in her life with that of her parents: "By resurrecting me, you are more familiar to me than my own parents." In her place one simply cannot afford to be so prodigal with such praises, since the identity of her parents' child turns out to be a question of life and death significance. This conflation of parent and husband, unsettling though it is, casts further light on Du Bao's hostility towards Liu Mengmei. And what does it mean when she rewards her parent-equivalent (Liu Mengmei who has given her life itself) by marrying him? Keeping family relations straight, the most literal meaning of *zhengming*, is an integral part both of Confucian society and of the play's end, but at times it seems a hopeless task.

If Du Liniang is haphazard about attributing parentage, her parents too are promiscuous in deciding who their child is. Both parents lament the prospect of losing their only descendant: "In this half-child is our whole family's life."[47] A complex series of identifications takes place here: of course, Du Liniang is entirely their own child, and normally, it is a son-in-law who is called a half-child. But in such a wealthy family with only a single daughter, a son-in-law would likely have married in, eventually passing on his wife's surname to their children. And so the lives of both Lady Zhen and Du Bao are equated—and some metaphorical life of the family beyond that as well—in roundabout but explicit fashion, to an as yet unseen, unknown, nonexistent son-in-law.

In some ways, the kind of uncertainty and inaccuracy implicit in that comment prefigures one of the strangest moments in the play. Why, when he introduces himself to Du Bao, does Liu Mengmei not identify himself by name, but instead only as his son-in-law? In Liu Mengmei's place, I might have tried to explain more carefully the unusual history of their marriage. But the greeting is singular for more general reasons as well—it is impossible to imagine another circumstance in which a stranger would introduce himself to somebody as his son-in-law, since in virtually all cases, the son-in-law's relationship to the father would precede any relationship with his wife. Only through knowledge of one's father-in-law (or more precisely, through a young man's knowledge of his own father who would then make the initial contact with the prospective father-in-law) would somebody come to know his wife. Just as the two parents imply at their daughter's deathbed, their son-in-law, in fact, can be just anyone.

Finally in this context, a conversation which takes place after Du Liniang's death further undermines any confidence we might have had in the potential of family structure to identify individuals with any certainty. Three years after Du Liniang's death, her mother and her maidservant set up a little ceremony to her memory, which serves as the focus for a long conversation between the two as to what it is to be someone's child. In the course of the conversation, during which Lady Zhen bemoans her own lack of descendants repeatedly, Chunxiang comforts her with alternatives, and the two explore ways one might have a son without actually physically bearing one. It becomes clear that even the beloved daughter was only a necessary means to a grandson.

Lady Zhen dismisses the possibility of having her husband take a concubine. The child resulting from such a union would be considered Lady Zhen's, no different according to custom and ritual from Du Liniang. But Lady Zhen suggests otherwise: "Now is the child of a concubine the equal of a child born of oneself?"[48] Chunxiang responds that parenthood is not a biological bond, but an emotional one, which can be forged with anyone, within or outside of a family: "Lady, you have graced me with your care, so that even if not of family, we are of family. If you can do so with a concubine's son, will you not have a son, even if you do not have one?"[49]

We have had ample evidence that in some ways Chunxiang can substitute for Du Liniang. For example, if identity is to be equated as it so often is with responsibility, early on, Du Bao tells the tutor Chen Zuiliang to punish the maidservant for the transgressions of her mistress. It is hard to know whether Chunxiang's comforting words are flattery, gratitude, or even sarcasm. At various points in the play, Chunxiang complains quite vociferously and graphically about just how different the position of a beloved only daughter is from that of her maidservant. Nonetheless, this maternal promiscuity certainly casts a peculiar light on Lady Zhen's relationship with her biological daughter.

Chunxiang concludes that by loving an adopted child, Lady Zhen will be able to have a son without a son. These words of comfort prefigure Du Bao's later fears that without a child he will be forced to accept a demon as his flesh and blood. His extreme reaction at the end of the play suggests that the reduction of familial relations to metaphor demands caution. Unlike his wife, any child of Du Bao's would have to be biologically his own. Late imperial legal codes contained numerous prohibitions against adoption, allowing only adoptions of children of the same surname, to keep pure each patriarchal constituent of the polity.

Chunxiang and Lady Zhen have this conversation about parenthood at a private ceremony to hasten Du Liniang's reincarnation. As Lady Zhen prays for her child's speedy rebirth, her prior obsession—with blood relationships, that she herself not die without descendants—disappears, since what is obvious to us seems of no importance to her: that at the instant of Du Liniang's rebirth, this new creature will of course cease to be Lady Zhen's child and become somebody else's. In other words, her love for her child ultimately does not depend at all on her child's being her child. And if she is praying for Du Liniang's speedy reincarnation, any child is equally deserving of her affections, since any little child born could be her own daughter, resurrected through reincarnation. In other words, just as her son-in-law can be anyone, anyone could be her child; but even her child might not be her child (and instead, the reincarnated soul of someone else's child).

As she yearns for her daughter and prays for her reincarnation, Lady Zhen finds herself in a not uncommon position. How can two beliefs as incompatible as reincarnation and kinship be sustained simultaneously? To believe in reincarnation is to believe in the rootlessness of the soul; to believe in kinship is to believe in the fixity of identity. The dilemma has faced Chinese people since the introduction of Buddhism; Buddhists' seeming disregard for family led Han Yu, for example, to decry them as inhuman. Chinese Buddhist literature, almost obsessively focused on family matters, seems all about resolving this paradox, as Alan Cole's *Mothers and Sons in Chinese Buddhism* suggests.

Love of a child and filial piety must somehow square with Buddhist devotion and the transmigration of souls, and this paradox produced untold reams of sutras, plays, prose narratives, illustrated tales, and *baojuan*. Tales that simply valorize filial piety and chastity often deliberately downplay the emotional bond between the parent and child, or the husband and wife, lest love and not duty be seen to be the motivation for good behavior. In contrast, Buddhist depictions of family are frequently characterized by effusive outpourings of feeling. Perhaps the most famously filial Buddhist, Mu Lian, descends to hell to perform the ultimate filial deed of saving his mother from eternal torment. Cole translates a passage from *The Pure Land Ghost Festival Sutra* describing the reunion of mother and son:

> Mu Lian's joy was like [when one] searches for a piece of gold among the sands of the Ganges and suddenly finds it. Or like a filial son hearing news that his deceased mother has come back to life. Or, again, it was like a congenitally blind person suddenly opening his eyes. It was like [the joy of] a dead person coming back to life.[50]

Where ardent belief in kinship seemingly always contains a strain of distrust in feeling, a belief in reincarnation can admit for passionate love of an individual in the bond between mother and child.

Similarly, Lady Zhen's prayer for her daughter's reincarnation underlies perhaps the most moving moment of the play. After that creature who so resembles her daughter fails each of the tests meant to determine whether she is a ghost or not, her attendant Daoist Shi shines the lamp into the face of her mistress and says, "Cease your worrying: move the lamp or go into the moonlight and look her over closely. Is it not the human face of yesteryear?" It is another moment when Du Liniang is recognized by the lineaments of her face—and against all logic, since a ghost would certainly look the same.

But at this moment, Lady Zhen makes the decision that whether her daughter is human or a ghost simply does not matter: "Child, even if you are a ghost, mother couldn't bear to give you up!"[51] The bond here might have its origins in parental regard, but after the girl's death it is by her own admission changed. Lady Zhen's feelings for Du Liniang follow the opposite trajectory as Liu Mengmei's: there, a love between two individuals stripped down virtually to their consciousnesses ends up integrated into society as a marriage sanctioned by the Emperor. And here, that fully orthodox love between mother and daughter asserts itself finally as a love between two individuals, where—since Du Liniang is possibly a ghost—there can be no assurance that she is Lady Zhen's daughter.

In the end, both halves of the Emperor's promise—human identity and identity within a family—have each already been given to Du Liniang by her husband and her mother. Each has loved her into being, as daughter and as wife. Lady Zhen addresses herself to her daughter: "Child, even if you are a ghost, mother couldn't bear to give you up!" She refers to herself as "mother"—a mode of speech this woman, past her reproductive years and her only child dead three years ago, surely thought she could never use again—and a mode of speech peculiar with a ghost. If this woman has already allowed that she could be a mother to any human child at all, she here admits the possibility of being a mother to a ghost. But can one mother a ghost? To acknowledge this creature as her daughter is not only to recognize her as human, but to give her a place in the human world—and also to refuse to ask this question of her identity any longer. At first distrustful and wary, the sight of her daughter's familiar face kills all questioning of her daughter's humanity—she does not address it again in this act, and not ever again. It has become simply unnecessary to ask.

Of course, if Lady Zhen expresses her love for Du Liniang by making her human, Liu Mengmei does so much more literally. At its most literal level, when Liu Mengmei calls Du Liniang by that Ming endearment, "my person," it is precisely his love that has made her a person (and vice-versa, given his own unique circumstances as well), and both lovers articulate this sentiment. Since that is the case, tests can prove nothing: how can one test for humanity—when here it is precisely the examiner's relationship to the examinee that makes her human?

Upon resurrection, after he is pointed out to her, Du Liniang's first words to Liu Mengmei are enigmatic and can be translated in one of two ways. He has done as he has promised, and so "Master Liu is truly a trustworthy person," but also because he believed that she would in fact rise human out of the grave, "Master Liu is so trusting a person."[52] Since these are among the first words she has spoken as a person, they suggest what Liu Mengmei will say literally a few acts later. After Du Liniang tells Liu Mengmei as complete a version of events as he will ever hear, he sighs in response, "This explanation has rendered me speechless, and so I, irrational through passion, believed your person into existence."[53] And then in the same aria, in reference to his disinterment of her, he sings: "Out of the earth I brought you and made you a person."[54] First he believes her back into life among mortals, and then by marrying her, he makes her human.

And so we end where we began, with the figure of Du Bao, resisting and still skeptical. Surely the Emperor cannot force belief on him. And yet without Du Bao's approval, despite all that they have been through, it is not clear that the marriage of the two young lovers can stand—if the roles conflict in their demands, how can Du Liniang be a filial daughter and a loyal wife? The position in human society her mother and her husband have so laboriously created for her, as daughter and as wife, is all for naught if her father will not accept her.

Surely he should have as strong an inclination as his wife to recognize the creature as his daughter—or if he is simply a skeptic all around, he should have just as strong an inclination to consider his wife a ghost as his daughter. Du Bao enters the last act believing his wife to have died; when she enters to testify, he is shocked. After the Emperor decrees that father and child, husband and wife should all recognize each other, a grand reunion seems to be set in place when Lady Zhen congratulates her husband on his promotion and he eagerly and affectionately greets her after their long separation: "How could I ever have thought to have found my lady well?"[55] But when Du

Liniang then addresses her father familiarly *wode die* (which can only translate as "Daddy!"), she is cruelly rebuffed.

With no more proof than he has for his daughter, Du Bao willingly recognizes his wife as human and as his wife, whom he just as easily could regard a ghost. So for him, too, with his wife, these recognition scenes can be a kind of resurrection scene, except that he withholds that very scene both from us and from his daughter—though we all yearn for such a scene.

But then again, why should we be surprised? His treatment of her at the end of the play in no way differs from it at the beginning; even before her death, she could not prove her humanity to him. Much earlier, Du Liniang's lovesickness elicits two very different reactions from her parents. Immediately, her mother regrets having not married her daughter off earlier, leaving her vulnerable to the passions that killed her. Du Bao dismisses Lady Zhen's concerns, saying, "She is too much of a child; what does a little girl like that know of the seven emotions?"[56] As is written in the Book of Rites, and as Tang Xianzu and Du Bao must know: "What are the so-called human emotions? Joy, anger, grief, fear, love, hatred, and desire. These seven—even without learning—one can feel."[57] *The Book of Rites* hints at another prescriptive definition of humanity; no person, howsoever mean or young she might be, lacks these.

This version of human nature is one with which by now we are familiar, since it reprises much of what Liu Mengmei, Du Liniang, and Lady Zhen have been articulating. It is a prescription for human nature, a recognition that human nature is not something preexisting to be tested but only action and feeling—and how significant then that Du Bao should mention the seven emotions. For if this play is indeed not a comedy, its tragedy lies in Du Bao's refusal to recognize his daughter as human and to participate in the recognition which gives the other characters such joy. And if this is so, even as he presides over his family, he can never enjoy that marriage of human society so beautifully suggested by the play in which all abide "not in forced cohabitation and counterfeit performance of duties, but in unfeigned love and peace."[58]

PART TWO

Taohua shan

Introduction to *Taohua shan*

Questions of identity are ultimately decided in *Mudan ting* by the Emperor, a character whose presence is profoundly important to the play, but who is never seen. Instead, like the dead Du Liniang at the scene of her disinterment but before she is resurrected, he is represented by an offstage voice, as if like the disembodied spirit he exists on a different plane from the rest of humanity. And he is carefully kept offstage, lest he experience the vagaries of identity that afflict or threaten to afflict the other characters: the possibility of misidentification, of refusals to recognize, of substitution by another.

After *zaju*'s popularity grew, it became the official court entertainment of the Ming Emperors. Imperial troupes were established, and censors checked through scripts to make sure that nothing that might cause offense appeared onstage. Most *zaju* texts that have survived to the present day passed through the court and the hands of the censors. In these plays the presence of the Emperor onstage is carefully excised. Two Emperors, one onstage performing and one offstage observing, seems one too many, especially when the first few decades of the new dynasty were filled with controversy over the proper succession.[1] To comply with the new regulations, extensive rewrites were undertaken in the Ming to modify plays from the Yuan dynasty; for example, a messenger carrying an edict could substitute for the imperial presence itself.

In *Mudan ting*, all the other identities revolve around that of the Emperor: it is he who decrees that Du Bao, his own minister, should serve as father to Du Liniang and father-in-law to Liu Mengmei, so that all three come to be defined in relation to him. "Father and daughter, husband and wife will all recognize each other," he commands in the final act. What remains unspoken is that they will recognize each other as family only because first they recognize him as Emperor. They obey him and become a family. Ultimately, the fixedness of human identities within this society rests on the Emperor.

What happens if in a world like that of *Mudan ting*, where personal identity is so vulnerable to confusion and where the confusions have so much to do with the liberating powers of the theatre, the Emperor himself is brought onstage? For in contradistinction both to *Mudan ting* and to *zaju* convention, in *Taohua shan* the Emperor is an onstage presence, played by an actor, one character among many others. That is one way of articulating the central challenge *Taohua shan* poses to its predecessor, *Mudan ting*. For the climactic moment in *Mudan ting*, when the offstage imperial presence sorts out all the problems and assigns each person to his or her proper place, can never take place in the play's great epigone, *Taohua shan*. *Taohua shan* tells the story of the Ming dynasty's fall, when the identity of the Emperor was anything but clear.

By a conservative count, at the end of 1644, there were seven men with strong claims to being Emperor. First, the last Ming Emperor to live in Beijing's Forbidden City, Chongzhen, whom some stubborn souls still believed to be alive (but who had hanged himself when it was clear the imperial compound was about to be breached). Second, third, and fourth, his three sons, any one of whom had the right to succession in the event of their father's death and of whom it was known only that they had all fled the palace, but not where they had gone. Fifth, the Hongguang Emperor, the imperial cousin who was eventually chosen to rule in the provisional capital of Nanjing and with whose reign *Taohua shan* mostly concerns itself. Sixth, Li Zicheng, the bandit at the hands of whose army Beijing fell and who by the end of 1644 had declared himself Emperor just as he himself was about to lose control of the capital to the Manchus. And seventh, the Shunzhi Emperor, the young Manchu lordling (who incidentally as a ten-year-old child ceded all authority to his uncle, the Regent Dorgon, a final candidate for the wielder of supreme power).

Without an Emperor—or more accurately, with too many—the moment of imperial judgment that fixes everything in *Mudan ting* cannot take place. Yet the absence of such a scene, and the way it incontrovertibly places people where they ought to be, haunts the later play as it explores the question of what happens to the identity of all people when even that of the Emperor is uncertain.

In its account of the fall of the Ming dynasty, *Taohua shan* focuses its attention on a young couple, Li Xiangjun and Hou Fangyu, and their experiences in this time of political turmoil. But they are only two figures in a large cast, consisting mostly of real-life historical figures, who range from the most exalted—the Hongguang Emperor and powerful ministers of state—to the humblest entertainers and courtesans. Yet despite the disparity of their backgrounds, many of these characters know each other, and all of them are tied together through complex emotional, economic, and political bonds.

The play begins right before the fall of Beijing. Li Xiangjun, a teenaged prostitute living with her adoptive mother, Li Zhenli, has her first customer recommended to her by Yang Wencong, a family friend who is both an art connoisseur and an official. He suggests Hou Fangyu, a young scholar of good family but humble means, and the match is agreed upon. Hou and the two women have no idea that all the while the entire affair is being bankrolled by Ruan Dacheng, an official disgraced by his association with the corrupt eunuch Wei Zhongxian and ostracized by the decent society typified by Hou Fangyu. After a facsimile of a marriage ceremony—in the presence of other prostitutes and entertainers and the absence of his parents—the couple pledge their troth on a fan and repair to a night of bliss. The next morning, Yang Wencong confesses Ruan Dacheng's involvement. Outraged, Li Xiangjun insists upon returning her dowry, earning her the praise of Hou and his friends from the Revival Society, a political group dedicated to reforming some of the corruptions of late Ming government. For a little while, the young lovers are ecstatically happy.

The romantic interlude is brought to an end when General Zuo Liangyu's troops threaten Nanjing. Zuo is a basically loyal general, but his troops are rioting for want of supplies. Yang Wencong enlists Hou Fangyu's help to save the city. They come up with the idea of forging a letter in the name of Hou's father, an old acquaintance of Zuo's. The letter convinces Zuo Liangyu to stand down his troops. After the crisis is defused, Hou Fangyu is forced to flee the city for his part in the affair. At their tearful parting, Li Xiangjun vows to remain loyal to Hou, who rushes off to become an aide-de-camp for Shi Kefa (later to be renowned as the great loyalist general).

At this time of personal turmoil, news from the northern capital arrives, reporting the fall of Beijing: the rebel Li Zicheng has stormed the Forbidden City, and the Chongzhen Emperor has killed himself. Officials in Nanjing hurry to set up a makeshift government, whose first task must be to replace the Emperor. Ma Shiying and Ruan Dacheng take advantage of the situation and rise to power, backing the dissolute heir to the Prince Fu as their candidate. Hou Fangyu, however, vehemently disapproves of this choice and advises Shi Kefa accordingly, but to no avail. Ruan Dacheng and Ma Shiying succeed in welcoming into the city their choice, the erstwhile heir to the Prince Fu, Zhu Yousong, and now the new Emperor Hongguang.

Of course, the new Emperor's old backers, Ruan Dacheng and Ma Shiying, are the real powers in Nanjing, and they promptly begin to abuse their new positions, promising Li Xiangjun to a colleague of theirs despite her repeated refusals. She means to keep herself chaste for Hou Fangyu, and when the sedan bearers arrive to bear her away, she resists despite the urgings of her mother and Yang Wencong. Finally she resorts to marring her own face by beating it against the ground. With sedan bearers knocking at their door and a powerful and vengeful Ruan Dacheng behind them, her mother has no choice but to go in her place. The next morning, in checking up on Li Xiangjun, Yang Wencong finds that the fan (the very same one on which she had pledged her troth with Hou Fangyu) has been bloodstained from the night's troubles, and he, with skillful use of pigment, transforms the bloodstains to peach blossoms, creating the eponymous *Taohua shan*, a peach blossom fan.

But not even this sacrifice is enough to purchase Li Xiangjun's seclusion: all entertainers are to register at court so that the new Emperor can cast the players in a production of his favorite play, Ruan Dacheng's own romantic comedy *Yanzi jian*, or *The Swallow Letter*. Ruan still holds a grudge against Li Xiangjun, who scorned his dowry, and so when she arrives, he promptly casts her as a clown; the Emperor, though, overrules him, casting Li Xiangjun instead in the lead role.

Meanwhile, Hou has returned to Nanjing, and after failing to find Li Xiangjun, looks up his old Revival Society friends, with whom he is arrested straightaway, since he has had the bad luck to return during a crackdown. To rescue Hou from prison, once again Zuo Liangyu is persuaded to move his troops. Zuo's advance leaves the Yangtze River open to any attack from the north, and with that entire flank open, the great city Yangzhou is doomed. After that, it is only a matter of time before Nanjing itself falls.

Shi Kefa kills himself after the Yangzhou massacre, and with his whole government fleeing or in hiding, Hongguang seeks refuge with General Huang Degong but is then quickly taken captive. Unbeknownst to each other, Li Xiangjun and Hou Fangyu each take refuge in the same remote Daoist retreat far in the mountains, where they find many of the members of their makeshift family: Li Zhenli, the musicians, and friends from the Revival Society. All seems set for a final reunion, until the Daoist priest (an erstwhile Ming official) dissuades the young lovers from marrying, rips the fan to shreds, and sends them each away.

Even with many subplots necessarily elided and the names of some of the most important characters yet to be mentioned, the play resists—as you may have noticed—simple plot summary. It is enormously complicated, an attempt to represent something monumental, the experience of dynastic change and how it affects a whole cross section of people. Its dramatic form notwithstanding, *Taohua shan* is one of many unofficial histories on the fall of the Ming dynasty (and in fact, in the prologue the Old Ceremonial Assistant compares it with the most hallowed of all the histories, *The Spring and Autumn Annals*, which tradition attributes to Kong's ancestor Confucius).

Consequently, one critical problem scholars have long addressed is the accuracy of the play's version of events.[2] The play also reflects on historiography: what it means to record events, how a certain version of them comes to be chosen, whether events are predetermined, and how the perception of events is changed by how they are recorded. But I am concerned only tangentially with the play as either history or historiography. Instead, my discussion of the play begins with how *Taohua shan* responds to some of the questions about identity posed by its predecessor *Mudan ting*. When I consult some of the numerous unofficial histories reflecting on the same events as *Taohua shan*, my concern will not be accuracy, or the degree to which the texts correspond with each other and with the play, but rather how they each articulate different ideas about identity.

The singing instructor Su Kunsheng persuades Zuo Liangyu to attack the capital for personal reasons; he wants somebody to rescue his friend Hou Fangyu from prison. Kong Shangren's audience would have known just how disastrous the effects of this attempted rescue will be. The movement of Zuo Liangyu's troops leaves the entire Yangtze River vulnerable to attack and ultimately dooms the Nanjing regime, spelling the end of serious Ming resistance. Naturally Su Kunsheng does not tell Zuo Liangyu that he is recommending the self-destruction of the Empire simply out of loyalty to a friend. Instead, he claims a public goal, specifically, the liberation of a more exalted prisoner: the putative Crown Prince.

The Chongzhen Emperor had three sons, all of whom disappeared shortly after Beijing's fall and whose claims to the throne would naturally have superseded those of Hongguang, a mere cousin. Reports that the Crown Prince or either of his two brothers had survived dogged the Nanjing regime for the entire length of its existence. One young pretender, whose claims the Manchus had to dismiss repeatedly, turned up in the north, and an even more persuasive candidate presented himself in the south.

The appearance of the southern claimant set off rumors Hongguang's government had to dispel. Officials who would have known the prince in happier times were brought in to quiz him. Unfortunately, however, the results of these tests of identity were interpreted very differently by different people, leading to the formation of two irresolvably opposed factions: one firmly convinced that the young man was a clever impostor, and the other just as sure that the Crown Prince—the rightful occupant of the throne— was being treated as a common criminal. According to *Taohua shan* and other accounts, ultimately it was this dispute as much as the continued military pressure from the north that caused the fall of the Nanjing regime. With rumors afoot of the Imperial Princes' survival, Hongguang was never able to consolidate support. As we well know from *Mudan ting*, there are times when on matters of personal identity, compromise is not possible.

The Emperor who renders judgment on identity in *Mudan ting* is one whose facelessness reflects his lack of individual characteristics, and whose timelessness, ahistoricity, and ultimately incontestability are such that even his dynasty remains nameless.[3] There is simply no way to regard him as an individual. Whatever he decides with regard to Du Liniang's identity will have no impact on him at all; the decision is entirely impersonal, unswayed by any personal considerations, which is suggested by the fact that he can and does rule in favor of the penniless young scholar and against the powerful, established official.

Hongguang shares neither his remove nor his infallibility. At a memorial service for the dead Chongzhen Emperor, the Old Ceremonial Assistant reads Hongguang's proclamation in which the new ruler attempts once and for all to debunk the rumors that the Crown Prince survived the fall of Beijing and to resolve the thorny problem of the pretender's identity. The proclamation addresses the dead Chongzhen Emperor but is read aloud for the benefit of the gathered officials: "The empire collapsed. Your Majesty was sacrificed for the country, and the Empress and Crown Prince both died amidst the troubles of their lord and father."[4] Yet we know that though embedded in ritual and couched in appropriately elevated language, this assertion does not command belief at all. A few scant months later, the conviction that Hongguang was lying will help to topple him from his throne.

Self-interest manifestly motivates Hongguang; if the young pretender's claims are true, then Hongguang's own position as Emperor can never be secure. In reflecting on the young man's identity, Hongguang is in essence reasserting his own. Or, as Ruan Dacheng says more directly: "If we recognize the Crown Prince as real, where will we stick the lord that we welcomed in?"[5] It does not in the least matter to Ruan who the young man really is, for all of them—Ruan, Ma Shiying, and the Hongguang Emperor—stand to lose too much if he turns out to be the Crown Prince.

This monarch is no impersonal judge around whom others can define themselves, but only one member of a faction whose opinions will be read in partisan context. By such logic, Hongguang's position on the question of the young pretender's identity proves nothing one way or the other, except what is known already—that he is a puppet in the hands of the Ma and Ruan faction. The Emperor no longer rises above and adjudicates identity, but is himself embroiled in a vicious dispute over identity.

If at its end *Mudan ting* faces a crossroads and chooses comedy—a conclusion where everybody finds his or her right place in society—it is unclear in *Taohua shan* where such right places might be. In a world where all things turn out right, where should someone like the Hongguang Emperor end up? Perhaps there is no right place for him.

Du Liniang's unexpected resurrection and the Barbarian Prince's aggression have the disruptive—and liberating—effect of unrooting the identities of the whole Du family, but when all is over, everyone is back where he or she belongs. In contrast, the possibility of comedy is never open to *Taohua shan*'s society. We know a little bit about what happens after the play ends: the Qing will consolidate its power, and Hou Fangyu will find his way back to his family. But no such return to home avails itself to Li Xiangjun. Unlike Du Liniang, her counterpart in *Mudan ting*, Li Xiangjun is no daughter of privilege, but a prostitute, and there is neither father's nor husband's home for her to return to.

The play is scrupulously grounded in the historical past. Not only are the major political figures—Ruan Dacheng, Shi Kefa, Ma Shiying—thoroughly researched, but the entertainers are also based on historical figures. Because Kong Shangren invested so much emotion in this period more than a generation earlier than his own, seeking out surviving eyewitnesses and doing considerable amounts of research, *Taohua shan* has often been read either as loyalist literature or, at the very least, as deeply colored by nostalgia for the *ancien régime*. I disagree strongly with such interpretations.

I have summarized the play with what may strike the reader as painstaking detail partly to make the following chapters easier to follow, but also to suggest how the play resists such a nostalgic reading. Even in the third of the play that takes place before Beijing's fall and Chongzhen's death, all is not well in Nanjing. And the fault lies not—as some of the characters argue—with the actions of a few identifiable, evil individuals, but with an entire polity where things have gone terribly awry. It is hard to imagine where one could begin to fix it.

In other words, what is cast on Nanjing is not a rosy, nostalgic light, and there is profound moral ambivalence even about historical figures traditionally regarded favorably. To name one example, Shi Kefa, valorized by loyalists and Manchus alike, comes across in *Taohua shan* as a decidedly imperfect individual.

Nor does our hero Hou Fangyu come off particularly well. At a moment when rebels and foreigners threaten the nation's borders, when corruption has reached the point that rations and materiel disappear on their way to Zuo Liangyu's army, Hou Fangyu's friends at the Revival Society conceive of themselves as heroes saving the country. But they never engage in any action beyond embroiling themselves in petty factional disputes that have been emptied of all subject matter. Like Hongguang, whose assertions can be read only in terms of his alliance with Ma and Ruan, it is difficult to read the Revival Society as standing for anything other than disdain for Ruan Dacheng. The sign they hang inadvertently reveals the emptiness of their position: "The Revival Society is meeting; non-members stay out."[6]

This sense of things gone wrong is borne out otherwise as well. A play entitled *Peach Blossom Fan* can scarcely avoid evoking the great Six Dynasties' poet Tao Qian's account of the mythic Peach Blossom Spring, *Taohua yuan ji* ("The Record of Peach Blossom Spring"). A number of characters strengthen the connection by making explicit reference to Peach Blossom Spring: the painter Lan Ying is working on a painting of it (in the studio that was once Li Xiangjun's boudoir); the official Zhang Wei calls his own country house by that name; our hero Hou Fangyu refers to it when he is imprisoned.

Our play has a very complicated relationship with the famous prose piece, which tells of a fisherman wandering upon a community that has lost touch with the rest of the world. He marvels at the peace and calm of the isolated community, and after he leaves, he is unable to find his way back to it. Many writers have interpreted "Record of the Peach Blossom Spring" simply as an account of a utopia, or even more simplistically, as a cipher for all things good and pleasant. But in *Taohua shan*, as an old polity is being destroyed in preparation for the birth of a new one, Peach Blossom Spring has all sorts of resonances, many of them entirely applicable to the situation at hand: can one society break off from another? Can people truly flee politics and the structures of government?

From the beginning of the play, well before the fall of Beijing, the main characters of *Taohua shan* participate in a political culture in which the ugliest of conspiracies have credence and where purges and public humiliations presciently violent are regular events. The blame cannot be laid at the feet of a single villain or a single villainous clique, but instead must be ascribed to a political dynamic. If Ma Shiying and Ruan Dacheng prove gratuitously cruel and vicious when they come to power, when we first encounter the conflict between them and their Revival Society enemies, it is Ruan Dacheng who is being bullied by his enemies. It becomes impossible to tell whether Ruan Dacheng is actually wronging his opponents or merely exacting vengeance. At any rate, a cycle of vengeance provides much of the energy for political action.

Certainly, the brutality of Act 3 (instigated by Hou Fangyu's friends) matches that of any later act. Ruan Dacheng breaks his self-imposed exile to witness the annual spring sacrifices. The ritual is interrupted not by Ruan's appearance, but by four scholars, including Hou Fangyu's close friend, Wu Yingji, who protest Ruan's presence. First they taunt him, and then, joined now by those officiating at the ritual, they pummel him and tear his beard. All the while, surrounded by those bent on his humiliation, Ruan Dacheng defends his past actions, albeit somewhat weakly and self-servingly. Finally he is reduced to protesting weakly: "You have torn out my entire beard; how am I to face people? Oh, this is so dreadful."[7] Even the sympathetic Old Ceremonial Assistant joins in on the beating.

Then after Ruan Dacheng has been cruelly humiliated, Wu Yingji sighs with pure satisfaction: "What we did today was revenge the Donglin and give glory to the Nanjing Academy. Was it not refreshing!"[8] *Shuangkuai*, "refreshing" or "pleasant," is chilling in its casualness—a term that might more usually be applied to a cool breeze than a beating, and I think, key to Kong Shangren's condemnation of the Revival Society. Factional politics, devoid of content, have simply become a way for men (and those who engage in these ugly acts are those claiming to be the good guys) to express their very basest instincts: a brutality which serves no purpose, since after all, Ruan Dacheng is at the moment entirely powerless, having long since been dismissed from his office. Beating him serves no particular political end, but it does feel good.

This kind of political culture looks much like a trap where one alternates between taking vengeance and experiencing the vengeance of others, or between beating and being beaten. A person in such a culture might well find himself attracted by the promise of a Peach Blossom Spring, since what it represents is an escape out of the cycle.

Zhang Wei is sufficiently obsessed by Peach Blossom Spring that he commissions a painting of it from Lan Ying to be placed in his country retreat (which Zhang also refers to several times as his Peach Blossom Spring). Although he does not appear in many scenes, Zhang Wei is actually a centrally important figure in the play, partly in that he ties together its many locales: he is the official who had overseen Chongzhen's proper burial before fleeing the north and who, frustrated with his assigned role as henchman, absconds with one of his prisoners (Cai Yisuo, a Revival Society sympathizer), leaving for the mountain hideaway where he is eventually joined by Hou Fangyu, Li Xiangjun, and Li Zhenli. Finally at the end of the play, as a Daoist priest, Zhang rips apart the fan.

In this retreat, Zhang Wei would seem to have recreated his longtime obsession, Peach Blossom Spring. He and his band of followers have succeeded in escaping from the invaders, much as the people in Peach Blossom Spring escaped the Qin dynasty. The people beyond the Spring explain to Tao Qian's visiting fisherman how they got there:

> They said their ancestors had run from the chaos of the Qin dynasty, and taking their wives, families, and other villagers, had come to this remote area, never leaving again, and then cutting off all ties with outsiders. They asked what era it was, and they did not know even about the Han dynasty, much less the Wei or the Jin.[9]

And yet once he has left Nanjing for the mountains, Zhang Wei never again mentions Peach Blossom Spring.

It is he who refuses to allow Li Xiangjun and Hou Fangyu to wed, arguing that in a group of people broken off from the larger polity, marriage itself cannot take place. In other words, he tells them the dream of Peach Blossom Spring—that one can escape from oppressive political circumstances and recreate everything good about society elsewhere—is only a fantasy: "Fie! You two crazy little lovebugs! Look about you: where is the country? Where is the family? Where is the Emperor? Where are the fathers? And all you have is this root of passion in flowers and moonlight, and you can't sever it?"[10] Marriage promises continuity, whether of a family, or of a society. Refusal to allow Li Xiangjun and Hou Fangyu to marry means that this band of refugees can never form their own society, but instead are destined to return to the larger polity, to rejoin and accommodate themselves to the whole.

Rather than protest his unreasonableness, all the characters accede to his judgment, and the two young lovers part for the final time. It is curious that it takes so little to persuade the lovers—who have been through a great deal for each other—to give up. Why cannot this isolated mountain area become their Peach Blossom Spring? It seems such a tempting ending: Li Xiangjun and Hou Fangyu's children could be born and grow up and have their own children without ever knowing anything of the ugliness on the outside, and the leader of this community would be Zhang Wei. But at some point between leaving Nanjing and reaching the mountains, Zhang Wei has come to disbelieve in the dream of Peach Blossom Spring.

In this play, the yearning for Peach Blossom Spring—a cliché in Chinese if ever there ever was one—never escapes moral ambiguity. Tao Qian's prose piece suggests that one cannot approach Peach Blossom Spring deliberately; the fisherman finds the spring accidentally, and once he tries to return, he cannot. In *Taohua shan*, this anxiety is translated into questions about staging. *Taohua shan* recurrently juxtaposes actions that can be staged without losing any of their meaning and those actions that cannot be staged.

The isolated temples where Li Xiangjun and Hou Fangyu find themselves reunited under Zhang Wei are not his first refuge. Instead, as an official in Nanjing, he carefully prepares a country home which he repeatedly refers to as Peach Blossom Spring, a refuge from his political life that he prepares as carefully as a stage set. Before heading off, he gauges the appropriateness of his own costume: "Without taking off my official hat, belt, robes, and boots, costumed like this—how can I be a person of the Peach Blossom Spring?"[11] As he is an official based in a bustling city, we can only figure that all of these objects he has set aside for this purpose—dress-up utterly foreign from his workaday clothes—are store-bought: a bamboo hat, straw shoes, a dried-reed sash, and a coat of feathers are neatly stored at his mountain retreat in a trunk.[12] He costumes himself and designs a set in accordance with his own imaginings of Peach Blossom Spring.

Ultimately, what prompts his real flight from this vacation home into the unknown is the realization of how far his surroundings differ from his imaginings: "With a yamen runner going through my flowers and a criminal chained to my pine tree, what kind of a 'Peach Blossom Spring' can this be?"[13] No matter how eremitic the setting, there is no escape from politics. He invites the prisoner, Cai Yisuo, to flee with him, and the Daoist garb that had been dress-up for his country house becomes his real clothing, as if Marie Antoinette found herself actually herding sheep. But instead of being convinced that this escape allows him to find the true Peach Blossom Spring, Zhang Wei gives up on that dream of escape, never mentioning it again.

Three acts after Zhang Wei's escape into the unknown with prisoner in tow, Hou Fangyu and his musician friend Liu Jingting invoke Peach Blossom Spring as well. In prison, the two have just been reunited in a scene of surpassing ugliness and violence: Liu, with his hands shackled together, is defecating in the prison courtyard as other prisoners, also political enemies of Ma and Ruan, are taken out to be executed in the middle of the night. In the darkness, the warden and some guards go through the prison population looking for those whose placards match up to the names on the doomed list. In the midst of all this, Hou sings to Liu, alluding to the prose piece by Tao Qian: "Forgetting how tired we are, we laughingly look at the round moon—it is like the cave with the peaches in Wuling. There are men of the Qin dynasty, who have fled from that chaos, and fishermen in their boats talking to each other."[14]

Hou Fangyu and Liu Jingting, helpless at the hands of the corrupt government of Ruan Dacheng and Ma Shiying, identify themselves with those who successfully fled from the Qin dynasty to Peach Blossom Spring. And yet this yearning seems to contradict the deep sense of political engagement both men have professed so earnestly; they have long associated themselves with the Revival Society, and the fate of the Ming turns on their actions and decisions.

But what is wrong with two good friends taking delight in each other's company, even if all around them is misery? Why shouldn't they take whatever pleasures they can as individuals? To appeal to Peach Blossom Spring now is to reveal the ultimate emptiness of the earlier conflict between Ma and Ruan and the Revival Society. To turn now to Peach Blossom Spring suggests that the only real alternative to the ugliness all around them is total escape, an imaginary life as fishermen.

For these two to claim they are innocent individuals who may grasp at whatever simple delight might come their way is a bit disingenuous. Dreaming of Peach Blossom Spring obscures the fact that the mess is at least partly their own making. Hou Fangyu, good friend of Wu Yingji and the Revival Society, and on whose behalf Su Kunsheng is just now inciting Zuo Liangyu to move his troops, is hardly an innocent party to the chaos besetting Nanjing. After all, it will be he, as much as any Ruan Dacheng or Ma Shiying, who will have caused the fall of the dynasty. At this moment, rather than mourning the dead Emperor or the terrible trials the people are suffering, the two friends evoke those imaginary fisherman, so out of touch with history that they think the Qin still rules. Their blindness troubles us, suggesting a terrible irresponsibility.

What is taking place all around them in the prison represents the quintessence of one sort of political identity gone wrong. Suggestive of his twentieth-century avatars, a warden, who himself is neither good nor evil, but simply a minion of Ma and Ruan, obeying their orders, matches names on a list with the names on the placards each prisoner is required to wear. Something like this takes place in *Mudan ting* when the Underworld Magistrate consults official records to see where Du Liniang belongs, and the Record of Successful Candidates comes to establish Liu Mengmei's identity.

In this play, however, the relationship between bureaucracy and identity is much darker. Once he takes over de facto power, Ma Shiying can appoint himself and his co-conspirators to whichever official positions he wishes, making them literally whatever they want to be with a flourish of the imperial pen. After he creates an Emperor out of Zhu Yousong, he makes high officials of all his cronies.

And this nightmarish vision of identity, where tallies and lists determine who one is—even sometimes taking over who one is—culminates in the scene at the prison, where everything about identity is reduced to the simple act of matching up slips of paper with placards. Commenting on the scene before him, a horrified Hou Fangyu sings: "A slip of paper flies by, but no one sees it; in the dead of night they are dragged away, in bounds, to be executed. It startles my heart and shakes up my insides."[15] I have chosen to render this "no one sees it," but it could just as easily read "there is no one to see." Either way, this much is clear: except as physical items to be dealt with, the people have been elided out of this process—the pieces of paper and the matching of tally to placard are what matter.

In this bureaucratic machine, the warden's task is simply to match lists with placards; neither we nor anyone else ever sees the unfortunate Zhou Lu or Lei Yingzuo. Nor have we—or any of the characters—any idea what these men have done or who they are, only that the bureaucracy has deemed them deserving of execution. It is a scene that might have been taken from the darkest moments of our own century.

But does, as Hou Fangyu suggests hopefully, Peach Blossom Spring provide a satisfying alternative to such a dark vision of bureaucratized identity? The community in the Peach Blossom Spring has no Emperor; they are there precisely because they fled from the first Emperor, Qin Shihuang. But the escape is only the beginning; no Zhang Wei stops them from getting married, and no Zhang Wei tells them that ultimately they must rejoin the world outside. Instead, they flee and start new lives, with new families, the old and the young enjoying themselves, the men and the women engaged in the work of small scale agriculture. It is a land where Hou Fangyu would have been able to marry Li Xiangjun. Here, however, Zhang Wei stands in the lovers' way.

Nightmarishly, the society in Peach Blossom Spring mirrors both the Nanjing regime and the social milieu of which Hou Fangyu and Li Xiangjun are a part. Like Ma Shiying and Ruan Dacheng, the residents of Peach Blossom Spring have established their own community ex nihilo, with no concern that it be a part of the preexisting social and political order or possess legitimacy. Far from having their identities defined by the Emperor, they do not even know which dynasty is in power; Ruan and Ma, of course, have defined who the Emperor is, and they do not think the question of which dynasty is in power to be a matter of great importance.

In some ways, the same description—of a society with no preexisting political order—might cover *Mudan ting*'s idyll as well: the family granted recognition by the Emperor is one created by choice, whose focus is a young husband and wife who have chosen each other. And the same description might also be applied to the community of Nanjing refugees led by Zhang Wei—*except* that Zhang Wei insists otherwise, forbidding Li Xiangjun and Hou Fangyu to marry in the absence of country and monarch.

Hou Fangyu defends his desire to marry Li Xiangjun with a vision of humanity grounded in the natural: "Men and women have always created households together; that is the great principle of mankind, coming together and going apart, sorrow and happiness, to have someone to love—how can you meddle with that?" Something like this belief—that the natural needs of a person cannot be contravened—motivates Du Liniang and Liu Mengmei as well; for his efforts to oppose human nature, Du Bao is punished.

According to this vision, people are defined first and foremost not as members of a hierarchy, but as free-floating individuals, capable of choosing and forging their own social ties. But this vision of human identity—at once tempting and frightening—is not allowed to prevail in *Taohua shan*. Instead, after Zhang Wei's response, both Li Xiangjun and Hou Fangyu themselves recognize that this claim simply does not hold. He reprimands the two young lovers: "Where is the country? Where is the family? Where is the Emperor? Where are the fathers? And all you have is this root of passion in flowers and moonlight, and you can't sever it?"

For what Hou Fangyu proposes—and part of what underlies the fantasy represented by "The Record of Peach Blossom Spring"—resembles too closely the nightmare that has already seized Nanjing. In Nanjing, too, hierarchies have been disrupted, people are unencumbered by any political identity as citizen or civil servant, and finally, in Nanjing, too, no one knows who the Emperor is or even which dynasty is in power. Hou Fangyu's dream—that one can just run away from this chaos and simply be a person, following the natural desires and feelings of a person, those *qiqing* so important in *Mudan ting*—turns out ultimately not to differ so much from the sickness that grips Ma Shiying and Ruan Dacheng.

In the hands of Ma and Ruan, this vision of identity makes them think they can make of any man the Emperor. For Hongguang, like Hou Fangyu, a conviction that beneath all the trappings of status and social position lies a natural person manifests itself as a fantasy of escape. If Hou Fangyu can marry because he chooses to, because the coming together of man and woman is natural, then Hongguang too might cast aside his identity as an Emperor and join those farmers at the Peach Blossom Spring, whose only obligations are to themselves and personal happiness. Seeking refuge from Manchu troops, Hongguang delivers his version of the same dream. He tells Huang Degong: "You don't have to worry—all We want is to manage to survive. As for that imperial role, I don't want to play it anymore." According to this way of looking at things, identity is simply the continued existence of the body, with its natural urges and desires. I will be exploring what Kong Shangren proposes in the place of such a vision. Or, as someone with better sense might well have asked of Hongguang: if you run away from being the Emperor, who is doing the running?

CHAPTER 4

The Prostitute's Fan

By the middle of *Mudan ting*, the identity of Du Liniang has fragmented into four versions—corpse, sacred tablet, portrait, and ghost—each with a different and competing claim to being Du Liniang. By the end, two identities are accounted for: the girl who becomes the wife of Liu Mengmei combines characteristics of the ghost and the corpse.

As for the third possible locus of identity, its survival is not so problematic, since one supposes the sacred tablet is not an absolute loss. If the tablet serves no purpose now, it can be of use later after her eventual death. No one claims that any of her identity is currently invested there, so long as Du Liniang is shown to be living. The coexistence of the live woman and the sacred tablet is no more troubling than a coffin bought years in advance for future use.

But what happens to the portrait, painted before her death, that brought the two lovers together? We can account for its fate only until Liu Mengmei's detainment in prison, by which time it is his sole remaining possession. When the Emperor grants recognition to Du Liniang and reunites her with her family in the final act, the whereabouts of the portrait go unmentioned. What for many acts was the most important artifact in the play, in which her identity had magically been invested, simply disappears. Worse yet, no one even seems to notice it is gone—a very troubling forgetting.

One way in which *Taohua shan* responds to *Mudan ting* is by taking apart the conditions of the earlier play's idyllic conclusion—sometimes with almost punitive vigor.[1] Throughout the play, Li Xiangjun echoes Du Liniang, sometimes literally. Twice, she sings Du Liniang's arias from *Mudan ting*: the first time with her singing master Su Kunsheng, and the second in her audition before Hongguang. The first time, she is singing a newly learned text and responding to the instructions of her teacher as she runs through a lesson; there is no necessary tie between her and the character whose words she sings.

The second time, she sings Du Liniang's part only after she has refused to play all other roles and at a moment when Du Liniang's words apply equally to her own situation. As when the young actress Shang Xiaoling died with Du Liniang's words on her lips, it is hard to tell in the singing of this second aria who exactly is doing the singing—Li Xiangjun or Du Liniang; their two identities are confusingly intertwined. Nonetheless, even though Li Xiangjun echoes Du Liniang, the young courtesan is not allowed to marry her lover.

Du Liniang's portrait vanishes without anyone taking notice, while *Taohua shan* climaxes with the fan's destruction—or to be more accurate, when Zhang Wei talks about ripping up the fan, he makes sure that it loses whatever importance it once had. It was once so fetishized that several characters have asserted that they value the fan more highly than their own lives. Zhang Wei ends the scene in which Li Xiangjun and Hou Fangyu go their separate ways forever by saying: "See how those two part, without letting drop a last glance. It's all because I ripped up this peach blossom fan into shred after shred; it will never again allow those crazy lovebugs to entangle themselves up myriad times with their own spun silk."[2] The fan's destruction parts the young lovers forever.

Zhang Wei's final lines not only account for the fan's end, but they also make clear at least one reason that destruction must take place. *Mudan ting*'s arithmetic defies easy understanding, but *Taohua shan*'s is aggressively straightforward. The play, Zhang Wei explains, will abide by a strict conservation of fiber. Once the fan is destroyed, then there will be no silk left for the lovebugs to entangle themselves up. Karma, we are told in Chinese, unspools like silk, tangling and knotting. To make sure there is no fiber left, the fan must be taken apart.

Without asking her, Yang Wencong takes Li Xiangjun's fan and transforms the bloodstains into peach blossoms, painting in stems and leaves. Upon waking, Li Xiangjun thanks him: "These peach blossoms have unlucky fates, floating here at the bottom of my fan. Thank you, Master Yang, for painting my portrait."[3] If, as she says, the blood-spattered fan is Li Xiangjun's portrait, the purposefulness of the fan's destruction forces us to return to the earlier play and ask the question: where does the portrait in *Mudan ting* go? And where does the part of Du Liniang's identity that had its locus in the portrait go?

The disappearance of the portrait implies an erasure of responsibility, as if the forbidden passion disappears alongside the portrait. When it disappears, perhaps so too does Du Liniang's accountability for those actions associated with it. Of course, if it had survived, that figure for illicit desire would occupy an awkward position in her new identity as respectable young matron—perhaps even rendering that new life an impossibility. This is precisely *Taohua shan*'s point.

There are other ways to phrase this question. After her disinterment, Du Liniang claims to have been reborn a virgin, allowing her an opportunity that is for all other people an impossibility—the chance both to have fornicated with Liu Mengmei and then to marry him later on with propriety. We could put the equation this way: she dies of grief, earning in the eyes of the world and of the underworld administration the reputation for giving her everything to a single passion; and yet she then gets to go on to live, reaping all the pleasures and honors of our own world. In other words, by living she earns credit for an action she doesn't exactly see through to its end. Something about the mathematics is not quite right: if there is a choice to be made—life as opposed to death, or license as opposed to propriety—can one avoid the inconveniences of both alternatives and enjoy the comforts of both?

The way these problems simply cannot be worked out seems to have troubled Kong Shangren as well, since *Taohua shan* restages each of these equations, making a point of having each of them come out evenly. In other words, Li Xiangjun, the heroine whom it is sometimes difficult to distinguish from Du Liniang, undergoes versions of Du Liniang's experiences, but with some crucial differences.

One might suppose that *Taohua shan*'s critique of the earlier play is simply leveled at the supernatural. Instead, *Taohua shan*'s critique has only a little to do with the empiricism one might expect of a historical play's treatment of a fairy tale predecessor. *Taohua shan* reacts to *Mudan ting* by taking apart the conditions of Confucian idyll—everything upon which the restoration of Du Bao's family rests—and this particular critique extends to practically every aspect of the earlier play, many having nothing at all to do with the supernatural.

Near the end, after searching in vain for each other for most of the play, Hou Fangyu and Li Xiangjun actually share the stage without being aware of the other's presence. The lovers have separately fled Nanjing, seeking refuge in the hills. The date marks three years since their first meeting at the hamper party and in some ways consciously restages that first encounter. The three-year anniversary is an important one; the same period of time elapses between reunions in *Mudan ting* as well—between Du Liniang's dream of Liu Mengmei and then her appearance to him in the yamen. In their first meeting, the courtesans cavorted in a sort of tree house, sharing delicacies in hampers, pretending to be ignorant of the potential customers watching below. In fact, attracting customers is the entire motive of the hamper party. It is a staged moment of spontaneity, set up for voyeurism.

What was assumed ignorance in Nanjing is genuine ignorance now. This time Li Xiangjun is truly ignorant of Hou Fangyu's presence. Just as on the first occasion, there is another mother figure at hand, Bian Yujing, also an entertainer, but one who has turned her back on the old way of life and become a Daoist priestess. In Nanjing, the mother welcomed Hou Fangyu's attentions, looking forward to the possibility of profit. This time, Bian Yujing sends away the men looking for a place to stay the night. She tells them: "This is just like a cloister for virgins." And Li Xiangjun concurs: "That's so; this is not like those days in the brothels."[4]

Li Xiangjun has a choice to make. She can do as Bian Yujing does—repudiate her former lifestyle and become a nun—or she can continue as an entertainer. But she cannot have it both ways, turning her back on her old lifestyle *and* still ending up Hou Fangyu's honored wife. She cannot, as Du Liniang does, reap both the benefits of the life of license and of Confucian restraint. Asking about the fate of Du Liniang's missing portrait then is another way of asking what happens to Du Liniang's virginity. Her portrait disappears without a trace; her virginity appears again with no explanation. How can such things happen?

Li Xiangjun's profession makes tallies of debits and credits explicit. The fan is the obvious center for one arithmetic: different layers keep being added to it, first of ink (Hou Fangyu's contribution), then of blood (Li Xiangjun's), and finally of plant pigment (out of which Yang Wencong paints the stems and leaves of the peach blossoms); and as they accumulate, the value of the fan correspondingly increases.

It starts off ordinary and blank. During the wedding festivities, a guest offers to fetch pen and paper for poetry; but Hou Fangyu responds that paper won't be necessary: "I won't be using poetry stationery, since I've got a fan on me. I'll inscribe it for Xiangjun, and it will serve as a pledge object forever."[5] It certainly sounds as if Hou Fangyu simply improvises a present for Li Xiangjun out of what he has on his person; the fan was not predestined for such a purpose, and the only value it possesses is sentimental.

But the bloodstains turned to peach blossoms are another matter altogether. They give the fan the appearance of value to many more beholders: Yang Wencong, Su Kunsheng, Li Zhenli, Hou Fangyu. For these onlookers, the fan takes on value at Li Xiangjun's expense. The bloodstains gesture towards a displaced defloration, and they also change the value of the fan, because they diminish the value of the prostitute whose blood it is. An expensive prostitute, worth several hundred taels of silver, destroys her face in a show of chastity, so as to withhold the very services for which she will be paid. To Li Zhenli, the fan may not be worth three hundred taels of silver, but that is certainly what its creation cost her: the sum of money the minister was willing to pay for Li Xiangjun was lost when she bled onto the fan instead of going. Such is the context—ineluctably, given Li Xiangjun and Li Zhenli's profession—when we are told, as we are repeatedly, that the fan is priceless.[6]

This kind of value is inextricably tied to human suffering. The more suffering is attached to an object, the more valuable it is. The model for this arithmetic is He's jade disk, later the focus of the struggle between the kingdoms of Qin and Zhao. After finding a stone that he was convinced had a precious jade embedded in it, Bian He presented it to the king, who was told by an expert that it was just a stone. Bian He was punished by having one of his feet chopped off. After the king died, Bian He presented it to his successor, who was told by another expert that it was just a stone. Bian He's remaining foot was chopped off. Finally, after the second king had died, Bian He presented the stone once again; and with no feet left, this time he was risking his neck. The stone turned out to be jade, and Bian He was vindicated. Generations later, the state of Qin offered Zhao a staggering fifteen cities for the single jade disk. The story of He's jade disk sets up conflicting equations of value.

After the girl entrusts Su Kunsheng to deliver the fan to Hou Fangyu, Su

Kunsheng is pushed into the river and comes close to drowning. The image on the fan survives only because the fan is in a bundle on Su's head and because Su himself is saved in the nick of time by Li Zhenli, who just happens to be in a houseboat on the river. In Hou Fangyu's hands, the fan makes it through enemy territory, a jaunt in prison, and a trek to the mountains. But if indeed the play is deeply concerned with all sorts of economies and making them come out right, how is it that the fan—made priceless by Li Xiangjun's sufferings and further made incrementally more valuable by each of its subsequent narrow escapes from destruction—survives only to fall into Zhang Wei's hands, where it is transformed into an utterly devalued object?

In this peculiar work of art—a mix of artifice and the natural substances of blood and plant sap—Li Xiangjun sees a portrait that says something fundamental about who she is. To Li Xiangjun, the peculiar picture on the fan makes an argument about personal identity: "These peach blossoms have unlucky fates, floating here at the bottom of my fan. Thank you, Master Yang, for painting my portrait."

According to poetic trope, as a young beauty she corresponds to the flowers, whose blooming season is all too short and will soon fade. And the words Li Xiangjun has chosen to describe the peach blossoms reinforce this connection; these red flowers have "unlucky fates" (*boming*), just as according to the cliché a rosy-faced beauty does (*hongyan boming*). The rosy faces might belong either to her or to the red flowers. But these are connections Li Xiangjun might draw between herself and any red flowers—while what makes these noteworthy is precisely that they are unique, having been painted in her own blood.

Du Liniang's *xiezhen* is different in kind from Li Xiangjun's *xiezhao*—not just in appearance, but in the very way it seeks to represent its subject. Du Liniang's is a supremely successful metaphor, her identity invested, translated even, into an altogether different substance—paint and ink standing in for flesh and blood. In contrast, Li Xiangjun's portrait is painted of her own blood, synecdochical in the most literal of ways.[8]

While Du Liniang's possesses a high degree of verisimilitude, Li Xiangjun's portrait does not look like peach blossoms, except in a highly metaphorical sense; the object and the image are manifestly different: no picture of peach blossoms looks like a girl. And indeed the fan perpetually runs the danger of being seen simply as a decorative picture of peach blossoms. While both Liu Mengmei and the prison guard initially make the mistake of regarding Du Liniang's portrait as one of Chang E or Guanyin, Hou Fangyu by contrast mistakes the blood-spattered fan as simply a painted fan. Without explanation, it fades into decorative insignificance.

After Du Liniang paints herself, there are two Du Liniangs—one painted, one the painter. But if the painting has assumed so much of the painter's identity, and if the painter remains the same after the painting's completion, then aren't we left with more than what we began with, two where we started with one? Moreover, there seems to be nothing to stop Du Liniang from continuing this process forever, repeating Act 14 over and over again and producing ever more self-portraits, each of which possesses something essential about the painter. And how would we treat copies of each of those paintings? Produced of the same substance as the original painting, could a ghost emerge out of any of those (or each of those)? The conclusion of the play assures us of the singularity of Du Liniang's identity. But without any assurance that identity is conserved—and so long as producing more paintings appears so easy—how can we pin down a single Du Liniang?

A portrait painted from its subject's blood answers these objections. The fan resists copying and proliferation, since Li Xiangjun could hardly make many copies of such a portrait. This portrait bears an altogether different relationship with its creator, while maintaining a similar claim of privileged relation with her. In that sense, the self-portrait on the fan resembles not so much Du Liniang's self-portrait as Michel de Montaigne's. In one famous passage, Montaigne claims about his self-descriptive writings, that they were "consubstantiel à son auteur"—meaning not that Montaigne regarded himself as made out of ink and paper, but rather that no easy distinction presents itself to tell the author from his writings. The subject cannot maintain distance from the representation, since by the very act of describing oneself, the self being described is changed.

Montaigne describes his literary self-portrait as "consubstantiel" in a passage about what it means to write about the self (incidentally, with characteristic playfulness, the essay is called "Du Démentir" or "On Giving the Lie"). He explains his relation to his writing: "Je n'ai pas plus fait mon livre que mon livre m'a fait, livre consubstantiel à son auteur, d'une occupation propre, membre de ma vie; non d'une occupation et fin tierce et étrangère comme tous autres livres."[9] Just as he has made his book, the book has in turn also made him the person he has become. Similarly, Li Xiangjun makes the bloodstains on the fan; but they also change her, literally by draining her blood and scarring her face, but also making her a new person, since they commemorate and prove her transformation into a chaste woman, willing to sacrifice her life for her honor.

Montaigne was writing in a great age of self-portraiture, and he introduces this section by equating his project with a portrait: "Me peignant pour autrui, je me suis peint en moi de couleurs plus nettes que n'étaient les miennes premières."[10] Like Montaigne's self-portrait, the painting of the peach blossoms takes what had been internal and private and renders it external and shared. By becoming visible, those traits of Montaigne and that blood of Li Xiangjun become something wholly different from what they were before. The fan is transformed into a material token of what was formerly unverifiable—her desire to keep herself chaste for Hou Fangyu. For both Montaigne and Li Xiangjun, self-representation changes the subject; their self-portraits are no mere copies of a preexisting artist.

Montaigne's claims for his writings—that he has created them, but that they too have created him—suggest an arithmetic in which both the self and the self-representation figure: the self-depiction and the person add up to a single whole. Once the self-portrait has come into being, the author has no particular claim to anteriority. The *Essais* and their author have the same claim to being the *real* Michel de Montaigne.

This very specific sort of arithmetic—that the representation and the maker of the representation should together form a whole—directly addresses the problems raised by Du Liniang's portrait in *Mudan ting*. Specifically, this version of the portrait counters that peculiar sense of proliferation discussed in the first chapter, where what seemed to be one Du Liniang suddenly turns into three—reflection, painting, and painter—with no promise that this proliferation could not continue indefinitely. The making of the peach blossom fan (and of Montaigne's *Essais*) argue for another model of self-representation, which foils infinite replication. The way Du Liniang paints her self-portrait augurs—even predetermines—the troubles that plague the end of the play; if it is so easy for her identity to proliferate near the beginning, it is no wonder that the climax concerns a test of identity and an effort to pin down a single Du Liniang.

In Li Xiangjun's case, the arithmetic is made explicit because she is a prostitute. Converting Li Xiangjun's person into hard currency is central to the play, and different characters repeatedly make those calculations for us. Indeed such calculations are central to the play. When Li Xiangjun mutilates herself in the face and takes herself out of the market, Li Zhenli's reaction reflects not only a more maternal concern, but also her awareness as a procuress of the economics of this act: "Oh dear! Wake up, child. You've taken your flower-like face and smashed it all up."[11] One suspects that in a similar situation, Du Liniang's mother would have been more concerned about her daughter's health than her beauty.

Since the blood splattered from these wounds becomes the peach blossoms on the fan, the creation of this consubstantial painting marks externally her transformation from a prostitute on the market to a woman unavailable and thus necessarily chaste. Of course, there are plenty of prostitutes less palatable than Li Xiangjun, even with the scabs on her face; but once so marked, Li Xiangjun, celebrated for her beauty, is no longer the famed courtesan she was before. And when we are told later that the fan is "beyond price," we cannot fail to associate its value with what has been taken—if only temporarily—from Li Xiangjun's value. An arithmetic like Montaigne's is at work here. The girl with the unbloodied face is precisely equal to the sum of the fan with its bloodstains and the girl with her marred face. Nothing has been added.

Both portraits share a certain anxiety about their connection to their subjects. Li Xiangjun's demands commentary, lest it be mistaken for just any painted fan. Du Liniang's threatens to be misread as a portrait of Chang E or Guanyin. No matter how much faith we have in a given representation's possibility for verisimilitude, the link between subject and portrait can never be absolute. The highest quality photograph in the world might have been doctored—and thus represent no specific individual—or might become stranded from its subject. Are we simply not seeing how that portrait correlates to that woman? Just as we cannot prove a certain tie between a specific person and a specific representation, we cannot prove that any two are not related.

During the Han, the Emperor chose the woman he thought to be ugliest of his concubines to present to a barbarian chieftain as a goodwill offering. In fact, Wang Zhaojun was the most beautiful of the Emperor's wives, but the only one who failed to bribe the portraitist. Nevertheless, it is the nature of portraiture that we cannot be absolutely certain if the portraitist painted her as he did out of vengeance, or ineptitude, or even whether he simply painted her as he saw her.

The faith our age has in photographs, that they unquestionably bind a person to a representation, does not stand up to much scrutiny. For when it comes down to it, there is no particular reason to trust photographers to label their portraits accurately or for subjects to identify themselves correctly. Even that claim of the photograph, that if nothing else it faithfully depicts something real, is a fiction. The possibility of computer doctoring (or even simple airbrushing) makes photographic portraits no more certain than any to be rooted in a real person and not an imaginary one.

And what of portraits of someone who has since died or aged or changed in any way? How then to prove the link between the portrait and its subject? (This problem presents itself to me whenever I have to insist that the picture on my driver's license—with its different haircut and slightly dazed look—is indeed of myself.) Montaigne's and Li Xiangjun's extravagant claims of consubstantiality are cries into the wind. Portraits always contend with the possibility of being separated from their subjects. The fear extends to literary self-portrait, too. Binding a specific author to a specific text is no easy task. For imitators, or forgers, are clever; they copy precisely what makes a given author's voice distinctive.

If all portraits at least implicitly acknowledge the possibility that they cannot be bound irrevocably to a single subject, they must also deal with a related, even broader anxiety. Portraiture implicitly articulates an argument about individual difference—that differences between individuals are meaningful and distinctive. But what if it turns out that people are simply not sufficiently different from one other to sustain a different portrait for each person?

Even if one knows for sure whether or not the subject of a painting has an identical twin, one can certainly never assume that the subject does not have a double, whether perfect or only approximate enough to deceive some people. These concerns are particularly evident in drama, where the possibility of having a double does not seem quite as farfetched as it would in life. Doubles are a staple of multiple dramatic traditions (in our own, *Twelfth Night* and *Comedy of Errors* are probably two of the most canonical examples). The plot of Ruan Dacheng's *Yanzi jian*—mentioned repeatedly in *Taohua shan* as the play that Hongguang takes such care to cast—hinges upon just such a pair of doubles. The two heroines (both of whom end up marrying the hero) just happen to look almost exactly like each other; the play starts when a portrait of one is confused for the other.[12]

Doubles complicate the question of individual distinctiveness, but they are not necessary preconditions to doubting the ability of any portrait to represent an individual adequately. We might also blame the medium we use to try to capture distinctiveness. Perhaps there are no true doubles, but only functional ones—made to seem identical because of the inadequacy of representations. The fear extends much further than he gives it credit for, but the art historian Richard Brilliant explores one of its dimensions, whether beyond markers of class and society, portraits can ever express differences between people.[13] Can the portrait that is taken to be Chang E's, Guanyin's, and finally Du Liniang's be said to show anything other than an attractive female clad in diaphanous robes?

Certainly, one might reasonably wonder whether Chinese portraiture of the Ming dynasty possessed the wherewithal—or even the real desire—to capture subtle facial differences that set individuals apart, beyond superficial ones such as those of clothing and setting.[14] But there is no particular reason to target the flaws and limitations of late imperial portraiture. Perhaps all portraiture is inadequate to the task of representing individuals; and this suspicion cannot be purged from any portrait that purports to be that of an individual.

It could be the case that someone like Du Liniang is touched less by the fear that a person's appearance may not differentiate her from all others. Her singularity at least partially rests on her being the only daughter of Du Bao and Lady Zhen, and her identity is later granted by the Emperor and not on the basis of her appearance. In contrast—quite apart from issues of portraiture, as will be discussed at greater length later—as a woman with no husband and no father, there may in a Confucian polity be no way at all to pin down Li Xiangjun as an individual, distinct from all others. Du Liniang invests tremendously high hopes in her portrait, that something of and unique to herself might survive after her death; but on Li Xiangjun's portrait, the peach blossom fan, ride hopes just as great—and perhaps just as fantastic—that a prostitute might become not only a chaste woman, but an individual, different and unmistakable from all others.

Portraits are reasonably good at allowing us to match one face with another. All those I have seen, for example, of the Kangxi Emperor are recognizably related, showing a slender man with a narrow face. Nonetheless, even when one has gathered together a number of representations of a single individual, who is to say that someone else's has not somehow slipped in? An impostor might well choose to imitate a portrait, parroting precisely those circumstantial details with which one usually matches a subject up to his portrait. Such an imitation leaves anyone seeking to verify a person's identity in a particularly vulnerable position. Facing a problem like this might make some adopt an approach like David Hume's and make the problem one of authority: all we need do to resolve the resulting problem would be to appeal to those in a position to know—to go, for example, to somebody who knew the individual personally. But such a strategy has its obvious failing: even some close Romanov relatives and family intimates were taken in by Anna

Anderson, who claimed to be the Grand Duchess Anastasia, basing their judgment on wishful thinking and, tellingly enough, on her superficial resemblance to *photographs* of the dead girl.

What portraits can never do very successfully is link that face with a specific identity—a single name, a single position in a family and in society. Among all those portraits of the Kangxi Emperor might be one in which a double posed, and I would never be the wiser. A person might look a great deal like someone in a portrait; but we are still far from assured that any given document that ties that face to a identity—a driver's license, say, or a passport—is authentic. And we have no indication at all that such an individual is the only person to possess a rough facsimile of that face. We know this failure to be the case from *Mudan ting*: matching the face of the ghost with that of the portrait takes but a moment; proving that both of those faces are those of Du Liniang takes the entire rest of the play.

Far more than most subjects of self-portraits, Li Xiangjun counts on hers to make known her own uniqueness. The fan's creation allows this young prostitute to make extraordinary claims: that she is not fungible, that she cannot be readily substituted, that she is unique. Therein the paradox, for Li Xiangjun has chosen a peculiar medium to make known her own singularity: they are just bloodstains—the blood of any other person would look precisely the same. The ties between subject and portrait are so strained and remote as to be largely an act of the imagination.

There is one portrait we know irrefutably to be tied to a specific subject. For what is magical about Du Liniang's portrait lies in its very exemption from these fears assumed by other portraits: while claiming individuality, it manages to link itself irrefutably with its subject. Even if the process of its creation does not guarantee us its singularity, what happens afterwards in the play seems to. Alone among people, she is secondary to her own picture—which is yet another reason, perhaps, that it cannot survive her reintegration into normal human society.

On the other hand, the greater problem—tying this particular face to a single identity—remains unresolved for many acts. And even this magical painting seems more hindrance than help to that particular project. For though the portrait does manage to tie itself to a specific face quite admirably, it does so only because that face is in fact *not* singular: the ghost looks like the painting, and the resurrected girl looks like the ghost.

By contrast, Li Xiangjun's fan is decidedly mundane, always in peril of separating from its subject and dissolving not into a portrait of a goddess, but a decorative object. The girl bleeds to make herself a person and not a commodity, but it is unclear whether she succeeds. The act of changing the bloodstains to peach blossoms has the effect of distancing Li Xiangjun from the fan, even of disguising her presence on the fan. Without intervening stems and leaves, the red stains would undoubtedly more readily be recognized for the bloodstains they are. Yet the transformation of her most precious possession takes place without her permission: Yang Wencong modifies the fan while Li Xiangjun is still asleep, without waking her, even though he knows full well the fan's significance for her.

Even though she calls it a portrait, metaphorically tying her own fragile existence to that of the blossoms, that interpretation does not seem to have occurred to Yang Wencong, even as he was painting around her bloodstains. The fan embodies everything important about her life: her love of Hou Fangyu and her intention to retain her chastity, even if it means sacrificing her life. And yet when Yang Wencong adds to it, he seems to have nothing in mind beyond the merely decorative. Instead, his impulse derives from an aestheticism gone out of control, to the point where it is contrary to morality. To him, the blotches are noteworthy not as human blood, but as aesthetic object. He examines the fan and muses: "These traces of blood are extraordinarily vivid red. I'll have to add some stems and leaves and dress them up a bit for her."[15]

When he encounters the fan for the first time, Hou Fangyu is not that much better at figuring out its significance. Through some instinctive sympathy, Liu Mengmei gathers from the portrait of his love that most salient feature of hers—her passion. But Hou Fangyu fails to understand the fan until its whole history is told to him explicitly, even though he is given enough of the story to piece its history together.

Li Zhenli explains what has happened since his departure from Nanjing: "Xiangjun would not remarry, and she was so afraid that she beat her head against the floor." Hou Fangyu replies: "My Xiangjun! Did she die from that?"[16] Li Zhenli answers that Xiangjun did not die, but was so bloodied that she herself had to go in Xiangjun's place. Having been told that rather than betray him, Xiangjun bloodied and mutilated herself, Hou Fangyu then asks no more about her, but instead turns his attention to Li Zhenli and what happened to her next. His comments about his former lover come off as mere politeness, and in turning immediately to asking about Li Zhenli, he implies that the two women have commensurate claims on him, members of an old circle of friends.

Then Su Kunsheng presents the fan to him, and Hou Fangyu has no idea what it is, other than the fan he had given her in bygone days. One supposes that a more sympathetic lover, having heard Li Zhenli's narrative of Li Xiangjun's experiences, might guess the true nature of the red splotches. After all, Su Kunsheng gives Hou Fangyu plenty of hints to figure things out. He holds out the fan and sings: "Look at the peach blossoms, all red and misty, how sincere the emotion! A thousand, ten thousand locutions would hardly exhaust it."[17] Hou Fangyu already knows that Li Xiangjun beat her head against the floor, bled profusely, and then passed out. Moreover, Su Kunsheng has just told him that he is bearing a message for Hou Fangyu from Li Xiangjun. This subsequent aria is filled with hints over the fan's true nature. *Yun* has two meanings, both mistiness and the dead faint Li Xiangjun falls into. "A thousand, ten thousand locutions" refers to the emotion embodied by the peach blossoms of blood—the graphic letter Hou Fangyu has been promised.

And yet given all this information, Hou Fangyu still fails to see the fan for the portrait it is. Indeed, the portraitist Li Xiangjun has ample reason to fear that her own identity might become untethered from the picture on the fan. If one measures sincerity by the directness of the connection between a person and a expression, there could hardly be a more sincere painting than this one, whose pigment is literally the artist's lifeblood. In classical Chinese, one would say that such a painting embodies her sincerity (*shen qi cheng*). But this sincere expression does not immediately find a receptive audience. Su Kunsheng finally has to resort to telling Hou Fangyu what the fan is in the most explicit terms possible. Hou Fangyu reacts, not with the sorrow one might expect of him, but with a chilling delight, in a passage I will discuss at greater length later in this chapter: "So it turns out that they are drops of blood! And Yang Wencong embellished them—why that's marvelous. This peach blossom fan is now my treasure."[18] If anything, *youqu*, which I have translated as "marvelous," has even more lighthearted connotations: "entertaining" or "amusing" might also do. One cannot tell from the context whether *youqu* refers only to Yang Wencong's contributions; at any rate, the comment does betray a certain cold-bloodedness. His amusement certainly seems incommensurate to the occasion.

Li Xiangjun sends the fan to her lover as a message, hoping that through it he will understand her. But what is the message, and who is this person she means him to understand? Surely Li Xiangjun, who has embarked on this path precisely to resist being treated as a commodity worth exactly three hundred taels of silver, who ruins her face precisely so that she can no longer be so evaluated, would not be pleased to find out that her fan has become Hou Fangyu's "treasure." If Li Xiangjun meant the fan as a way of expressing her identity, of speaking for her in her absence, of standing in for her individuality and irreplaceability, his initial reaction suggests that it has sorely fallen short of that goal.

Portraits can gesture towards two different kinds of identity: who one is, a specific identity which can be differentiated from that of all other people, and what one is, one's personality traits and character. If Du Liniang's identity is different in kind from the entertainer Li Xiangjun's, perhaps it is the case that they cannot be painted the same way.

Du Liniang's mother, is referred to simply as *Zhen Shi*, which I have been translating as "Lady Zhen." *Zhen Shi* refers simply to her father's surname, a way of naming which allows us no way to differentiate her from her sisters and her cousins. This appellation is the usual and official way for referring to women of good family; for example, local gazetteers in recounting virtuous deeds ascribe them to *Chen Shi, Zhang Shi, Li Shi*—there is no cause to use personal names in describing these women. In official registers later in life, Du Liniang, wife of Liu Mengmei, the top examination candidate and high official, will simply be *Du Shi*. Their surnames indicate a position within the polity, as daughters within a specific clan.

Li Zhenli's name serves quite a different function. As a courtesan, she will probably never be referred to as *Li Shi*, because Li is not the important component of her name; it might not even refer to her father. There is nothing about the surname that positions her within a patriline, as is indicated by the fact that her daughter, too, is named Li. Surnames are grounded in knowledge of paternity. They allow people to be classified according to specific identity, who they are relative to other people; in the world of the brothel, not organized by patrilines, personal names are the ones that have importance. Writing on late nineteenth-century prostitutes in Shanghai, Gail Hershatter argues that courtesans named themselves as part of general self-presentation.[19] Such names, suggesting personal qualities, lending cachet, more closely resemble modern-day brand names than surnames or even the personal names given by parents.

In *Taohua shan*, the distinction between these two kinds of identity is embodied in the contrast between two characters—the Hongguang Emperor of the Nanjing regime and Li Xiangjun. Here, with imperial identity on the line, the distinction between these two sorts of identity is perhaps the clearest: the prostitute and the Emperor represent two poles in the question of what makes a person who he or she is.

The Emperor is leader of an empire but also head of a family: for

Hongguang to be Hongguang, he must be a specific individual—of the imperial clan Zhu, the son of the Prince of Fu, and the grandson of the Wanli Emperor. It is uncertainty about this kind of identity that throws Nanjing into turmoil when the young man claiming to be the Crown Prince shows up—no accounts I have run into make any mention of the young man's personality or his character traits. Although it is presumed that he would make a better Emperor than the incompetent Hongguang, that matter is beside the point. Ultimately, the whole dispute is nothing that an appropriately supervised DNA test would not have cleared up.

In contrast, a DNA test would tell us nothing important about Li Xiangjun. No one cares who her parents are (Li Zhenli, of course, is an adoptive mother). What makes her important in her world and what everyone talks about when they mention her are precisely the sorts of things no one ever mentions about the young claimant to the throne: her personal characteristics, her appearance, her accomplishments.

Imagine two people: one who closely resembles Hongguang and another who closely resembles Li Xiangjun. Each seeks to pose as his or her double. To what extent can they succeed? What would happen if the two were found out? If he is found out, the one who closely resembles Hongguang will naturally be decried as an impostor and will probably be executed for his attempt to usurp the throne. Proximate equivalence might prove of use in certain circumstances—as with a body double in the heat of battle—but as viewers of Kurasawa's *Kagemusha* know, that double is by his nature eminently disposable. He is meant as a backup for an irreplaceable original; his whole purpose is to be used and then dispensed with. For no one can ever truly substitute for the liege, however like him in the externals of appearance—and even the internal qualities of attainments and temperament—he might be.

In fact, the controversy surrounding the young claimant suggests precisely the fears that such an impostor might instill. For those who were convinced that the claimant was an impostor claiming to be the Crown Prince, the young man suggested the frightening possibility that just anyone—armed with a few facts and the ability to persuade enough people—could slip in and usurp the position of Emperor.

Hongguang's hypothetical double who challenges him for his identity does exist in the play then, only he doesn't need at all to look like Hongguang, since that isn't what is important about Hongguang. Instead, all his double needs is a similar claim to the throne. What makes Hongguang Hongguang, the core of this version of identity, reveals itself in what sort of challenge can be posed to his identity. Such a challenge can take one of two forms. First (and this is the possibility *Taohua shan* does not take up) the man we have known as Hongguang himself might be an impostor. One of the unofficial histories examined in the next chapter proposes this possibility, arguing that a manservant of the Prince of Fu ran off with the official seals and presented himself to the relevant authorities as the prince himself. Or second—and this is the attack on his authenticity *Taohua shan* takes up—someone else can claim a closer degree of consanguinity to the Chongzhen Emperor, for it is upon his degree of relatedness to the deceased man that his own claim to the throne and his very identity rest.

And what about Li Xiangjun's double, our imaginary girl just as well-spoken, talented, and pretty as our heroine? Once again the play suggests an answer. When it comes to somebody like Li Xiangjun, a proximate equivalent will do quite nicely. In fact, even highly imperfect substitutions can take place, as happens when Li Zhenli takes her daughter's place after she mutilates herself. Afterwards, when the Emperor summons all the entertainers to court, Li Zhenli's absence forces Xiangjun to take her mother's place. Her hard-fought identity, as chaste woman who might be thought of as Hou Fangyu's wife, is given up with nary a protest, and she reverts to being simply an entertainer, whose name is hardly important. Of course, observers know something is up (for one thing, Li Zhenli could hardly be mistaken for the girl of sixteen who appears at court), but the messenger in charge cannot be bothered to figure out any of their specific identities.

Armed with a billet, a *piao*, that lists the names of performers who must report to the Emperor, he does not bother checking the identity of the prostitutes he has come to summon, taking each at her word, and checking off the appropriate name. All of the other entertainers obviously know that the person who shows up here is Li Xiangjun, so naturally there is a little confusion about who she really is; she says she is Li Zhenli, but her colleagues suggest otherwise. The messenger, though, does not care; none of these concerns are part of his job: "Well, mother and daughter are always of a type anyway; so long as I don't run short of the quota, I'll be fine."[20] Partisans are willing to tear the empire apart over the exact identity of the stranger who claims to be the Crown Prince; no one bothers if one prostitute takes the place of another.

If Li Zhenli successfully passes as Li Xiangjun, and then Li Xiangjun successfully passes as Li Zhenli, it hardly makes sense to ask about a more precise double. Defined by her personal qualities, someone who sings just as well, shows the same allegiance to the Revival Society, and is just as pretty might as well be the same person.

What makes Du Liniang herself? Surely Du Bao's anxieties of the last act revolve around a notion of identity not dissimilar to that which defines Hongguang: Du Bao worries that an impostor—but one who perfectly resembles his daughter—has taken her place. Without any positive proof that this creature is his daughter, he will not accept her. Like the Emperor, a substitute identical in all respects (both internal and external) simply will not do.

But even if the Emperor grants her this sort of identity—making her the daughter of Du Bao all over again—this version of identity isn't the reason she has found her way back from the dead to the imperial court. The young matron at the end of the play owes her identity to the self-portrait. And the portrait succeeds in bringing her back to life only because it establishes the other kind of identity, showing to Liu Mengmei her beauty and her passionate nature. He doesn't fall in love with the girl in the portrait because it depicts Du Liniang, daughter of the high official Du Bao (anyway that knowledge only comes much later in their relationship), but because of what the portrait reveals her to be, beautiful and passionate.

If Li Xiangjun wants Hou Fangyu to know how sad she is and how much she misses him, why doesn't she just paint a conventional portrait of herself, looking melancholy? Sending a portrait is a well-established way of jogging a forgetful lover's memory, both in life and in plays. She might even show herself clutching his fan, the symbol of their love. After all, such a strategy works for Du Liniang. Li Xiangjun decides to send him such an unconventional portrait precisely because the conventional one would emphasize the assumptions about her identity she hopes the fan will counter.

Prostitution and portraiture share a complicated history. Marc Shell has suggested one possible origin of the modern portrait: patrons of brothels would begin their visit by examining different portraits of prostitutes, choosing one based on her portrait, and then conclude it by going off with the appropriate prostitute.[21] Japanese *ukiyo-e* sometimes served a similar function. Gail Hershatter mentions the late imperial habit of prostitutes' painting portraits of themselves, either to decorate their own quarters with or to give to patrons.[22] In the late nineteenth century, prostitutes quickly adopted photography, with its possibilities of mass reproduction, having portraits of themselves made in a variety of different costumes, to be sold both at photography studios and at the brothels. Such photographs were circulated widely.

The only kind of identity that portraits can ever truly indicate is what most prostitutes rely upon. Even if portraits do a very unreliable job of tying a person to a specific bureaucratic identity, they can still indicate physical characteristics. And of course this is precisely the sort of identity at the center of prostitution as a profession. Any individual prostitute is chosen on the basis of physical appearance, especially one whose portrait is picked out of a lineup. One chooses a prostitute, in part, based on those qualities a painting is best at expressing, what a person's face looks like, the shape of a person's body. What portraits cannot do—associate a specific face with a specific identity—is not important for prostitutes anyway. In a prose piece on the trade in "Skinny Horses" in Yangzhou, Zhang Dai writes about the effect of watching prostitute after prostitute paraded in front of one's eyes:

> After seeing fifty or sixty girls, all with their fair faces and red shirts, endless variations on the same rule, it's like someone learning calligraphy. If you write a single character a hundred times or a thousand times, you won't even be able to recognize that character. The mind and the heart debate, neither holding the reins, and in the end there is choice but to compromise, and pick a single person.[23]

One can only pity Li Xiangjun's desire to establish singularity, while condemned to a profession where she might seem, no matter how beautiful, as only an "endless variation on the same rule."

In short, Li Xiangjun, who desperately wants to be and may even think of herself as Hou Fangyu's wife, has very good reasons for not sending him a picture of her face. If the Hongguang Emperor had some sort of accident and scarred his face, none of his courtiers would care. If Lady Zhen's experiences with the bandits had somehow caused her face to be scarred, Du Bao would have been reunited with her in the final act with no less joy and gratitude. In contrast, Li Xiangjun's scarring of her face is a matter of serious import to how those nearest to her will see her.

Rather than send him a representation of her beauty, she sends him something that indicates that she does *not* look as he remembers her. She assumes—or rather hopes—that a Li Xiangjun with a scarred face will paradoxically mean more to him than Li Xiangjun the storied beauty, since her chastity and constancy will be marked on her face. In other words, she hopes that it is her specific identity that matters to him—that a double, no matter how similar, cannot substitute for her. The bloodied fan is her effort to stake uniqueness, her argument that no one else can substitute for her. Nonetheless, her efforts to prove her uniqueness might be doomed from the start.

Let me pause for a moment to compare Li Xiangjun's portrait, the fan, with a hypothetical portrait—that of Hongguang, whose reign spanned so brief and turbulent a time that perhaps no official portraits were made. If portraiture's strengths are perfectly attuned to the kind of identity one associates with prostitutes, where does that leave portraits of an Emperor? Nobody bases loyalty to an Emperor on those specific qualities portraits represent. Making a portrait of the Emperor—which emphasizes what is important about him, precisely the qualities portraits cannot capture—seems an almost oxymoronic project.

Of course, imperial portraits were made; most readers have probably seen a number of them. The portraits of Emperors and Empresses most often displayed in museums were originally destined for special ancestral temples and painted for official state purposes (a notable exception are portraits of the Yuan rulers before Kublai Khan, who naturally were not concerned with Confucian rituals, and which consequently look much more like conventional portraits). These ritual portraits are life-size or larger, and from the beginning of the Ming to the end of the Qing—a period of more than five centuries—the portraits change remarkably little.[24] In portraits of the Emperors from the two dynasties, the differences between Ming and Qing dress are hardly noticeable, though for commoners these changes—in hair, in the neck of the garment—were of life and death importance. Historians like Philip Kuhn and Norman Kutcher have written about the political minefield surrounding hair in the Qing dynasty.[25]

In these portraits, however, the emphasis is not on these crucial differences, but on how imperial garb differs from that of all others. Headdress covers up the telltale hair, and the garments are displayed not in such a way as to emphasize their cut, but so as to show off imperial insignia, five-clawed dragons, or any of the other stylized symbols of imperial sovereignty (sacrificial cups, millet, sun and moon, and the like), which were the same for both dynasties. One can usually tell immediately in portraits of male commoners which dynasty is in power; curiously, in portraits of the Emperors, one must look twice.

The predominant effect in all of these imperial state portraits is of a very large picture, mostly of imperial yellow. Much more attention has been devoted to getting perfect the patterns of the textiles—robes open slightly to reveal yet another layer of fabulously ornate brocade underneath or the complicated patterns of imperial carpeting—than to depicting any individual features of a specific person. No individual lives forever through the creation of such a portrait: no artist makes himself known, since no individual style can manifest itself in this setting; nor is any single imperial face given rein to imprint itself on a viewer unforgettably.

Leafing through a folio of official imperial portraits of the Qing Emperors and Empresses, one is left with the distinct impression that the face is the least important part. These portraits focus as much on the depiction of rugs and robes as facial features. In fact, one feels as if all the faces could be transposed without much difference of effect. Ultimately these are portraits of an institution and not of specific individuals. Looking at the subject of such a portrait, underneath all his robes, seated stiffly on a throne, we cannot glean the sort of information we are used to getting from a portrait (and which any portrait of a prostitute would be expected to provide): is the individual in question short or tall? thin or stocky? fairskinned or swarthy? Is his skin pockmarked or smooth? What would he look like standing next to another individual? These are not the sort of portraits used to pick someone out from others.

In other words, imperial portraits have the opposite effect of those of prostitutes. Their focus is not on individual distinctiveness, those physical characteristics that set one person apart from another; in fact, studying these portraits, one can hardly find a distinguishing characteristic. I can barely match up, for example, an official portrait of the Kangxi Emperor with more informal portraits of the same man. In informal portraits, he is slender and intense, easy to pick out; but in official portraits, his distinctive narrow face with its full lips and wary eyes seems to fade away in the midst of all that yellow brocade. The portraits suggest that while no other individual can substitute for the Emperor, all Emperors might be able to substitute for each other. One is pretty much like any other.

In the Qing dynasty, at least, many Emperors commissioned portraits of themselves in a variety of more casual contexts and styles. Among many other portraits of him, the Kangxi Emperor had one painted in a style associated with the Jesuits, complete with shadows on his face and on the walls, his simple blue gown shaded so that its folds appear three-dimensional. Sometimes the Emperors are dressed in costume: his successor the Yongzheng Emperor had himself painted in three-quarters pose, dressed like the Sun King, complete with brocade vest and (unforgettably) curled wig. In others of these portraits, the various Emperors sit, dressed in casual clothes, sometimes surrounded by their children, other times by the accessories of either a scholarly life or a reclusive one.

Naturally, the Qianlong Emperor, an insatiable collector of all sorts of painting and calligraphy, was particularly fond of these casual portraits. He was also evidently fond of playing dress-up. Among his portraits, for example, is an ornate picture of Buddhist deities, done Tibetan style, more than a hundred lamas in circles connected to each other, all touching a center, a lama with the face of the Emperor Qianlong.[26] In another, he is a Daoist immortal, once again on an elevated throne, surrounded by fairies and other immortals. Evelyn Rawski has examined some of these portraits in the context of imperial politics. Portraits such as these stake the Qing Emperor's claim as leader not only of the Confucian polity, but also of a multi-ethnic imperium, of Tibetan lamas and Mongols as well.[27]

But the demands of imperial politics cannot account for all of these portraits. For example, one portrait depicts the Qianlong Emperor dressed in open-neck Ming garb, practicing calligraphy outdoors, with only two young servants in attendance. The portrait, embedded within a landscape, carefully hides all clues as to its subject's imperial identity: no five-clawed dragons here, nor even a queue (hidden discreetly beneath a Ming style hat).

The official portrait will find a place in state and family ritual, where it will be seen as one in a sequence of like portraits, revealing an unbroken succession of Emperors in official poses and garb. Such a display would have created an impression of dynastic continuity and inevitability. Casual portraits serve more mysterious functions. Surely no ritual purpose is served in showing the Qianlong Emperor painting in a garden. The state imperial portraits emphasize the trappings of the monarchy and the continuity of that institution. But nearly the opposite is taking place in these portraits of the Qianlong Emperor, where the same face appears embedded in a vast array of costumes—one almost wants to say disguises. The viewer learns to look for his face in even the most improbable of contexts. Their very profusion indicates a certain faith in portraiture, in its abilities either to manifest a subject's qualities or to make new claims about the subject. Does a painting of himself on horseback shooting down a mighty stag with a single shot show him to be a great hunter or make him one?

I suspect that this series of portraits was meant for the Qianlong Emperor himself and that they were painted to make a complicated assertion about the Emperor's identity. They articulate claims the Qianlong Emperor made about himself, which go something like this: Yes, I am the Emperor, but at the same time I am also a father; I am a hunter; I am a gentleman scholar; I am a connoisseur of the zither; I am a Buddhist monk; I am a Daoist immortal.

I have stacked the claims from those we believe to be true—that he was a father, for instance—to those that are self-evidently false. He certainly was no Buddhist monk; the completely shaved head shown in that particular portrait was not his.[28] Such claims suggest a version of identity where what on the surface is a lie may still be true if it represents an internal state. The picture of the Qianlong Emperor as Buddhist monk asserts that even if his position in society belies it, inside he is as devout and humble as a Buddhist monk, or a scholar whose true pleasures are derived from gardening and calligraphy.

In other words, a very different assertion about identity is being made in these casual portraits, which contrasts strikingly with those made by the official ones. These portraits claim to manifest an interior life, which is more important than the external one: I am not what I seem to be; the person underneath is the one who counts. Surely Hongguang, for his part, identifies with this internal person—defined against the trappings of status—when he contemplates running away from his position.

Of course, I don't believe that these paintings say anything true about the Qianlong Emperor's identity; and I certainly do not expect my reader to. A portrait of him dressed as a Buddhist monk and with his head shaven does not convince *me* of his truly pious nature. Instead, after flipping through a folio of such portraits, searching for his face in each one, no matter how unlikely the setting is, I feel that the real claim these portraits make when seen together is one that would not have amused the Qianlong Emperor at all.

For one thing, the problem of establishing individuality in a portrait becomes a different one. In the official portraits, we had difficulty figuring out which individual Emperor was being depicted, but none at all in discerning that the subject was the Emperor. But what distinguishes the portrait of Qianlong painting in his garden from thousands of portraits of Ming and Qing gentlemen practicing calligraphy outdoors, all of them claiming to express their true and natural selves (where such a self has supposedly nothing to do with the cultural apparatus that might help us identify the person)? Certainly, without its being included among imperial portraits, there would be no telling that its subject is none other than the Qianlong Emperor. Looking at the portrait, then, resembles something like examining the young claimant, trying to discover whether the individual in question is the Emperor, even though he is plucked out of his imperial surroundings.

Something just as invidious but unexpected also takes place: the line between honesty and flattery is important even for the viewer, and it has been crossed when one can no longer find credible the claims the portraits make about the Qianlong Emperor's identity. If one doesn't believe him to be a Daoist immortal, there is nothing to distinguish the setting from a stage and his clothing from costume. After looking at enough of these informal portraits, they start collectively to be making the following statement: all costumes are equally interchangeable and equally meaningless in determining who I am, because all I really am is this face. And recall that this claim is the one Li Xiangjun fears so much that she paints her portrait with blood, so that its painting literally effaces her own visage.

A line of inquiry that begins with the fan and its contrast with the imaginary portrait of the Hongguang Emperor's leads us almost inexorably to ask important political questions. What, for example, sets the Emperor apart from all other people and how can this be represented? Surely his distinctiveness does not entirely lie in a set of bright yellow clothing; but it also does not lie in a set of interior qualities, like a love of music or Buddhist piety.

Another step from here, and we have arrived at one of the hoariest of all political problems, which lies at the heart of imperial China: is the specific identity of the Emperor important? The play repeatedly circles around the problem of how the Emperor's specific identity matters, interpreting it in two related ways, both of which by now will certainly seem familiar.

First, does it matter which specific individual sits on the throne? Or, to phrase this question in the context of portraiture, does the face of the individual in the official state portrait matter? To the shameless prostitute Zheng Tuoniang, the face in the portrait could not matter less. She puts her response to this question baldly when she gleefully regards the fall of the dynasty as an opportunity to ply her wares: "Why, Master Yang, don't you know? Those camps of soldiers are the place to grab some money. I'll sell these songs elsewhere; in the palace of Sui, the willows fade; in the palace of Wu, the flowers die."[29] To her, whether a member of the Aisin Gioro family or a member of the Zhu family sits on the throne is a matter totally without import.

And second, do the Emperor's personal traits matter? Or was there a point to those casual portraits the Qianlong Emperor had painted, of himself as horseman, as contemplative hermit, as scholar? The loyalist Shi Kefa gladly sacrifices his life to the cause of that wholly inadequate sovereign Hongguang. In contrast, Hou Fangyu gets himself into trouble by insisting that the heir to the Prince of Fu cannot become Emperor because his personal history shows him entirely unworthy. Which is it? Do those casual portraits have anything to do with being Emperor?

I began this section by drawing a distinction between two different kinds of identity: *what* one is—physical traits and personal characteristics, so important to Li Xiangjun's career as a courtesan—as opposed to *who* one is, the specific identity of someone like the Emperor. By now, though, it should be clear that this bipartite division keeps breaking down: the fan is part of Li Xiangjun's greater project of establishing who she is, to be Hou Fangyu's wife, regardless of how she looks; and Hongguang, who by the end of his disastrous reign longs to escape his position, dreams of an identity that has nothing to do with his being a prince of the blood royal.

Li Xiangjun calls the fan her portrait and a letter, both metaphors of communication; she hopes it will speak for her. In one of the prefaces to the play, Kong Shangren explains that the fan also serves a different function: "those peach blossoms are the bloodstains of a beauty; with those bloodstains she guards her chastity and awaits a proper marriage."[30] In other words, the fan transforms her from courtesan to maiden; as a sign of chastity and as her most important possession, it even takes the position of a proxy dowry—as if to replace the dowry secretly provided by Ruan Dacheng and then rejected by Li Xiangjun.

Having removed Li Xiangjun from the immediate necessity of selling her body, the fan participates in other external economies as well. Her lover immediately recognizes this fact about the fan. Hou Fangyu's first reaction upon receiving it from Su Kunsheng is to call it "his treasure"; with his second, he reveals that he regards the fan not only as something of value, but as something that limits his own behavior and obligates him to respond: "Xiangjun! Xiangjun! Now how will I ever be able to requite you?"[31] There is an economy dictating the relationship between Li Xiangjun and the fan, but having been created, it circulates in other economies as well.

In late imperial China, after a bride married into her husband's family, her dowry was considered her own to dispose of at her discretion. Even if her husband's family found themselves in dire financial straits, she was under no legal obligation to contribute her dowry. Of course in practice, once she had joined her husband's family, the money helped start the newlyweds on their lives together. Nonetheless, having a dowry was tremendously important. James Watson argues that in traditional Chinese societies the dowry brought in by the bride differentiates her from all other women who might enter the household. Those women—servants, prostitutes, and secondary wives, among whom, of course, Li Xiangjun would normally have been counted— were simply purchased; women, like any other form of property, could be exchanged for money or other goods.[32]

But even the most orthodox marriage also revolved around the transfer of goods and money. In contrast to the simple purchase of any other woman, the introduction of a primary wife into a household took several steps, all subject to mediation by outsiders and negotiated carefully. According to canonical texts like the *Book of Rites*, there could be as many as six separate exchanges involved, where the families of the bride and groom alternated presents to each other, each exchange deepening the ties between the two families and making it increasingly difficult to tell who was in debt to whom.

Even with fewer exchanges of gifts, the traffic of goods makes it impossible to break down the transactions into the simple exchange of money for a woman. For rich families, after the groom's family gave the bride's family a bride-price, the bride's family sent the bride off with a dowry of approximately the same value as the bride-price, but consisting not of money but of clothing, jewelry, and sometimes household goods. Even a very poor family marrying off a daughter would be sure to send her off with some meager possessions—a pillow, perhaps, or a blanket.

Once the two families had been united in marriage, these possessions were used in daily life, perhaps incorporated into other dowries, and gradually absorbed into the groom's family. In other words, just as the two families cannot be easily separated once the marriage has taken place, the entire process resists articulation as buying or selling, since neither family can boil down their various expenditures to net gain or loss. The groom's family loses a bride-price, but gains a dowry; the bride's family gains a bride-price, but must pay a dowry. Even for a poor family, the pillow or the blanket stands in the way of viewing the transaction as purchase.

In a marriage between two wealthy families, neither family gains or loses in terms of money and goods; but given the market situation, the bride's family has lost, since a woman who could have been sold as a prostitute or servant has instead been given away—for free, essentially—as a wife.[33] Marriage rites seem to discourage tracing the path of the goods and money. But if we insist, the dowry and the bride-price—roughly equivalent in value—have been exchanged. They cancel each other out, and the bride herself is a gift.

It makes sense. When all women other than wives are bought and sold, the only way to differentiate a wife from chattel is to make of her a gift. Dowries, in other words, provide another answer to the question of exactly what a marriage is, as distinct from all other types of sexual relations between men and women. A dowry—a collection of trinkets and clothes—is part of a greater set of exchanges, each gift continuing the process of uniting two families. Amidst these exchanges between the two families, the passage of the woman herself from one household to the other cannot otherwise be accounted for, except as some sort of a gift.

A dowry is part of a network of exchanges—either the response to a bride-price or the culmination of a series of gifts presented from one family to the other—strengthening the bonds between these two families about to become one. All of these exchanges highlight the fact that the central transfer of a bride into her groom's home ends up being a gift. Here Marcel Mauss's *Essai sur le Don* (*The Gift*) is highly suggestive; Mauss describes the important position in many cultures of the gift and its relation to requital. He envisions the gift as a locus for the magical integration of self-interest and disinterested generosity. Yet unlike a purchase, after the response to the gift has been made, the bond between the participants is strengthened rather than ended. Gifts lie at the center of marriage, since it is defined against purchase.

But there is nothing remotely approaching gift-giving in the scene of Li Xiangjun's wedding. Unlike a dowry, the money Ruan Dacheng contributes towards the match counts as a purchase, both of a woman and of Hou Fangyu's friendship. Ruan Dacheng's money ties together a group of people economically, but unlike the ultimately unanswerable gift of the dowry, it ties them together impermanently. At the end of the play, once all these purchases are completed, once everyone who owes pays up and everyone who is owed receives payment, all of these figures can and will simply disperse. Nothing else—no magical combination of generosity and self-interest—ties them together. Zhang Dai writes that after a man has picked a concubine, "the girl's establishment produces a red receipt, and on it is written how many lengths of colored silk, how many gold ornaments, how much money, how much cloth [they expect of the customer]. It's all written in ink and then sent to the customer for his inspection."[34] Except that the play's transaction is implicit, nothing much distinguishes it from Zhang Dai's.

In fact, the brazen prostitute Zheng Tuoniang negotiates a price of ten coppers for her sexual favors right in the midst of the marriage proceedings, setting the tone for the ritual and suggesting something of their true nature. It is difficult to decide in all of this buying and selling who exactly *is* the prostitute. Ruan Dacheng has Yang Wencong broker a deal for him. Yang Wencong does not work for free, either; after Chongzhen's death and Ruan Dacheng's rise to power, Yang Wencong will call in this favor for a pretty sinecure. Ruan is prepared to pay two hundred taels for Hou Fangyu's friendship, buying him the prostitute he himself cannot afford. None of our characters can pretend to complete ignorance of what is going on—not even Li Xiangjun, who has grown up in a brothel and is being trained as an opera singer. Hou Fangyu, Li Xiangjun, and Li Zhenli all pretend to ignorance: each knows somebody has paid, but none of them asks about the source of this considerable sum of money.

The return of this dowry, which is just a purchase price, leads to some outstanding debts that the young couple have to pay off. But in addition to money, there is also a debt of *chou* which must be repaid as well. *Chou* refers not only to enmity, but also requital—useful in this situation where enmity seems to imply requital. Li Xiangjun earns Ruan Dacheng's enmity when she returns his dowry; he resolves this sense of being wronged by forcing her into a match with Tian Yang. Moreover, Ruan Dacheng's need to avenge himself on Hou Fangyu explains his almost irrational behavior later on, when he invents a plot against the state masterminded by Hou. And in so doing, even though Ruan has no idea about the consequences of his actions, he drives the young couple apart. In other words, the debt they incur by beginning their relationship—that enmity owed Ruan Dacheng—ends it.

The play never says so explicitly, but of course the two hundred taels worth of jewelry and clothing are intended to be a payment to Li Zhenli, in return for her having fed, clothed, and raised the adopted girl. Our understanding of the dowry necessarily colors how we see Li Zhenli's relationship to Li Xiangjun. She is not simply the girl's adoptive mother nor simply her madam. Even though she tries, Li Zhenli does not in fact make a red cent out of Li Xiangjun's sexual services. The dowry provided by Ruan Dacheng is returned, and the match with Tian Yang does not come off as expected. Nonetheless—unlike Lady Zhen, for example—Li Zhenli had intended to be recompensed for the costs incurred in Li Xiangjun's upbringing. Most parents do not call in this debt.

At any rate, Li Zhenli looks on her daughter's rejection of the goods regretfully and a little disbelievingly. Understandably so—when the dowry is returned, she is the obvious loser: even if he has failed at his objective, Ruan Dacheng at least has his money back (less the price of the tasty banquet already consumed); Hou Fangyu has the young beauty (he gets the girl without charge, having gotten out of paying Ruan Dacheng with his friendship); but poor Li Zhenli has no money to show for the loss of her daughter's virginity. In other words, Li Xiangjun turns out to be a free gift, but not the way a wife is. With a wife, the exchange of gifts promises exclusivity; giving her sexual favors free of charge here only implies what her mother assumes—that she may then bequeath such a gift on anyone.

Before he knows the origin of the trousseau, Hou Fangyu exults that these new jewels and dresses make her more beautiful than she was before. He tells Yang Wencong: "In her natural state, Xiangjun is one of the great beauties of the land; but today, with a few pearl and jade hair ornaments, wearing this rich brocade, that ten parts flower visage has another two parts added to it."[35]

Clothes and jewels like these are entirely necessary in Li Zhenli's profession. Properly plying her trade requires an initial investment, since only a courtesan dressed in such gorgeous wares could command higher prices—perhaps, to indulge in a bit of literalmindedness, even the twenty percent Hou Fangyu suggests.

Once the dowry has been rejected, Hou Fangyu turns tack, reassuring Li Zhenli that this is a temporary setback and that the reputation Li Xiangjun will gain from this incident will more than offset the loss. With the same trope by which beauty is quantified, he rephrases: "With all that fancy garb taken off, her naturally beautiful face—a perfect ten—adds another ten to it; I find her even more charming."[36] It is difficult to figure out how the arithmetic works out: ten, plus two, minus two, does not equal twenty. Moreover, once numbers like twenty are being bandied about, the notion of a perfect ten experiences some devaluation.

But with a little explanation, the mathematics *does* work. Li Xiangjun, who has rejected the dowry, might look like a girl who simply has no dowry—the perfect ten, plus two, minus two, looks just like ten. But in fact it is the act of rejection that matters—a girl whose very unadorned appearance represents her rejection of Ruan Dacheng might be worth much more than a girl without a dowry. Reputation counts. Incidentally, there is some small suggestion that he might be right, when we learn Li Xiangjun's precise value at the moment when she mars her face; Tian Yang offers three hundred taels for Li Xiangjun. Ruan Dacheng's dowry was worth only two hundred taels. Evidently, her celebrity has added a hundred taels—or fifty percent and not Hou Fangyu's twenty percent—to her price.

But something goes wrong here. The fan symbolizes her remove from circulation—much as a dowry would have—but then she returns to her old life as an entertainer. By all rights, when Hou Fangyu rushes back to Nanjing after receiving the fan, he should find his lover still waiting for him, so that all three may be reunited: the young man, the girl with the scarred face, and the fan commemorating the scarring. The play would then be a morality tale whose ending rewarded Li Xiangjun for her chastity.

Instead, when armed with the fan, Hou Fangyu comes to find her, she has healed, been restored to her full beauty, and gone to the palace. One suspects that even with all the other impediments, if she had sustained permanent damage, even a comely discreet little scar—anything to tie her to the fan permanently—she and Hou could have been married, and the fan preserved, all three of them to live on happily ever after.

For what stands out in the context of contemporary texts is not the scarring, but the healing. What the peach blossom fan has in common with the dowry is that both represent the removal of a woman from straightforward economic transaction; she is not to be simply bought with a sum of money. This remove from transaction can also be accomplished through much more gruesome means in late imperial literature.

In the hands of another writer, the wound Li Xiangjun sustains in the fan's creation could have been quite different. Ming and Qing readers seemed to derive a delicious frisson from accounts of women who sacrificed everything for chastity—not just married women, but unattached virgins as well—and not just for chastity, but also loyalty to the state and filial piety. In *Yangzhou shiri ji*, Wang Xiuchu makes note of the women who willingly go off with the Manchu conquerors, but many more writers detail other women's sacrifices for chastity.

The local gazetteers are filled with stories of such sacrifice. Take, for example, this account of a particularly noteworthy paragon of chastity:

> A woman surnamed Tan who was a native of Jiading was engaged to Sheng Tianyou. Before the marriage, he died. Her parents tried on numerous occasions to marry her to someone else. After waiting for an opportunity, she threw herself into a pond behind their home. Her family rescued her. After that, she cut her hair and ruined her face and went to live with her fiancé's family to preserve her chastity and to fulfill her wifely role.[37]

Miss Tan and Li Xiangjun find themselves in similar positions, both resisting matches their elders wish to impose on them. The two young women hit upon the same solution—ruining their faces. My guess is that Miss Tan's scars were permanent; parents undeterred by even a serious suicide effort would certainly not stop trying to marry her off until she had made herself thoroughly—and permanently—unmarriageable.

One popular historical account, summarized by Frederic Wakeman, features yet another chaste woman and yet another scar. It provides both an extreme example of this sort of gruesomeness and an especially interesting contrast to Li Xiangjun's experience. Lady Li, sister-in-law of the real-life Shi Kefa, was arrested by the Manchus after their victory; while in custody, a Manchu noble saw her. Smitten by her beauty, he sent a messenger with engagement gifts, among them a golden box. Lady Li withdrew to her chamber with the box. Her maid came out a few moments later with the box and Lady Li's thanks. When the messenger opened the box, he found inside her nose and ears, which she had sliced off herself.[38]

Only the level of the violence done to the self differentiates the creation of the fan from this moment. Reading a number of stories like these in quick succession results in a peculiar misogynist inflation, in which all three of these narratives participate. In a genre rife with suicides—by suffocation, by hanging, by drowning—and self-mutilation of all kinds, if one wants to prove a sincere desire to preserve one's chastity, more and more extreme measures are demanded. If Li Xiangjun had been truly serious about keeping her chastity, so this reasoning goes, she would have mutilated herself much more terribly, amputating her nose and ears or gouging her eyes rather than simply scarring her skin. In the case of Miss Tan, a failed suicide attempt was seemingly insufficient to prove her sincerity; her next attempt must escalate in violence against herself, as if only permanent damage will state her decision not to remarry with enough sincerity. The fan, with its bloodstains made into aesthetic pattern, has its place among these narratives, resting on the very threshold of this kind of violence. It reserves the potential of these narratives.

Why then after the creation of such a portrait (which represents her chastity in such a direct way) does Li Xiangjun's face heal? If her face had been permanently damaged, the fan would in fact be the portrait that truly captured the moment, truly Montaigne's portrait, which itself had changed the colors of its subject, permanently and demonstrably tied through the scar to its subject. Like the dowry to which Kong Shangren compares it, the fan would symbolize marriage, making her incapable of selling herself.

How after such a painting can the subject just be the same? Shouldn't such a painting change the identity of its subject? For indeed the magic of *Mudan ting* is such that Du Liniang somehow does remain just the same; even after painting a portrait that is supposed to be her last statement to the world, the girl at the beginning of the play who is daughter to Du Bao is continuous to the woman at the end of the play who is wife to Liu Mengmei.

The fan continues to represent Li Xiangjun to Hou Fangyu as the woman who has sacrificed her beauty for chastity, even after she heals and returns to sexual circulation. For healing, she must pay the price; the instant we know her to be good as new, the reader sensitive to Kong Shangren's arithmetic concerns knows the relationship between these young lovers to be doomed. Only one possible fate awaits such a symbol after the beauty of its owner has returned. If she is to remain the same, then the fan must be destroyed.

The fan, then, is an important element in circulations of capital and of karmic obligation. In this play, these circulations are mostly articulated in terms of reciprocity (*bao*). *Taohua shan*'s vision of the processes of history is deeply concerned with how various exchanges and circulations—for example, vendettas and personal debts—must be paid out and how they end up affecting an entire society. In other words, as part of Kong Shangren's vision of society as an organic unity, the enmities generated by a young prostitute's refusal to accept some clothing and jewels have everything to do with the fall of the mighty empire.

And so, the source of the conflict between Ruan Dacheng and the Revival Society is simply that they are in conflict. When Cai Yisuo is arrested, he naturally wants to know why, but he phrases that question tellingly: "Where do we owe this debt?"[39] He knows that they have been arrested to fulfill some personal vendetta; in their world, punishment and retribution are indistinguishable. Through a cycle of vengeful acts that demand requital, the men of the Revival Society are inextricably bound to the Ma and Ruan clique. This vendetta consumes all their energy, leaving none left for any other activity.

This kind of tie is mirrored in the relationship between Hou Fangyu and Li Xiangjun: unlike their counterparts in *Mudan ting*, there is very little evidence of deep passion between the two. In place of passion is what seems another kind of inextricable bond, that of obligation. No song attests to Li Xiangjun's love for Hou Fangyu as an individual. Instead, she is concerned with her obligations to him. As Yang Wencong persuades her of the wisdom of going to Tian Yang's household, she responds by pointing out the lovers' vows: "How may one sway a sworn vow?"[40] Anyone who had been her first customer could have elicited precisely the same feelings. In contrast, no other individual, or so the claim of romantic passion goes, could have summoned Du Liniang from the grave.

If her feelings seem strangely divorced from him, Hou Fangyu seems frequently even to forget her existence. From the time he flees Nanjing to Su Kunsheng's presentation to him of the fan, he does not even mention her. Each time he talks about the fan, Hou Fangyu's response consists primarily of worry about how he can possibly reciprocate such an action. I have mentioned already first his failure to recognize what the fan is upon first receiving it, and then his inappropriate glee at its rarity and worth.

Immediately thereafter, still mostly concerned with the fan's value, he worries that he will not be able to requite such a present: "Xiangjun! Xiangjun! How can I ever recompense you?"[41] Near the end of the play as well, during their brief and temporary reunion, Hou Fangyu returns again to this concern, saying to Li Xiangjun: "Just take a look at the peach blossoms on this fan—how can I ever recompense you?"[42] To Hou Fangyu, the fan represents something he cannot reciprocate. If he could reciprocate it—find the precise response that would answer it—then their relationship would be over. A relationship that ends once the proper recompense changes hands is not that between husband and wife, but that between client and patron. Their relationship is more like that between enemies—with its possibility of being ended by the perfect act of vengeance—than that between husband and wife, which by definition can never be satisfied and so ended.

The beginning of their relationship sets the tone for all the rest. Even though Yang Wencong has long had Hou Fangyu in mind as the perfect match for Li Xiangjun, the two young people only meet in the fifth act. Li Xiangjun is not at home, but at a hamper party, where prostitutes gather, each bringing a box of dainties to share. The whole party takes place on an upper story, because as Liu Jingting says, "what they fear most is the intrusion of men; that's why they lock themselves up, allowing us only to watch from below."[43] The party takes place on a platform, which serves as a stage, and there is an established procedure for a man to express his appreciation for a particular courtesan.

Liu explains to Hou how he can set up an assignation. The routine goes like this: "If someone strikes your fancy, throw a trinket upstairs, and she'll throw down a fruit."[44] Since Hou Fangyu knows in advance what he is supposed to do, when the moment actually comes, his claims of being swept up in the moment do not exactly ring true, instead sounding more than a bit rehearsed: "These strains of flute hold me spellbound. I can bear it no longer and will make my offering."[45] Moreover, having been primed first by Yang Wencong's and then by Liu Jingting's suggestions, he comes with the very purpose of meeting Li Xiangjun and arranging a meeting with her. It is according to custom and not uncontrollable passion that he throws the pendant.

Hou throws up to Li Xiangjun a fan pendant made of imported sandalwood, which is reciprocated by an equally rare and valuable gift of out-of-season cherries, wrapped in a fine handkerchief. The cherries inspire Hou Fangyu to new flights of feigned surprise—"I wonder who threw this down? If it were Xiangjun, wouldn't that be wonderful?"[46]—when of course everyone present—Hou, Liu Jingting, Yang Wencong (who just happens to show up), Li Zhenli, and Li Xiangjun—knows that this occasion has been set up especially to introduce the two young people.

The fan inspires in Hou Fangyu neither love nor remembrance, but instead only a desperate desire to recompense (*bao*). The exchange of pendant for cherries takes place at a moment when recompense is possible, but it colors and dooms their relationship, for the recompense for which Hou Fangyu yearns sets up problems that allow for no resolution. No Confucian redemption is possible with this relationship; nothing can render this illicit affair a true and orthodox marriage. Before all the ensuing complications, recompense ties the two young people together. The pendant demands the return gift of the cherries. One guesses the cherries and the fine handkerchief were prepared in advance, awaiting the toss of the pendant. Later, their relationship will become held together by what is not recompensed, first the rejected dowry and later and more importantly, the fan.

Before all this, though, she is simply a prostitute, albeit an expensive and inexperienced one, and they both follow prearranged rules. The exchange of pendant and cherries allows all the parties to meet and negotiate terms. The exchange restages—though with crucial differences—an epithalamion in the *Shijing* (or *The Book of Odes*), "Mugua," a canonical formulation of courtship and marriage. Li Xiangjun and Hou Fangyu go through the steps of the following dance, more or less:

> My love threw me a quince,
> I returned with a jade pendant.
> Not as a recompense,
> But as a statement of eternal love.⁴⁷

Both texts mark a moment of early courtship. In "Mugua," the first lover throws a fruit, which is answered by a trinket. The order is reversed in *Taohua shan*: first Hou Fangyu throws a fan pendant, and Li Xiangjun answers with cherries.

The gifts in *Taohua shan* reflect a world whose material and social circumstances are infinitely more complicated than those of the *Shijing*—no humble, hardy quince here, but cherries in early spring, as Liu Jingting marvels, costly and fragile, certainly imported to Nanjing from some even warmer clime. The simple jade pendant has been replaced by a sandalwood ornament, also rare, also imported; Hou Fangyu calls it "exotic ware from Hainan."

And suggestively, the order of the exchange has been reversed. The quince might have been thrown spontaneously—seized from a nearby tree at a passing stranger who caught one's eye—and then reciprocated by another spontaneous gesture, a jade pendant removed from the neck. None of that spontaneity has any part of Li Xiangjun and Hou Fangyu's first meeting. This exchange was, as we know, a prearranged code (as the objects themselves, rare and specially prepared, hardly conceivable as things just at hand, seem to indicate).

"Mugua" reflects back upon courtship, from a point when it has already concluded and marriage has begun, describing the progression from love to marriage—or how the natural attraction of man and woman is transformed to a vow, with all of its social implications. Somehow, mysteriously, what seems the spontaneous exchange of quince and pendant ends up articulating a statement of eternal love. One can imagine many uses of such a poem in its early days, as a song with a dance attached to it, or perhaps as part of a custom where a vow between two lovers itself is articulated through the song.

This extremely simple poem consists of almost nothing but one adamantly and repeatedly insisted idea: that the exchange of quince and pendant not be understood as recompense, that exchange not be confused for a purchase of one object for the other. To emphasize this point, the last two lines are repeated in each of the following stanzas (each stanza describes the exchange of a different fruit and created object). The quince was not thrown with the intention of earning a jade pendant in return, but instead as an uncalculating expression of feeling. The jade pendant is thrown back not as payment for the quince, nor even out of gratitude for the quince, but as a gesture of fully and spontaneously reciprocated admiration.

There are very good reasons, in other words, that a statement of eternal love and the notion of recompense be so fundamentally opposed. Recompense and reciprocity according to this formulation are somehow antithetical to marriage. In fact, each of the fundamental human relations—between lord and servant, father and son, husband and wife, elder brother and younger brother, even that between friends—is threatened in different ways by being reduced entirely to a relation of recompense. People ought to treat each other in certain, prescribed ways not because of what one person has done, but because of who that person is: husband, father, lord, brother. A truly filial son would be no less devoted and obedient to a loving parent as to a cruel one.

Reciprocity even seems to be a specter to be purged in the relation of friends, which of all the fundamental human relations would seem to be the one where it is most central. After all, one chooses one's friends, based partly on how they have treated one in the past. Two of the truest friends in Chinese literature do their best to rid their friendship of all suspicion of reciprocity. The friends in the story "Wu Baoan" go to unbelievable lengths for each other. The one renders himself penniless to redeem the other before they even meet each other. If they had shared a history of friendship with each other, this generosity might be construed as paying back an old debt.) True friendship, it seems, like true filial piety, must be as little based on the individual nature of the object of devotion as possible. There is nothing particularly honorable in venerating a loving parent or being loyal to a friend one has known for decades. The true test lies in showing devotion untainted by recompense.

Yang Lien-sheng has discussed some of the political ramifications of reciprocity and how canonical views of its centrality changed. Under certain conditions, for example, both Confucius and Mencius allowed children to murmur against their parents and subjects to revolt against cruel lords. But, he points out, by the late imperial period, the ethics of reciprocity had changed radically: "The son or the subject was always the one to blame, no matter whether there was kindness from the parent or the ruler."[48] Some of *Ershisi xiao* (the Twenty-four Paragons of Filial Piety), for example, have terrible parents, so that the challenge lies precisely in treating these abusers with the utmost respect—an implicit argument that filial piety lies precisely in refuting reciprocity. Loving treatment of a loving parent might arise not out of filial piety, but simply be reward for services rendered.

In one of the most famous stories of filial piety, Min Sun's stepmother shows blatant favoritism to her own sons, padding his winter clothes with dried grass, but her own sons' clothes with cotton silk. The cold makes Min Sun clumsy at his chores, and when he is beaten by his father, his clothing is torn, and its inadequate padding shows. Enraged, his father intends to divorce his wife, but Min Sun intercedes on her behalf: "If mother is here, one son will be cold; if mother leaves, three sons will be left forlorn." To our biological parents we owe the gift of life, which can never be fully recompensed; but Min Sun does not owe his stepmother that. Nor since she treats him badly does he owe her for anything else. His deference is due entirely to her position; no reciprocity taints his behavior.[49]

Reducing filial piety (or loyalty, for that matter) to recompense opens up deeply troubling possibilities. Confucius, for example, suggests a direct relationship between how a parent cares for a child and how the child will one day treat the parent. He explains that a child ought to mourn his parents for three years because they cared for him for three years when he was an entirely helpless infant: "A child ceases to be nursed by his parents only when he is three years old. Three years' mourning is observed throughout the Empire."[50]

Confucius only slips this explanation in at the very end of a long defense of the three-year mourning period. It is one thing to suggest the parallelism and interdependence at the heart of the family that allows for its continuation, but it is quite another to imply that children should be filial to their parents only because they were cared for as infants.

Even in this weak version, linking filial piety and reciprocity opens up all sorts of unwelcome possibilities. Let me choose an extreme case from which to argue: what if a person had been kidnapped at the first moment of birth? Would that person be obliged to treat his kidnappers with filial love, even knowing that they were not his natural parents? After all, the kidnappers would have cared for him as a helpless infant.

The reasoning of reciprocity leads one to all sorts of conclusions that are not tenable in a Confucian society. It gives license to people with bad parents to treat them with equally bad treatment, and it puts parents in a position of needing to earn filial treatment. Are bad, unloving parents less deserving of filial treatment than good, loving ones? The hypothetical child snatched away at birth should not treat the kidnapper and the parent equally, because it must matter who one's parent is (just as it should always matter who the Emperor is). Du Bao adamantly refuses to accept what might not be his daughter, but instead a perfect double. For in such cases, a double will not do; somebody who has done for one everything one could expect of a father will not do either.

If Confucian society is to make sense, fathers must be treated with the respect and obedience accorded to fathers simply on the basis of their identity as fathers. Consequently, the importance of preserving the uniqueness of the father's position has been an important part of Confucianism since its beginnings. Mohists who argued that in the ideal moral world all elders would be as revered as one's father were countered by Confucians who responded with horror. Where everyone was as good as a father, then the unique position of one's own father would be diluted beyond recognition. For by treating everyone as one's father, one ceases to treat one's true father as he deserves.

Let me return to "Mugua" and *Taohua shan* and why the quince cannot be an exchange for the jade pendant. The logic of reciprocity is as destructive of the relationship between husbands and wives as it is for parents and children. For it reduces the relationship of any husband and wife to simply that of prostitution.

It is simply unacceptable to explain marriage according to reciprocity: if the husband treats the wife well, rewards her generously for duties performed, then she in turn will compensate him for his efforts with good housekeeping and chastity. Such an arrangement would be not conjugal harmony, but consumer loyalty. Consequently, the wives most honored for virtue in the late imperial period had sometimes never even met their husbands, thus rendering inconceivable any reading of their services as compensation. These were the young fiancées whose intendeds died before the marriage day and who nonetheless joined the young man's households, taking care of his parents and family and, of course, preserving their chastity. The less the tie to the "husband," the more a woman who preserved her chastity was valorized. Recompense has no part in the relationship between husband and wife, and that is why in "Mugua" the jade pendant cannot be recompense for the quince. To be meaningful, each gesture must be made independently.

The exchange of the cherries for the sandalwood pendant colors the whole rest of their relationship. If Li Xiangjun were indeed his wife, the creation of the fan—though it would no doubt move him deeply and arouse compassion and perhaps even deeper love—would not inspire profound anxiety about recompense. If she were his wife, her loyalty to the point of death would not in any way change his obligation to her or demand a reciprocal action, for his obligations to her would be based solely on who she was and not what she did. The pendant and the cherries bode no good.

One fundamental relation I have still not discussed is central to *Taohua shan*—that between lord and vassal. Reciprocity's anxieties hold true in this relation as well. The fan casts a pall over the world of politics as well as over the world of romance. Sinologists, particularly those of a popular variety, frequently invoke the Mandate from Heaven, possessed only provisionally by the Emperor, to be revoked by improper behavior. *Taohua shan* will have none of that. Instead, this brand of reciprocity is completely dismissed. The logic of reciprocity can only corrupt loyalty and eat away at the stability of the polity; ultimately the flexibility of this sort of reasoning can accommodate virtually any action, no matter how obviously treasonous.

It justifies, for example, Zuo Liangyu's move on Nanjing, which to many eyes must have seemed a clear-cut case of treason and revolt. Su Kunsheng convinces Zuo that it is his duty to turn his troops on Nanjing and rescue the putative Crown Prince. Once again, Zuo Liangyu proves easy to manipulate: "That's right. I, Zuo Liangyu, am a general of the old Emperor. And since Chongzhen has a Crown Prince, it is he who is my lord. When that Ma and Ruan seized control of the coronation of Hongguang, I was far away and didn't receive the decree."[51] It goes without saying that not receiving an imperial decree does not let a person off the hook when it comes to loyalty. Hongguang either is or is not the Emperor—regardless of whether all individual generals received or understood the decree.

In Zuo Liangyu's mind, loyalty to an Emperor is an entirely personal matter; because Chongzhen granted leniency to Zuo when he was an outlaw, Zuo will in turn pledge allegiance to Chongzhen and his own. But personal loyalty has its limits; particularly in an enormous, complicated state, generals cannot decide against rebellion only because of personal obligations, because one individual Emperor might have extended special kindnesses. In *Taohua shan*, this version of loyalty reflects what is by now a familiar problem. It is almost as if Zuo Liangyu came to his misapprehension by seeing the wrong portrait of Chongzhen—not the picture to be used in state ceremonies of the sovereign in his formal robes, but instead the casual portrait of the man in his garden.

To Zuo Liangyu, the Emperor is a person just like any other. Because one man—who happened to be the Chongzhen Emperor—was kind to him and the other man wasn't, he will choose which one to pledge allegiance to—and which one to rebel against. Casting the right man in the imperial role is the subject of the next two chapters.

CHAPTER 5

The Actor's Stage

This chapter focuses on *Taohua shan*'s treatment of the theatre. The next concentrates on the play's treatment of politics, specifically, the effect that dynastic turmoil has on the legitimacy of the Emperor. These last two chapters are meant to be read in conjunction; at the same time that the theatre sheds light onto the political world, monarchy (in its guise in *Taohua shan*) seemingly cannot exist without employing the language and tools of the theatre. In *Taohua shan*, the magic and energy of the throne and of the theatre are interconnected and inseparable.

The play suggests that by allowing for repeatability, the theatre allows for the proliferation of what ought to be singular, indiscriminately cheapening and intermingling the inauthentic with the authentic. Li Xiangjun invests all her hopes in the singularity and uniqueness of the fan. But the fan is not unique in the play; there is, remarkably, a second peach blossom fan, offhandedly thrown to Li Xiangjun during her audition before Hongguang. Lest the reader be confused, let me reassure her that other than in this play, fans with peach blossoms painted on them are not a major trope in Chinese literature.

The appearance onstage of the second fan is disturbingly casual, never mentioned again by any of the characters, and not foregrounded in either the arias or in the action onstage. Nonetheless, its brief presence entirely undermines the singularity of the play's central artifact. After she is brought into the palace compound along with all the other entertainers, Li Xiangjun refuses to sing before the Emperor, claiming not to know the play he is casting, Ruan Dacheng's *Yanzi jian*. Impressed by the beauty of the young entertainer, Hongguang asks her what operas she does know. She tells him *Mudan ting* but then refuses to sing. Hongguang remarks appreciatively: "Look at her powdered face blushing pink, looking as if she were shy. Give her a fan with peach blossoms."[1] The stage directions emphasize the carelessness with which this second fan is treated (keep in mind the way that the first fan calls on several characters to risk their very lives): "A *za* [bit part] tosses a pink fan to the *dan* [female lead]."[2]

Everything Li Xiangjun does in this scene is meant to emphasize her refusal to fake anything. The situation cries out for dissimulation: as an actress it is called for; flattering the Emperor would buy her great favor; finally she finds herself in a situation where what is onstage and offstage seem impossible to distinguish. Nonetheless, she manages to carve out a moment of unimpeachable sincerity. It would strain the abilities of even the most talented and skilled actress to feign blushing, even when the Emperor's reaction to it shows just how impossible sincerity is in this environment. She follows the blush with an aria from *Mudan ting* chosen to express her own feelings. In it, Du Liniang muses on her dream—and the way the beauty of flowers, like that of young girls, can be wasted, without anyone even grieving.

And yet in the midst of everything we would like to see as sincerity—a blushing actress who refuses to assume another role but insists upon singing about herself—the second fan intrudes. The second fan inevitably cheapens the first, whose salient characteristics are the sincerity of its creation and its inviolable connection to Li Xiangjun. The creation of the first fan out of her own blood involved enormously high stakes. That another fan can simply be summoned as a prop cannot fail to weaken our faith in the possibility of the first. To what extent was the first peach blossom fan merely a prop for a performance?

The second peach blossom fan is only one in a series of embedded performances in an intensely metatheatrical play. For example, the preface and each of the first three acts all contain embedded performances, as if collectively reflecting on the nature of performance and whether experience can ever be abstracted from it. Can events ever be experienced without any mediation, separated from any frame of performance? Unmediated experience must be a possibility if one is to retain the hope of purging some of the disturbing qualities of performance from society as a whole.

In the second act, Yang Wencong gives Li Xiangjun her name and observes her singing lesson. The first words Yang utters as he walks onstage propose a troubling relationship between representation and the world represented, between what is onstage and offstage:

> The scenery of the Three Mountains offers itself for paintings.
> The elegance of the Six Dynasties enters poetic evaluation.[3]

If we know landscape and history only through representation, does it then follow that the Three Mountains and Six Dynasties exist only through and for representations?

In the next act, Ruan Dacheng's presence disrupts a Confucian ritual, which is set up like a performance. That scene begins with two ritual attendants preparing the altar, gathering together the items they will need, and going over what they will need to do: in short, they are rehearsing and preparing the stage within a stage (complete with the Old Ceremonial Assistant, whose presence from the preface onwards is associated with metatheatre). The ritual begins with the Old Ceremonial Assistant's calling out of instructions, immediately obeyed by all the scholars present. Into this scene, Ruan Dacheng intrudes, less participant than spectator, as if—like a play—all who pay to watch are welcome to attend. He explains his own presence, providing a reason that seems more suited for attending the theatre than a ritual: "Living in leisure here in Nanjing, I've come to watch this grand ceremony."[4] This act, in which political ritual not only takes place onstage, but itself seems so closely to resemble theatre, down to props, cues, and a responsive audience, suggests one way to approach the convergence of the theatrical and the political.

These two final chapters explore how the theatre—both in its workings and as an idea—disturbingly affects the realm of the political. For sincerity and singularity, foregrounded by the stage, are matters of import offstage as well. How can one tell if loyalty is sincere? How is it that loyalty can be transferred from the Chongzhen Emperor to his successor Hongguang as soon as Hongguang appears in the proper costume and setting?

After the Hongguang Emperor ruled him an impostor, the putative

Crown Prince was imprisoned. As the victorious Manchu armies approached Nanjing, Hongguang and most of the members of his government fled, and a large crowd of people broke open the prison to liberate the mysterious young man. The *Mingji nanlue* records his impromptu coronation:

> The people bore the Crown Prince on to a horse through the Xihua Gate and into the Wuying Palace. They brought him into the West Palace, but he had not yet been ritually bathed nor his hair dressed. At the time, because of the rush there had been no preparations, so they took a headdress from a trunk of theatrical props to put on his head, and he took his place on the Wuying throne and the crowds cried out, "Myriad years!"[5]

In this anecdote, as in *Taohua shan*, the theatre and the throne dovetail. The crowds gathered before the young man take on two identities at once; they are both subjects expressing allegiance to their Emperor and an audience gathered to watch a performance. The young man is both performer and Emperor; even his crown is both a theatrical prop (a crown was an important part of any troupe's accoutrements, since so very many plays are political) and a very real symbol of sovereignty, entirely meaningful to the subjects watching.

Although they are integrally related, tied together at a number of points, neither the theatre nor the monarchy completely frames the other. In other words, the political cannot explain away the theatrical. The gravity of the young man's coronation in the *Mingji nanlue* is partly dependent on the magic of the stage. One cannot fully account for the episode by simply summarizing it as a minor uprising on the part of people wishing to free the rightful heir to the throne and return him to his proper position. Such an explanation misses out not only on the energy involved, but the very mechanism of this insurgency. A world in which the theatre was not central to perceptions of reality would simply have been unable to comprehend why a fake crown and an audience have any legitimacy in the creation of an Emperor, why such a performance must be carefully staged, why it bears more resemblance to the performance of a play than to any conventional investiture. For of course, ceremonies of imperial investiture were not performed before crowds of citizens, but instead in the seclusion of the imperial compound for an audience of officials.

Nor can the political completely absorb the power of the theatre in *Taohua shan*, though throughout there is a suggestion that such a thing might be possible. All of the major characters who are entertainers quit their professions by the end of the play (some minor characters continue on, like

Zheng Tuoniang, but primarily as prostitutes, and not as actresses, we gather). It seems that the new world order has no place for these people. Of course, the theatre in some guise continues on, as the prologue indicates, since we the audience only come into contact with the play when the Old Ceremonial relates a performance of it; but *Taohua shan*, a play about history and the fall of a dynasty, differs from *Yanzi jian*, say, or *Mudan ting*.

Still, *Taohua shan* neatly straddles two mutually exclusive intimations. On the one hand, there is the possibility that the political can fully account for the world onstage. The corollary to this version of theatre's subordinate relationship to the political world is that once problems in the political arena have been fully resolved, the theatre might no longer have any reason to exist. Before comparing the reigning Emperor Kangxi to the Sage Kings of antiquity Yao and Shun, the Old Ceremonial Assistant tells us about the Kangxi Emperor's reign: "Sons are filial, ministers loyal, myriad affairs all just so. No need even to bother seeking the fruit of eternal life."[6] When even the notion of eternal life holds no more charms than the present, surely imagined worlds onstage are no longer compelling. It seems this golden age has no room for actors and performers like Li Xiangjun, Liu Jingting, and Su Kunsheng, whose unstable identities and failure to fit within a single patriline do not allow them to conform neatly to Confucian hierarchies.

And yet on the other hand, these very people who might seem to have been phased out by the advent of the new order are presented here in a positive light—and far more unequivocally so than conventional heroes like Shi Kefa, for example, the defeated general canonized by Manchus and loyalists alike. The entertainers prove themselves to be ardently loyal defenders of the old dynasty. Perhaps more importantly, the play suggests that the actors are not simply bastards in an empire of sons, nor mere dissimulators in a world where specific identity is so important, but instead are engaged in a project much more meaningful than lying or make-believe.

One could ask the question the way the play does: how is it that Liu Jingting and Su Kunsheng, a storyteller and an opera singer, are reconciled into the new dynasty? They end the play as hermits, on the run from a buffoonish yamen runner wanting to turn them in; they are no longer professional entertainers, but now a fisherman and a woodsman—two of the four traditionally honorable professions (along with scholar and farmer).

The young man in the anecdote might seem simply to be playing the role of the Emperor, costumed in a crown that is just an abandoned prop, cast in his role by an audience. This is a politics turned into burlesque: a deserted capital ruled by a so-called prince in makeshift robes. His reign lasted all of a day or so, before the Manchus arrived, captured, and executed him. In that single day, the young man engaged in acts of empty largesse, freeing various officials from prison (including many of those who had refused to recognize him earlier) and bequeathing high office on them. But these acts, couched in the high-flown language associated with acts of imperial amnesty, read like farce, because they were totally ineffectual. No sooner did he free them than they wisely fled from the Manchus.

How can this scene be interpreted in such a way that it does not cast doubt on the very institution of monarchy, when the Emperor can be created by so simple an act as looting a box of theatrical props? It is not clear how we can maintain a fundamental difference between this young man and the hundreds of other actors performing the role of the Emperor on other stages, every day, all over China (in plays like *Taohua shan* or *Changsheng dian*). Or conversely, how can we distinguish between this Emperor and all the others claiming rule over all of China? How do we tell the difference between him and someone to whom we grant more legitimacy? The young man's stage costume can be donned or doffed with equal ease (he will shortly be captured by the Manchus, who assuredly do not allow him to continue as Emperor).

The costume and the role-playing it suggests remind one of Hongguang's shortsighted desires as he explains to Huang Degong, with whom he seeks refuge: "You don't have to worry—all We want is to manage to survive. As for that imperial role, I don't want to play it anymore." He regards the position of Emperor as no more fixed a marker of identity than a theatrical role, to be assumed and divested at will. And yet these subversive suggestions are embedded in surprisingly orthodox contexts. Hongguang, after all, fails in his attempt to return to life as an ordinary prince; the imperial robes do not prove so easy to divest himself of as he hopes. A faith in the theoretical redeemability of the polity forms an integral part of the play's description of the late Ming's utter corruption: the play is deeply committed to the ultimate possibility of a Confucian order as an organic and successful whole.

Just as Hongguang's threats to the legitimacy of the throne are defused, the episode of the putative Crown Prince's investiture ventures uncomfortably close to farce but manages to defer it. Despite describing a scene that appears to cast a skeptical light on the whole institution of monarchy—never mind the one individual—Ji Liuqi, the author of the *Mingji nanlue*, expresses with some warmth his belief in the young man's authenticity.

Ji Liuqi presents an array of evidence to buttress the young man's claims that he was in fact a son of the Chongzhen Emperor. According to his interpretation, the mysterious young man was the victim of conspiracy and of rigged tests of identity.

Imagine how this account of the investiture would read if the writer believed the pretender to be a mere impostor. His belief in the truth of the young man's claims allows our author to back off from the scarier possibility, which reflects not just on this individual, but on the idea of the monarchy. While serving as Emperor does share some potentially disturbing features with playing a theatrical role, we ultimately return to a world where the person underneath the costume matters, a world in which the identity of the Emperor must be and can be known.

This young actor who might also be the Emperor (or is he an Emperor forced temporarily to take on the guise of an actor?) bears a strong resemblance to Hongguang. Hongguang is another monarch whose questionable legitimacy is bound up with the theatre. He is cast in the role of Emperor partly by Ruan Dacheng, a civil servant who happens to be a master playwright. Throughout the play, Hongguang's status resides somewhere in the awkward in-between. He lacks the unquestioned authority and legitimacy of either a Chongzhen or a Kangxi. But then again, even if Shi Kefa does not approve of this buffoon's being chosen as Emperor, the general does martyr himself in Hongguang's service, in an act of loyalty to his liege, while we understand Liu Liangzuo's betrayal as basest treachery and treason.

Hongguang's unusual relationship to the theatre further complicates his status—and not just in his eagerness to discard the role of Emperor. Another man might have spent his time in Nanjing attending to the many pressing matters of state. Instead, Hongguang turns amateur impresario, spending his time casting the parts for his production of Ruan Dacheng's play *Yanzi jian*. His obsession with the theatre influences the way we gauge his legitimacy (and also contrasts with the next Emperor of the Southern Ming—the earnest Zhongli, who wholeheartedly dedicated himself to recovering the north). The young man in the *Mingji nanlue* who is both actor and Emperor finds his counterpart in *Taohua shan*'s Hongguang, who cannot wait to get out of his role of Emperor and return to his real life, that of the theatre. As enemy troops besiege Nanjing, Hongguang's greatest concerns are onstage, with properly staging Ruan Dacheng's play.

The play's structure suggests a connection between the way the past is framed as history and the way reality is framed onstage. In adherence to dramatic convention, the *fumo* (in the role of the Old Ceremonial Assistant) introduces the play. What is unusual in this case is that he does so from a point in time forty years in the future of the events related by the play. Now an old man, he tells us of a play he has seen, by the name of *Taohua shan*, in which he himself is a minor figure. Remarkably he sees a character onstage in the role of himself:

> Yesterday, at Peace Garden, I saw a new play called *Peach Blossom Fan*, which related the recent historical events of the fall of the Ming Dynasty in Nanjing.... And most delightful—they'd dragged up my wizened visage onto the stage, to play a *fumo* role, which made me at times cry, at times laugh, at times rage, and at time grumble. That whole theatre was full of audience members. How could they know that I was one of the people in the play?[7]

And so we are introduced to a play about history and politics; it begins with the intimation that political memory and the theatre are somehow related. His grumbling—perhaps at the performance, perhaps at what is being performed—hints at the inadequacies of the framed reality, whether memory or stage.

On the one hand, as I have discussed in the preceding chapter, the play highlights the importance of knowing a person's specific identity, a core issue in any debate on legitimacy in a monarchy. And yet on the other hand, many of the characters are actors, both professional and amateur, inhabiting the stage, a space especially designated for dissimilation and disguise. Are not all fixed identities threatened by the existence of such people and such a space? What happens to the identity of the Emperor when it rests on a space where identity is infinitely fungible?

One thing that happens is that the Emperor's identity starts to converge with that of an entertainer. Li Xiangjun and Hongguang share a remarkable amount in common. They are the two characters who are treated as commodities by others, both creatures of this particular historical moment, with all of its attendant instabilities: a loyalist actress and an impresario Emperor.

Hongguang and Li Xiangjun are afflicted with matching misapprehensions about identity, that their stations in life do not matter so much as who they really are inside. This is a strikingly peculiar position for an Emperor to take, since after all he did not become a prince because of his tastes. But it is not such a surprising position for an actress. For the idea that one is really who one is on the inside depends on the faith that one can perfectly distinguish internal from external—and that faith is obviously informed by the theatre, which also relies on people showing a different face from who they really are.

What makes Li Xiangjun who she is ought to be very different from what makes the Emperor who he is. First of all, to claim to be the Emperor ought to imply a claim to uniqueness, as so much of the imperial paraphernalia implies. The Emperor's physical location in the Forbidden City foregrounds his singularity, living in a miniaturized version of the capital city surrounding it—a box within a box within a box, aligned according to absolute north and south, so that it occupies a uniquely privileged position in the cosmos. Being the Emperor entitles one to wear a color no other individual in the polity may wear, imperial yellow, and to have gowns decorated with five-clawed dragons, a motif exclusive to him. In the ethics of sacrifice, the Emperor is the one person in the polity who never has any obligation to sacrifice himself for another.[8] A prostitute by contrast is a commodity, by her nature meant to be replaced.

But in the world of *Taohua shan*, these distinctions collapse. Throughout the play, the deep parallels between Hongguang and Li Xiangjun mark the degree to which things have gone wrong. They are the two characters who are cast into their roles before our eyes. In Act 37, "Plundering Treasure," Liu Liangzuo and Liu Zeqing, about to surrender to the Manchus, plan to turn in Hongguang to sweeten the deal they hope to cut. Huang Degong, with whom Hongguang has sought refuge, wants to keep him in his camp. What ensues is quite literally a tug of war, where Hongguang is the rope: Liu grabs at his arms, and Huang pulls at his legs.

This scene represents more than a vivid display of the imperial institution degraded; it also specifically echoes a previous scene in the play. Hongguang fails to escape the fate that might so easily have been Li Xiangjun's. She must batter her own face to avoid being dragged out of her home with bodily force and being treated as an object to be bundled up and delivered for a price. If we know to the tael Li Xiangjun's price, Hongguang also possesses a value, which can be transferred from one set of hands to another. Liu Liangzuo betrays Hongguang and prepares to cash in with the Manchus. His brash comments at the end echo Ruan Dacheng's much earlier: "Turn in Hongguang to the Northern Dynasty, and we'll all be enfeoffed as great princes—isn't it like offering up a treasure?"[9]

Li Xiangjun and Hongguang seem to have been created out of whole cloth for the use of others. But for an improbable confluence of events (everything leading up to the fall of Beijing, capped off by his own survival in the uprising that killed his father), Hongguang would merely be one of tens of thousands of obscure imperial princes. It appears that he has been improbably cast into the role of Emperor: "I, Ruan Dacheng, secretly went to Jiangpu and sought out Prince Fu, came back the next night and have been plotting his coronation with Ma Shiying."[10]

The play gives us no reason to believe that Hongguang is not the imperial prince and grandson of the Wanli Emperor he claims to be. And we are not told about other princely candidates for the throne. But according to some unofficial histories, the casting of Hongguang in the role of the Emperor was as seemingly arbitrary as Li Xiangjun's casting. In the version of events told by *Hongguang shilu chao*, Ma Shiying dispatches Yang Wencong to seek out the new Emperor.

> Ma Shiying sent out his own man Yang Wencong with a blank letter, telling him that no matter which prince he encountered—so long as he was the first—he should fill in the name and welcome him [as regent]. Wencong arrived at the Huai River, where he saw a broken-down boat on the river with a person inside, of whom someone said, "That's Prince Fu." Wencong entered to see him and explained Ma Shiying's intention to have him crowned.[11]

Any prince could have become Emperor—and there were many (the fertility of the Zhu clan was one major contributing factor in the bankrupting of the Ming government). But the man in the broken-down boat might not even be a prince. Other than the casual testimony of one bystander, there is no evidence one way or the other: no seal, no royal appurtenances at all.

In yet another account, Hongguang himself turns out to be an impostor. Having made off with the seals of the real prince during the chaos of military revolt, he is a mere attendant who in Nanjing passes himself off as the erstwhile Prince Dechang. If any pretty, talented girl could have just as easily become Li Xiangjun, any one of hundreds (perhaps thousands) of princes could equally easily have become Hongguang, according to Ma Shiying's instructions in the *Hongguang shilu chao*. Whether these stories are true or not (almost certainly not), they reflect a deep and abiding anxiety about the specific identity of this particular Emperor, who does not succeed to the throne so much as he is chosen for and cast in it.

As for Li Xiangjun, either no one knows or it is a matter of no import who her biological parents are or where she comes from. When we first see her, at sixteen years old, she seems to be an entirely blank slate, not even possessing a name. Her only connection is with her madam Li Zhenli—a relationship that neither contributes to her specific identity nor is even inviolable. Later on, we discover that their bond can be quite easily dissolved, as when Li Zhenli herself goes to join Tian Yang's household and loses touch with Li Xiangjun. Contrast their relationship with that between Lady Zhen and Du Liniang, which even death does nothing to dissolve. Knowing that Li Zhenli has taken the girl under her wing tells us nothing about who Xiangjun is, since Li Zhenli might have developed a similar bond with anyone.

Her lack of identity even has an impact on dramatic convention. Most characters in this and in other plays identify themselves when they appear onstage for the first time. For example, earlier in the same act, the heroine's mother in a few words economically reveals her name and her high status within the community of entertainers: "My surname is Li; I am called Zhenli; and I am of the fine division of the 'misty flowers' and in a famous troupe of the 'wind and the moon.'"[12] Or to choose another character, whose more conventional family background allows him to introduce himself as one does subjects in a standard biography, where one's place of origin follows on the heels of one's name as an identifying feature: "My last name is Hou; my personal name, Fangyu. My style is Chaozong, and I am from Guide County in Henan Province."[13]

One noteworthy feature about the characters in *Taohua shan* is how many of them cannot be introduced as conventionally as Hou Fangyu introduces himself, since they go by professional names. For example, Su Kunsheng, as Yang Wencong tells us, was born with the surname Zhou. But in the absence not only of a proper name such as Hou Fangyu's or even of a professional name such as Su Kunsheng's, our heroine cannot introduce herself in this fashion, since lacking any sort of a personal name when she first comes onstage she cannot really refer to herself. Her surname is no more her own, but rather passed on to her by an adoptive mother (whose own hold on it can be said to be tenuous).

The heroine's lack of a name has seemingly widespread consequences. Not only does she fail to identify herself in this act, but she also does not say anything on her own, instead volunteering as little as possible in response to the others' questions and singing only at Li Zhenli's urging, and then words written for Du Liniang. If she had indeed been brought up by Li Zhenli for a life as a courtesan, why does she at this late date require an explanation of how they make their living? Not having a name seems to leave her with no means of regarding herself and her own position, no subjectivity that can contextualize its own place in society.

She comes by her name in casual, almost accidental fashion. Her naming parallels the creation of the peach blossom fan, both arising out of Yang Wencong's paintings. In both cases, he is motivated by aestheticism and blithely unburdened by the significance of what he is about to do. Yang Wencong enters her quarters and sees the walls decorated with poems inscribed by some famous contemporary literati and proposes first to add a poem, using the rhymes of those by Zhang Pu and Xia Yunyi. At the last moment, he changes his mind, opting to paint an orchid instead, and only then does he discover a rock painted by Lan Ying by which he will place the orchid. Like the peach blossom fan, the painted orchid that inspires the name Xiangjun seems to arise in entirely serendipitous fashion.

Yang Wencong needs to know the girl's name so that he can dedicate the picture of the flower to her. To his question, she answers: "I am young and have no name."[14] In tellingly casual fashion, Li Zhenli asks Yang Wencong to name her adoptive daughter: "Won't you give her a name?"[15] Literally, she asks him for the "gift of two words," since most Chinese personal names consist of two characters, which underscores the casualness of this act—as if a name, like an object, might simply be broken down into its component parts. Yang Wencong agrees to the request, naming her after his own painted orchid and citing as allusion from the *Zuozhuan*: "The orchid is most fragrant in all the land; people love to adorn themselves with it."[16] But though the quotation is taken from a passage rich with significance about naming and kinship, the allusion seems almost irrelevant to this name—"Fragrant Lady" is after all a plain and unadorned name (the girl is known in some records by the extraordinarily bland name of Li Xiang).

Without giving it very much thought, Yang Wencong twice gives her something—her name and the fan—to define herself by. The transformation of bloodstains into blossoms arises out of a whim. Her name is arbitrary, inspired by an impromptu painting of a flower and attached to the surname of her madam. Since she is named after one painting of a flower (rather arbitrarily so), her hope later on that she may pin her identity on another painting of flowers (the peach blossoms painted of her own blood) strikes one both as seemingly circular—and consequently perhaps futile. For one thing, if she is named after one and then claims another embodies who she is, shouldn't some kind of transitive property between the two paintings hold? And yet it clearly doesn't: in no way does the orchid on the wall seem commensurate to the peach blossoms. The first is glib; the second, tragic.

By late imperial standards (and anyone who has done even a little work on the period knows just how many names one person might accumulate through a lifetime), Li Xiangjun possesses a meager scrap of a name. In fact, she still has no *ming*, a name to place within a family, nor a *zi*, a style she herself has chosen to express her own identity within an intellectual community. Late imperial people gave themselves and were given names for all sorts of reasons: to commemorate a Buddhist conversion, or a move into a new retreat, for example. Through Yang Wencong's efforts, she now has a *hao* with an obvious function; she is a prostitute about to go out onto the market, and Xiangjun will serve nicely as her stage name. The name Li Xiangjun fails to root her to any patriarchal bedrock. Nor does she herself choose it to emphasize some physical or temperamental characteristic. But for chance, she might have been named something else, or somebody else might have received the name (some other little girl acquired by Li Zhenli).

Later in the act, she will assume the role of Du Liniang as easily as she does her new name—which leads one to wonder who, if anyone fixed, lies under the role and the name. To answer that underneath the role of Du Liniang lies some discrete entity or unitary being called Li Xiangjun strikes us, under the circumstances, as rather inadequate, since we have just witnessed her take up her name.

Unfortunately for the Nanjing regime, Hongguang turns out to be just as inadequate a name as Xiangjun. Any prince selected would have been called Hongguang. As for his *ming*, the sort of name Li Xiangjun lacks entirely, he is never mentioned by it, even though it is the one name he holds exclusively. He is called only once the Prince of Dechang, the title he unequivocally holds and the only title that refers to this particular man and to him alone.

Instead, Zhu Yousong is usually referred to by names or titles with which he has at best an uncomfortable relationship, sometimes a name that refers to someone else in addition to him. If one took exception with Hongguang's very legitimacy, what would one call him? When he becomes a candidate for the imperial throne, he is repeatedly referred to as Prince Fu. However, the title is entirely new to him. Before the current insurrections, he was never called Prince Fu—a title he presumably was meant to inherit upon the death of his father. Yet in these times of turmoil, no investiture has taken place. Moreover, the title refers to the enormously wealthy fiefdom in Henan now occupied by enemy armies, whose fruits Zhu Yousong will never have the opportunity to enjoy. Strictly speaking, the prince elevated to the throne is Prince Dechang, though no one refers to him by the title (and perhaps the death of his father makes the title inappropriate). His many names all fit him imperfectly, like the imperial robes and crown that remain more of a costume than a signifier of the identity underneath.

Of course, Hongguang ought not be used to refer to the man, since Hongguang is actually his reign title, serving an entirely distinct function from a personal name, which is meant to place a person within the context of a family or distinguish one person from others. Since the Emperor does not need his name to distinguish him from other people, a reign title refers not to an individual, but to the time of his reign.[17]

And yet in speaking of the man, almost everyone in the play calls him Hongguang (to his face, he is usually referred to as "His Sageliness"). Except in this play and a few other historical texts, no one writing in the late seventeenth century refers to 1644 as the first year of Hongguang. All the name Hongguang does is to distinguish this particular Emperor from the others in contention at the time. Hongguang ends up serving as an inadequate name and an equally inadequate reign title.

Our playwright Kong Shangren himself had both professional and personal experience with genealogy. Keeping track of names and people within his clan was no trivial activity. All male descendants of Confucius were supposed to be named (and many still are) according to a genealogical order, so that all of the same generation share not only the same surname, but also one of the two characters in their personal names. A sixty-fourth generation descendant of Confucius, Kong Shangren had been put in charge of compiling a genealogy of the entire Kong clan—an enormous task not unlike putting together an official history (although not of a country, but of a family). Richard Strassberg explains that the genealogy included charts of the clan organization, a chronicle of Confucius's own ancestors, biographies of leading lights among the Kongs, and a list of how all living clan members were related.[18]

Kong Shangren's own relationship to his name and to his clan was exceptional in its very orthodoxy; of all Chinese clans, his is the most famous and the one where patrilineal descent has been most scrutinized and recorded meticulously—not just over the centuries, but over millennia. The ideal to which I have been referring—that a person might be knowable because he occupied a specific position within a specific patriline—was largely a fiction for most people. Go back just a few centuries, and most clan genealogies become shrouded with mists of uncertainty. Even for someone like Kong Shangren, such a lineage was laboriously constructed, maintained only through prodigious amounts of labor and well-placed leaps of faith. Nonetheless, he seems not only genuinely to have believed, but to have spent many years of his life on the faith that people—within his own patriline at least—could be organized within a genealogy.

Even to outsiders, our playwright's name and place of origin—Kong Shangren from Qufu—indicated a great deal of information: first and most importantly, that he was a descendant of the Sage himself, but also how many generations removed and to which cousins he was most closely related. In our own day, many educated Chinese can still identify the current head of the Kong household (who retains his ducal title and resides in Taiwan) and recognize descendants who have been named according to the genealogical order.

In other words, Kong Shangren's name itself roots him securely in an order, one among cousins, preceded by ancestors and to be followed by descendants. Possessing that name and proving ownership of it implied many material privileges, including exemption from corvée labor and some kinds of taxes. This kind of identity sets him apart from some of the most important figures in the play—like Liu Jingting and Li Xiangjun (and to some extent, Hongguang)—whose names are taken on later in life, and who lack roots in a clan or in a location like Qufu. Kong Shangren's work as the genealogist for the clan was to place all the Kongs with respect to each other, even if mistakes had been made before about their exact place within the family. The genealogical project is predicated on the idea that each person has a normative place within the clan and that finding that place allows us to know who that person really is.

Lacking such normative places within society and within a family, the identities of the entertainers and Hongguang seem more like theatrical roles; these characters either invent themselves or are invented, assuming and divesting themselves of roles at whim. In contrast, the playwright's own claim to his name was meticulously corroborated through many separate sources—it could not simply be made up. At this time of turmoil, when the identity of the Emperor was up for grabs, the head of the Kong clan remained secure in his identity.

The presence of people like the playwright and Hou Fangyu forms a necessary backdrop to the convergences between Li Xiangjun and Hongguang. If we are somehow to end up in a new dynasty, where "Sons are filial, ministers loyal, myriad affairs all just so," as the Old Ceremonial Assistant tells us at the beginning of the play, all identities cannot be as seemingly arbitrary as the experiences of Li Xiangjun and Hongguang suggest. Beneath the face paint and costumes, someone whose identity is fixed and determinable must exist who can be precisely positioned within the polity.

These uneasy relationships to their own names creates a resemblance between Hongguang and Li Xiangjun in ways that set them apart from people like Kong Shangren of Qufu or Hou Fangyu of Guide. The prostitute and the would-be Emperor regard their social roles as theatrical ones. Not only do the démimonde and this imperial court parallel each other, but they are also tied through complicated causal relationships.

Hongguang is fascinated by the theatre, surrounding himself with entertainers and playwrights like Ruan Dacheng and exerting most of his energies on a production of *Yanzi jian*. More importantly, though, the theatrical metaphor thoroughly permeates his court, as Yang Wencong's career shows. Act 17 begins with his gloating over his new position in the Ministry of Rites, bequeathed to him by Ma Shiying and Ruan Dacheng. We know that Yang Wencong has curried Ma and Ruan's favor partly by setting up Hou Fangyu's match with Li Xiangjun. Later on, he means to arrange a match between Li Xiangjun and a colleague of his, Tian Yang, also the recent recipient of an office. So the giving and receiving of prostitutes strengthens ties between officials; eventually Yang Wencong parlays his ability to bridge these two worlds into a position as Minister of Rites. In that position, he actually has administrative control over these very prostitutes; professional entertainers were under the supervision of the Bureau of Instruction, which was under the Board of Rites. When Li Xiangjun refuses the match with Tian Yang, another entertainer points out his complicated interests: "Now that Master Yang is at the Board of Rites, he's in charge even of you 'officials.' He could have you taken in tomorrow and your fingers pressed!"[19]

After being sent off on an errand, one of Yang Wencong's underlings insists that he is unable to find the brothel where Li Xiangjun resides, explaining that this is not his usual beat. His reluctance we see not as upright, but as self-righteous and self-deluding: "I only recognize each of the officials' residences; those johns and whores I have no way of finding."[20] The musicians, who recognize the artificiality of such a distinction, respond immediately with a mocking riposte: "In the brothels, often old court ministers remain; and at the imperial court great courtesans are newly given engagement presents."[21] In other words, prostitutes and officials mingle in both settings. Neither world—that of government or that of pretense and fantasy—can claim to be the real one, as the message runner would like to think. One of

Yang Wencong's employees, he too owes his employment to the brothels he scorns.

The politics of *Taohua shan* converges with the theatre—a space, as I have said, where things both are and aren't, where people can simultaneously be themselves and somebody entirely different. Both in politics and onstage, people do not say what they mean, and what they say cannot be taken at face value. As previously suggested, there is an obvious political dimension to the question of whether there is any necessary relationship between what a person does and what he believes. But there is a theatrical aspect to that question, too, which I have already proposed the play poses with regard to Li Xiangjun and Hongguang: can anybody play any role? One might ask essentially the same question from another perspective: does it matter what an actor really believes and who he really is?

Some actors claim to be impersonators; others, that they express complex truths through performance. One way the hybrid history of the English language expresses this problem is in the contrast between two words that both have their sources in the theatre: *hypocrite*—from the Greek *hypokrites*, meaning actor—and *persona* (or *per sona*)—from the Latin, which possibly refers to the mask an actor used to speak through. Is an actor nothing more than a liar, as the Greek suggests? Or does he speak through his role, as the Latin suggests? How can we tell the difference between the role and a person underneath? And assuming we could tell the difference, which should we find more credible—the role or the person underneath?

While some philosophers working on the problem of personal identity have used science fiction and other fantastical narratives as a starting point, others have taken up examples from psychopathology. According to some experts on Multiple Personality Disorder (MPD), one human body might be occupied by many separate and independent persons. The debate continues as to whether MPD even exists, and if it does, whether the aim of treatment should be integrating the various personalities or allowing one finally to triumph over the others.

One school of skeptical experts compares MPD to acting, regarding patients as playactors and not as the site of an involuntary battle among true, independent personalities. One school of acting compares itself to MPD, practically a pathology with one self warring against another—as if the young actress Shang Xiaoling can be seen to have been possessed and eventually killed by some Du Liniang from within herself. This version is practically a trope, especially in film. For example, *A Double Life* (1947) makes this point, equating inspired acting with a psychological problem: after a mild-mannered actor takes on the role of Othello, the role takes on a life of its own. Flying into jealous passions, he begins to threaten his ex-wife, who cannot believe this is the gentle man she has known for years.

And certainly, when Constantin Stanislavski, best known for training actors according to the Method, discusses how the actor should inhabit a role, his comments make an actor sound like a cross between someone possessed by spirits and a compulsive confidence man. For the actor is no mere impersonator, but changed by the very process of acting:

> Just think: You prepare with logic and consistency a simple, accessible line for the physical being of your role, and as a result you suddenly feel inside yourself the life of a human spirit. To find in yourself the same kind of human material as the author took from life, from the human nature of other people, when he wrote your part—isn't that a wonderful piece of conjuring![22]

This actor and teacher of actors in his description of the craft evokes spirit possession, but it isn't clear whether the actor is the one possessed, seized by the role, or whether instead she is the spirit possessing "the human nature of other people." The magic of which Stanislavski writes rests on a frightening fluidity of personhood—that one person might inhabit other people's bodies, that we cannot tell who is doing the inhabiting and who being inhabited. Such a version of acting seems incompatible with any belief in the possibility of discrete and fixed individuals.

The acting profession contains the seeds of a threat. On some level, all of the craft's practitioners, both amateur and professional, are essentially impersonators; and because of their filiation with prostitution, the professionals have only an uneasy place in a society so invested in patrilines. Since prostitutes are those without fathers and husbands—or more properly, those to whom all men might be father or husband—they have something in common with actors, who pretend to be many different people: both groups are frightening, because it is impossible to tell who they really are—they might be anyone. *Wei gongzi* ("Young Gentleman Wei") from *Liaozhai zhiyi*, Pu Songling's Qing collection of stories, suggests at least one reason prostitutes are so troublesome to the fabric of society. After years spent sporting with prostitutes, Wei discovers that one of his liaisons is actually his own daughter, illegitimately begotten of another prostitute a generation earlier.[23] After a lifetime of debauchery, the improbable event is not that he has accidentally engaged in sexual relations with his own daughter, but that he actually managed to find out her identity. With prostitutes, the possibility of such incestuous liaisons is omnipresent. Each new customer might be a father, or a brother, or a cousin, or a son.

If it is so hard for others to figure out who actors really are, either in contradistinction to the roles they play or within a society where so much depends on one's family, then how do they themselves lay claim to a single, fixed identity? The actors in the play face considerable difficulty in defining themselves, and yet, to a man and a woman, they insist that they can—first, that it is easy to distinguish the person inside from the role (much as such an assertion denigrates their craft), and second, that a person who performs the role both exists and matters.

All share an ardent faith in sincerity, a conviction approached in different ways. Su Kunsheng, Li Xiangjun's singing master, makes it clear to his pupil that acting is simply a matter of proper technique, that a person and a role bear no stronger relation of identity than any other craftsman does to his work. If one school of Chinese literary criticism seeks to conflate a writer and his writing, Su Kunsheng would argue that acting less resembles writing than it does wheel making or pottery. Li Zhenli urges the reluctant Li Xiangjun to show off her singing skills to Yang Wencong so that he will make a match for her. Still a complete innocent in the ways of the world, the girl runs through the part of Du Liniang, in a longing reminiscence about her excursion in the garden, excerpted from a scene that more than perhaps any other in Chinese drama has become associated with passion.

By the late seventeenth century, Du Liniang had become much more than just another dramatic role. Her love for the young man met in her dream and her willingness to die for that love made her someone with whom other young girls and women identified powerfully. They compared their own lives to hers, casting themselves in her part. First among these, Xiaoqing, mentioned in the earlier discussion of *Mudan ting*, is perhaps the most famous example, but scores of young poetesses had the same relationship to Du Liniang, too, among them Ye Xiaoluan, a young girl of literatus background who wrote a number of poems about Du Liniang and died tragically young.[24] And we recall Shang Xiaoling, famous for dying onstage midperformance, having entirely embodied the role of Du Liniang.

In this cultural context, then—and especially the marked contrast to Shang Xiaoling's experience of the role—we return to Li Xiangjun's singing lesson, where any desire she might have to compare herself to Du Liniang is quickly quashed by her mother and her teacher. Li Xiangjun initially does not want to sing for Yang Wencong (this is the only time this professional entertainer will perform on command). She frowns, but more out of petulance than principle: "But there is a guest here; how can I practice my singing?"[25]

The mother responds with an interpretation of performance as purely instrumental, focused solely on making money for survival. Singing exists as a means to an end. In taking this position, Li Zhenli shares with Zheng Tuoniang a lack of interest in acting in itself and an equating of it with prostitution. Li Zhenli repeatedly describes singing as an item in an exchange, making it clear that it is a bodily act to be sold for profit. She dismisses Li Xiangjun's reluctance to perform in front of Yang Wencong: "Nonsense! For people of our caste, our sleeves for dancing and skirts for singing are like our storehouses of grain."[26] And then again, in the next aria, singing figures in another conversion—this one even more evidently close to prostitution—where a body part actually morphs into currency: "This tuneful throat strung together is our source of money!"[27]

The measure word Li Zhenli uses for throat (which I have chosen to render as "strung together") is *chuan*, referring to any string of things, like a neck as here, but most frequently in late imperial China referring to one of the commonest forms of currency, coins strung together, with the value of a thousand coins or a single silver tael. Li Zhenli suggests a perfect conversion of flesh into money, a pretty throat somehow the same as a string of cash and as a source of many more strings of cash. This version of singing is literally a trade in flesh.

If society is to be organized around families headed by patriarchs and divided among scholars, farmers, craftsmen, and merchants, how do entertainers (who are not craftsmen in that they do not make anything) fit in? Li Zhenli's admonishments to her daughter about their position as entertainers suggests a heterodox answer. She repeatedly intimates a connection between their work and that of farmers. First, their "sleeves for dancing and skirts for singing" are literally "storehouses of grain," *zhuangtun*. And then again in the next equivalence, the association with agriculture is repeated; what I have translated as "source of money" (*jinqian di*) might more literally be rendered "ground for wealth," as if money is to be found directly in the earth—the source of agricultural wealth.

In short, in a few quick strokes, Li Zhenli makes it sound as if prostitutes and actors have more in common with farmers than with anyone else. She implicitly elevates prostitutes and actors from practitioners of a profession (one even approaching an inherited caste) that does not figure in traditional formulations—since it might be purged from society with no ill effects—to one on a par with farmers, the very bedrock of society. Practitioners of both occupations, she suggests, are somehow primary: both make a living from natural process, and unlike artisans or merchants, who ultimately rely on agricultural production, neither has to consume other goods in order to produce.

The other professional entertainer present at the lesson, the tutor Su Kunsheng, is just as adamant as Li Zhenli about separating the craft of singing from anything individual about the singer, so that singing does not reflect anything internal about the singer. Yet unlike Li Zhenli, he remains interested in acting as an end unto itself. He does not sing (or teach singing) simply to make a living, or rather, other ways of making the same living would not adequately substitute for it, as they would for Li Zhenli. Viewing singing as merely a craft that does not reflect on the moral character of its practitioner does not stop him from finding the details of the craft fascinating and significant in and of themselves.

Like the girl's mother, Su Kunsheng doesn't allow his pupil for a minute actually to identify with Du Liniang as untold numbers of other teenage girls did. *Taohua shan* so repeatedly invokes *Mudan ting*, especially with the two heroines each with her own portrait, that Li Xiangjun's singing of Du Liniang's words right at the moment when passion has been born seems potentially weighty. After all, *Taohua shan* is the story of a prostitute who thinks she is Du Liniang and that she too can at once enjoy passion and maintain propriety.

Su Kunsheng's instructions allow her no room for such an interpretation. Instead, he focuses exclusively on craft. The teacher does not teach like Stanislavski—nothing here on projecting emotion or delving into the subtleties of Du Liniang's feelings (theories of acting practiced by Li Xiangjun's contemporaries, like Shang Xiaoling). Instead, he keeps interrupting with a running commentary on technical details. First he corrects: "No, that's wrong. 'Beauty' takes one beat; 'how' another. Don't blur them together. Do it again."[28] He waits for her to sing again, only to stop her again at another point to interject more instructions: "No, that's not it either. The word 'silken' is the focal point of the line; you have to sing it from your diaphragm."[29]

But perhaps drawing some kind of equivalence is inevitable between these two *dan*—both sixteen-year-old ingénues, one about to experience love for the first time, and the other, singing right after the erotic dream whose memory will soon kill her. The power of *Mudan ting*'s Du Liniang is such that perhaps the mere presence of Su Kunsheng's comments cannot defuse it. But is Li Xiangjun the only one singing during the lesson? The play offers ambiguous stage directions: "The *jing* and the *dan* sit facing each other and sing."[30] And there is no indication before the sung parts of who is doing the singing, whether it is the *jing* or the *dan*. Su Kunsheng urges her to begin her lesson: "While Master Yang is sitting here, follow my cue and let's run through it, so that we can ask him for pointers."[31] Who exactly in this setting is responsible for the singing—the teacher offering instructions or the student responding to commands?

The scene could be staged so as to confound any equivalence between singer and role, with Su Kunsheng not only interrupting, but actually joining in on the singing with Li Xiangjun. Su Kunsheng, a grown man, a professional opera singer and a dabbler in politics, has absolutely nothing in common with Du Liniang. Yet he sings the part with authority, better than his pupil, who so resembles Du Liniang, another sixteen-year-old girl, also new to love, also willing to stake everything on her feelings, with no regard for the consequences.

Su Kunsheng will make this point even more clearly later on: acting is a challenging craft worth learning well but in no way different from any other, like carpentry or lacquerwork. It reflects on the proficiency of its practitioner, but not on who he is inside—either his beliefs or the substance of his character. Of course, this version of acting's relationship to its practitioner relies upon the possibility of differentiating both the external from the internal and the extrinsic from the intrinsic.

The great singer Su Kunsheng has only taken on this student because he has resigned from his former post, along with Liu Jingting, as one of Ruan Dacheng's private musicians. He will not serve a master whose politics he disdains, no matter how great the rewards. Ruan Dacheng, a member of Wei Zhongxian's clique, has even become a godson of the eunuch (an act that strikes bystanders as more egregious by far than anything else he has done). Su Kunsheng introduces himself before the lesson (not without a touch of sour grapes): "Ever since I left Ruan's establishment, I have joined up with this brothel. Isn't providing tutelage for this beauty better than being the protégé of that godson?"[32] Later on in the play, Su Kunsheng will enthusiastically embark on a series of events he knows will bring down Ruan Dacheng and Ma Shiying's government.

But as a craftsman, Su Kunsheng still continues to miss his former employer, even when as a political being he slanders Ruan Dacheng and plots his downfall. As we know, Ruan Dacheng is a fellow artist and afficionado, an important playwright, and even after Liu Jingting and Su Kunsheng's defection, patron of one of the best troupes in Nanjing. Ruan Dacheng tries to buy the friendship of other literati by lending out his own troupe to perform his play. Su Kunsheng plans to convince Zuo Liangyu to move his armies on Nanjing, and as he attracts Zuo Liangyu's attention by singing, he remarks regretfully to himself: "Such a good song, and other than Ruan Dacheng, there is no one to appreciate it. Enough! I'd rather be buried in floating dust than throw my lot in with that type of bandit."[33]

Such a comment cannot fail to invoke the very model of friendship in classical Chinese—those two friends of antiquity, Bo Ya and Zhong Ziqi, another musician and avid music lover. Zhong Ziqi's appreciation of his friend's playing gave rise to the term "knower of the tone," *zhiyin*, which expresses the very height of what friendship can be. When Bo Ya played the lute, Zhong Ziqi knew exactly what his friend was expressing with his music—whether lofty mountains or overflowing waters—so that at Zhong Ziqi's death, Bo Ya put his lute away forever. After the only one who truly understood him and his music had died, there was no point in playing to less understanding audiences.

Su Kunsheng might almost be speaking for Bo Ya at Zhong Ziqi's death: "Such a good song, and other than Ruan Dacheng, there is no one to appreciate it." And yet there is one critical difference between Bo Ya and Su Kunsheng: Bo Ya and Zhong Ziqi were a unit, never invoked except together. Zhong Ziqi is just as important to the creating of music as Bo Ya, since after his death there is no point to playing anymore. Finally, one feels that the craft that they shared in common implied much about what they *were*. The music is primarily a means for friendship to be expressed, for these two greatest of friends to prove their shared essence. One can hardly imagine Bo Ya and Zhong Ziqi breaking off relations over a question of political allegiance. Su Kunsheng's version of the privileged listener is someone he otherwise disdains and whose downfall he works towards, as if singing no more expresses whatever is crucial to himself than any other craft would.

Su Kunsheng has a vision of his craft in which opera singing and play-acting are extrinsic to a person's true nature. He himself is not a sixteen-year-old girl, and yet he can teach a sixteen-year-old girl how the part of someone much more like her than himself ought to be sung. According to Su Kunsheng, his political beliefs—his support of the Revival Society and opposition to Wei Zhongxian—are what define him.

His self-identification needs to be grounded on a profound faith that the distinction—between the interior and exterior—can be sustained. But his political career makes us question that faith. To what extent does behavior reflect either compliance or rebellion? By persuading Zuo Liangyu to move his troops, Su Kunsheng, who repeatedly avows sincere loyalty to the Ming dynasty, probably actually does more than any other character in the play—and certainly more than the vilified Ma Shiying and Ruan Dacheng—to bring the dynasty down.

So is he truly loyal? To what extent do the motivations behind his actions matter when their results prove so monumentally disastrous? Or to move that question back to the stage, what allows him to classify his singing "external" and his protestations of loyalty "internal"? For there is no particular reason to regard his singing as performance and his political protestations as sincere. There is no way to establish one as merely going through motions when we only know his internal state through his behavior. Perhaps the internal state is as much a performance as the external one. In his own way, even though he is one of the great actors of the day, Su Kunsheng turns out to be a Confucian moralist distrustful of the theatre. By basing his theory of performance on the idea that a person has an inside and outside and that both can fully be known, Su Kunsheng is bent on nullifying the power of the theatre.

Before they are first introduced, Hou Fangyu is informed that the famous storyteller Liu Jingting led the walkout from Ruan Dacheng's service when he found out that Ruan Dacheng served the eunuch Wei Zhongxian. Hou Fangyu and two of his friends visit Liu Jingting and are treated to a performance about ancient musicians who under the influence of Confucius leave their own unworthy patrons. The story he tells is really, of course, his own veiled autobiography. The story's significance is explained to Hou Fangyu, who sighs admiringly: "I see that Jingting is of such high, peerless character, his bosom so free and easy, that he truly is one of us, and storytelling is just an additional skill of his."[36] In other words, Hou Fangyu would like to adopt Su Kunsheng's paradigm of the performing artist. He prefers to think of his new friend as just a plain person who happens to be a storyteller, whose profession is basically incidental to who he really is—someone like Hou Fangyu himself.

Liu Jingting has a decidedly different vision of his relationship to his craft. Of course, he is a storyteller and not a singer performing specific roles; but nonetheless, if he were Li Xiangjun's teacher, one suspects he would not be so diligent as Li Zhenli and Su Kunsheng are at preventing her from identifying with the role of Du Liniang. When Hou Fangyu surprises Liu Jingting at home, he finds Liu Jingting telling stories even though there seems to be no audience (except for the unacknowledged one watching offstage). Hou Fangyu chuckles at him, for who ever heard of something so ridiculous as a storyteller telling himself stories? Just imagine Li Zhenli's response if she had caught Li Xiangjun singing to herself; what a waste of effort, she would say, to sing if no one is paying. But Liu Jingting quickly rebukes him: "This storytelling is my vocation; it's just like when you are sitting in your study, you might strum on a lute or chant a poem—do you need someone to be listening?"[35]

I have chosen "vocation" to translate Liu Jingting's characterization of storytelling. But no single English word is adequate to the challenges presented by the term *benye*. Like Li Zhenli's *zhuangtun*, "storehouses of grain," and *jinqian di*, "ground for wealth," *benye* also suggests agricultural pursuits. These intimations of the agricultural are important, since at heart the question is where entertainers fit in a world mostly consisting of *liangmin*, the commoners who are largely farm workers. Referring to society as a whole, *benye* alludes to the single pursuit—the "root occupation," literally—indispensable to the survival of the group, agriculture. *Moye*, by contrast—the "branch occupations"—live off agricultural production and include artisans and tradesmen, who are engaged either in secondary production, as in the case of the artisans, or in no production at all, as in the case of the merchants. Of the four traditional occupations, this schema omits one, the scholars (*shi*), or those who would be contrasting these two categories, *benye* and *moye*, in the first place.

What then does *benye* mean when applied to an individual and not society? Liu Jingting suggests that his talents are intrinsic to and inextricable from the self. Storytelling to him is like agriculture to society, in that there is no way to conceive of himself without it and in that no other means of making a living can be substituted for it. In short, he appropriates for himself the very claim Confucian scholars have long made about their own contributions to society. While others—artisans, farmers, merchants—*do* something, scholars, by their nature, *are* something. Their contribution is themselves, which is why when they chant poems or play the lute, it isn't for anyone else's entertainment, but instead to communicate their own nature.

He also subverts the usual privileging of the written over the spoken. According to Liu Jingting, the written word—the purview of the Confucian—cannot compare with the storyteller's story. Hou Fangyu is forced to flee Nanjing and part from Li Xiangjun after he forges a letter in his father's name to General Zuo Liangyu. But after the letter is written, there still remains the crucial step of delivering it to Zuo Liangyu. Gently prodded by Hou Fangyu and Yang Wencong, Liu Jingting volunteers; however, he makes it clear that his role is not secondary, but indispensable. He sings:

> I don't need to explain carefully the meaning of the letter. Why should I clear things up and waste the labor of my lips and cheeks? Even if I went empty handed, it would be just the same, and I would seize the opportunity. Just relying on the sharpness of my tongue, I could drive back his troops and cavalry and push them back eight hundred *li*.[36]

Hou Fangyu would have it that Liu Jingting is just like a literatus, only somehow lesser, since he lacks family and learning. In contrast, Liu Jingting regards himself as something more than a literatus like Hou Fangyu, who feebly has to depend on the written word, which can always be separated from its author. With Liu Jingting the storyteller, the message can never simply be detached from the messenger.

When Liu Jingting compares his own abilities with those of Hou Fangyu, he suggests that it is Hou's skills—and not his own—that are simply a craft that anyone could master (in other words, his theory of literature closely resembles Su Kunsheng's on opera singing). Liu's case is strengthened by the circumstances: since the letter in question is a deliberate forgery, it really could have been written by anybody. Hou Fangyu certainly hopes that no one will be able to discern its author from reading it. According to Liu's line of reasoning, his own skills of persuasion are unique to himself. While anyone might have been able to write the letter, only one man can deliver it. The written word, Liu Jingting argues, detaches the writer from what is written, as if the writer were simply a craftsman, like the maker of wheels or pots. In contrast, no such separation can ever be made between a storyteller and his stories—his stories are consubstantial with himself in a way that the writer can only regard with envy.

Hou Fangyu does not agree with Liu Jingting's evaluation of storytelling. According to Hou Fangyu, spoken words function as mere commentary: "We'll succeed if you take what's said in the letter and explain it."[37] After Liu Jingting leaves, Hou Fangyu needs to dismiss his friend's abilities once again in a backhanded compliment: "I often praise him as being one of us; storytelling is just an extrinsic skill."[38] Hou refers to Liu's skill in storytelling as *yuji*—literally an extra skill, somehow detachable from the person, where what would be left would be simply a plain person (compare this to Hongguang's version of personhood, where the role of Emperor can likewise simply be divested). Nothing could be further from Liu's own description of storytelling as *benye*, according to which storytelling is absolutely central to and inseparable from Liu Jingting, superior to all other abilities in that it rises from himself.

Moreover, by calling storytelling a mere *yuji*, Hou Fangyu implies what can only be regarded as an insulting equivalence between their two contributions: bearing the letter to a general at the head of a potentially hostile army, Liu has generously offered to risk his life by venturing behind lines, while Hou himself has spent a few minutes writing a letter for which he does not even bear responsibility, since it is in his father's name (after all, he does not yet know that there will be any political repercussions to his actions). Hou Fangyu has condescendingly admitted Liu Jingting to his own company; by sharing the same political beliefs, Liu Jingting has become, as Hou Fangyu puts it, *wobei*, "one of us" or "our sort." If their contributions are commensurate, what Hou Fangyu has to contribute has much more to do with skill and education, whereas Liu Jingting has only his body to sacrifice. In other words, storytelling (and storytellers) cannot be worth much.

Even more of an affront, though, is that Hou Fangyu's comparison deliberately misrepresents Liu Jingting's own attitude towards his storytelling—and at a moment when Liu has just exited the stage and cannot defend himself. Liu himself has made grandiose claims about the importance of storytelling and boasted that the success of their enterprise rests on his own services (an assertion which turns out to be accurate) and that the letter is entirely irrelevant: "Just relying on the sharpness of my tongue, I could drive back his troops and cavalry and push them back eight hundred *li*."

Storytelling is intrinsic to his person, Liu repeats again and again; try as Hou Fangyu might, there is no way of separating the identity of the man from his craft. When Liu Jingting introduces himself to the audience, he first makes it clear that he fits into society in no conventional fashion, by revealing not his home and family name, but instead his profession. The name Liu Jingting does not mark membership in a family, but identifies him as a renowned storyteller: "I am Liu Jingting. Since youth I have had no steady residence but wander among the rivers and lakes. Though I am a storyteller, I am not simply someone who does this merely to eat and drink."[39]

He tells us first that unlike Kong Shangren, say, or Hou Fangyu, he has no established place of residence; the next most salient fact about himself is that he does not sing solely for the sake of earning a living. In attempting to demarcate the internal from the external, Su Kunsheng finds himself in the contradictory position of having to act out the internal. There is a problem at the heart of Liu Jingting's assertions about identity, too: he is, he insists repeatedly, in his essence a storyteller, and not someone who just happens to tell stories to make a living. Ultimately the claims he makes about his own essence are tautologies: he is nothing but a storyteller, and a storyteller is what he is. He defines himself not against other people, but against the backdrop only of himself. In the new order, such an artist can only become a hermit.

Of course, compared to Li Xiangjun, Liu Jingting has it easy. Especially after they have become famous, storytellers may choose their stories, selecting ones with appropriate morals or other qualities—as did the historical Liu Jingting. Among his descriptions of noteworthy people, places, and events of the bygone dynasty, Zhang Dai includes one of the real-life Liu Jingting's repertoire: Wu Song's fight with the tiger, a vigorous, manly narrative for a vigorous, manly storyteller.[40]

Unlike storytellers, however, actors, even if by great good luck they can choose which roles they are to play, surely cannot expect to identify perfectly with each one of them, unless their identities are infinitely fungible, malleable, and polymorphous—or unless their identities simply do not matter. One suspects that Su Kunsheng—who denies any kind of equivalence with the roles he plays—would sing any role given to him, pouring into it his wealth of experience and craft. An actor like Li Zhenli would never aspire to a single true portrait like the fan, but rather would supply each client different ones for every occasion—each in costume, whatever the client preferred. But asked for a self-portrait, Liu Jingting would appear in the humble garb of a storyteller, while Su Kunsheng would choose that of a literatus (all the while suffering the niggling suspicion that ultimately that garb itself is just another costume).

Their attitudes about money further reflect these differences on acting. Su Kunsheng has no qualms about making a living off his craft; that was not the reason behind his leaving Ruan's employ, and we presume Li Zhenli compensates him for Xiangjun's lessons. Li Zhenli and Zheng Tuoniang act for the sole purpose of earning money. Liu Jingting insists that he simply happens to make a living from his performances. But Li Xiangjun takes it a step further; remuneration does not even seem to figure in her version of performance.

If one is paid to perform, as I have said, one cannot always, as Li Xiangjun desires, draw perfect equivalences between oneself and the roles one plays. For her, playacting, where there is a fixed difference between the role and the actor, is the same as lying. The second time Li Xiangjun sings from *Mudan ting*, she is not passively obedient, but stubbornly defiant.

Forcibly brought out of seclusion, she and the other actresses are paraded before Hongguang. Each in turn is asked whether she is familiar with *Yanzi jian*; Li Xiangjun denies knowing anything about that piece of romantic fluff, so she chooses for her own audition an act from *Mudan ting*, "Seeking the Dream," an aria that directly applies to her own situation, lamenting the helplessness of flowers and of young girls, who suffer seemingly in vain.

Others try to force Li Xiangjun into roles she has no intention of playing, but even when she can choose her own roles, equating oneself to a dramatic role is no simple matter. As she prepares to confront Ruan Dacheng and Ma Shiying, she comforts herself with this thought: "When Zhao Wenhua flattered Yan Song, he painted his face and sat at the front of the reed mat in his eagerness to please. With ugly songs and nasty postures, I'll act out a real 'Calling Phoenix.' I'll be a female Mi Heng, and when I play the Yuyang drum song, with each sound execrating my enemies, let's see if they understand."[41]

Li Xiangjun makes two allusions here, the first to the play *Mingfeng ji*, *The Record of the Calling Phoenix*, a historical play about events a century earlier than those of our play. Contrasting herself with the obsequious Zhao Wenhua, who curried the favor of Yan Song (a villain because he earlier seized various powers from the Emperor), she compares herself with the honest official Yang Jisheng, who publicly charges Yan Song with crimes and corruption and is later put to death for his affrontery. The second allusion refers to events more than a thousand years earlier; Mi Heng was a scholar and writer humiliated by Cao Cao, the powerful figure from the end of the Han dynasty whose son would found the short-lived kingdom of Wei. Cao Cao forced Mi Heng to be a drummer at his banquets, but Mi Heng contrived to avenge himself through his music.

For a girl who so prides herself on sincerity and authenticity, even the most passionate and spontaneous action is curiously mediated by multiple layers of performance. When she confronts Ruan Dacheng and Ma Shiying, she will be giving them a piece of her mind—only that will involve playing Yang Jisheng's role. But since she will be denouncing real-life officials and it will be an offstage performance, she will be starring as she says in a "real 'Calling Phoenix.'" Maintaining her belief in the stage as false, while at the same time evoking dramatic roles she can play, she is drawn inextricably into a paradox—her own life is the "real 'Calling Phoenix'" and the play itself (which since it is the original ought arguably by definition to be the real version) is the false "Calling Phoenix."

The second allusion introduces its own problems. In facing Ruan

Dacheng and Ma Shiying, Li Xiangjun will also be playing the role of Mi Heng, a real-life scholar humiliated by being forced to play the role of someone he is not—a musician. Li Xiangjun will be an actress playing an official, who himself plays an entertainer. Refusing to be caught up in any false role-playing does not make things any less complicated for a person who sees all reality in theatrical terms.

Who is the Zhao Wenhua to whom Li Xiangjun refers, the creature in the face paint sitting at the front of his mat? Ma Shiying is clearly Yan Song; each is a corrupt official with special access and control over his Emperor. If Yan Song corresponds to Ma Shiying, and Yan Song's lackey is Zhao Wenhua, then clearly Ruan Dacheng is Zhao Wenhua, who "painted his face and sat at the front of the reed mat in his eagerness to please." But of course the face paint here is metaphorical, suggesting that acting itself is dissimulation. The true actor, Li Xiangjun wants to argue, is not herself, the person really wearing face paint, but instead Ruan Dacheng—not an actor at all, but just a garden variety liar and flatterer. According to this metaphor, real face paint—representing attempts to deceive and dissimulate—isn't even actually there, while the actual face paint worn by Li Xiangjun isn't real, since she does not attempt to deceive.

These then are some of the stakes when an actress conceives of playacting as containing the possibility for privileged truth telling. For Li Xiangjun, to be indignant is not simply to be an indignant Li Xiangjun, but instead to play Mi Heng or Yang Jisheng. And if one's identity is, as Li Xiangjun argues it is, some inviolable core that can be fixed, then penetrating beneath the layers of playacting to a sincere interior that exclusively represents Li Xiangjun takes us through layers and layers of role-playing. Small wonder, then, that her portrait—the fan depicting that fixed identity—cannot show a face lest it be accused of being mere face paint.

Acting and the effort to stake out uniqueness can come into conflict: actors earn fame for their ability to lose their own identities. They earn fame, in other words, for their ability to impersonate, but even more for their claim to lose themselves within their roles, if in a distinctive way. Many contemporary actors, for example, not only have disfigured their very bodies—some by gaining or losing tremendous amounts of weight for different roles, for example—but have also claimed to submerge their identities in more fundamental ways, boasting that afterwards it took them weeks, even months, to find "themselves" again, while the character given rein offstage has wreaked havoc with their own lives.

In a short prose piece, the real Hou Fangyu wrote about the rivalry of two actors who each specialized in the same role—that of the corrupt official Yan Song (the villain whom Li Xiangjun elliptically compares to Ma Shiying). The two actors set up a competition in which two performances of *Mingfeng ji* take place simultaneously, one featuring an actor named Ma in the role of Yan Song and the other with an actor named Li in the same role. The actors use the reactions of the audience to judge, and when it is obvious that the audience is directing its full attention only to Li's performance, Ma slinks off the stage in humiliation and disappears for three years, only to return and challenge Li to a rematch.

This time, surprisingly, Ma is victorious; the audience applauds his performance and not Li's. Afterwards, the actors from the other troupe ask Ma how he was able to triumph. Ma explains:

> Naturally, there was no way to replace (*yi*) Li, and he also refused to teach me. But I heard that Prime Minister Gu Bingqian is a match (*chou*) for Minister Yan. So I went to the capital and became his doorman for three years. Every day I served him in the court waiting room; I examined his behavior, and I listened to his speech. After a while, I got it, and that was what served to teach me![42]

Acting is indeed technique, as Su Kunsheng says, something that can be learned from another actor, but it is also imitation, since Ma ultimately prevails by imitating not another actor, but an official like Yan Song himself.

Much is staked on the idea of people possessing a certain kind of uniqueness—finding out the single greatest actor is the point of the competition. And yet for individuals with such name recognition, they seem remarkably able to substitute for each other. Ma's first strategy to achieve victory is to exchange himself for Li. Only when that fails does he pursue a real-life person Gu Bingqian, who is a perfect cipher (another translation of *chou*) for Minister Yan; and all of these substitutions have been accomplished in pursuit of celebrity, based at least partly on the notion of individual singularity. In both cases, the loser slips offstage unnoticed, as if once one has been proven superior, then the other has been rendered unnecessary.

So far I have been discussing characters who are professionals in role-playing. But in the sort of political culture I have been describing, officials as well as professional entertainers have strong opinions on this very same question: namely, whether there is any necessary relationship between an actor and his actions. And the officials are just as helpless when it comes to demarcating what is onstage from what is offstage. In most plays, someone who insulted two of the most highly placed officials at the court—to their faces, no less—would be executed. Instead, Ma Shiying and Ruan Dacheng subject Li Xiangjun to a virtual death, casting her as a clown. A few lines later in the same act, Ruan Dacheng discusses the relationship between an actor and his role.

The gathering Li Xiangjun interrupts has been arranged carefully by Ruan Dacheng for the express purpose of currying Ma Shiying's favor. He admires the arrangements for the party, telling his hosts Yang Wencong and Ruan Dacheng that the party's simplicity marks their good taste. Ruan Dacheng responds: "Today I'll sweep the snow and boil some tea, and we'll have some pure conversation, which will manifest your lofty-mindedness and refinement, and we too on our part will skip a few strokes of face paint."[43] He means that he and Yang Wencong will act more spontaneously with Ma Shiying than is their wont, but once again this lack of face paint points to a paradox. For Ma Shiying speaks first, telling us that he prefers lack of adornment; Ruan Dacheng and Yang Wencong have removed their face paint, so to speak, for no other reason than better to please him. The face paint suggests straightaway the question all of Ruan Dacheng's musings on the theatre end with—whether anything in fact lies beneath the paint, and whether the face without the paint is any truer than the painted one.

In the same vein, Ruan Dacheng takes a peculiar tack in flattering Ma Shiying: "You, sir, do not like flattery; it's just that I truly respect you."[44] What room is there under such conditions for the truth ever to be known? If a statement pleasing to the listener is made, then it lacks credibility since it looks like mere flattery; but might not an insult be also flattery, of the listener's insusceptibility to flattery? The next chapter will explore the ways in which the case of the putative Crown Prince suggests some of these problems. Perhaps there is no action that cannot be considered a performance.

The metaphor of the face paint leads the three into a discussion about the theatre, whose power Ma Shiying fears because it convinces people so thoroughly of its version of the truth: "My, that face paint is so powerful! Once it's on your face, you can never wash it off, and even a filial son or a loving grandson will refuse to recognize you."[45] Ma Shiying attributes to the theatre what others attribute to the decline of society. So much of this play concerns the circumstances under which the ties of the family and of the polity can be broken. Under what circumstances will someone refuse to recognize his

Emperor? What will make Li Xiangjun give up the idea that Hou Fangyu is her husband? Is the relationship between Li Zhenli and Li Xiangjun as indissoluble as that between a real mother and child? Here the power of the theatre is explicitly connected to the polity's breakdown, to the notion that the stage can so malign—or disguise—a person that his own sons will choose not to recognize him. An exact counterpart to the sort of slander that makes people deny their own fathers is the flattery that would lead Ruan Dacheng to become the godson of a eunuch.

The discussion turns coincidentally to *Mingfeng ji*, *The Calling Phoenix*, the same play Li Xiangjun imagines herself in, in the part of Yang Jisheng as he attacks sycophants and opportunists. Not surprisingly, the three officials have a strikingly different interpretation of *Mingfeng ji*. Ma Shiying regards Yang Jisheng's diatribe as slander against Yan Song. Ma Shiying defends Yan (the corrupt official Li Xiangjun compares him to) as a cultivated man painted and costumed into the role of a clown. His stand on Yan Song is of a piece with his beliefs on other matters too: if Yan Song can be turned into a bad man with face paint, then Li Xiangjun can also be punished for her effrontery by making her a clown, as Ma Shiying and Ruan Dacheng decide to do in a fit of pique.

In contrast, Yang Wencong argues that the stage adequately represents these historical figures, although he lacks the self-awareness to place himself and his colleagues in their context. In other words, he shares Li Xiangjun's belief in the fixity of role types, that there are *chou* and *dan* offstage as well as on. That painted face represents something about the person: "But though the face paint is powerful, it's also fair. It's meant to warn entirely unscrupulous little people and not for people like us."[46]

Ma Shiying's fears about the power of the theatre are related to the core of his and Ruan Dacheng's essential villainy: namely, their belief that what is underneath a costume is irrelevant, and that anybody can play any role (Yang Wencong, who in most of his actions is almost every bit as bad as they, at least feels that the theatre is representing *something*, which may be his saving grace). Naturally, Ma Shiying fears the theatre because he recognizes its political power: he and Ruan Dacheng can dress up just any old prince in the right garb, make him the Emperor, and make others recognize him as such. It stands to reason that by dressing another man as a villain, they might actually make him so, and certainly prevent his family from recognizing him. But what about the person playing the role? To what extent does his or her identity and character matter?

Ruan Dacheng, the dramaturge, playwright, and enthusiastic patron of the theatre, also regards himself as a playactor and is thoroughly imbued with a faith that he too is open to infinite transformations of this sort. When the play begins, he is distressed and humiliated by his demotion; but all it takes for him to transform himself from shamed, exiled partisan of Wei Zhongxian to honored official is a simple change of costume.

All states share a loathing of disguise; impersonating a police officer, for example, exacts a heavy punishment. Especially in the transition from Ming to Qing, clothing served the very important function of identifying its wearer and asserting allegiance, since men of the Ming wore loose-fitting clothing that tied around the waist, while Manchu garb was more form-fitting and buttoned at the neck. In Qing politics, a man's outside revealed important things about him. If a long queue and a shaved pate expressed loyalty, then was stubble to be interpreted as mere sloppiness or actual subversion?

Clothes continue to identify their wearers in peacetime: both dynasties, like those before them, had sumptuary laws, designed to prevent Ruan Dacheng's numerous quick changes. Wearing the uniform of an office to which one was not entitled earned a grievous beating and immediate and permanent dismissal.[47] Recall again those external markers of the Emperor's singularity: his exclusive rights both to a color, golden yellow, and to certain logos, especially the five-clawed dragon. In such a world, costuming in the theatre itself might well provide a little frisson; for, of course, any actor walking off the stage garbed as he was onstage is transformed into a criminal, whether for masquerading as an official or for daring to arrange his hair in a Ming style.

Ruan Dacheng finds himself in a predicament as the arrangements are being made for Hongguang's investiture. Ma Shiying and Ruan Dacheng discuss the tricky problem of how to costume Ruan, because technically he remains disgraced and is thus barred from wearing court dress, even though, of course, he has played a great part in masterminding this coronation ceremony. How then to create an identity for him so that he can participate? He asks Ma Shiying:

> "Sir, may I ask you, how should I be costumed?"
> "The grand ritual of welcoming the Emperor is of course not to be compared with a private visit, so you'll need both cap and gown."
> "But I am a dismissed official—what sort of uniform will I have?"
> "That's so. Well, there's no choice. Why don't you just for the moment take the office of Bearer of the Petition, though that's a bit of a fall for you."[48]

The need for costuming precedes any substantial notion of the office. Ruan Dacheng needs some sort of uniform to participate in the ceremony, so Ma Shiying gives him an essentially meaningless office for the sole purpose of providing him with something to wear.

This episode reveals a certain persistent, sartorial quality to Ruan Dacheng's aspirations. He finds shouldering the petition demeaning, but not because he finds anything wrong with their conspiring to choose the Emperor or with his own taking the task on as Ma Shiying's yes-man. Instead he is disturbed by having people see him in the costume of a petty official, and he soothes his battered ego with the prospect of those same people seeing him later in a position of glory: "Don't laugh; in days to come when my picture hangs in the Hall of Meritorious Officials, then I'll be the proud one."[49] And later, when he has become the Emperor's favorite, his exultation seems to be primarily directed towards his new costume, the uniform of a high official (and a contrast to his garb in his days of disgrace): "Spanking new black hat and a red robe, black leather boots sewed up with green."[50] In other words, his moments of greatest triumph—both real and imagined—consist of these: to wear the costume of a high official and to see his own portrait hung up among those of other officials. Both reveal a life committed to a specific version of playacting, where experience is secondary, and the self is to be perceived through the eyes of imagined viewers.

Like the portraits of the Emperor made for ritual purposes, Ruan Dacheng's imagined portrait would focus on its subject's social position, pictorially emphasizing his new hat, robe, and boots. The portrait allows Ruan Dacheng to imagine himself inhabiting that dream role forever, painted for all time with all the accoutrements of that role. Of course, the figure would possess his own face, with its characteristic lineaments; but neither this portrait nor any other can be said to be definitive, since we do not really believe in the legitimacy of the costume he has assumed. He has no particular right to it.

In a political and artistic world where a person's actions and beliefs exist in such problematic relation to each other and where the idea of a fixed and true inner self is so troubled, all externals start to look like face paint and costume. Small wonder then that Li Xiangjun's portrait, her peach blossom fan, which articulates who she really is, should so thoroughly reject verisimilitude. Perhaps the only way to depict a person's true essence is to move what lies literally inside her to the outside.

Unlike the professional entertainers, Ruan Dacheng simply does not bother to demarcate performance from non-performance; instead, playacting goes on all the time, and onstage or off, there is no role that Ruan feels he cannot play. In his efforts to flatter, he thinks himself capable of any transformation. This problem plagues him from the very beginning; after all, he is publicly ostracized and censured because he feels he can play what is literally an impossible and paradoxical role—that of son to a eunuch. His position as Wei Zhongxian's son evokes a visceral anger, incommensurate with Wei's corrupt behavior; Ruan Dacheng outrages onlookers with his willingness to assume the unnatural role of son to a castrated man.

Later, when his new patron Hongguang worries that he will not be able to cast his production of *Yanzi jian* in time for the Lantern Festival, Ruan Dacheng succumbs once again to his belief that he might become anyone. He even seems to feel that anyone can be cast into any role type: Li Xiangjun as a clown, or *chou*; himself as a romantic female lead, or *dan*. Recognizing one's own role type demands an awareness of one's relation to other people—which Ruan Dacheng, for all of his interest in how he appears, lacks entirely. At the very beginning of the play, the Old Ceremonial Assistant has the peculiar experience of seeing his younger self onstage, where he is transformed into a *fumo*, a supporting male role type. Often the author, as a *fumo*, himself appears in the introduction of a *chuanqi* (as Tang Xianzu does, for example, in the introduction to *Mudan ting*). Even if he wanted to, the Old Ceremonial Assistant could not see himself as the center of the events unfolding, but rather knows—simply by observing his own makeup and costume—that he occupies the position of the observer and commentator.

When Hongguang expresses worry over the difficulty in properly casting *Yanzi jian*, Ruan Dacheng tries to comfort his sovereign, offering to change himself into whatever the Emperor desires. He even proposes himself, outrageous *fujing* and middle-aged male, for the part of a *dan*, the female lead: "I regret that I cannot paint my cheeks with powder and makeup, and I would gladly clutch a lute to my bosom."[51] And since he himself cannot play the lead female role, he ends up being responsible for casting someone almost as inappropriate, the old whore Zheng Tuoniang.

Ruan Dacheng's desire to please—and his faith in his illimitable capacity for self-transformation—makes him a very dissatisfying enemy, as his initial response to the Revival Society reveals. He cannot even make up his mind simply to oppose them and instead defends himself by claiming he was one of them all along. Such a convoluted claim draws on a version of loyalty and identity that will be discussed at length in the next chapter—one that presumes a world full of secret plots and conspiracies, where things are not as they seem and people do not say what they mean. He tries to ingratiate himself with the Revival Society, saying that even though to all appearances he sided with Wei Zhongxian's faction, in fact his was the ultimate sacrifice, since the whole time he was actually working on the inside for the Revival Society. According to this version of events, despite all of his well-publicized gestures of allegiance to Wei Zhongxian, Ruan Dacheng was secretly Wei's opponent, willing to brave the ire of Revival Society supporters who did not know that he was a double agent: "I first came to know Wei Zhongxian so as to save Zhou and Wei; thus I took my good name and gladly ruined it."[52]

There is no evidence to support his story other than his very success at infiltrating Wei's faction; on the other hand, Wei Zhongxian's two opponents, Zhou and Wei, were ultimately both executed at the same time that Ruan Dacheng was happily acting as the godson of Wei Zhongxian. Perhaps Ruan Dacheng has even convinced himself of this patently false account. From his perspective, it is clear that these changes of allegiance are alarmingly easy, as if the opinions that supposedly motivate them either cannot be determined or ultimately do not matter.

These contortions still fail to win him friends among the Revival Society. No extreme measure of ingratiation—not even a beautiful prostitute worth two hundred taels of silver—will win Hou over (I am retelling the circumstances from Ruan Dacheng's perspective, since actually, of course, Hou Fangyu is all too willing to be won over, and only Li Xiangjun's outrage prevents him). For someone so concerned with getting credit for his actions and with acting only when the eyes of an audience are upon him, Ruan Dacheng seems remarkably close-lipped about his role in funding the match; Yang Wencong admits it only after Li Xiangjun pressures him to do so.

One is tempted to interpret Ruan Dacheng's gift to Hou Fangyu as the ultimate faith in the self's malleability: first, he purchases Li Xiangjun and then gives her to Hou Fangyu, using her to win his friendship. In some sense, in this episode, Li Xiangjun serves as Ruan Dacheng's proxy; he reads her as a blank ground onto which he can project himself. Many acts before his offer to Hongguang, Ruan Dacheng tries to make himself into that beautiful *dan*. There is someone else to do it for him—so that in order to charm Hou Fangyu, he himself does not need to "paint my cheeks with powder and makeup" and "clutch a lute to my bosom." Li Xiangjun's willful return of the dowry shatters this illusion, though, proving that she is the *dan*.

There is something sadly empty about such a way of life, relegating a person to the position of spectator of his own life. The uniform worn to the coronation ceremony resembles a costume onstage, with no necessary relationship to the body underneath. And yet, like the imagined portrait hanging among those of the meritorious officials, it somehow validates and confirms for him his own identity, or at least one momentary fantasy of what he might become. His identity in some part consists of imagining himself being seen. When he fantasizes about his imagined portrait, the real Ruan Dacheng is its viewer and not its constantly changing subject.

If a portrait is a way to articulate identity, so too, as Caroline Walker Bynum has argued, is a last judgment, a final summation of one's life.[53] In Act 40, Zhang Wei has a vision of Ruan Dacheng's and Ma Shiying's fate in the hereafter. Ma Shiying identifies himself one final time, summing up who he has been. Satisfyingly, he voices his recognition of the punishment's appropriateness: "I, Ma Shiying, have spent my lifetime doing pernicious things; how could I have known that I would end up in this mountain range in Taizhou?" And then as the thunder god chases and smites him, he calls out: "Spare me! Spare me!"[54]

In contrast, at his moment of judgment, Ruan Dacheng cannot confess what he has been. Who is this man who even at the moment of last judgment cannot say anything meaningful about himself? Just as earlier he cannot recognize his own role type, so now he cannot take up his punishment. At the end, he cannot stop himself from continuing to pose for an audience, even at the moment of eternal judgment, when there would be no point in impressing or flattering. Once again, speaking about himself in the third person, he boasts about his own achievements, still eager to get credit, even alone and fleeing for his life, when credit should be the last thing on his mind: "Great indeed! I, Ruan Dacheng, have crossed the Xianxia Chain of mountains—that should be accounted a preeminent achievement."[55]

At that very moment, a mountain god and an ogre drag him off the mountain. Ma Shiying satisfyingly confesses what he is, but Ruan Dacheng reveals nothing except yet another pose. So who is there—simply an admiring observer of this new pose? In his ruthless and ceaseless political machinations, but also in his attitudes to the self, Ruan resembles another politician of questionable morals and claims to legitimacy—Shakespeare's Richard III—except that Richard, unlike Ruan Dacheng, does try to stop acting for just a moment. In the fifth act of that play, the night before the climactic battle he will lose, Richard undergoes a moment of terror and contrition. He looks inside himself to reflect, and rather than seeing a contained, unchanging self on whose behalf he has been ceaselessly machinating, he sees nothingness, the proper conclusion to a life dedicated to endless plotting and deception:

> What do I fear? myself? there's none else by:
> Richard loves Richard: that is, I am I.
> Is there a murderer here? No;—yes, I am:
> Then fly. What, from myself? (V.iii.182–85).

In the next chapter, I will discuss how closely some forms of political paranoia approximate Cartesian epistemology. After all those virtuosic transformations meant to deceive one victim after another—Clarence, Anne, the English people—he is left unable to answer the question of who Richard is underneath all the disguises and duplicity. But Ruan Dacheng's emptiness goes one step further, barring him from even this kind of self-understanding.

Each character I have discussed—Li Xiangjun, Su Kunsheng, Liu Jingting, Ruan Dacheng—has a different notion of what kind of relationship a role has or ought to have with the person playing the role, but all beg the question of internality, providing no answer to what really lies inside. The entertainers, in contradistinction to Ruan Dacheng, insist that what is on the inside matters, but they can neither prove that the inside exists nor provide an adequate answer for what it might be.

In one of the prefaces he wrote to the play, Kong Shangren himself suggests this problem: "Through role types we distinguish between gentlemen and mean people; also there are times when the straight characters are not enough, and then painted-face characters are used. Unpainted-face or painted-face characters are like ugly or beautiful human beings—they should be judged and appreciated by something beyond being a stallion or a mare, or black or roan."[56] "Beyond being a stallion or a mare" refers to a story in the *Liezi* about Duke Mu of Qin, who sent out the horse specialist Jiufang Gao to buy a horse. Jiufang Gao reported that he had bought a roan stallion. The horse turns out, however, to be a black mare. The Duke was about to become very angry, when the other great horse specialist of the time told him that Jiufang Gao was correct and that this black mare's true essence was indeed that of a roan stallion. On the one hand, the allusion refers, of course, to characters like Liu Jingting and Su Kunsheng—painted-face characters who prove themselves to be unstereotypically heroic, people who on the surface appear humble and unimportant, but are, as Hou Fangyu says of Liu Jingting, "one of us" after all, willing to sacrifice themselves just like the great men of the age.

But push just a little bit, and this kind of statement begins to fall apart. Ultimately, it doesn't account for what people really are, but instead replaces an external description of their exteriors with an external description of their interiors. What does it mean for a black mare to be a yellow stallion on the inside? Is that internal yellow mare then something else again on its true interior? This model of identity resembles nothing but Russian dolls, one enclosed within the other, where the interior is simply deferred infinitely.

CHAPTER 6

The Emperor's Throne

Let me begin this chapter with what by now is familiar territory—the trials of the young man claiming to be the Crown Prince. For ease of exposition, I speak of both *Taohua shan* and the various *yeshi* sources upon which I have drawn as describing a late Ming epistemological climate. In fact, of course, both *Taohua shan* and the *yeshi* sources were written in the early Qing, reflecting on the causes of the Ming's fall.[1] *Taohua shan*, written at the very end of the seventeenth century, postdates by a few decades the other texts, which were written mostly by men who had personally experienced the fall of the dynasty. I am using these texts more as a conduit to understanding some strains of Qing political thought and historical understanding than to access the late Ming itself. Specifically, I will be examining the epistemological conditions that to these particular Qing writers characterized the late Ming. These texts attempt to make sense of a recent past, musing on the reasons the Ming fell and placing the blame squarely on moral failures.

The play mentions the young man who professes to be the Crown Prince only in passing. Su Kunsheng wants to save Hou Fangyu and lists a whole series of grievances to Zuo Liangyu to try to persuade him to turn on the Nanjing government. Huang Degong, one of the generals present, adds that the Crown Prince "has been confirmed by tutors and high ministers, but now they want to consign him to a prison. Everyone is furious and wants to grind Ma and Ruan into mincemeat for the sake of our late Emperor."[2] We know what happens afterwards: Zuo's actions lead to the fall of the Southern Ming. According to the play, the uncertainty surrounding the young man's identity leads directly to the fall of the dynasty.

After the young man's arrival in Nanjing, he was subjected to rigorous grilling by tutors who in the old days would have had frequent contact with the young prince and also by highly placed officials who would have seen the prince with his father, the Chongzhen Emperor. I will be turning to the precise content of these trials momentarily as well as to precisely how they fed into fears of conspiracy—and how in turn the same fears and concerns underlie much of *Taohua shan*.

In recounting the young man's trials, writers of *yeshi* end up recapitulating the different positions taken up by contemporaries, some arguing for the authenticity of the young man's claims, while others insisted that he was an obvious fake. Just as one might expect, to determine the worth of his claims, the unofficial historians evaluate the accuracy of his responses to questions on such subjects as his lessons and their order. The young man was also tested on the names and titles of his family members and where the quarters of each were in the imperial palace. Finally, officials present at different specific occasions asked the alleged Crown Prince questions about how he and others had reacted at those particular moments.

His partisans felt he passed the tests as well as might be expected of a prince whose memories of the palace might naturally have faded with time and who had obviously undergone great trauma since his escape from the palace. But on the same evidence, those who opposed him concluded that he was a clever impostor, backed by conspirators who had prepared him with answers to likely questions. According to proponents of this position, his correct answers to relatively esoteric questions indicated only how far-reaching and well-connected his co-conspirators were. If the young man could answer questions about his lessons with only minor inaccuracies, someone—or perhaps many someones—with privileged access to the imperial family must be helping him pass. The more the young man knew, the more his knowledge suggested infiltrators at even the highest levels of government. Any success the young man might have with the questions fueled the suspicion not that he was the Crown Prince, but of wider conspiracy, revealing hidden treachery and rot in already beleaguered Nanjing.

But then at some point in the interrogations, according to some accounts, the young man's composure finally broke: his name, he confessed, was Wang Zhiming, and he knew some key facts because he belonged to a family with minor connections to the imperial court. In *Mudan ting*, the Emperor's verdict on Du Liniang's identity does not seem to have convinced Du Bao; in Nanjing, the young man's confession did nothing to resolve the disagreement between the two positions. On the one hand, it confirmed the suspicions of those who were already convinced that he was an impostor. On the other hand, to those in the other camp his confession suggested only a great horror, that the prince had been coerced into falsely confessing through terrible torture. Certain witnesses later reported hearing cries of pain coming from his cell.

Moreover, to his supporters, the name he disclosed, Wang Zhiming, held clues to his real identity. According to those who believed him, when his real name and status were not believed, the prince had secretly continued to insist upon his true identity, repeated in simple code: read backward, *ming zhi wang*, the prince of the Ming. Since it did not appear to change anyone's mind, the torture of the young man does not seem to have accomplished very much.

I have introduced the final chapter with this incident because the kind of torture that people suspected had been practiced on the young man seems an extension by practice of the theory of identity proposed by so many of the actors. If indeed a person might possess a true, inner identity not suggested by external appearances (as Su Kunsheng proposes), then how are outsiders to gain access to that privileged interior? Or is such access forever denied?

After the government fled, the same young man is said to have decked himself out in theatrical props to claim the powers of the Emperor as his own. The necessary counterpart to that young man—and the frightening fluidity of identity the theatrical element introduces—is the tortured prisoner here, joints being pressed in an effort literally to extract his true identity, to fix it as one thing or the other. In *Mudan ting*, all other identities are held in place by the fixity of the Emperor's; that normative vision has been so perverted that a man who might be the Emperor has his tenuous claims to that identity tested through torture.

Torture forms a very natural partner to playacting. Like theories of playacting, what motivates the use of torture is a presumption about the relationship between a person's identity and his behavior—that the two can be out of joint, disconnected with each other—coupled with an insistence that one can go beneath the surface and establish a single identity to explain those actions.

And yet the promise of torture is transparently flawed, as every false confession attests. The confession achieved at such a high price might just be another gesture that might also deceive. Most *gongan* literature is quite scrupulous about relating torture's limitations; if incriminating information is divulged in the course of torture, it will only have to be corroborated separately (sometimes through magical means) to convince the reader that the perpetrator has truly been identified. Torture does not appear onstage in *Taohua shan* (although random executions and imprisonment do). But its use is central both in traditional Chinese literature and legal systems (*xing*, which means punishment or penal, can also refer simply to torture).

Nonetheless, a false confession extracted by torture is commonplace in the literature. Writers can allude offhandedly to false confessions elicited by torture, confident that their readers will understand. In other words, every reader and every audience member understood that an innocent man or a woman being tortured could be forced to lie, confessing only to stop the torments. It was often the work of a Lord Di or a Lord Bao to exonerate the innocent after a confession had been forced through torture.

In the case of the young claimant, what are we to make of the fact that torturing the young man in the end resolves nothing, merely hardening people in their different opinions? Perhaps stripping away one lie only reveals another. Here too, thinking about acting provides a close parallel; as both Su Kunsheng and Kong Shangren intimate in their discussions of role-playing, stripping away one layer of face paint might reveal nothing but another layer of performance, affected for another purpose. Instead of being composed of an exterior characterized by assumed behavior and a truthful and sincere interior, a person might be instead an infinite series of nested performances, one inside another.

In "De la Conscience," Montaigne summarizes the problem of torture: "C'est une dangereuse invention que celle des gehennes, et semble que ce soit plut't un essai de patience que de verité. Et celui qui les peut souffrir, cache la verité, et celui qui ne les peut souffrir. Car pourquoi la douleur me fera-elle plut't confesser ce qui en est, qu'elle ne me forcera de dire ce qui n'est pas?"[3] Su Kunsheng and Kong Shangren suggest a similar problem with regard to playacting: regarding what is onstage as mere performance does not in fact promise that what takes place offstage will be truth telling, but may suggest instead that it, too, is yet another performance.

A freely elicited statement might be a lie, but then again so might be one extracted by means of torture. Like many others, the Chinese legal tradition privileged confessions made freely (similarly, during the Spanish Inquisition, any confession extracted by torture had to be repeated twenty-four hours after the cessation of torture to prove that it had been made freely—even though, of course, if retracted the torture would begin anew). In China, theoretically at least, a person could not be tortured if he confessed before the crime had been discovered. Some scholars have argued that other legal traditions, including that of the ancient Greeks, took the opposite position; in the case of slaves, ancient Greek law regarded testimony made under torture as more likely to be truthful than that given freely.[4] But at any rate, as Montaigne points out, there is no particular reason to privilege or devalue a confession extracted by torture: if torture is only being used because one cannot distinguish between truth telling and deception, one certainly cannot tell a true confession from a lie told to stop the torture.

In retrospect, using torture on the young claimant seems to have been inevitable; the nature of his claim to a specific identity is precisely the sort of possible deception that torture promises to resolve. In Chinese law, torture was used to get information, of course, but primarily it was used to force confessions, without which a defendant could not be punished. In Montaigne's time, too, throughout Europe, torture was regularly used not only in quotidian criminal investigations, but especially in religious persecutions.

A comparison between the Spanish Inquisition—where torture was used extensively—and the English campaign against secret Catholics—where torture was used far more sparingly—suggests some reasons why our would-be Crown Prince's case invited torture. In Spain, after many Jews had been forced to convert, the Church was afraid that these recent, reluctant converts might still consider themselves Jews and continue to practice their ancestral faith. Most of the persecutions and tortures were designed to flush out secret Jews. Edicts of Faith that circulated in the fifteenth and sixteenth centuries included elaborate descriptions of Jewish practice (explaining a number of Jewish holidays and the dietary restrictions of *kashrut*, for example), so that servants and casual acquaintances might be able to identify even fragments of practice as clues to the person's real identity (overscrupulous housecleaning on Friday or preparing special dishes, for example, often invited the attentions of the Inquisition). The suspected Judaizers were then tortured until a confession could be extracted.

But by the middle of the sixteenth century or so, actual religious practice seemed sometimes beside the point. Many of those burned at the stake were probably descendants of Jews who themselves knew nothing about Judaism. Others, several generations removed from conversion, admitted that they derived everything they knew about Judaism from published accounts of the crimes of Inquisitional victims.[5] If the goal had been simply to ensure that everyone in Spain participated in Catholic sacraments, that could have been accomplished easily enough, simply by requiring attendance. Instead, the point was to detect a secret identity that did not accord with outward, observably Roman Catholic behavior (which simple surveillance could monitor). When there exists the possibility that actions disguise an internal identity, torture promises to resolve this conundrum (so familiar to us in our explorations of playacting), forcing a statement that speaks for the inside. But there is no way out of the dilemma, as Montaigne points out, since that extracted statement is no more and no less a performance than what came before it.

In contrast, contemporary English persecutions relied on torture not to identify ordinary Catholic faithful, but instead Catholic priests (usually to encourage them to point fingers at other priests). For in England, Catholicism was defined in contrast to Protestantism—the former marked specifically by external works and practice, the latter marked by what cannot be known by others—faith, that substance of things unseen. One could only be a Catholic by avowing the faith. Such an identity need not be pried out of a person, for if one denied the faith, then ipso facto one was not Catholic. If a man says he is not a Catholic, there is no need to torture him, since by making the statement he makes it true.

The problem of the would-be Crown Prince's identity resembles that of the suspected Judaizers. Both cases rest on a two-pronged belief—that people have true and knowable inner identities, and that a disjunction between false actions and some true, internal identity can be resolved. By scourging the flesh, torture promises to purge away those false actions, leaving only what is true behind. And so the Crown Prince's claims at once welcomed the use of torture—and at the same time dramatically resisted being resolved by it.

Contrast, for example, the Crown Prince's identity with the crisis facing millions upon millions of ordinary subjects precisely at this time, as their allegiances shifted from the Ming to the Qing dynasty. The Qing government had no interest in torturing all of its new subjects in an effort to determine their true identities (such a project would wait for the eighteenth century, when Ming loyalists—like the Judaizers—knew to hide themselves). Instead, for the most part, a new subject of the Qing only had to prove himself with actions, displaying physical markers of loyalty, the most important of which were the queue and the shaved pate. However, men were punished (and tortured, if they refused to confess their guilt, so that they would disclose the names of any confederates) for failing to display these proper gestures.

When Su Kunsheng speaks of a true self that can be separated from actions and behavior, he means that one should not judge who he is from the roles he sings or from his circumstances in life. In the political world, a great deal is at stake when the same issue—namely, the relationship between an actor and his actions—is introduced. Such a version of identity calls forth elaborate tests of loyalty and torture to determine who a person might really be.

At a certain point, subjected to certain pressures, every fundamental relation we see in *Taohua shan*—identity as father, as wife, as subject—breaks down. What appears to have been a tightly knit community falls apart before our eyes, leaving two unrelated individuals where before there was husband and wife, mother and daughter, lord and subject.

Where *chuanqi* conventionally end with reunions, Kong Shangren concludes with an anti-reunion. In the epilogue, Su Kunsheng and Liu Jingting, now a woodcutter and a fisherman, gather together in the woods with the Old Ceremonial Assistant to reminisce about old days. We think we are about to witness a reunion not of a family, but of its counterpart in this play—the old network of friends. In the community of entertainers, relations of choice can take the place of orthodox familial ones. At one point, Li Zhenli even calls them all a family. The pseudo-familial ties dissolved, all that seems to remain is friendship, the single normative Confucian relation grounded in choice.

But at the end of the play, even that relation of friendship disintegrates, as all are chased off the stage by a Qing informer. Under the Ming, as entertainers, Su Kunsheng and Liu Jingting had only a troubled, usually peripheral position within the polity (although with occasional access to the great and powerful); under the Qing, their ties to the rest of society have become further attenuated, and they have become loyalist recluses. We begin the epilogue with atomized individuals coming together in the forest, hermits separated from the rest of the human community; we end it looking at an empty stage.

Mudan ting ends with a magical coalescing of the polity, but exactly the opposite process takes place in *Taohua shan*. In *Mudan ting*, through choice, trust, and the power of the Emperor, a family is forged out of what might seem an unlikely collection of characters: an orphan, a dead girl, and two childless parents. In contrast, by the end of *Taohua shan*, this very fluidity—the fact that identity has become a matter of choice and an act of mind—proves to have a fatally corrosive effect on the polity. Choice itself, so sanctified in *Mudan ting*, turns out to be the culprit.

All the ties to which we have been privy have dissolved, no matter how firm and binding they once seemed. Even friendship seems not to have withstood the dynastic change. There is no trace of friends like Hou Fangyu, who has rejoined society under the Qing, and when the two entertainers flee, they go off separately. There is no place for Su Kunsheng and Liu Jingting to go together. In the remainder of this chapter, I will explore some of the ways in which that theatrical model of identity permeates and eventually dooms the community in *Taohua shan*.

In evaluating the evidence for and against the supposed Crown Prince's claims, many unofficial historians devote just as much attention to speculating on the motivations of the examiners as they do on the actual content of the examinations. Let me begin by returning to the *Mingji nanlue* (the same *yeshi* that recounts the young pretender's coronation in theatrical garb). As the young man confidently answers one question after another, one of the bystanders makes an innocent observation (precisely the sort of straightforward, seemingly objective evaluation one might expect from the *yeshi* itself):

> "Even if he isn't the Crown Prince, he is still someone who has long knowledge of court affairs." An official beside him said, "If you talk like that, you'll lose your position tomorrow." After that, none of the officials at court dared again to affirm that he was the Crown Prince.[6]

In other words, according to Ji Liuqi, because no one dares offend Hongguang, no one will speak the truth. Moreover, the paranoia expressed by the official—"If you talk like that, you'll lose your position tomorrow"—supports the case of the young man. After all, if the unnamed official wasn't commenting truthfully, why should Hongguang interfere?

In fact, this kind of environment disables all testimony, no matter its content. On the one hand, as Ji Liuqi explains, these trials are designed not out of an impartial desire to uncover the truth, but instead to prove the young man in question an impostor, since all the witnesses' testimonies will be coerced. But on the other hand, since the tests are rigged, there is also no way to prove the other possibility either—what Ji Liuqi actually believes, that the young man really *is* the Crown Prince.

In other words, foregrounding the environment of the tests of identity—specifically the way that Hongguang seems to have stifled any possibility for dissent—makes ever more remote the possibility of conclusive proof one way or the other. The original goal was to uncover who the young man might really be (with the understanding that his appearance might deceive), but the problem seems to have grown. Knowing what we do about the way those tests have been conducted, the task suddenly includes many more adjudications of identity and rests upon the possibility of truly knowing the examiners, too (and their true political allegiances), since they also have the capacity to deceive. Should each examiner then also be quizzed to determine his allegiances? When tests are performed under these circumstances, determining the identity of the young man implies multiple other tests of identity, of each of the multiple examiners, to determine their sincere beliefs, with the understanding that in each case a person's beliefs and his public behavior might not correspond.

This further adjudication—not of the young man's identity, but of his examiners—can take on central importance. To properly understand the tests administered to the young man, this argument goes, it is important first to determine the intent of his examiners and whether they are actually in Hongguang's pocket. For example, Wen Bing's *Jiayi shian* relates a memorial presented by Huang Degong, who, since he has been stationed away from the capital for the duration of the controversy, has been able carefully to maintain a neutral stand. He expresses no opinion one way or the other on the young man's identity, but only on whether the conclusions reached by the various examiners can be trusted: "I fear that of the many ministers at court, there are many currying favor and few who would calmly and fearlessly tell the truth—so that even those who clearly recognized him would also not dare stick their heads out and invite disaster!"[7]

In the short term, the belief that people who disagree with the state will not voice their disagreements out of fear benefits those in power. Such a belief implies that one cannot tell from others' behavior what they are thinking and instead only that they are being controlled. If a person believed that everyone else was being intimidated into lying, he would surely hesitate before speaking his own mind.

Taohua shan scrupulously does not rule on the putative Prince's identity, a lacuna I will turn to later. Other historians, however, have passed judgment, and it does seem likely that the young man was a mere impostor. Let me play the role of the historian for a moment, then, and venture this guess: the young man's efforts to claim the identity of the Crown Prince were laughable, but Hongguang's government still did everything it could to prevent people from speaking out on the case, based on the belief that even mentioning the possibility of an alternative sovereign might further weaken the Ming dynasty at a time when it could hardly withstand any more threats. The effort to shut down any discussion bolstered a belief among the populace and intelligentsia that there was a cover-up of the young man's true identity.

In other words, a widespread belief in a cover-up—that dissenting opinions are not a possibility and that witnesses will testify, not to express their own opinions, but instead to fulfill some prearranged role—creates a pervasive and poisonous cynicism. When the political world is nothing but a stage, no one can say anything that commands belief.

In several of the *yeshi* accounts, Hongguang ends up helplessly protesting his innocence and avowing that there has been no cover-up. But because he has done such an effective job of suppressing dissent (and this would have been the argument of a suspicious observer), we cannot know whether he is guilty of a brutal and total cover-up, or entirely innocent and wrongly maligned—or somewhere more plausibly in between. Since this epistemological environment provides no check at all on stories—allowing them to grow ever more incredible, with no internal means to check them—it allows the accusations leveled against Hongguang to grow ever more exaggerated. Closer to our own day, the secrecy surrounding the personal life of Chairman Mao has fostered the extreme and mythological quality of stories about his life, with their hundreds of young virgins and decades without toothbrushing.

Consequently, in his own defense, Hongguang is reduced to pleading in vain that these stories are simply beyond belief. Of course, he insists, both the so-called Lady Tong—a woman who emerged claiming to be his consort—and the reputed Crown Prince were impostors seeking to take advantage of the chaos of the moment: what unnatural monster would he be to imprison, interrogate, and torture his own wife and cousin? The true monster would have been the man who accepted a false wife and cousin simply to keep the people happy. That such a plea to credibility failed to sway people speaks both to the way in which political upheaval disrupted normative ways of identifying people and how the politics of Hongguang's Nanjing had disabled the usual mechanisms for judging whether a story is true or false.

Like Hongguang's repeated insistence on his own innocence—which is either monstrousness or a declaration of what is manifestly true—the putative

Crown Prince's treatment in prison is variously interpreted by proponents of different factions. According to some accounts I have already touched on, the young man was tortured to extract a confession, but according to others, the young man's treatment was remarkable, since not only was his life spared, but he also managed to escape torture. Why should this young man be singled out? The generous treatment accorded to him fueled a frenzy of rumors that he was the authentic Crown Prince, detained by the nefarious Hongguang and Ma Shiying, who might have sunk low enough to imprison, but not so low as to kill or torture, the rightful occupant of the throne.

On the other hand, for those who believed him to be a brazen impostor, his having been spared torture and execution did not strengthen his case. Instead, according to this faction, he was kept alive and treated well precisely to prevent his popular support from rebelling. Any execution—or even report of mistreatment—would simply have given his supporters an excuse to rise up against Hongguang's government. Partisans of both positions regarded the same piece of evidence—his relatively merciful treatment in detainment—as support for their two mutually exclusive positions.

In such a world, there is no way to take an objective position without its looking like partisanship. Even Shi Kefa, virtually canonized as a patron saint of loyalty both by Ming loyalists and by the Manchus who defeated him, had his motivations scrutinized in this way. A posthumous reputation for unflinching loyalty to a lost cause is no match for this sort of all-pervading suspicion of corruption.

The *Hongguang shilu chao* records a rumor about the general. As Prince Dechang was brought into Nanjing to be installed first as Regent and then as Emperor: "Ma Shiying took Shi Kefa's memo 'Seven Reasons Against' and had it printed out as a case, and after this, Shi Kefa in all matters was blackmailed by Ma Shiying."[8] Before the new Emperor had been chosen, Shi Kefa opposed Prince Dechang—hence, the memo. But once the new Emperor has been installed, that memo becomes evidence of retroactive treason.

A hint of such a connection between Ma Shiying and Shi Kefa remains in *Taohua shan*. In Act 14, Hou Fangyu convinces Shi Kefa that Hongguang will not make an appropriate Emperor; Shi Kefa seems entirely persuaded by Hou Fangyu's "Three Crimes and Five Reasons Against His Elevation" (which incidentally sounds very like the *Hongguang shilu chao*'s "Seven Reasons Against"). And yet a few acts later, Shi Kefa remains in office and is now mysteriously committed to the government of Ma Shiying and Ruan Dacheng. For his connection to factions that opposed Prince Fu's candidacy and for humiliating Ruan Dacheng by refusing to parley, Shi Kefa is punished only with a small demotion in rank. A man of power and reputation, he cannot be punished with impunity (as Hou Fangyu can, for example); but despite his political sympathies, he remains in power, as if there were some unspoken alliance between him and Ruan and Ma.

Moreover, their relative generosity to him contrasts with Ruan's and Ma's treatment of far more imaginary opponents. After Hou Fangyu refuses to accept Ruan Dacheng's gift of a dowry, the younger man becomes the older man's sworn enemy. Later in the play, Ma and Ruan expend considerable energy masterminding ruthless purges designed to rid Nanjing of anyone possessed of dubious connections (the prison in which Hou Fangyu and Liu Jingting find themselves in Act 33 is filled with political prisoners at a time when Ma had far more pressing concerns).

According to the *Hongguang shilu chao*, Shi Kefa sent back to Nanjing a report about the northern claimant, another would-be Crown Prince who resurfaced after the fall of Beijing to Li Zicheng's armies. This young man turned himself in at his would-be sister's house in Beijing. According to a handbill posted by the Manchu authorities, an impostor claiming to be the Crown Prince appeared at the Princess's home. She came out to see him; initially she was convinced and wept to see her brother. But upon closer inspection, she determined that he was in fact an impostor, whereupon he was then taken into official custody. The handbill concludes with a plea to the populace: that the real Crown Prince turn himself in, since the falseness of this claimant leaves the real Crown Prince still unaccounted for.

Shi Kefa reports to the Nanjing government on this young man's claims. According to Shi Kefa's interpretation, the handbill accurately reports events but deliberately misleads with its conclusion. In fact, the young man at the Princess's house was indeed the Crown Prince, and all of the Manchu government's actions following their encounter constitute part of a cover-up. Shi Kefa supports this theory with a rumor that many key witnesses who recognized the Crown Prince have since been executed. He interprets the scene at the Princess's residence:

> When Lady Yuan [one of Chongzhen's concubines] and the Princess saw him, at the time they were surrounded—and so they said he was false, as even the stupidest of people would have done. And when Zhou Kui and the Princess saw him, they embraced him and wept, and only later, fearing those who would do them harm, did they not dare to recognize him.[9]

In a turnabout, his would-be sister decides she does not recognize the young man, but paradoxically, that merely strengthens Shi Kefa's conviction that the young man is truly the Crown Prince. For of course if he really were her brother, she would want to protect him by failing to recognize him. Any Manchu operatives that might want to turn in the Crown Prince might lose interest if she managed to convince them that he was a mere impostor.

Shi Kefa leaves no room for the possibility that the young man might truly have been an impostor. The Princess' refusal to recognize the young man fails to convince Shi Kefa that the young man is an impostor. By what means, then, could she have signified true and sincere lack of recognition? One is led to guess that no reaction on the part of the Princess could have conclusively dismissed the young man's claim. Shi Kefa argues that the Princess must pretend that the young man is an impostor because their meeting takes place in public, in the presence of witnesses; but once again there is no room to disprove this contention, since no one could possibly ever know about a reunion that happened in the absence of anyone else. Is there room in this world for a recognition—or even a failure to recognize—which we have no choice but to believe and which can only be seen as sincere?

The Princess' refusal to recognize the young man might mean any one of a number of things. It is nested in such a way as to make her motivations and beliefs inscrutable. We cannot confidently translate the Princess's action into an understanding of her beliefs. Perhaps she does not recognize the young man. Or perhaps she really knows very well who he is but must pretend not to so that she can protect her brother.

Under these circumstances, the claims of the young man cannot possibly be disproven. Moreover, in a move we will observe in *Taohua shan*, any piece of evidence that under normal circumstances would serve to debunk his claims instead becomes part of an ever changing (and growing) conspiracy. Therefore, the Princess's refusal to recognize her would-be brother proves not that he is an impostor, but instead her fear of the Manchus and the omnipresence of operatives lurking around observing her.

In the same vein, the author of the *Hongguang shilu chao* frames Shi Kefa's observations themselves in the context of a greater conspiracy. The complicated situation is further complicated by an added twist: this entire passage begins by explaining that Ma Shiying (who wields that document proving Shi Kefa's original opposition to Hongguang) had coerced Shi Kefa into submitting this report.

To protect his own position as the highest official in the land, Ma Shiying has no choice but to find the southern claimant false, without regard for the true facts of the matter. Consequently, Shi Kefa—under Ma Shiying's thumb—must show that the northern claimant was real, because that would in turn prove the southern claimant false: there can, after all, be only one Crown Prince. Shi Kefa's interpretations are themselves coerced—not a free and impartial evaluation of the facts at hand, but instead determined by *Realpolitik* in Nanjing.

The author of the *Hongguang shilu chao* believed that the southern claimant was the true Crown Prince, which sets up a complicated chain. Once one believes the southern claimant, any piece of evidence or interpretation that argues against his veracity instead becomes part of an increasingly complicated conspiracy to deprive the young man of his rightful inheritance. Instead of casting any light on the real identity of either the northern claimant or the southern claimant, Shi Kefa's memorandum proves only his secret collusion with Ma Shiying and the fact that no one involved with that government, not even Shi Kefa, can tell the truth. Indeed, the rot runs deep.

There is a broader effect as well: if the seemingly unimpeachable Shi Kefa, the loyalist whose bravery and integrity attracted deep respect even from the Manchus who defeated him, cannot be trusted because he lacks sincerity, then is there anyone whose word can be taken at face value? At least two issues are at stake here: first, to what extent does loyalty to a morally questionable system inevitably become complicity and collusion? And second, how is a sphere for sincere speech and action to be established in a world where so many are convinced that everyone is simply playing a role?

What the *Hongguang shilu chao*, among many other similar accounts, ultimately expresses is an unsettling, profound epistemological uncertainty, verging on paranoia. Not only does Shi Kefa's memorial turn out to mean exactly the opposite of what it purports to mean, but Shi Kefa himself becomes the model of a paranoid reader, always on the lookout for a potential cover-up and for words that mean the opposite of what they say. And the author in turn calls on us to outdo even Shi Kefa's paranoia, framing his actions and interpretations themselves in a further context of conspiracies and blackmail. Political chaos has profound and far-reaching epistemological implications.

Naturally, the author of the *Hongguang shilu chao* had no hard evidence of the document Ruan Dacheng purportedly held over Shi Kefa's head and instead based his theory of their collusion entirely on rumors, which themselves must have been grounded in perverse paranoia. To some, Shi Kefa's cooperation with the nefarious Ma Shiying must have seemed to beg an explanation: how could two such different people possibly cooperate? One answer might be that Ma Shiying must have had something with which to blackmail Shi Kefa. And so arises this peculiar proof that the northern claimant was false: because Shi Kefa argues that the young man of the north is truly the Crown Prince (an evaluation paradoxically based on his would-be sister's refusal to recognize him), and because Shi Kefa as someone working for Ruan Dacheng's government can no longer be considered reliable, then the young man in the north must be an impostor, since Shi Kefa must be lying.

If only one person thought like this, there would be little to distinguish such thinking from a paranoia that is simply pathological. But what separates it from sickness under these particular circumstances is that so many people seem to have shared the same idea.

Let me put it in another way. A sick polity like this one reproduces some of the uncertainties of a Cartesian consciousness. There is nothing that can be truly known—and nobody who can be truly trusted.

Mudan ting also highlights epistemological questions: centrally, how one might be able to distinguish between dreaming and waking or *any* two frames of reality. In the world of *Taohua shan* and the *Hongguang shilu chao*—where a girl who shakes her head and does not recognize a young man proves a widespread conspiracy to hide the truth, or where a seemingly innocent letter sent from one man to another proves the presence of agents provocateurs—lie indications of an extreme version of skepticism, where everything must be approached with suspicion. One man's ruling on the identity of another might suggest that he is in secret collusion with his enemy. Things are not as they appear. Skepticism and political paranoia are close cousins.

In Nanjing, it seems normal to doubt everyone and to entertain all possibilities. Even apparently familiar people might not be who they seem to be, either because a person might be a simple impostor, as the alleged Crown Prince was accused of being, or because a person might hide his true identity in another way, acting as a partisan of one faction while secretly serving another. Descartes looks out his window and fears that what he sees might not be what it appears at first glance: "What do I see from this window, other than hats and cloaks, which can cover ghosts or dummies who move only by means of springs?" In Nanjing, fears almost as counterintuitive turn out to be reasonable.

In *Meditations*, Descartes runs through different kinds of knowledge, seeking to find something that can be trusted absolutely. He evaluates all that one might know through the senses but decides that even sensory knowledge might be illusory. For there is the possibility that everything perceived is but deception:

> I shall suppose, therefore, that there is, not a true God, who is the sovereign source of truth, but some evil demon, no less cunning and deceiving than powerful, who has used all his artifice to deceive me. I will suppose that the heavens, the air, the earth, colours, shapes, sounds and all external things that we see, are only illusions and deceptions which he uses to take me in.[10]

Descartes writes of this extreme version of skepticism as if it were purely an epistemological and theological question—that everything he perceives around him might be an elaborate lie, meant specifically to deceive him.

But the possibility that nothing is as it seems clearly has political ramifications. There is an obvious parallel between a good monarch and Descartes' benevolent God. In a universe ruled by a good deity, the senses do not deceive. One can believe that what one sees and hears does in fact exist. Likewise, in a land ruled by a good monarch, public pronouncements are reliable. If an imperial proclamation declares an individual to be an impostor, one can believe it.

And if everything—"the heavens, the air, the earth, colours, shapes, sounds and all external things that we see"—might be illusions under the reign of an evil demon, then something similar takes place in the world of the bad monarch: none of the state's versions of "external things," those public pronouncements and official versions of the news, are to be trusted. If the government's version of reality cannot be relied upon, then the sort of paranoia to which we have been witness is entirely appropriate. Descartes worries that one's eyes and ears might lie. In reflecting on the Southern Ming, commentators argued that government had become so corrupt that Hongguang and his henchmen were lying about a whole range of affairs, including the identity of the putative Crown Prince and the secret collusion of Shi Kefa with Ma Shiying.

As we have seen in the case of the *Hongguang shilu chao*, the possibility of such deception can lead to terrible consequences—a paranoia that makes all actions and statements appear as performances and lies, so that simple tests of identity become elaborately nested in explanations of different lies. And finally, not far down such a path, one arrives at an Emperor who cannot defend himself against any charges, no matter how appalling.

An unfortunate person in such a world might find himself in the position of Shi Kefa. If he is telling the truth in his memorandum, then he has decided that sensory evidence is unreliable (that the Princess's refusal to recognize the young man constitutes true recognition). And if, as the author of the *Hongguang shilu chao* believes, Shi Kefa actually thinks the northern claimant is genuine (and that in fact the Princess's initial recognition was sincere), he has been forced to disavow what he knows to be true. If this imagined Shi Kefa, under the thumb of Ruan Dacheng and forced to say what he knows is not true, is not under the control of an evil demon willing to play games with his mind, he is not far from that predicament. Certainly, Descartes himself, born into a world torn apart by religious wars and persecutions, where false confessions were often made after torture and under threat of death, had rather more to fear this epistemological violence from terrestrial sources than from any evil demon.

But beyond the fact that *Taohua shan* tangentially treats the case of the would-be Crown Prince, what does any of this have to do with our play? These accounts in the unofficial histories and *Taohua shan*'s version of the same events share the same concerns and a backdrop of paranoia, conspiracies, cover-ups, and corruption.

I have suggested how peculiar it is that Shi Kefa, a friend to Hou Fangyu who resists Ruan Dacheng's efforts to have him endorse Prince Fu's candidacy, should only a few acts later—and with no explanation at all—be serving Ma and Ruan's government in a position of power. Given the persecutions and random arrests that befall the supporters of the Revival Society in Hongguang's Nanjing and the constant machinations and forging of new alliances that characterize politics in the play, we are absolutely within our rights to wonder why Shi Kefa should be bound so inextricably to this government.

The play usually only gestures towards these dark undercurrents (although there are times when it foregrounds their results, as in Act 33, when Hou Fangyu and Liu Jingting reunite in prison while opponents of Ma Shiying's government are dragged out to be executed). But in Act 12, which describes the events leading up to Hou Fangyu's forced escape from Nanjing, we are shown precisely how the ideas of such plots are hatched. Conspiracies are suggested, but we are never clear as to their participants, their scope, and even their existence. In the preceding act, Yang Wencong proposes that Hou Fangyu forge a letter to forestall Zuo Liangyu's move on Nanjing. In Act 12, in a conference with Ma Shiying and Shi Kefa, Ruan Dacheng—still seething over how Li Xiangjun and Hou Fangyu humiliated him by refusing his dowry and his friendship—deliberately misrepresents Hou Fangyu's participation, making him seem like a conspirator who must be expelled from the city.

The audience has been privy to the letter's writing. We have observed that Hou Fangyu writes the letter only at Yang's suggestion and that it seems to have been done on the spur of the moment. If Ruan Dacheng is ready to take this as part of a conspiracy, any act—no matter how seemingly innocent—might be construed so. Act 12 consists of three parts, each of which might have constituted its own act: Ruan Dacheng's political machinations, Shi Kefa's protests against them, and finally, how both of these lead to the separation of the two young lovers. Instead, all three parts are mixed together, as if to imply covert connections.

In quick strokes, Ruan Dacheng outlines a conspiracy of unknown dimensions. However, all the evidence of our senses and experiences points to Hou Fangyu's innocence. The letter is the first Hou Fangyu has ever written to Zuo Liangyu, whom he knows only through his father, and then not well; furthermore, it was Yang Wencong's idea all along for Hou Fangyu to write it. Nonetheless, in Ruan's hands, the letter starts to look like the deceptively innocuous surface manifestation of a dark plan of unknown dimensions, suggesting the presence of hidden enemies, ready at some opportune moment to betray Nanjing.

While Shi Kefa and Yang Wencong, the other two characters present at this conference, congratulate each other for having averted Zuo Liangyu's invasion, Ruan Dacheng and Ma Shiying talk about the instrumental letter in quite another way. Ruan Dacheng hints that it indicates a secret plot spearheaded by Hou Fangyu: "Don't you know, my Lord—he is very tight with Zuo Liangyu. They often exchange private letters, so that if we don't get rid of him soon, he will certainly be a man on the inside for Zuo later."[11] It goes without saying that his theory of an imaginary cabal makes no sense; if Hou Fangyu had really wanted Zuo Liangyu to take over the city, no planning would have been necessary. His intercession was meant to prevent just such an invasion. Nonetheless, through casual speculations (which never claim to be anything that might be substantiated by careful scrutiny), Ruan Dacheng has raised the possibility of an infiltrator who would surrender the city to Zuo Liangyu, and this idea immediately takes on a life of its own.

Shi Kefa contributes to this discussion inadvertently, but with chilling effect. In a histrionic gesture, he proclaims, almost to himself, that all he can do for the country is this: "I cannot but wholeheartedly sacrifice this weakened, sick body."[12] As Ruan Dacheng suggests, Hou Fangyu might be an enemy agent; and as Shi Kefa suggests, one should sacrifice the life of an individual to save a community—so that one is not surprised to hear Ma Shiying combine these two suggestions. Ma Shiying submits that they ought to sacrifice Hou Fangyu for the sake of the city: "How could we value one man's life to the point of sacrificing the city?"[13]

Without batting an eyelash, Ma Shiying seems to take it for granted that such a plot really exists (when it came into being mere seconds ago with Ruan Dacheng's ungrounded speculations). Ma Shiying agrees that Hou Fangyu must be sacrificed, since he might be a traitor who would surrender Nanjing. Once mentioned, the conspiracy between Hou Fangyu and Zuo Liangyu seems to be real, or at least it is not subject to the normal procedures of proof and disproof. Under more normal circumstances, we would regard Ma Shiying as having skipped a step—going directly to how he is to deal with this conspiracy, without any effort to verify that it in fact exists. Here, though, even the outrageous seems possible. That Ruan Dacheng can set up the outline of a conspiracy so quickly and have it so readily believed bespeaks a society already poisoned with distrust. Only those practiced at paranoia can leap to conclusions so quickly.

Yang Wencong, at whose behest Hou Fangyu had written the letter, naturally feels a responsibility to intercede at this point and a fear that he might be the next to be implicated. Still careful lest he reveal too much of the role he has played, he attempts to exonerate Hou. Yang Wencong presents the obvious defense—that he himself was present at the letter's writing and read it and therefore knows that it is entirely innocuous: "But that is maligning him a bit too much! It was I who sent Liu Jingting, and when the letter was being written, I was there. He was writing sincerely—how can we turn around and suspect him?"[14]

Under most circumstances, Ruan Dacheng's makeshift theory would simply be laughed out of consideration, and Yang Wencong's explanation would no doubt exonerate Hou Fangyu. But not under these circumstances; here the rumor of a conspiracy is not so easy to dispel as Yang Wencong hopes. Ruan Dacheng's rejoinder seems almost to condescend to Yang Wencong's naïveté and emerges from the *yeshi*'s world of paranoia. Addressing him by his *zi*, Ruan Dacheng says: "But, Longyu, you wouldn't even know if there had been a secret code in that letter; how could a person know?"[15] Appearances deceive, and knowledge gained through sensory perceptions means nothing, Ruan Dacheng tells Yang Wencong. Even a letter one helped to write might contain a secret coded message—*anhao*, a secret signal or password—just like a person apparently familiar might retain the capacity to deceive and dissimulate.

By this point, proof one way or the other seems beyond the point, as is demonstrated by the futility of Yang Wencong's efforts to exculpate Hou Fangyu. Ma Shiying chooses to disregard all evidence and act as if Ruan Dacheng's theory of conspiracy is correct, or rather cannot reliably be discounted. Surely Yang Wencong is not convinced by so unpersuasive an explanation. How could the letter have been in secret code? After all, Hou Fangyu allowed Yang Wencong to read it before it was sent and suggested that they pass it on to a third party for editing. Yet even though he knows his friend has been wronged, Yang Wencong goes along with Ruan Dacheng's proposal. His silence is tacit recognition that conspiracies will indiscriminatingly feed on any evidence; anything will do, and words, as I have said, can mean exactly the opposite of what they say.

Even some of the play's black humor rests on the effect of this kind of political culture—namely, the impossibility of knowing what is taking place. Sensory input and experience are inadequate, and rather than inform or explain, other people's accounts of events are so embedded in their own interests that they obscure as much as they illuminate.

Early on in the play, Zuo Liangyu turns his troops to Nanjing not because he has carefully planned out a rebellion, but because his troops are hungry and restive, which we may take as yet another sign of widespread corruption: food and funds diverted to the armies simply disappear, lining the pockets of petty functionaries along the way. Inside his camp, Zuo Liangyu hears loud noises issuing from the troops and asks an adjutant what is taking place. His adjutants have decided that impassivity is the safest position.

    ZUO: What is all the clamor going on outside?
    ADJ.: Sir, outside all is quiet—who would dare clamor?
    ZUO, angrily: There is clamor; how dare you report that there is not!
    ADJ.: Those are hungry troops demanding food—it's not clamor.[16]

His adjutants have no intention of being blamed for the troops' insurrection and so refuse to admit that it exists, lest any admission be taken as an admission of guilt.

But then how is someone like Zuo Liangyu to know what is going on if he cannot trust or even understand his own adjutant? He cannot rely on the reports of his aides, and when he does rely on Su Kunsheng, he is essentially tricked. But the whole empire (both now and later) depends on his full awareness of his circumstances and the consequences of his actions; and that awareness and, consequently, his judgment is terribly—even fatally—compromised.

This is a culture of doublespeak. Who is to say whether the noise outside is truly clamor? The question of what is really happening seems virtually inaccessible—buried not just in suspicion and mistrust, as we have seen with the purported Crown Prince, but also in suspicion's companion, flattery.

The epistemological conditions created by a morally bankrupt state recapitulate some of the qualities of Cartesian consciousness. For the subject living in such a state, everything—including evidence from the senses and the sworn testimony of others—must be approached with suspicion. Everything must be subjected to minute scrutiny before it can be trusted, and even then paranoia is never quelled, but only fueled by obsessive musings. Both the senses and the testimony of reliable people seem eminently impeachable.

In short, the realm of the knowable contracts to what is inside oneself. And faith in that realm depends on a claim we are all too familiar with from the last chapter: that one's inside—as distinct from external roles, which can be assumed and then discarded—is what truly matters. As *Taohua shan*'s entertainers assert, this is an internal essence not accessible to others, bearing a complicated relationship to a person's behavior. Descartes articulates a similar claim: "I think, therefore I am."

In one of the prefaces, Kong Shangren ties the question of whether people are truly at their core one thing or another to the problem of role types. He compares role type to physical appearance, an external phenomenon that may not correspond to an internal identity. And in fact the play proposes a number of different miscastings, as if to test the extent to which an actor can stretch herself to play a role, and also wrestles with the political dimension to this question. For example, what does Ruan Dacheng's status as a painted-face character have to do with his true nature? Since Zheng Tuoniang is a *chou*, or a clown, is she prevented from playing other roles onstage? As punishment, the leading lady Li Xiangjun is cast as a clown. If Hongguang had not rescued her, would she have been able to play that role?

In the grossest miscasting, Ruan Dacheng imagines himself as a female lead. By this point, we are asking ourselves whether some inviolable core of his identity stands in the way of his taking on that role. After all, the very act in which this imagining takes place begins with a conversation involving some of the minor entertainer characters, comparing the attributes of the Emperor's male favorites with his female ones. The group assumes that gender distinctions are fundamentally unimportant. Finally, they conclude that (except that they can achieve official status as concubines) females do not stand any advantage, at least in pleasing the Emperor, which is Ruan Dacheng's ostensible concern.

In the same act, Ma Shiying laments the power of the stage to break up families; with face paint on: "even a filial son or a loving grandson will refuse to recognize you."[17] For a man in the singular position of having handpicked an Emperor, he uses a peculiar figure to express his concerns about the fragility of identity. After casting Hongguang into the role of the Emperor, Ma Shiying makes his own fears about the theatre come to pass. For by making Prince Dechang the Emperor, he denies the would-be Crown Prince of his birthright, preventing his subjects from recognizing him. From the perspective of the Crown Prince, Ma Shiying has indeed made it so that rather than being recognized as the Son of Heaven, he is instead imprisoned as an impostor.

Ma Shiying's concerns come to pass in many other relationships as well. For as I have said, *Taohua shan* concludes with the dissolution of all normative relations: his subjects cease to recognize the Hongguang Emperor; parents and children no longer recognize each other; husband and wife become as strangers. And just as Ma Shiying suggests, the theatre seems to bear some of the blame.

Throughout the play, tremendous attention is paid and great value given to the possibility of knowing a person. Can we think of people as being authentically one thing or another, despite their ability both to deceive and to impersonate? In the case of the monarch (and those who would be the monarch), this problem has two related parts: first, whether the specific individual is who he claims to be (the kind of authenticity at stake in the case of the putative Crown Prince and in many anecdotes about Hongguang), and second, what sort of person he truly is, or the true color of his character. The first kind of identity informs much of the play's discussion of legitimacy, while the second kind is taken up with special passion by the more plebeian characters: a great deal is staked on what sort of a person Ruan Dacheng, for example, or Liu Jingting really is.

Throughout the play, sympathetic characters (Su Kunsheng, Li Xiangjun, all of the Revival Society) espouse a faith in the possibility of knowing people in the second sense—what sort of character a person might possess. In Chinese, *shi*, "to recognize," an action fraught with tension and the possibility of failure in this play, can also refer specifically to knowing a person's character.

A pair of ideas—that there are good people and bad people, and that the two categories can be distinguished from each other—animates the discourse of the Revival Society and their supporters. A cynic observing the actual behavior of the Revival Society would see first their utter conviction that they are good people and second, the license this conviction allows them. Even the cruelest and pettiest of their actions—the public humiliation of Ruan Dacheng—can be transformed by such a conviction into a righteous act. As Ruan Dacheng slinks off in disgrace, the whole crowd of Revival Society supporters (including Wu Yingji and the Old Ceremonial Assistant) sings together: "We separate the wicked from the righteous, and the traitorous from the virtuous."[18]

And yet their confidence in being able to tell apart "the wicked and the righteous" seems ill-founded, divorced from the actual workings of politics in Nanjing. For the volatility of the actual situation undermines any claim that people might be—in their essence—one thing or another. Some characters, such as Zuo Liangyu and Gao Jie, for example, defy such easy categorization by their switching of allegiances. Gao Jie was a bandit who surrendered to the Chongzhen Emperor but was allowed to keep his troops. In return, he agreed to serve the Emperor, with the same troops. In other words, in one moment, with a flourish of the imperial seal—in that curious tie between ontology and bureaucracy I discussed with regard to *Mudan ting*—Gao Jie changes sides and identities, going from traitorous bandit to loyal retainer. However, his fellow generals retain some doubt about the sincerity of his about-face, suspecting that at another moment of crisis, he will again choose expediency, and throughout the play, he never escapes that reversal's lingering moral taint.

Zuo Liangyu's position is even more ambiguous. Early in the play, this well-meaning man comes within a hair's breadth of moving his restive troops on Nanjing. And later on, by moving his armies on Nanjing with the intent of freeing the Crown Prince, he directly causes the fall of the very dynasty he has sworn to uphold. Nonetheless, despite his central role in the downfall of the dynasty, he still retains some hold on our sympathies and is even included with Huang Degong and Shi Kefa in Zhang Wei's vision of the good generals' reward in the afterlife.

In a world as chaotic as this one, Zhang Wei's vision seems markedly out of place. It is predicated on the idea that complicated lives—with multiple turns of allegiance, partial innocence and partial guilt, possible deception and double-dealings—might be simply boiled down to good or bad. Perhaps we agree with the judgments passed on Ma Shiying and Ruan Dacheng, that the sum total of their lives merits punishment. But why is Zuo Liangyu rewarded, when he twice threatens Nanjing, once with disastrous results? It is unclear whether his complicated career *can* be reduced simply to a quantifiable reward of the sort he receives: "I am the Marquis of Ningnan, Zuo Liangyu. By the command of the Heavenly Emperor, I have now been enfeoffed Soaring Heavenly Emissary. I gallop to my posting."[19]

At Su Kunsheng's suggestion, Zuo Liangyu moves his troops, exposing the entire Yangtze River to the Manchu armies. Shi Kefa's consequent refusal to surrender Yangzhou incurs the Manchus' wrath, which they take out on the citizenry of the city in the bloodiest episode of the dynastic transition. Forget the *Hongguang shilu chao*'s account of Shi Kefa's secret pact with Ma Shiying (according to which Shi Kefa is a clear-cut weakling and villain), and Shi Kefa's career according to *Taohua shan* is still far from unblemished: serving an Emperor whose selection he had first opposed, cooperating with Ma Shiying, and contributing to the death of thousands of innocents.

Moreover, like so many of the characters who are not directly connected with the stage, his behavior bears the unmistakable marks of theatre. On the turrets of Yangzhou, with his troops deserting, Shi Kefa finds himself in the position of an actor needing to win back the attention of a distracted audience. Beating his breast, he pretends to speak to himself; of course, the troops below are his real audience: "Shi Kefa! Shi Kefa! Having spent your whole life in vain reading the classics and talking abstractly of loyalty and filial piety, you are actually helpless!"[20] First he weeps tears. Only an aide notices. Then he escalates to tears of blood, finally drawing the attention of soldiers who gather around him. Moved, the soldiers agree not to desert.

As many characters, Li Xiangjun and Liu Jingting among them, would insist, sincerity and performance do not mutually exclude each other; I do not mean to impugn Shi Kefa, but I would argue that *Taohua shan* does portray him as a self-conscious performer, unceasingly acting for an audience. The scene on the turrets of Yangzhou makes it clear that determining a single Shi Kefa is as difficult as figuring out which monarch one ought to direct one's loyalties toward: is Shi Kefa the weeper, with sorrow so deep and sincere he produces tears of blood? or the calculating general who must do whatever he can to prevent his troops from deserting?

Shi Kefa even manages to put off committing suicide until an audience arrives. The Old Ceremonial Assistant shows up to bear witness, so that the world will know what has happened to the great general.[21] When Zhang Wei envisions a heavenly reward for Shi Kefa, he is assuming the possibility of purging the complications of performance. Zhang Wei would have us believe that there is a single Shi Kefa, simplifying a character whose words and actions are not only calculated, but generated for effect.

And what of Hongguang, who was also dead by the time of Zhang Wei's vision? Why does Zhang Wei not include him in his vision of the afterlife? For of course such a vision would have to resolve once and for all whether Hongguang was legitimately the Emperor or a usurper wrongfully occupying the throne. But given that of the three generals rewarded in the afterlife for loyalty, one fought against Hongguang and two for him, no resolution of his identity can take place.

Zhang Wei's vision is pure wish fulfillment: first, in the sense that the good are rewarded and the bad punished, a kind of justice the world of the living does not mete out. As a historian, Kong Shangren's concern for this problem has an honorable and long lineage; the inequity of earthly deserts has plagued all Chinese historians since at least Sima Qian.

But Zhang Wei's vision also expresses a wish that there might exist a realm where all the complexities of political life are ironed out and eliminated. In that realm, Zuo Liangyu, who betrays Hongguang, and Huang Degong, who dies to protect him, are both rewarded because they are both loyal, albeit to opposing causes. Hongguang can have no place at all in such a vision. And to accommodate Shi Kefa, Zhang Wei creates a space where a person might finally speak without anticipating the response of an audience. In heaven, there is no one to please or impress; in announcing his position in the world of the dead, for once, Shi Kefa, every bit as much of a performer as Ruan Dacheng, is not playing to an audience.

The intersection between playacting and politics also plays itself out in expressions of loyalty. Obedience, the hallmark of loyalty, bears a strong structural resemblance to playacting in that it necessarily involves doing something one doesn't believe in (adhering to a script, as it were). Simply behaving as one wants—or listening to one's inner self, as one of the actors might put it—does not constitute obedience.

In an earlier chapter, in speculating about whether Hou Fangyu can possibly reciprocate Li Xiangjun's gift of the blood-splattered fan, I have written about the fear that filial piety and chastity might be confused with mere recompense. To differentiate filial piety and chastity from reciprocity, one might choose to express devotion in so extreme a way that it could not possibly be interpreted as recompense. In the case of chastity, this extreme is often suicide (or remaining chaste for a fiancé never even encountered in person). With filial piety, since life itself was the gift bestowed, simple suicide was not an option, but self-mutilation was. In late imperial times, local gazetteers frequently reported on filial women's cutting off bits of flesh (usually from the area around the thigh) to prepare medicinal broths for a parent or a parent-in-law.

Obedience finds itself in the same difficult position, needing to mark itself off from other behavior, so that it cannot be confused with simple reciprocity—or even a coincidental convergence with personal desire. For it stands to reason that a person might by chance want to do what is asked of him by a superior, especially if that superior conducts himself wisely.

How then can one tell if any action is true loyalty and not simply reciprocity or even coincidence? A subject might obey for any number of reasons that have nothing to do with true loyalty—out of desire for reward, say, or out of fear of punishment. Obeying a manifestly unwise superior might help to demonstrate loyalty. Or an action might seem to be loyalty precisely when it appears to be counter to or, at least, different from the desires of the subject—hence, one reason that paragons of loyalty, like Shi Kefa or his late Song counterpart Wen Tianxiang, can generally only be venerated posthumously. Once a person is dead, it has been proven that his actions were not determined by self-interest. To a dead man, rewards for loyalty have no value.

Playacting and obedience can inform each other powerfully. Thomas Hobbes's vision of what obedience entails, for example, is concerned purely with dissimulation for political purposes, but clearly there are theatrical implications to his discussion of the relationship between performance and belief. Hobbes explores questions of obedience, and after concluding that all actions are subject to control, he comes to the question of belief.

He sets himself a hypothetical situation that is at once extreme and yet entirely within the realm of imagination for a European living in the midst of a century of religious civil wars. *Leviathan* had to be composed in Paris, where Hobbes sought refuge from the Civil War raging in England; the question of belief and allegiance and how they are to be expressed through behavior must have cut very close to the quick for an Englishman in his position. Hobbes asks: "But what . . . if a King, or a Senate, or other Soveraign Person forbid us to beleeve in Christ?"[22]

Hobbes poses the question of whether a king could command a person to relinquish Christian belief, but he might have chosen far less hypothetical religious questions, which his contemporaries believed important enough to stake their lives on: whether the state could force a person to reject internal allegiance to the Pope, for example, or stop a person from believing that only a Catholic priest could properly administer the sacraments. Had he wanted,

Hobbes could also have chosen to frame the same issue with questions lifted more directly from seventeenth-century England. Without changing the gist of the question at all, he might have asked whether a Protector and a Parliament could alter people's belief in the Divine Right of Kings.

The question has obvious resonances with a situation closer at hand for us. Ruan Dacheng, as we know from the beginning of the play, wants to be loved and respected; he offers the dowry and lends his troupe precisely to win friends in Nanjing. But once he has reached a position of power, how are he and Ma Shiying to know that they are truly respected and not secretly loathed? For Kong Shangren the question is both of historical and contemporary relevance: we know the Qing state could and did scrupulously mandate multiple outward signs of allegiance—to begin with, queues, change of clothing, and participation in various state rituals—but what is the relationship between these outward signs of allegiance and belief? Could the state actually change the strongly held beliefs of Ming loyalists, convincing them that the Qing indeed was the legitimate government? And did a shaved pate have anything at all to do with such a belief?

Hobbes's response on the matter of state control of belief is unequivocal. To him, the powers of a sovereign govern only behavior, not belief, so that belief always lies outside the control of any state. He answers his own hypothetical question about whether the state might forbid a person from believing in Christ by affirming that no state can do such a thing: "To this, I answer, that such Forbidding is of no effect; because Beleef and Unbeleef never follow mens Commands."[23]

But even if a sovereign cannot control belief per se, any action that could conceivably serve to express belief—whether through speech, writing, or ritual behavior—is fully within his purview, as Hobbes goes on to ask: "What if wee bee commanded by our lawfull Prince to say with our tongue, wee beleeve not; must we obey such command?" He responds in the affirmative: "Profession with the tongue is but an externall thing, and no more then any other gesture whereby we signifie our obedience."[24] Anything that purports to express belief and thought is ultimately an action like any other and thus falls under the potential jurisdiction of the state. A person can believe what he wants and yet be forbidden all means of expressing that belief and compelled to disavow his beliefs. As every character in *Taohua shan* is all too aware, people can lie, and there is no reason to tie any gesture to a belief.

Hobbes's hypothetical Christian is asked to refuse recognition to Christ: should such a disavowal be considered apostasy? Hobbes intimates it is not, citing the precedent of Elisha:

a Christian, holding firmly in his heart the Faith of Christ, hath the same liberty which the Prophet Elisha allowed to Naaman the Syrian.... Here Naaman beleeved in his heart, but by bowing before the Idol Rimmon, he denyed the true God in effect, as much as if he had done it with his lips.[25]

To comply with the authorities in Syria, Naaman needed to deny the one God and make all the gestures of worship to the idol Rimmon. Afterwards, the prophet Elisha sanctions Naaman's apostasy.

Although Hobbes seems convinced that Naaman truly believed in God, there is no evidence one way or the other except for those very gestures that we know from Naaman's own experience have the potential to deceive. No one other than Naaman himself—not even the Prophet Elisha who allows him to worship Rimmon—can ever truly know the real reason for his actions or what he "beleeved in his heart." Why should we privilege Naaman's conversation with Elisha over his bowing before Rimmon? And after he has paid obeisance to Rimmon, how can we trust those same gestures to reflect belief in God? After all, it may well be that Naaman's professions to Elisha are the real lie and his obeisance before Rimmon the truth. All that can be known is that "he denied the true God in effect"; whatever his true, sincere thoughts on the matter were must remain forever a secret.

If a monarch may control all action, but not belief, then what takes place inside a person's mind is beyond the control of anyone else. But if belief cannot be expressed, it isn't clear that this Cartesian space does a subject much good. Hobbes approaches Descartes from the outside, imagining a state that might be an aggregate of thousands of atomized Cartesian consciousnesses, each one convinced of the inviolability of his own thoughts—that interior which even Descartes' evil demon cannot penetrate.

Mudan ting meditates on whether dreams or waking have primacy. Hobbes rules for the shared world of gestures and speech over the private one of dreams and beliefs. Unknown to anyone else, a belief might as well not exist. If no one acts on beliefs about his identity, even if the young man really were the Crown Prince and everyone around him knew it, then like Naaman's real beliefs, the young man's real identity does not matter. Actions, then, may or may not reflect belief, but belief itself may not be of much importance.

The putative Crown Prince's case has a central, if subtle, role in *Taohua shan*. Kong Shangren clearly was familiar with the details of the case. As he himself explains, Kong did copious research on the period, and most writers of unofficial histories do treat the case, although with varying degrees of attention. Why, then, when it is obviously so important, does the play withhold judgment on the question of the young man's identity?

Like Hongguang's absence in Zhang Wei's vision, the absence of any ruling one way or another on the young man's identity should immediately alert us. Even though Hou Fangyu opposes Prince Dechang's elevation, he does not express any belief on the identity of the mysterious young man claiming to be the Crown Prince. Offering one judgment might have implied the other. For example, if Zhang Wei had included Hongguang's punishment alongside Ruan Dacheng's and Ma Shiying's, as a usurper (and not a mere incompetent), such a vision ostensibly sanctioned by heaven would point us to the real identity of both would-be Crown Prince and Hongguang. In that case, the confusing inclusion of both Huang Degong and Zuo Liangyu as paragons of loyalty would have to be cleared up.

This play is deeply concerned with a person's true identity—both how he fits within his family and the polity and what he is like inside—and yet it neglects to resolve arguably the most important identity of them all, who the Emperor is, leaving a vacuum in the very center of things. Nowhere does the play provide any kind of definitive ruling on whether Wang Zhiming—the name the young man confessed to, perhaps under torture, perhaps not—was really the eldest son of the Chongzhen Emperor or an impostor. And without knowing the answer to that question, we cannot know whether Hongguang ought to be regarded as the Emperor.

It is not just Zhang Wei; all characters in the play withhold judgment on these two vital questions. For example, even though Su Kunsheng is responsible for stoking the flames of Zuo Liangyu's outrage over the mistreatment of the Crown Prince, his goal in doing so is the rescue of his friend Hou Fangyu and the downfall of his enemy Ruan Dacheng, not a mercy mission inspired by the young prisoner's status. His belief in the young man is decidedly secondary; if he could accomplish Hou Fangyu's rescue by some other means, he would no doubt choose it. For his part, Shi Kefa simply never expresses any opinion one way or the other, even though, of course, he continues to treat Hongguang as the legitimate Emperor, only committing suicide after he is told Hongguang has fled from the capital. The three loyal generals whose fates in the afterlife Zhang Wei relates serve two different Emperors; at least one (and possibly two) of these three paragons of loyalty must be considered a traitor and a rebel.

I would argue that the play's omission of a judgment on the matter of the young man's identity is entirely deliberate. Partly, as a loyal Qing subject,

Kong Shangren allows the absence at this moment of an indubitably legitimate Ming monarch to smooth the dynastic transition. As a result of this ambiguity, the Kangxi Emperor, the Sage King of whom the Old Ceremonial Assistant sings, does not inherit his throne through a Manchu murder of a Ming monarch. The Chongzhen Emperor, we might recall, hanged himself at the approach not of Manchu armies, but the renegade troops of Li Zicheng. If we cannot adjudicate on the identity of the young man, then the Manchus are neither usurpers nor regicides, but pacifiers and unifiers.

But the absence of a judgment on the young man's identity also underscores issues more directly pertinent to our concerns here. At the heart of the play is a vacuum that speaks to Hobbes's concerns. For nowhere can we know what Kong Shangren would have us believe on the question of the would-be Crown Prince (and consequently of Hongguang's legitimacy). It is almost as if *Taohua shan* by omission makes the argument that in this world where the identity of the Emperor is beyond what can be known, all political behavior is staged.

Achieving any certain knowledge of the young man's identity might simply be impossible in this atmosphere; for reasons I have discussed, normal proofs and disproofs have been disabled. The play suggests what might follow: if even the Emperor's identity is truly something beyond what can be known, if he might be in some sense an impostor, then how are the other characters' identities to be rooted? Once legal identities and identities positioning a person within a patriarchy have been disabled, what is left? We have seen that many of the characters define themselves according to internal qualities—not by who they are relative to a family or a polity, but by what they are like. In a world where even the Emperor cannot be known, such highly problematic self-identification may be all that is left.

If one cannot know whether Hongguang is the legitimate monarch, then gestures of obeisance to him are curiously empty—not what is due to him according to the cosmic order, but simply expedient gestures, like Naaman's worship of the idol Rimmon. In determining how we interpret behavior, context is all. Ruan Dacheng treats Wei Zhongxian with elaborate respect and decorum; we expect that Hou Fangyu would do the same to his father Hou Xun. And yet Hou Fangyu's behavior we would call filial piety; Ruan Dacheng's, sycophancy. We can only give the same behavior two different names because we know Hou Xun is a true and legitimate father, while Wei Zhongxian is merely Ruan Dacheng's boss and adoptive father.

In Nanjing, as the southern regime began to dissolve, the identity of the

Emperor seemed unknowable. Under such circumstances, the entire political arena becomes a stage, where loyalty and sycophancy are impossible to distinguish. Instead, everything dissolves into performative gestures.

Not knowing whom they ought to serve, people assume the posture of loyalty. But in fact the cardinal virtues of loyalty (*zhong*), trustworthiness (*xin*), and sincerity (*cheng*) only make sense in the context of an absolute certainty in a person's identity, whether he is father or sovereign. For it is not the behavior itself that is singled out for praise, but its context, specifically, the relation between lord and subject. Otherwise, loyalty is meaningless, simply a behavior as easily assumed and potentially meaningless as Naaman's worship of Rimmon, indistinguishable from a role that can be assumed and divested at will.

Mistakenly or not, Hongguang regards himself as the Emperor, which leads him to confuse expedient service to him with loyalty. Hongguang recounts what he has suffered in the days between his flight from the capital and his seeking refuge with Huang Degong. Evidently, General Huang is not the first from whom Hongguang has sought refuge: "Yesterday I went to the Duke of Wei, Xu Hongji. He pretended he didn't know me and kicked me out of his camp."[26] Hongguang says that Xu Hongji pretended not to know him, and he uses the word "to know," *shi*. He could also have used "to recognize," *ren*, a word whose use in *Mudan ting* I have discussed at length. In that case, however, the line would have to be rewritten, because this sentence simply does not make sense in Chinese: "he pretended not to recognize (*ren*) me."

As Xu Hongji does, a person can pretend not to know the Emperor by acting as if he were confusing the Emperor with another person (in that case, of course, he must treat the would-be Emperor as a shameless impostor, much as Hongguang treated the would-be Crown Prince, or the Princess treated her would-be brother). But pretending not to recognize the Emperor is a purely political matter and almost a contradiction in terms (except perhaps for an ardent republican, who understands that this particular man is Emperor, son of such-and-such, heir to so-and-so, but refuses to recognize his special status). A person can pretend not to know the Emperor, confusing him with someone else, but one simply cannot pretend not to recognize (*ren*) the Emperor: if a subject does not go through the motions of recognizing the Emperor, then de facto he does not recognize the Emperor as Emperor.

A brazenly turncoat general could, for example, have known who he was—that the pathetic creature at his mercy was Zhu Yousong, the former

Prince Dechang, heir to Prince Fu, and grandson of the Wanli Emperor—while at the same time denying that this particular man was Emperor, withholding recognition from this man and saving it for another (say, another Ming claimant or the young Aisin Gioro princeling). Such a general might have known the individual (*shi*) without recognizing his status (*ren*). But open rebellion of this variety is not the subject of Hongguang's complaints.

There is also an incidental, additional complication: technically, it is only through Hongguang's generosity that Xu Hongji holds the title of Duke of Wei, by which Hongguang refers to him and complains about his behavior. It is only possible for the Duke of Wei not to know who Hongguang is (*shi*); it is impossible for the Duke of Wei (but not for Xu Hongji, a name he holds through his position in a family and independent of his relationship to Hongguang) not to recognize the Hongguang Emperor. Without recognizing this Emperor, there is no Duke of Wei.

Xu Hongji is involved in two separate and distinct acts of deception: first, he pretends to confuse the Emperor with another person. But not knowing him (*shi*) is just a cover for not recognizing him; he also does not own up to his refusal to recognize the person Hongguang as the Emperor. We cannot know whether he really knows Hongguang to be the person he is. Besides, what he really *knows* is entirely beside the point and can never be proven. Only his behavior counts.

Having taken on the position of Emperor under unique circumstances, Hongguang is disabled in his dealings with other people, incapable of seeing how people might feel differently than they act. In his circumstances, where some are sycophants and others are loyal but there seems no way to distinguish between the two, one alternative is simply to disregard the link between belief and behavior and to focus instead solely on behavior (another solution in such circumstances would be to distrust all behavior as potentially masking betrayal, as other monarchs of questionable legitimacy—like Qin Shihuang—have done). Concerned not with belief, which he cannot control, but with behavior, Hongguang is perhaps uncoincidentally enamored of the theatre.[27]

After Hongguang rescues Li Xiangjun from being cast as a clown, she delights him with her audition piece, an aria from *Mudan ting*. Crowing exultantly, as if at a new toy, the Emperor gloats: "Look at her powdered face blushing pink, looking as if she were shy." What he says defeats her entirely (as does his presentation to her of the second fan). She has chosen this aria to explain who she is, how she feels, to underscore that she is no common actress. And yet for his part, he is interested solely in how she appears, not whether she is in fact shy or not, but that she looks shy. At first reading, one is tempted to substitute "methinks" *xiang* for "looks like" *xiang*: "Methinks she is shy." But functionally there is no difference between Li Xiangjun's appearing shy and Hongguang's thinking her shy. How could you tell between someone who simply looked shy and someone who actually was?

More importantly, would it matter? Throughout the first half of the play, Li Xiangjun has comforted herself with thoughts of who she really is, a person separable from her status as an entertainer and defined by her character and the friends she has chosen. Confronted by the possibility brought up by Hongguang that the person underneath is a performance as well, she no longer resists. After this point, she simply accedes to Hongguang's desires. The presentation of the second peach blossom fan confirms that this has become a world where there is no offstage. All behavior consists of expedient gestures with no necessary relation to belief; all clothing is costume; and even the peach blossom fan is only a prop.

Kong Shangren does not provide any kind of definitive answer to the young pretender's identity, because in some important ways that question does not hold in the world he represents. What is the true identity of that young man who presents himself at court claiming to be the Crown Prince? In this world, the question is ridiculous; for as Hobbes points out, the proper focus is obedience and not ontology.

Hobbes has only disdain for those martyred for their beliefs. He ends up countenancing apostasy: "Here Naaman beleeved in his heart, but by bowing before the Idol Rimmon, he denyed the true God in effect, as much as if he had done it with his lips." According to Hobbes, even if belief matters to the person, it does not matter to the state: functionally, an action performed sincerely and the same action performed simply to comply with regulations are equivalent. One would not judge whether the true God existed by Naaman's testimony, and one certainly ought not judge whether the young man is an impostor or not by the testimony of those called on to examine him.

Where Kong Shangren differs from Hobbes is that to Kong Shangren, this state of events—where the loyal and the disloyal cannot be distinguished—is horrifying, a reflection not on the nature of power and truth telling, but instead on how terribly far Hongguang's Nanjing has diverged from a healthy Confucian state. In the golden age of the Qing, as the Old Ceremonial Assistant describes it in the Preface, identity is fixed, so that sons can be filial and ministers loyal. All of those Confucian virtues—loyalty, sincerity, filial piety—can then refer not to a set of behaviors, but to an unchangeable relation between two specific people.

In life, the man Kong Shangren was known for being a lineal descendant of Confucius and for having personally escorted the Kangxi Emperor on a tour of the ancestral grounds in Qufu. In other words, his public life was grounded on a faith in the reliability and fixedness of patrilineal identity and identity within the polity. And yet a reader might easily (albeit wrongly) interpret his position in *Taohua shan* on the nature both of monarchy and patrilineal identity as radically cynical.

Other than *Taohua shan* and a draft of another play, Kong Shangren also wrote the occasional pieces common to many literati, including one long account of the Kangxi Emperor's visit to Qufu. In it, he relates his personal interactions with the Sage King, whose reign the Old Ceremonial Assistant describes in glowing terms. After impressing the Kangxi Emperor on his visit, Kong Shangren was given a special position in the capital, a sinecure won not through the examinations, but through his special connection to the sovereign, both as tour guide and as descendant of the Sage.

In his account of that encounter there is no trace of irony, no hint that he might regard the Kangxi Emperor in anything but the most reverential light. Even the physical details of the monarch deeply impress Kong Shangren. Walking around the grounds of Qufu, Kong Shangren looks at Kangxi's clothes: "I noticed that the lining of the imperial kingfisher robe had been mended after having been scorched and I looked up with admiration at our Sovereign's frugality and perfect virtue, qualities that matched those of the Sage King Yu."[28] These clothes could not differ more from the theatrical costume the would-be Crown Prince was decked out in, and this Emperor—whom Kong Shangren approaches with a real sense of the sanctity of his person—could not differ more from the pathetic Hongguang. Kangxi's humanity and individuality only reinforce a sense of his sageliness. In contrast, all the little details that bring life to Hongguang reveal simply how poorly he inhabits the role of Emperor.

Being assured of Kong Shangren's devotion to the monarchy leaves us with a serious lacuna, indicated by the absence of the legitimate monarchs in the play. Just as scrupulously as *Mudan ting*, *Taohua shan* keeps the indisputably legitimate monarchs—Chongzhen and Kangxi—carefully offstage.[29]

Other than the Old Ceremonial Assistant's comments at the beginning of the play, one has no sense of the world after the events of *Taohua shan*. The same play that scrupulously explains why Hou Fangyu and Li Xiangjun cannot marry never indicates what happens to Li Xiangjun after the play ends. We come to know in careful detail all that is wrong with the late Ming polity, but we have no indication of how all these wrongs come to be repaired. What happens to the remnants of the old world that cannot be incorporated into the new, healed society described by the Old Ceremonial Assistant? After a period of such confusion and an intensely violent dynastic transition, how can we return to a world where the Emperor commands authority simply because of who he is?

Kong Shangren finds himself in a conundrum. On the one hand, identity is of absolute importance and cannot simply be a question of choice, for the ideal political world is one where people—like the Kangxi Emperor and Kong Shangren himself—can be definitively positioned and hence known. But on the other hand, the world he actually depicts is entirely different, undermining this sort of fixed identity, precisely in its depiction of the theatre's relation to the political world. And perhaps this lacuna explains the ending of the play, where we are left after Liu Jingting's and Su Kunsheng's flight with nothing but an empty stage. The play ends with no one onstage, because the world the Old Ceremonial Assistant describes to us at the beginning cannot accommodate the world of Liu Jingting and Su Kunsheng. There is no place for them anymore, not even onstage.

What if a relationship between two people—whether between liege and subject, husband and wife, parent and child—has been entered into as the result of choice? Can one later choose simply to dissolve that same tie? The promise of organizing people along patrilines is that one can then rely perfectly on the correspondence between individuals and their positions within a clan and within a polity.

Liu Liangzuo chooses to be Hongguang's subject, but later on he changes his mind. In that relation, as in so many others in the play, there is no assurance that such correspondences work: people occupying political positions might regard them as roles that may be discarded when they become inconvenient, and even more frighteningly, they may occupy positions within a family that are equally arbitrary and unverifiable, convenient for the moment, but which may be shed later.

The family at the center of *Taohua shan*—would-be mother, would-be daughter, and her would-be husband—is characterized by such relations, grounded in choice, unrecognized by the world at large, not apparent to those on the outside. Where many people might look at Li Xiangjun and Li Zhenli and see a madam and a prostitute, they see themselves as mother and daughter. Li Xiangjun insists that Hou Fangyu is her husband (or, critically, *as good as* her husband)—that if not in the eyes of his family or of their shared acquaintances, they are nonetheless married because of a pledge each made to the other. But no one, not even those in her intimate family circle, will ever believe her.

Li Xiangjun's family drama mirrors the situation of the whole nation. For Hongguang's legitimacy is as shadowy as Li Xiangjun's marriage, and his relationship to his ministers has been contracted in entirely heterodox fashion; rather than choosing them, this Emperor was chosen by his officials.

Let me turn to another *yeshi* account of Hongguang's reign, this time relating a tie between mother and son contracted in precisely this sort of makeshift way. Bear in mind both the way this account resonates with *Taohua shan*, in which practically all ties between people have been entered into in equally heterodox ways, but also the way this account is a nightmarish version of *Mudan ting*. For here, too, a dead child has come alive again—not through magic, but through simple impersonation.

Among the many other refugees descending upon Nanjing from the north was a woman who claimed to have been married to the Prince Dechang who was later to become Hongguang. Lady Tong's story, like the putative would-be Crown Prince's, quickly gathered a number of followers (*Taohua shan* only elliptically refers to this morganatic marriage, in Hou Fangyu's explanation to Shi Kefa of why Zhu Yousong should not become Emperor). Nonetheless, despite the woman's repeated petitions, Hongguang refused to grant her an audience, claiming she was an impostor and pointing out the numerous errors and inconsistencies in her story.

This passage from *Mingji nanlue* chillingly recounts his advisors' reaction to the Emperor's behavior:

> Ma Shiying spoke to Ruan Dacheng: "Lady Tong is a former concubine of the Emperor, and yet His Majesty refuses to recognize her. Why?" Dacheng said, "We can only observe the intentions of the Emperor; seeing as he refuses to recognize her, we should just put her to death.". . . Shiying said, "With real or fake undetermined, we will just go along with the Emperor's whim."[30]

Hongguang's rulings on identity cannot be believed; he is simply one of a number of powerful people willing to do away with those whose existences are inconvenient to him. No one makes any effort to determine whether she is an impostor or the real thing: no one in power has the faith that it matters whether someone is real or an impostor. This, then, is one of the nightmares averted in *Mudan ting* come to pass: the resurrected Du Liniang risks death for reclaiming her own identity. Similarly the real Lady Tong might be killed simply for claiming to be herself. Ma Shiying does not care who she is; but if she makes herself an inconvenience, he will certainly have her killed.

Lin Shidui expresses this fear in his account of three identity disputes of the Nanjing regime. Lin writes of three people whose identities are in question: the putative Crown Prince, the would-be Lady Tong (who claims to have been married to Hongguang), and finally Hongguang himself. Unlike most *yeshi* writers (including Kong Shangren), who question only his legitimacy or suitability for the position, Lin Shidui actually wonders whether he is who he claims to be. Lin Shidui presents the possibility that Hongguang is in fact an impostor and not the former Prince Dechang at all.

> Justice Qian Shengren had seen the Emperor while in the ranks, and he told me, "People say that the Emperor is not really the prince, and that in the fiefdom of Fu there was someone in the disciplinary office who resembled the prince very much, which is how this one came to be recognized as such. He told the Dowager Empress not to say anything and that they would enjoy riches and rank together."[31]

For, of course, if the real Prince Fu had been killed, another imperial prince would have been chosen to become Emperor. In that case, Prince Fu's mother would be no Dowager Empress in the new regime, but only another refugee noblewoman. She doesn't stand to gain a great deal by unmasking the stranger posing as her son. So what will it take for a woman to recognize as her own flesh and blood a mere impostor? This question, as we have seen, is of tremendous import both in *Mudan ting* and in *Taohua shan*, where parents' ties with their children are sorely tried.

For this particular noblewoman, it doesn't take much to claim this stranger as her own son, only the promise of "riches and rank," in the words of the impostor. Afterwards, the two—false Emperor and equally false Dowager Empress—are tied inextricably, not by bonds of love and trust (as Du Liniang and her mother are, for example), but instead on terms of mutual suspicion. For each has the power to unveil and destroy the other. They are forced to cling to each other in a grotesque parody of filial devotion—not out of love, but out of deep mutual distrust.

> Qiao also told me that after she entered the palace, she was with the Emperor day and night. Now whether this is true or not is impossible to know; how-

ever, when she came, he did not greet her, and only after a little while did he bow and weep. Moreover, when they fled from the capital, they did not do so together.[32]

Once the contract is concluded, each may go his own way. Unlike the tie between a true mother and son, this one is precisely characterized by its limitations. Compare it to the relationship between Lady Zhen and Du Liniang: the pact between the would-be Hongguang and the would-be Dowager Empress comes to an end when it no longer serves their best interests. According to Lin Shidui, Hongguang is entirely untrustworthy, even—perhaps especially—on the question of his own identity; he himself might be an impostor, not the Prince Dechang, heir to Prince Fu at all, but just a double.

Virtually all the important relationships in the play resemble that between Prince Fu's mother and the impostor posing as her son, in that they too are contracted voluntarily, and under pressure, they too collapse. The play foregrounds these relationships, and they form the backbone of the group of friends in Nanjing, a makeshift family. But of course more conventional relations lie off in the distant background. Somewhere, families like Kong Shangren's must exist. We can only assume that these more orthodox, conventional relationships form the building blocks for the regeneration of society, but they are carefully kept offstage. There are no two onstage characters related to each other indubitably, in orthodox fashion.

These unorthodox relations repeatedly appeal to the language of the family in describing their own bonds. After many of our main characters have left Nanjing, there is a mini-reunion of sorts in Act 27: Li Zhenli fishes Su Kunsheng out of the river and saves him from drowning, and Hou Fangyu happens to be in an adjacent boat and recognizes their voices. The three joyfully greet one another, and each recounts the travails passed through to reach this point. And then Li Zhenli sighs regretfully: "I think of those old days in the brothel, when the whole family was living there together; now here in this boat, we're only missing Xiangjun. I don't know whether we'll see each other again in this life."[33]

There is no other possible reading for "whole family"—this is how she views her community. And perhaps as a prostitute, no other family is possible than this seemingly random assemblage of entertainers and customers. Nonetheless, the family upon which she reflects with such longing was hardly meant to be permanent, or even of long standing. Between Hou Fangyu's first meeting of Li Xiangjun and his escape from Nanjing is a period of only seven months. Nostalgia and the language of family both conspire to grant an impression of permanence to a grouping that was anything but, instead contingent on coincidence and happenstance, and destined to fall apart even if nothing had happened in the world outside.

Family relationships are being used metaphorically, which means that in other circumstances they might be abandoned. As was common in traditional China, many of the aggregations of male friends or associates casually use fraternal terms to address each other; they are, they claim, brothers to each other (or more accurately, just *like* brothers). Sometimes, though, these relations manifestly do not live up to their billing, and they break down irretrievably. And unlike brothers, the two men can easily end all relations.

There are other hidden dangers to the polity in the casual bandying about of familial terms. After Hongguang finds refuge with Huang Degong, another general, Liu Liangzuo, arrives and suggests to Huang Degong that the two share the riches that will surely be theirs if they turn Hongguang over to the Manchus. Huang Degong indignantly refuses, and a tussle ensues. As they fight over the stewardship of Hongguang, Liu Liangzuo ingratiatingly refers again and again to his fellow general Huang Degong as brother; finally, Huang Degong explodes at the hypocrisy of a traitor who persists in using the kinship terms: "Fie! You dog! You don't even recognize your lord or your father [or your father-lord]—what kind of a brother should I recognize you as?"[34]

Like Xu Hongji, the general who first turned Hongguang away by pretending not to know who he was, Liu Liangzuo has ceased to recognize (*ren*) his erstwhile sovereign Hongguang. Huang Degong logically asks him why the tie of brotherhood should remain if the bond between Emperor and subject can be so severed. Zhang Wei momentarily echoes this concern when he asks the young lovers how they can marry in the absence of an established Emperor. For the virtue of *ti*, devotion between brothers, relies just as heavily as filial piety and loyalty on a sure knowledge of another person's identity; the privileged relation that brothers have with each other rests on the sure knowledge of who one's brother is.

If the polity really is, as Huang Degong implicitly argues, a patriarchy, headed by a father figure, then only by recognizing the same father can they be brothers. Or to put it another way: in a society organized by patrilines, a person who does not recognize his father can hardly know who his brother is. For by definition brothers are those who share a father (half-brothers who share a mother belong to separate families—one reason widow remarriage was considered so transgressive). Marriage might (as Li Zhi proposes) supersede paternity as the central human relation, but brotherhood can never do so, since it fundamentally derives from paternity. Without knowing one's father, one can hardly know one's brothers; if a general does not recognize his sovereign, then he can hardly recognize his fellow generals.

By calling Huang Degong his brother, Liu Liangzuo suggests that he can still pick out different elements of the imperial power structure to continue to respect. But how can they be brother-generals while recognizing different father-lieges? Huang Degong correctly perceives that Liu Liangzuo's attachment to him is not fraternal but just as expedient as Liu's former loyalty to Hongguang. Huang Degong's response suggests something of the interconnectedness of the polity: that if Liu Liangzuo refuses association with Hongguang, then he also can no longer be colleagues with Huang Degong. But what about other normative relations? One cannot be a loyal brother without also being a filial son; but what about intersections between the state and the family?

In the final act, Zhang Wei counters Hou Fangyu's desire to marry Li Xiangjun with this objection: "Fie! You two crazy little lovebugs! Look about you: where is the country? Where is the family? Where is the Emperor? Where are the fathers? And all you have is this root of passion in flowers and moonlight, and you can't sever it?" Without an established, recognized Emperor, Zhang Wei suggests that more than just the relationship between two brother generals is at stake.

Zhang Wei's objection to their marriage is *Taohua shan*'s exact counterpart to the Emperor's promise in *Mudan ting*, where he establishes both the marriage of the two young lovers and the reunion of Du Bao's family. Like the Emperor in *Mudan ting*, Zhang Wei argues for a close tie between the state and the family. The Emperor in *Mudan ting* legitimates the unlikely union of Du Liniang and Liu Mengmei and through the certainty of his own identity fixes everyone else's relative to his own. And in *Taohua shan*, in the absence of any Emperor relative to whom subjects can define themselves, Zhang Wei suggests that entering into marriage is impossible.

In the absence of a lord and father, there are no authorities from whom Hou Fangyu can get permission to marry. His marriage to Li Xiangjun could form no part either of the polity or of his own family (since the country is in total disarray and his family hundreds of miles distant)—but instead would consist only of two individuals who have chosen to come together, in the absence of a greater framework.[35] What Zhang Wei prevents is that old fantasy of Peach Blossom Spring, where broken off from the rest of the human community, society can be formed again but with no sovereign, just decentralized apolitical families.

But what is to stop someone from applying Zhang Wei's argument to an already formed family? What is to stop someone from arguing that no marriages hold anymore, since each and every marriage forms part of the polity, and the polity as it was constituted before no longer exists? Why should a foot soldier obey his general if the general in turn has no Emperor whom he obeys? Could it even be the case that the absence of an Emperor somehow frees up sons to disobey their fathers?

In fact, these are relevant questions to ask about the end of the dynasty. Boiled down to their essence: on what grounds does anyone possess authority—whether father, husband, or master—when the Emperor is no longer? The period recorded by the play was marked by widespread slave revolts couched in these very terms. Bondsmen from all over the country demanded their freedom, or they simply ran off, knowing that a master who in peaceful times would immediately have reported the escape to the local yamen had in these exceptional circumstances no resort at all. A bondsman might shed his old identity and obligations and in the chaos of dynastic transition resurface in a new area, one of thousands of refugees, free of his old debts, ready to begin anew.

Some slaves openly revolted. A full scale revolt was led by one Song Qi, a slave turned bandit, who argued: "The emperor has changed, so the masters should be made into servants; master and servant should address each other as brothers."[36] Song Qi mixes his metaphors: if slaves are to be masters and masters to be servants, they can hardly also be brothers at the same time. Although the relation between brothers is hierarchical, with the elder taking precedence, the dynamic between master and servant is still not comparable. Nonetheless, his intent is clear; somehow the change of dynasty permits not just him, but all slaves to revolt from their masters.

Song Qi takes the extreme version of Zhang Wei's position. Huang Degong and Zhang Wei are not alone in suggesting that when there is no Emperor, all the hierarchical relations that make up society might potentially be disrupted. Like Song Qi, Ruan Dacheng acts on the license Chongzhen's death gives him to undermine the status quo. When he fails to win over Shi Kefa's support of Prince Fu's candidacy, Ruan Dacheng is initially discouraged, since obviously Shi Kefa outranks him (in the aftermath of his association with Wei Zhongxian, Ruan Dacheng has been stripped of any official position). Under normal circumstances, Ruan Dacheng would simply have given up, deferring to Shi Kefa's seniority: "Since this Shi Kefa holds the seal to the armies, if he should get stubborn on me, then this plan to receive and crown Prince Fu won't work." But Ruan quickly reassures himself with this thought and proceeds with his plans: "Well, I'm being stupid—if even the Emperor's jade seal has disappeared, what use does your little pebble of a seal have?"[37]

Ruan Dacheng's logic is similar to that used by Huang Degong to deny any relationship to Liu Liangzuo: Shi Kefa's seal of office has no authority on its own without the Emperor's to back it up; without the Emperor in his place, Shi Kefa has no right to command Ruan Dacheng. According to Ruan Dacheng's interpretation (as suspect and self-serving as that of Song Qi the rebellious slave), once the Chongzhen Emperor is gone, the hierarchy binding all of the officials who served under him simply dissolves, leaving a free-for-all.

One might consider the Emperor the only one who himself owes no one for his appointment, but who instead is responsible for all the appointments. But by such standards, Hongguang is no Emperor at all. Having been chosen Emperor, he is forever indebted to his benefactors. His hold on power rests on Ma Shiying—not the other way around.

The peculiarities of this political situation are the source of some irony in the play. In Act 16, in one of the first acts of the new regime, Hongguang reads aloud the imperial edict appointing Ma Shiying to high official positions: "Governor Ma Shiying, who led the welcoming of the Emperor and who is first in merit, is hereby appointed to fill the position of Grand Secretary of the Grand Secretariat and Chief Minister of the Military."[38] Normally such an edict rests on two related assumptions, both tied to the fact that the Emperor's position precedes that of his subordinates: first, the Emperor's own appointment has nothing whatsoever to do with one of an official; and second, the official's position is defined relative to the Emperor. In contrast, we have just witnessed several scenes in which this normative vision has been inverted, where various officials evaluate the various merits of different Emperor-candidates.

We know that if anything, this edict, which on the surface announces Ma Shiying's new appointment as the highest minister in the land, indicates the reality that this particular Emperor has been appointed by Ma Shiying and not the other way around. Ma Shiying and Hongguang give each other identity just as Du Liniang and Liu Mengmei do; each creates the other, puppet monarch and puppet master. In *Mudan ting*, that kind of circularity marks an idyll, a magical space of romance that at the same time can be integrated with society at large, a husband and a wife who are on some profound level equals.

Here in *Taohua shan*, this mutual creation of identity that undoes a central hierarchical relation marks a sick society on the brink of collapse. If ministers appoint the Emperor, then hierarchies no longer make any sense, and the Emperor himself will be forever beholden to one of his own ministers.

Indeed, Hongguang's grand welcome into Nanjing, where his recognition is carefully staged by Ruan Dacheng and Ma Shiying, foreshadows his future as a pathetic refugee turned away and refused recognition. Ma Shiying and Ruan Dacheng worry that they can hardly welcome the new Emperor into the capital with a mere handful of officials, so they gather together false signatures as a show of support. Later on when the situation grows dire, those officials can hardly be called upon. And one of the few high officials willing to offer his support in person is the same Xu Hongji who will pretend not to recognize Hongguang later.[39] Recognition that can be offered as a choice may also be taken away.

In describing the influence of a superior's behavior on his inferior, Confucius explains: "If the lord acts as a lord, his minister will act as a minister. If the father acts as a father, the son will act as a son."[40] I have translated this quotation as it is usually read, descriptive of a specific kind of causality; namely, if superiors act as they ought, they set a proper example and allow their underlings to act as they ought. And perhaps Confucius intends not two parallel causal statements, but a single one, where the lord's proper behavior spreads downward, influencing the behavior of sons in families. However, one might read the same statement as prescriptive instead of descriptive. Perhaps one is to understand that the minister is obliged to act like a minister only if the lord behaves properly (and by extension, the son is obliged to act like a proper son only if his father first behaves appropriately). In other words, to merit respect, the lord and the father must first treat their subjects and sons properly.

I have already discussed some of the implications of this insidious line of logic, which ultimately obligates parents to earn the filial devotion of their children and husbands to earn the chastity of their wives. This ethical problem proved troubling, as late imperial popular literature and popular history on the matter of filial piety and chastity make clear: if filial piety is simply the payment of a debt, is it not intrinsically finite? According to the counter position, parents are entitled to filial devotion simply by the fact of their *being* parents. Filial piety, chastity, and loyalty become matters of identity and not recompense, and this is why the world of *Taohua shan*—where a wife is not really a wife, a parent is not truly a parent, and a liege lord not really a liege lord—ultimately dooms filial piety, chastity, and loyalty.

And what happens when a sovereign like Hongguang owes his very identity as sovereign to one of his ministers? How can their relation not be permanently tainted by reciprocity? For even if Hongguang were a far wiser sovereign, making every honest effort not to favor Ma Shiying, there would always be at least the appearance of recompense in all of his treatment of Ma Shiying. According to some, the relationship between sovereign and subject admits no reciprocity. No matter what he does, the sovereign owes the subject nothing. No one, as Elizabeth I of England is reported to have snapped on her deathbed, may use the word "must" to a prince.

If there is a reciprocal relationship between sovereign and subject, something of the sovereign's nature is lost. Briefly, I return to Hobbes: for amidst all the subjects whose behavior and belief bear no relation to each other, there is a single person in his imagined polity—the sovereign—whose actions *do* perfectly reflect his beliefs. Consequently, the sovereign is absolutely responsible for his actions, since he—and only he—cannot have been coerced into them. In other words, if a sovereign states disbelief in Christ, it must reflect belief, since no Elisha need ever give a sovereign permission of the kind given Naaman. All of the sovereign's actions are governed by free choice.

This autonomy, a transparency between thought and action that makes the sovereign the only person whose beliefs are mirrored by actions, allows the sovereign to be the only sincere person in a society of actors all playing for the approval of the monarch. Tang Xianzu and *zaju* censors at the Ming court were wise to keep the sovereign offstage. But such a privileged position is manifestly denied Hongguang; instead, he belongs onstage—a playactor in a society of playactors, both manipulated and manipulating in a political culture of machinations.

When it becomes clear that Bolingbroke means to replace him as king, Shakespeare's *Richard II*, with typical melodrama, mocks the proceedings:

> What must the king do now? Must he submit?
> The king shall do it. Must he be depos'd?
> The king shall be contented. Must he lose
> The name of king? a God's name, let it go. (III.iii.142–5)

Any obligation on the sovereign, Richard argues, contradicts the very nature of sovereignty. For if the king can be forced to do anything—to submit, for example—as Richard suggests, he might also be forced to relinquish his very kingship and lose his very identity. Richard finds himself in the position where Hongguang begins. To be sovereign is to recognize no obligations; if the Chongzhen Emperor rewards ministers for meritorious service, it ought to be solely because he chooses to do so, for all of the sovereign's acts take place out of choice. And it is difficult indeed to regard our Hongguang, who owes his existence as Emperor to Ma Shiying and who leaves our sight dragged off like a sack of potatoes, in that demanding light as any monarch at all.

Instead of being a natural-born daughter, Li Xiangjun is Li Zhenli's foster daughter. From Ruan Dacheng's experiences, we know very well what people think about adopted children: the eunuch Wei Zhongxian's adoption of Ruan Dacheng (admittedly somewhat different since both are grown men) inspires deep anger and disgust on the part of the Revival Society. Of course, the Revival Society hates Wei Zhongxian already, and his adoption of Ruan Dacheng strikes everyone as the height of sycophancy.

But part of the disgust comes out of what people think about adoption. Ruan Dacheng becomes Wei Zhongxian's *yizi*, a term I have earlier translated as "foster son," but which might more literally be rendered "sworn son"—intention is instrumental to the formation of this tie. The other common way in classical Chinese of referring to an adopted child puts it even more bluntly: *jiazi* or *jianü*, "artificial child" (where *jia* is the antonym of *zhen*, the "authentic" both *Mudan ting* and *Taohua shan* so relentlessly problematize).⁴¹

No one sneers at Li Xiangjun for having been reared by a foster mother; among prostitutes, such a state of affairs does not surprise and was quite common into the twentieth century. Nonetheless, the impropriety of the relationship between this mother and daughter is suggested at a number of points. They share a surname (which no legitimate daughter would with her mother), so that either Li Zhenli passed down her surname to her daughter—or just as bad, the father and mother shared the same surname (an endogamy bordering on incest to a Confucian moralist). They also come close to sharing a man, suggesting shades of an even more unpalatable incest. When Li Xiangjun refuses to become Tian Yang's mistress, Li Zhenli goes in her place to join his household, so that in making love to the mother, Tian Yang thinks he possesses the daughter.

Like the union between Hou Fangyu and Li Xiangjun, the one between Tian Yang and Li Zhenli invokes the language of the orthodox relation of marriage, but unlike marriage, it is all too easily dissolved. Her prostitute friends might consider her to have found a safe haven, but in a few acts Li Zhenli is floating around in a houseboat, having been kicked out by Tian Yang's jealous wife—his real one, that is.

In contrast, the possibility of financial interest taints every maternal word or gesture of Li Zhenli. When Xiangjun rejects the dowry, Li Zhenli is at first understandably disapproving, since after all, a great sum of money is involved. She cannot help but sound mercenary when she urges: "To take nice things and throw them on the ground—that's a shame."[42] Later, when Li Zhenli urges her daughter to go with Tian Yang, she might be convinced that her daughter will find safety with the powerful man, or she might be afraid to protest Yang Wencong's plans, but again it can hardly avoid looking like selfishness. Whatever she feels about her daughter's best interests, the history of their relationship makes Li Zhenli appear a bit too interested.

Even if Li Zhenli were truly to regard her daughter with sincere, maternal love and selfless concern for her well-being, she has no way to prove herself. In fact, we know that the girl has been a terrible investment. Throughout the play, Li Xiangjun costs Li Zhenli money, while the older woman does not earn a penny from Li Xiangjun: the dowry supplied by Ruan Dacheng is returned; Hou Fangyu has no money of his own to give (or pay, perhaps one ought to say); Li Xiangjun refuses to become Tian Yang's mistress. In an earlier chapter, I have gone through some of the difficulties involved in proving sincerity and selflessness when reciprocity is involved; since she contracted their relationship, paying now in the hopes of gaining later, Li Zhenli finds herself in the same position, in a similarly tainted relationship. What binds them is not a necessary relationship but merely an expedient one.

We have returned to the same problem that Hou Fangyu encounters when he receives the blood-splattered fan and that Hongguang faces with each former subject who refuses him help at his moment of need. At what point can a relationship be completed and consequently terminated?

The question is particularly relevant in the case of the madam and prostitute. Their relationship begins with and is founded on economic transactions: the madam purchases the girl as an investment, but only after years of lessons in music and deportment would the girl be able to bring in any significant amount of money for the madam. In such a relationship, there is very literally a point at which the relationship between the two can dissolve. Late Ming and Qing literature is filled with prostitutes who ask for money from a favorite client or save enough money on their own so that they can buy themselves from their madams (who are referred to as mothers, just like Li Zhenli).[43] Once the madam is reimbursed the price of the girl—perhaps appropriately inflated to account for her earning potential—she will relinquish her hold on the girl. At that point, the relationship with the madam simply comes to an end.

Bonds of choice, Kong Shangren argues, are weak, burdened always with the potential of dissolution. James Watson's anthropological research concurs. In his study of adoption practices in the New Territories, Watson finds that while adoption is a complicated and expensive process, subject at every juncture to many obstacles, disowning an adopted son involves no formalities at all, just a statement from the adoptive father. In contrast, disowning a legitimate son is very difficult. Their claims to property and to rights are not subject to their fathers' personal whims.[44]

Mudan ting ends with the promise that identity—even if it cannot be fixed in advance—can be granted; *Taohua shan*'s ending argues that any identity that can be granted can also be withdrawn. *Mudan ting* ends with a remarriage of the human family—a reunion between mother and father, a marriage of daughter and son-in-law, a joining together of all four—all reunited through choice and the power of an Emperor's promise. And yet even that reunion shows strains at the seams, as I suggested in my introduction to *Mudan ting*. Despite the joyousness of the moment, Du Bao's reluctance to participate in the reunion foreshadows some of the difficulties involved in conceiving of a fifty-sixth act of *Mudan ting* where all return home, happy and reconciled with what has transpired.

Taohua shan takes up the doubts that color *Mudan ting*'s ending. The later play muses—obsessively, a critic might say—over what would happen in the "happily ever after" of its predecessor, that fifty-sixth act I find it so difficult to imagine.

Mudan ting concludes with a promise, made good by the Emperor no less, that these newly assembled familial identities are entirely adequate to the demands made on more conventional ones. Perhaps we might even think that these newly forged ties might be considered superior, having been sanctified by passion, *qing*. But are they? Or would they, too, like the ties that bind in *Taohua shan*, collapse when subjected to pressure? Would that unique family dissolve, just as all the associations in *Taohua shan* seem doomed to?

If *Mudan ting* is a play where recognition is a magical gift, given by a mother to her long-dead child, bestowed by the Emperor unto a subject, then *Taohua shan* dramatizes again and again the possibility that recognition might be refused. As Ma Shiying muses in his thoughts on the theatre, what would it take for someone who knows me perfectly well—say, my son or grandson—to refuse to recognize me? Only a little makeup would do the trick. (Or, as the ghostly Du Liniang might ask, what would it take for my mother to disown me?) In that sense, the prospect of a Crown Prince who has lost his place in society, whom many know but none will recognize, haunts every moment in *Taohua shan*.

Sometimes, the refusal to recognize has merely comedic effects. After Hou Fangyu has already persuaded Shi Kefa of Prince Fu's utter unfitness to be Emperor, Ruan Dacheng arrives with an eleventh-hour appeal that Shi Kefa support Prince Fu's candidacy. He never even makes it in the door to see Shi Kefa, because the doorman detains him. The doorman clearly recognizes Ruan Dacheng, since he has ready those all-too-predictable jokes that accompany each appearance of Ruan Dacheng: his surname sounds exactly like the word "soft," *ruan*, and to make matters worse, he happens to live in a Nanjing neighborhood called "Crotch of the Pants." The reader may imagine for herself the hilarity that ensues.

Ruan introduces himself and then sends the doorman off with a message for Shi Kefa, who keeps sending the doorman back to delay Ruan Dacheng. Finally, with his mind made up about Prince Fu, Shi Kefa tells his doorman that he will not see Ruan Dacheng. At this point, the doorman does something very peculiar. Rather than pass on Shi Kefa's message, he pretends not to know who Ruan is, even though he has just been bantering with Ruan Dacheng. Flabbergasted, Ruan repeats the errand that he has commissioned the doorman: "That's right. I just now sent you to ask your master—surely you haven't forgotten." And the doorman responds, as if he does not recognize him: "Who are you?"[45]

The doorman's question to Ruan Dacheng—face-to-face, when each man knows perfectly well who the other is—is one of our first tastes of a motif running throughout the play: what does it take for someone who knows who a person is to refuse to recognize him? Since they have no prior relationship, the doorman's refusal to recognize Ruan Dacheng speaks only of a sadistic playfulness and a recognition of Ruan's powerlessness to retaliate. In every other context, this question is dead serious.

Ma Shiying asks what it would take for a son to give up his father; Yang Wencong tells us what it would take for a parent to refuse to recognize a child. In many ways, Yang Wencong approximates a father in his relationship with Li Xiangjun: Li Zhenli turns to him for advice about the girl's future; he names her; he masterminds her match to Hou Fangyu, arranging the details of the dowry (if not actually supplying it); and when Li Zhenli goes with Tian Yang in her daughter's place, she leaves her daughter in Yang Wencong's care. Moreover, there is never even the slightest hint that Yang Wencong would pursue her sexually for himself.

Despite this shared history, when he flees Nanjing, their association comes to an end. He tells Li Xiangjun he can no longer keep an eye on her: "In such a state of chaos, even fathers and their children cannot care for each other."[46] If even parents and children are no longer to care for each other, then surely Yang Wencong is absolved of his obligations to her, for he is not even her father. Under pressure from the outside, their bond evaporates to nothingness.

Mudan ting imagines a rebirth of a family—this time begun not with the relationship between parents and a child at its center, but with a husband and wife, who have chosen and created each other. The stakes are just as high in *Taohua shan*; isolated in the mountains, having fled the turmoil of dynastic transition, Li Xiangjun and Hou Fangyu are finally reunited. If they marry, it seems that the promise of Tao Qian's Peach Blossom Spring might be achieved. Society might indeed be regenerated by breaking away, starting over again with families at its center, no part of the totalizing imperium. A family might begin when a man and a woman choose each other and—with no authority's sanctioning power—marry each other.

I have already discussed Zhang Wei's refusal to endorse their desire. He insists on placing the two lovers in the context of the greater polity and on making marriage not a question of two individuals' feelings, but instead a part of preexisting families and society as a whole. After Zhang Wei's speech, the two lovers make no further protest, and they who have been entangled together for so long finally realize that they have no future.

However, it is not enough for them simply to concede that their affair has come to an end. After all they have been through, Li Xiangjun turns to the man she claimed to be her husband, for whom she has sacrificed and pined. No recognition is now possible, and she blankly asks: "Who is that across from me?" Only then, after denying all recognition, does she allow herself to be dressed in the robes of a Daoist initiate, and then she and Hou Fangyu are separated forever. It is gain, not loss, the first step to the rule of the Sage King. For to her, neither daughter nor wife, without the kind of promise the Emperor of *Mudan ting* made to Du Liniang, he can be no one but a mere stranger.

EPILOGUE

The Spider and the Snake

This book has been thoroughly informed by something I sensed intuitively to be true as I began my studies of late Ming and early Qing literature: how accessible I found the concerns of late imperial literature, especially when compared to those of earlier Chinese literatures. In this book, I have focused especially on questions posed about individuals, including how simultaneously difficult and yet absolutely imperative the task of identifying an individual is, and whether a person can define himself or herself without falling back on relations with others, either in a hierarchical context or in a familial one. Who am I, if not someone's sister or someone else's student?

I was also struck by the confluences between two very different strains in my studies of sixteenth- and seventeenth-century English literature and Ming and Qing literature. In short, I am interested not in explaining, but in exploring the point at which Stephen Greenblatt begins *Renaissance Self-Fashioning* and how it relates to these two late imperial Chinese plays: the observation "as old in academic writing as Burckhardt and Michelet, that there is in the early modern period a change in the intellectual, psychological, and aesthetic structures that govern the generation of identities."[1] Even though one might question the strong association of that change with anything "early modern," many scholars have observed the same sea change in Chinese texts of the late imperial period as well.

I have examined identity in these two plays from a number of perspectives. The title *Persons, Roles, and Minds* reflects my interest in the interactions between different kinds of identity: philosophical minds, theatrical roles, and legal positions. I have discussed ways in which both plays deal with the state's formation of bureaucratic identities, suggesting the possibility that legal identities and physical ones might not mesh. I am primarily interested in *Mudan ting* and *Taohua shan* as literary texts that invite close readings, not for how they must have been adapted for the stage centuries ago.[2] Nonetheless, both texts are deeply concerned with the place of the theatre, as a place that legitimates the power either of imagination (on the one hand) or of dissimulation (on the other). Who, for example, is an actor really—his role or the low-status entertainer playing that role?

Let me end this book by taking a step backward. In this epilogue, I will focus mainly on the question of whether the way I have chosen to approach these immensely rich texts can be justified, touching only a bit on the two plays.

I begin with a snake in shadow and a spider in a cup, both figures for knowledge that kills. In Shakespeare's *The Winter's Tale*, Leontes becomes inflamed with the suspicion that his best friend Polixenes and his wife Hermione are cuckolding him. The suspicion torments him; but once it has been confronted, Leontes finds, it proves impossible to put away. He says, almost regretfully, as if recognizing his own insanity:

> There may be in the cup
> A spider steeped, and one may drink, depart,
> And yet partake no venom, for his knowledge
> Is not infected; but if one present
> Th'abhorred ingredient to his eye, make known
> How he hath drunk, he cracks his gorge, his sides,
> With violent hefts. I have drunk, and seen the spider. (II.i.39)

The spider is a figure for a sort of belief whose basis in fact is almost immaterial, a poison that kills only if seen, but does not harm if drunk unknowingly.

In *Mudan ting*, Du Liniang's maidservant Chunxiang marvels at the miracle of her resurrection, ruing only the sorrow her death caused her mother in the first place:

Your fragrant spirit has summoned forth the butterfly of the dream,
Making your mother brokenhearted over the snake in the shadow.³

The snake in the shadow resembles to a remarkable degree Shakespeare's spider, a belief that kills its possessor regardless of whether the snake is actually there. The snake exists at all for reasons that have nothing to do with the spider; since Chunxiang sings a parallel couplet, Zhuangzi's famous butterfly—the one of whom he dreamt and upon waking wondered whether he had dreamt of a butterfly or whether even now the butterfly was dreaming of him—demands an equally buglike companion ("snake," or *she*, is written with the insect radical in Chinese). Nonetheless, the similarity between the snake and the spider is still striking. In both cases, they turn out to be illusory, figments of the imagination; Leontes is utterly mistaken about his wife's faithlessness, and the dead child that Lady Zhen mourns reappears as a blooming bride.

As a literary critic schooled in these two traditions, what am I to make of this similarity? Of course, it is merely coincidental, whatever that means; and in setting side by side the snake and the spider, I have chosen a photogenic homology that could hardly result from anything but serendipity. Tang Xianzu happened to draw on a well-known allusion from the *Jinshu* (or the *History of the Jin*), and Shakespeare wrote Leontes' speech, in two independent actions, each entirely unaware of and uninfluenced by the other. This coincidence, the tie between the spider and the snake, gives me license to pursue a few questions that underlie my own practice of comparative literature.

As befits an exploration of the problem of identity, I have been inspired by a number of Western philosophers past and present. To name some who are important: Descartes, Hobbes, Locke, Derek Parfit, Amèlie Oksenberg Rorty. In this epilogue, I will allude to some of the problems involved in thinking about the plays in the context of the work of these philosophers. But for the most part, I do not think philosophical influence presents the same methodological challenge that historicism does.

The Winter's Tale hardly appears in this book except at its end, but my knowing that play has deeply influenced almost every nuance of my interpretation of *Mudan ting*. I can never be the same as a reader who had never encountered it. Even where Western literary texts have not consciously influenced me, literary critics thinking about those texts and philosophers participating in the same tradition have.

And even in the absence of those more direct sorts of influence, other sorts of comparison and translation are constantly taking place for all scholars of Chinese literature, wherever they happen to work. The techniques employed in literary studies—and even the selection of texts considered worthy of academic scrutiny—are basically inherited from intellectual forebears in the Western academy (hence, for example, the ongoing and remarkably wrong-headed search for the Chinese epic). Even sinological philologists owe as much or more in technique to their nineteenth-century German predecessors than to Qing evidential scholars. Every university-affiliated scholar of Asian studies in the country, for example, must position herself in an academy whose organization into departments representing disciplines (history, for example, or literature) and those representing areas (such as East Asian Studies, or my own department—Asian and Middle Eastern Studies) seems still to reflect some old Hegelian saw about China's not having any history (nor any real literature, it seems).

But to return to my immediate problem of the spider and the snake: by "coincidence," I mean a convergence that is causally and historically unrelated. How am I to approach a convergence that I am convinced is truly "coincidental"? Or, to take a step backwards, is the fact of their unrelatedness actually such a confirmed fact? Or is it in fact the case that even with this convergence—so apparently coincidental—the actual precise degree of historical relatedness or unrelatedness is sufficiently beyond the reach of proof that one had simply better drop the issue? There are far-reaching repercussions to such a decision. And even if I could assert the absolute unrelatedness of these two texts, what persuasive readings could be generated out of this accidental convergence? Or, to rephrase my question, what are the implications of thinking that these two texts are somehow homologues, which can be compared as such, and how can one justify the very notion of homology itself?

If I were Northrop Frye, or of his intellectual lineage, or even a structuralist cousin, this coincidence would not trouble me at all. The coincidence I have chosen, a figure of speech, is one of many that tie *Mudan ting* and *The Winter's Tale* together at practically every level. The two plays tell remarkably similar stories. Both highlight trust and belief and are set into motion by a patriarch's obtuseness and suspicion. Both plays center on the same social problem: in the absence of a son, how can a patrimony be passed on to a daughter? Both fathers choose not to take a second wife with the goal of producing a male heir (Du Bao does not take a concubine, and in all of the years in which Leontes thinks himself widowed, he does not remarry).

In two dramatic traditions where the conventional ending joins together a girl and a boy in marriage, both of these plays choose to end instead with a family reunion, where the girl's mother and father come back together, just as the girl and her lover do. Nor do the parallels end there: in both plays, a mother and a daughter thought to be dead—leaving the husband and father entirely alone—come back to life. The plays share another miracle as well, each featuring a woman who emerges from a work of art: Du Liniang emerges out of her painting; Hermione is a statue come to life.

To a disciple of Frye, then, both plays represent a specific literary archetype, although even that would hardly seem enough to account for all of the similarities. To that critic, their historical proximity (they were written within a decade of each other) is irrelevant. According to such a reading, neither when nor where they were written is important. No stronger tie than this one of textual resemblance binds *The Winter's Tale* to its own Jacobean contemporaries or even to other plays written by the same playwright. *Mudan ting* and *The Winter's Tale* form as natural a pairing as any. The problem of comparison is resolved, but the answer fails to satisfy me, since it rests on a faith I do not share—the unity of all literature across different cultures, languages, and literary traditions.

Most people who really like literature also value particularity, and that implies certain historicist questions—for example, how texts are tied to the specifics of a location and a period, or perhaps how different texts participate in different societies. There are ahistorical ways of reading the two texts in conjunction, not limited to something like Frye's approach. I have often said that I like to imagine a dialogue between two texts where neither is privileged over the other, and I am convinced that such an approach is possible, indeed unavoidable in any discussion I am likely to generate on either text, since through familiarity and study both texts have become a part of me. And so the convergence has some significance if only as mediated through me; in my mind, spider and snake can hardly be separated from each other.

But then there is also the problem of scholarly interest: I happen to find myself drawn to some questions that lend themselves to historicism, or rather ones that can hardly be addressed outside of a historical context. Of course, *Taohua shan*, the play I deal with in the second half of this book, is a work of history, an effort to relate the fall of the Ming dynasty onstage, and it grapples explicitly with questions of historiography: what it implies, for example, to choose one version and to exclude other, competing versions of what happened.

But I mean something very different about historicist questions. For example, in thinking about *Mudan ting* and *The Winter's Tale*, I want to ask how thinking about marriage informs comedy, as it certainly does in both these plays. For both plays force a reader to think about what constitutes a marriage. Both plays conclude with marriages so fantastical as to threaten to undermine the very institution. But to challenge that institution, both plays present versions deeply embedded in the particularities of their own times and places.

In *Mudan ting*, as I discuss at length in the first half of this book, the hero and the heroine are wed in a highly unorthodox manner. After a love affair during the course of which the heroine is actually a ghost, her beloved resurrects her from the dead and they elope. Later, when they appear before the Emperor, the heroine's father refuses to accept both her resurrection and her marriage. But the Emperor rules in favor of the young lovers anyway, confirming both their marriage and their identities. So what is it that makes them married? At what point have they become married?

By the end of the second act of *The Winter's Tale*, the marriage between Leontes and Hermione finds itself in a position that cannot be sustained. Leontes has become a husband so obsessed with an unfounded jealousy that only by forcing his wife into a position where she dies of misery can he believe again in her chastity. If he can only believe her when her sincerity is proven by her death, they obviously cannot remain married.

A second marriage also cannot quite come together until the end of the play. The lost daughter of Leontes and Hermione, Perdita, was raised by a humble shepherd after her abandonment and after sixteen years is now a maiden in love with a young princeling. But without knowledge of her true parents, Perdita cannot be married, since the prince's father will not sanction a marriage between his son and a humble shepherdess.

At the beginning of this project, I felt—and continue to feel—that marriage occupies a similarly special place in these two plays and that there is something to a comparison of the place of marriage in them. In both plays, marriage is an external condition recognized by others and necessary to the perpetuation of family and society, but it is something much more as well; both plays suggest that marriage can sometimes reflect an internal state, private and shared between two individuals, unknowable by others. Something internal repairs Leontes and Hermione's sick marriage. When it is contracted again, the marriage can no longer serve any procreative purpose, since Hermione's childbearing years have been spent in self-imposed exile from her husband. Liu Mengmei and Du Liniang's marriage can somehow be contracted in isolation, when her family thinks she is dead (and so obviously do not consent to the union), so that this marriage—one of the basic components of society—has begun in a vacuum. Moreover, in both plays, marriage attracts a number of epistemological problems; as an external reflection of an internal state, it highlights a number of problems associated with privacy. How can one trust that the person one loves is indeed who she claims to be? How can one know one's partner? Even such a seemingly innocuous comparison between the plays presents theoretical problems.

Those of us in the field of Chinese literary studies mostly operate with the assumption that different cultures arose independently and that homologous cultural traces can profitably be compared—even if we are sometimes troubled by the enormous leaps of faith demanded by each of these assumptions. Of course, there are scholars who avoid the theoretical issue by facing the historical one head-on, choosing instead a problem that actually has an empirical solution. Through careful philological and archeological work, they seek to figure out which specific features of Chinese culture arose through cultural diffusion (and which others, by default, independently). But such scholars are rare. For the most part, we assume that cultural differences can be accounted for by separate but parallel histories and that comparative development shows patterns it might be fruitful to study.

However, this idea itself—that cultures originate and develop separately and that similarities ought to be seen as parallels, that, in other words, morphological comparisons suggest a way to understand cultural difference—is far from something that can simply be assumed. Instead, this idea has been the object of an intense debate, embedded in the intellectual legacy of Western Europe. Moreover, the problem continues to touch on other important philosophical questions that remain the object of contention to this day.

At the end of the eighteenth century, Johann Gottfried Herder was one of the first thinkers to argue in any systematic fashion that cultures could not be understood according to a single scale, ranging from the civilized to the barbaric, but instead had to be understood on their own terms. In connection with this idea, he also suggested something resembling a morphological analysis, proposing that the patterns of cultural difference themselves revealed truths (an idea that underlies the social sciences to this day). In a book review responding to Herder's work, his former teacher Immanuel Kant disagreed vehemently, arguing that the proper object of study was not the patterns of development, but reason itself, which makes people see patterns in different cultures.

A belief that cultural differences ought to be viewed through a morphological lens seems to be strongly associated with a commitment to relativist ethics. Whether implicitly or explicitly, those who espouse relativist ethics frequently do so by deploying a historicist argument (albeit one that is not quite historical in that it eludes proof or disproof): that cultures arise and develop independently. The myth of separate origins underlies weighty issues.

It was on the subject of ethics that Kant truly broke with his old student, arguing that according to Herder's version of human origins, one could not make any meaningful statements about ethics, nor even about a single human nature. Kant asks a rhetorical question of Herder, choosing the most primitive peoples he can think of, the Tahitians, who were thought to use cannibalism in their religious rites:

> Does the author [Herder] really mean that, if the happy inhabitants of Tahiti, never visited by more civilized nations, were destined to live in their peaceful indolence for thousands of centuries, it would be possible to give a satisfactory answer of why they should exist at all, and of whether it would not have been just as good if the island had been occupied by happy sheep and cattle as by happy human beings who merely enjoy themselves?[4]

This dispute—with morphology at stake—recapitulated throughout the last two centuries, foreshadows some of the most important conflicts of recent history: Herder's side in the service of tribalism; Kant's, colonialism.

While homology now seems something to be assumed, its old companion questions, born simultaneously and out of similar assumptions—including ethical relativism—remain very much in hot dispute. All I mean to show here is that morphological analysis is neither innocuous nor as foregone a conclusion as is sometimes assumed. For example, one current apology for authoritarian Asian governments rests essentially on the old tie between moral relativism and a very Herder-like version of cultural origins and difference; scholars like Tu Wei-ming, to name one of the most prominent, sound very much like the Enlightenment scholars they claim to disdain. Tu makes a claim about ethics based once again on a theory of cultural origins, arguing that since Chinese ethics arose out of a wholly independent tradition, Chinese politics should not be held to the ethical standards of the West.

There is a very good reason that proponents of this particular moral theory are very uneasy with the possibility of cultural diffusion. Such a theory of cultural origin suggests that traditions cannot be thought of as discrete and that all traditions are created through exchanges with and borrowings from others. Similarities between cultures might merely be morphological, but they might also be the result of diffusion. And the degree to which traditions are in fact independent can never be proven; links of cultural diffusion can sometimes incontrovertibly be shown, but morphological similarity can only be suggested by the absence of any other explanation and thus perhaps never conclusively proven, except in the individual case.

Conceptualizing cultural difference morphologically (or rather regarding similarities as simply homologous) has also been an important part of various other debates also central to European intellectual history. Isaiah Berlin has famously traced the intellectual lineage of cultural history itself back to Giambattista Vico's and Herder's thinking on national and cultural difference and the extent to which a person from one culture can ever understand another's. Others have placed the rise of the modern nation in this intellectual context. Nor can this history of an idea be separated from a legacy of colonialism; Anthony Pagden has written extensively about how European encounters with Native Americans created the field of ethnology, founded on the notion of polygenetic origins and homologies.

In turning my attention then to this problem—what an intellectually committed comparison of marriage in *Mudan ting* and *The Winter's Tale* would entail and presume—I am interested in what is considered a serious theoretical problem in anthropology and history but very much less so in literary criticism (and even less in philosophy). Comparative literary studies began with a belief in morphological relations between texts and genres of different traditions; Goethe's notion of a *Weltliteratur* began with a Chinese narrative that he assumed belonged to essentially the same category as a German or French romantic novel. In contrast, anthropologists and historians of the last few generations have struggled mightily with the problems associated with morphological comparison: whether, for example, such a thing as a shaman exists in different cultures, or whether feudalism as a concept can be applied to Japan as well as to Europe.

In this epilogue, I am centering my discussion on the problems that confront such a treatment of marriage, but I could have chosen any of a number of other topics, too. Interesting cross-cultural parallels have informed my ideas on many other fields of inquiry in this work. A few of the most important that come to mind include portraiture, monarchy, dreaming, and the uses of torture.

It goes without saying that marriage—in the laws that defined it, in its place in religious life, and in its cultural significances—was something very different in seventeenth-century England than in seventeenth-century China. For more than a generation, various anthropologists have contended that the study of such a topic across different cultures (and marriage, along with kinship and shamanism, is frequently the test case) is simply impossible, that it is grounded in an untenable belief that marriage in two different cultures represents two homologous cultural traces. Ultimately, so the reasoning goes, such an analysis reveals more about the anthropologist's mindset than about any culture.

Many anthropologists now make a point either of never referring to any field of study by a translated name, or at the very least of problematizing the act of translation, sometimes by choosing an unexpected equivalent. Rather than translating a given concept as "magic," for example, one might choose to use an indigenous word, or perhaps choose to refer to it as "ontology" instead. In other words, from the level of nomenclature onwards, perhaps my use of "marriage" for *hunyin* is itself wrongheaded, since it implies by omission that *hunyin* and marriage are the same thing.

Such a position—that any deep structural tie between *hunyin* and marriage is only something that I, in talking about them in conjunction, grant them—is by no means extreme. Let me just throw out two details about the practice of marriage that immediately reveal a few of the difficulties involved in drawing any kind of parallel. As Ludwig Wittgenstein writes, suggesting that the study of any word draws in that single word's place in the entire language, "We must plow through the whole of language."[5] Two little furrows to begin with then—and a reminder that the problem I have outlined suggests infinitely more complications than that already troublesome comparison between late imperial and Jacobean marriage, which many anthropologists would already consider impossible. For in tying together the spider and the snake, we enter the further level of abstraction of the represented world, where marriage is not just itself, but also a narrative and dramatic convention; and we are forced to compare not just the cultural apparatus surrounding marriage, but also that of representation and the theatre and the position of each within its culture.

Let us then turn to the difficulties. Marriage in seventeenth-century England was, of course, a Christian sacrament, practiced within the institution of the Anglican Church. Roman Catholic weddings, which took place much more rarely, raise different problems, since the possibility of divorce is specifically excluded. Any seventeenth-century English discussion of marriage ineluctably draws on an immense shared body of religious knowledge and practice. Hermione emerges out of what we are told is a sculpture, but which turns out simply to be herself. Only after the sculpture comes to life can she and Leontes be joined together; this moment can hardly avoid recalling in some way the beginnings of the very first marriage, when God creates a wife for Adam by sculpting his rib into Eve. Doesn't the allusion to events in Genesis render meaningless the comparison to the moment in *Mudan ting* when Du Liniang emerges out of her portrait?

More than one historian has noted that the central events of the European Renaissance were a marriage and a divorce: those of Martin Luther and Henry VIII, respectively. One can imagine the deep historical resonances a play like *The Winter's Tale* must have had in Jacobean England; in marked contrast to Henry VIII, Leontes is a king fully prepared to leave his kingdom to his daughter and her husband. Even when it would have been entirely within the bounds of law and custom, Henry's counterpart chooses not to remarry.

In China, a man could marry more than one wife, although one was usually considered the senior or official wife, and only she would later figure in the rites of ancestral worship. This particular sort of marriage—or bigamy, as one might choose to call it—resolves many a romantic comedy; when two young ladies both have a claim on the same young man, like as not, he will end up marrying them both. One might legitimately argue that all Chinese plays ending in a monogamous marriage or two (like *Mudan ting*) always stand in contradistinction to plays that end in bigamous marriages, like Gao Ming's *Pipa ji* (*The Story of the Lute*) or Ruan Dacheng's *Yanzi jian* (*The Swallow Letter*). *Mudan ting*'s happy ending, in which a nuclear family is reunited, emerges out of an entirely different repertoire of possibilities from *The Winter's Tale*.

Given all these problems, where does one even begin making a comparison of the sort I envision? I find myself in the dicey position of doing just what I accused Northrop Frye of doing, comparing what I consider to be two homologous cultural traces, matching up elements in different cultures to each other—in other words, taking a stand that I will be the first to admit is intellectually troubled: English marriage is to English comedy as Chinese marriage is to Chinese comedy. This process of analogy should not be taken for granted; there are real problems associated with doing what comes naturally—namely, comparing *Mudan ting* and *The Winter's Tale* as comparable, homological cultural traces.

I hasten to reassure the reader that I am certainly not taking the position that one culture's version of marriage is truer or more legitimate than that of others. Nor am I asserting or assuming that one can fall back on a fixed definition of marriage, one that means the same to all people, no matter what their culture or age. Writing on the European Middle Ages, John Boswell warns of some of the difficulties involved in writing a history of marriage, even when one's goal is tracing out a historical lineage that concludes in the present: "it is difficult, perhaps impossible, to map onto the grid of premodern heterosexual relationships what modern speakers understand by 'marriage': nothing in the ancient world quite corresponds to the idea of a permanent, exclusive union of social equals freely chosen by them to fulfill both their emotional needs and imposing equal obligations of fidelity on both partners."[6]

Quite to the contrary, I am comfortable in taking the anthropologists one step further and suggesting that there is much less accord on the question of what marriage is at *any* time or place than one might suppose. Boswell also points this problem out when he describes the situation in present-day America (as part of his work on same-sex marriage in medieval Europe): "Even in modern cultures with vast and standardized legal establishments, the technical definition of 'marriage' is difficult to formulate, and at the time of this writing there are hundreds of legal battles under adjudication about whether given heterosexual couples are actually 'married' or not."[7]

Some of the disputed cases involve a division of property and claims on offspring (just as such cases frequently did in late imperial China). Others, however, reveal much more than clear-cut cases do about what is considered important and defining about marriage in any culture, or what is truly at stake when two people marry. For example, the lawsuits recently brought before the Supreme Court of Hawaii by two couples, one gay and one lesbian, asserted that a prohibition against these marriages constituted gender discrimination. One might argue that according to the plaintiffs' version of marriage, its essence is a free relation between two consenting adults. The lawsuit then only brings this version to its natural conclusion, for surely there is no reason that two men or two women are less able to embark on such a contract than a single man and a single woman. Similarly, Du Liniang and Liu Mengmei's marriage (heterodox as it is) brings up issues important to all Ming marriages, primarily, the extent to which choice can feature in a Confucian relationship.

Pinning down even a single feature that all marriages share, whether across different cultures or even within a single culture, will prove an impossible task, as Boswell's work suggests. Marriages are not all the result of choice; they do not all involve a single man and a single woman; they do not all aim to produce children; they do not all result in shared property. One of the most important twentieth-century scholars of marriage, Boswell himself focuses his work on same-sex, possibly celibate unions. The best one can do is trace a network of relations among these different forms of marriage, linking different versions to each other through features that overlap and crisscross.

In theory, at least, one knows that one ought to avoid exaggerating similarity between different cultures. In our own time, when confronted with such differences, some of the most important anthropological and historical writers (Michel de Certeau comes to mind, but so might many others) have spilled a considerable amount of ink on the problem of writing about the unfamiliar and the extent to which it is possible. But how is one to avoid the equally important companion problem, exaggerating difference? One senses intuitively that there is a range of difference; some cultures are closer to each other than others, if only because of a history of cross-cultural influences and exchanges.

The recent passion among historians of Europe for turning anthropological techniques on the past has had some inadvertent effects. One might almost feel that the passionate ethnographic energy directed in the last century towards describing other cultures—having nowhere else to turn—is now directed towards the exoticizing of the European and North American pasts. At any rate, that strain of historical enquiry leaves scholars of China in an awkward position. For if nineteenth-century England is beyond any kind of intuitive understanding, where does that leave the scholar of premodern China?

One might try to gauge a precise sense of the exact degree and quality of cultural difference—without falling back on the assumption that the two cultures are either totally incommensurate or essentially interchangeable—by analyzing records of cross-cultural encounters and seeing what happened during these moments where such communication is foregrounded. Is translation between these two cultures possible? What degree of understanding was there? What was misunderstood?

For example, studies of the late-sixteenth-century Jesuits who came to China (many of whom, like the famous Matteo Ricci, were astonishingly successful at mastering Chinese language and customs) frequently seek to ascertain precisely the degree of communication that took place. Since these Jesuits seemed to have no problem recognizing marriages between Chinese men and women, one might argue, there must have been some grounds of communication, and a scholar such as myself might indeed have grounds for assuming that marriage in seventeenth-century Europe is something like marriage in seventeenth-century China.

But accounts of cross-cultural encounters are notorious for leaving much ground for seemingly unresolvable dispute. Gananath Obeyesekere and Marshall Sahlins, for example, examine precisely the same documents and events—the circumstances leading to Captain Cook's murder by Polynesians—and arrive at precisely opposite conclusions.[8] According to Sahlins, where Cook's sailors felt their captain had been brutally and treacherously murdered, the Polynesians had for their part simply incorporated Cook into their own religious rites, with the result that there is no common ground at all on which these two versions of Cook's death meet. There cannot be said to have been a single incident, but instead a European version and a Polynesian one so different they do not speak at all to each other. In contrast, Obeyesekere maintains that basically the two groups' understandings of the relevant events did share some inviolable common ground. The Hawaiians and the Britons expressed their perception of the same empirical reality in different ways; but these expressions speak to the same conflict and the same experience. In other words, Obeyesekere concludes that the Hawaiians and the Europeans shared a single experience; Sahlins concludes the opposite.

Closer to home, I am deeply impressed by the degree to which the Jesuits seemed truly to immerse themselves in the culture of the Chinese literati. In the second chapter on *Mudan ting*, I discuss a passage from a Jesuit dialogue written in Chinese that explains the doctrine of the immortal soul in the context of dreams, since in sleep the body and mind seem indeed to be separate entities. Could not, then, the Jesuit argued, the soul live on after death, unburdened by the body, just as in sleep? Chinese intellectuals of the age were fascinated by dreams, partly as a way that memories could live on independent of their material context. The Chinese intellectual to whom this argument was directed found it (according to the Jesuit, at least) persuasive.

To me such a dialogue, recording a moment when communication is foregrounded and predicated on the goodwill (and imaginative efforts) of both parties, suggests one way in which we can envision a conversation between, say, Descartes and Tang Xianzu—or between *The Winter's Tale* and *Mudan ting*. But other scholars, like Jacques Gernet, interpret many of the same texts as a record of the Jesuits' failure to understand Chinese culture on its own merits.

Historicist visions of single traditions have their problems, too, also intimately bound up with the various justifications of morphology I have already mentioned. Like many other scholars who study marriage in literature, I have been deeply inspired by the work of the philosopher Stanley Cavell, and most especially his writing on Hollywood movies, the comedies of manners and melodramas of the 1930s and 1940s. These readings discuss in juxtaposition two kinds of expression not normally seen together—popular film and philosophy. For example, Cavell discusses how the film *Gaslight* and others like it worked through a set of problems filiated to versions of skepticism, tying the film to the ideas of Emerson, Descartes, and Wittgenstein. Cavell suggests that this set of films focuses on marriage, because it promises "a relation of equality between human beings." In the course of each essay, he proceeds from filmic text to philosophical text—and back again—with enormous facility and infectious pleasure, mediating and generating what he calls and what truly seems a conversation.

But how does he ground this discussion of such seemingly disparate texts—to choose an example, films by Frank Capra and philosophical writings of Immanuel Kant—since surely to many readers speaking of Capra and Kant in the same breath must appear just as radical as my lumping together of *The Winter's Tale* and *Mudan ting*? Of course, Cavell realizes that yoking together these popular Hollywood films and philosophy provokes strong reactions in readers, perhaps even courting dismissal as outrageous.

Cavell first suggests that these films and the project of philosophy share some intrinsic traits, making claims about the two sets of texts themselves and not their contexts. But then he goes on to make two additional related, but different, claims about the grouping: first, that Capra and Kant belong to the same historical lineage, through the concerns of German expressionism. Second, Cavell suggests that what is at stake is "the issue of our common cultural inheritance"[9] and what it means to experience both of these texts.

Let me sketch out a parallel dialogue in the Chinese case—and I hope the reader will excuse its inadequacies next to Cavell's readings. For such a parallel reading can be assembled without too much difficulty (unsurprisingly, since as I have said, marriage in *Mudan ting* seems invested with hopes as high as any in a Shakespearean drama or Hollywood comedy). Marriage, as an ideal relation described by Confucian thinkers, was not usually characterized by equality (as friendship was), but instead as hierarchical—an intrinsically unequal, albeit complementary, relationship. It goes without saying that my work does not concern itself primarily with the philosophical lineage Cavell treats, nor its particular history; but it is surely no radical move to contend that there is a comparable interest in marriage within the Chinese intellectual tradition as well, particularly in this period.

Just as Cavell argues to be the case in European and North American thought, in the China of the late Ming and early Qing, marriage became a location for exploring important philosophical questions. Li Zhi, for example, a late Ming writer and thinker (who incidentally was quite intrigued by the Jesuit he met), proposed that the relationship between husband and wife, rather than that between father and son, should be understood as the fundamental one upon which all other relations (and ultimately all of society) was grounded. In the same period, as historians such as Dorothy Ko have pointed out, certain people (and especially literate women) began to espouse the values of companionate marriage.

Marriage further occupies a peculiar place, both according to philosophical and legal precedents, since it is a relation different from the rest that form society (except friendship), in that it is at least partially a state of mind and not merely a description of familial relation. Moreover, it suggests that that possibility—of choice, of the importance of feeling—might be extended to all the other relationships. Mencius associated personhood, *ren*, with its homophone *ren* ("benevolence" or "fellow-feeling"), implying that to be human is to possess the capacity for empathy—or, as the composition of the character suggests, to understand that other minds exist (the problem of other minds is, according to Cavell, central to all the comedies he examines). Personhood is also associated with *cheng*, the quality of sincerity. We skip ahead a few thousand years and read in *The Great Qing Code*: "If the two spouses do not get along together, but wish to divorce, there is no punishment. (If in spirit they are already separated, how can they be united by force?)."[10]

The questions raised by Mencius are still very much alive not only in philosophy, but in the laws that determine more concretely how people are to lead their lives: marriage is, as much as friendship, a bond not formed by blood and dissoluble at any time, subject to the whims and complexities of free will; and yet unlike friendship, it is a fundamental constituent part of a society organized around blood ties. We recall the Taizhou School's interest in sincerity and the age's fascination with disguise and drama: issues related easily—and I suggest, perhaps even necessarily—to marriage. What does it mean to know one's spouse? How is that sort of knowledge like and unlike the knowledge one has of one's father or son?

But let us examine Cavell's claim a little more closely. On what grounds does he tie together Emerson and *Gaslight*, or Kant and *It Happened One Night*, so that they form part of an unbroken chain within the same tradition? Sometimes Cavell makes a claim of direct historical relation, as here in an essay on *It Happened One Night*, where Cavell writes: "The transcendentalism of [the hero's] vision of oneness with the universe is an exact response to the American transcendentalism of Capra's exteriors, a mode of vision inherited from German expressionism, both in the history of Hollywood and in the history of philosophy."[11]

A philosopher whose work indeed focuses on a single historical lineage might be tempted to conflate what are in fact two separate claims—the first, of our common cultural inheritance, and the second, of the historical ties binding these two kinds of texts—into a single one. But in fact, for the scholar of premodern Chinese, the two forms of relatedness are manifestly very separate: what constitutes a common cultural inheritance can change. At the beginning of the Italian Renaissance, Petrarch did not have the Greek to read Homer; fashions and canons are in a perpetual state of flux, but a claim of historical relatedness might be proven or disproven. Kant and *Mudan ting* might form a common cultural inheritance—for me, for example—without any historical tie at all.

Let me take a step backwards, returning to the spider and the snake once more. The problem of comparison might appear more intractable to the scholar of Chinese literature, but in fact the central intellectual problem—of the nature of coincidental resemblance or resonance, of whether it can be addressed in a scholarly context—pertains equally to all scholars with any historicist bent. The scholar whose work does not center on Europe might not, after all, be alone in experiencing this problem—instead only more sensitive to seeing how far the problem reaches. If I had read about the spider and the snake in two English texts, or two Chinese texts, in some ways, the problem would remain. Often enough, however, scholars like Cavell, who work within the parameters of only one tradition, make this argument only by omission—that there is no coincidence, that similarities between texts always represent some sort of historical connection.

As another example, Stephen Greenblatt's work (which I mention partly because of its tremendous influence on literary scholars working on a number of traditions) also deals with texts from a single literary tradition and also seizes on the resonances between unlikely contemporaneous texts, some literary and some non-literary. Like Cavell's, Greenblatt's work basically elides the entire problem of relatedness or unrelatedness. By positing what he calls a single "circulation of social energy" in which all texts of a specific time and place participate, he ends up suggesting a textual world frighteningly overdetermined, where textual convergences never have the potential simply to be coincidental. Coincidence would provide a relief, at least, from every echo, every similarity having to mean something. But the problem to me is that historical relatedness is simply assumed and thus remains unverifiable.

In theory, Greenblatt's work draws clear boundaries between texts internal to a culture and external, texts that participate in a certain culture's circulation of social energy and those that do not, in essence replicating a version of translation where it—and all cross-cultural activity—is decidedly external to all real cultural enterprises. In practice, in the academy, New Historicism ends up being a defense of regional studies departments (and here I include departments of English in that category), since it reinforces the notion of reading things that belong within to a single historical moment and space. But quite aside from its effects (institutional or otherwise), this categorization of texts—those belonging and those not—feeds a tautology, for ultimately, of course, the claim of a social energy circulating within a closed system is a tautological one, unverifiable and actually not a historicist argument at all (even if those claims are only to be made under certain historical conditions). For if a text seems not to participate in this exchange of power, then it does not belong within the system.

Sometimes an argument addressing the problem of relatedness between two or more texts will appeal to causation and lineage even when that distracts a reader from what is the central core of an argument—as is the case, for example, in Cavell's readings of Capra and Kant, where he carefully draws a lineage according to which Capra is indeed a lineal descendant of Kant, if only of a cadet branch of the family. Even more than biological paternity, metaphorical paternity resists proof. The same insistence on historical ties—specifically, genealogical ones—appears also in Cavell's readings of Shakespearean plays. In reading Shakespeare as wrestling with certain philosophical problems associated with skepticism, Cavell insists upon tying him to a historical lineage. I quote: "My intuition is that the advent of skepticism as manifested in Descartes' *Meditationes* is already in full existence in Shakespeare, from the time of the great tragedies in the first years of the seventeenth century, in the generation preceding that of Descartes."[12] But if there are any facts to support such a connection, Cavell does not marshal them.

And yet despite this particular explanation of Shakespeare's philosophical concerns, the claim of historical connection turns out to be unnecessary; Cavell's wonderful readings of the plays do not rely on Shakespeare's having had contact with certain philosophical texts. Whether or not Shakespeare participated in a tradition of skepticism that culminated with Descartes, Cavell demonstrates beyond any doubt that the plays certainly explore a problem we associate with Descartes. In other words, it is by no means clear that Cavell's investment in historicism pays off, nor even why he makes it. And all of this comes from the work not of a historian, but from a philosopher, whose argument does not really depend on any notion of historical relatedness.

As a scholar whose work focuses on a supposedly single tradition (or to be more precise, a tradition that can be read as being discrete) Cavell can do something I cannot. When two texts with no obvious historical connection speak to each other (a kind of conversation he so often demonstrates beautifully, with Capra and Kant, and Descartes and Shakespeare), Cavell can fall back on the comforting explanation that some kind of historical causation lies at the bottom of things.

In other words, by appealing to the idea of a tradition as a discrete entity, Cavell can elide entirely the very real possibility of coincidence, and of purely morphological similarity, without having to go into the details of the precise historical connection. If things look similar, in other words, then they must be historically related, even if the exact genetics of the similarity cannot be derived. By suggesting that similarities can result only from diffusion, Cavell can deny the sticky problem with which I began—the possibility of morphological coincidence. For the sort of coincidence with which I began—the spider and the snake—can take place within the confines of a single tradition just as easily as between ones that we consider separate.

Now it goes without saying that Cavell does not really know the exact mechanisms behind why Capra seems to have been interested in some of the same questions Emerson introduced to philosophy about a century earlier. Perhaps the connection is one of coincidence; perhaps, one might indeed, if one looked hard enough, be able to unearth some evidence that strongly suggested direct historical influence (although that does seem doubtful in the case of Capra and Emerson); or perhaps one can only attribute the similarity to something more complicated and in-between the other two explanations—that the two men were both Americans, living only a few generations apart, sharing many cultural values. But by posing this question—the extent to which coincidence is responsible for similarity even within what we call a single tradition—we have arrived at a separate but related problem central to the historicizing impulse.

For only rarely can one know exactly how a given similarity arises. With all those other convergences, how can a scholar make sure that she does not conflate coincidence with cause? How is one to distinguish between what happened and what must have happened? How can we differentiate the historically contingent and the necessary? In comments on James Frazer's *Golden Bough*, Wittgenstein comments about all historical writing: "The correct and interesting thing to say is not: this has arisen from that, but: it could have arisen this way."[13]

If neither Cavell nor Greenblatt provides room for texts from a putatively single tradition to bear a relationship of coincidence to each other (providing instead a genetic model, where similarity must be relation), Michel Foucault's version of the Western tradition is equally tautological, defining a tradition even as he proposes to explain it. Let me turn now at greater length to Foucault's "What Is Enlightenment?" essay, through which I will continue to examine some of the problems that a historicist approach encounters in dealing with a single tradition, as well as the ways in which such treatment seems to rely on a faith in the existence of other traditions, as more or less independent homologues to the West.

Scholars in the field of Chinese studies tend to mention only one Foucault when they affirm his influence: a theorist whose ideas about power, punishment, knowledge, and individuals (to name a few of the many subjects Foucault wrote about) can be abstracted and applied to a Chinese case. For example, in explaining their methodology in the introduction to *Body, Subject, and Power in China*, Angela Zito and Tani Barlow treat Foucault's work as if it consisted simply of a series of factual statements about the nature of power, more akin to political theory than to any other scholarly discipline. Zito and Barlow write, as if in application of Foucauldian ideas to a Chinese case: "Once society itself is understood as the never finished outcome of constant discursive negotiation and historical determination, analysts can glimpse power-as-relation."[14]

In fact, in so writing, they grant Foucault's work precisely the kind of universalism Foucault himself would certainly have sought to historicize, choosing to focus not on whether such a statement can accurately be made about all societies, but rather on the actual uses to which such a universalizing impulse had been put. For if a single common *methodological* thread can be traced through all of Foucault's writings, it is a profound resistance to ontologies and broad conceptual categories—such as "power-as-relation," to cite Barlow and Zito—choosing to locate instead, within specific historical moments, operational categories.

On the one hand, as scholars like Roger Chartier have suggested, the specific nature of Foucault's own work demands that all scholars (no matter what their area of expertise) regard his influence in a special light, even when they are also European historians working on a topic that Foucault himself discussed extensively—say, Friedrich Nietzsche or the history of French penal systems. By complicating what an author is and situating any notion of an author within a specific historical context, Foucault problematizes precisely the ways in which we usually try to assess influence: one must tread lightly and carefully in speaking of the influence of Foucault's work when his work itself dealt with the complicated ways in which an author's œuvre is distilled to produce his "work" and historicized the notion of an author, showing its historical contingency—with the precise goal of demonstrating that such a concept is not universal at all. As Chartier puts it, "Foucault removed the supposed universality of these operations by restoring their variability."[15]

But other serious obstacles appear when one tries to apply Foucauldian ideas, and these are perhaps more evident to a scholar of texts that fall outside of what Foucault himself regarded as his own intellectual lineage. Some scholars of China (and of other cultures, too, of course) have looked to Foucault's essay "What Is Enlightenment?" for definitions of modernity and its implications; for those purposes, the essay appears on the surface to be a particularly rich source, as it makes much less reference to specific historical events than so much of Foucault's writing. After all, Foucault provides very usable aphorisms, seemingly applicable to any cultural setting: "Modernity is not a phenomenon of sensitivity to the fleeting present; it is the will to 'heroize' the present."[16] But this quotation about modernity actually takes place in the middle of a discussion (liberally salted with quotations and close readings) of Baudelaire.

The article itself is named after (and large portions of it consist of musings on) a single specific text, Kant's essay "What is Enlightenment?" and positions Kant's work both within its own historical context and within Foucault's own genealogy. His conclusions about the Enlightenment turn out to resist application to other cases (say, what modernity might mean in China), since they are predicated precisely on his own belonging to the same tradition as those Enlightenment authors. Any examination of the

Enlightenment, according to Foucault, takes place with the understanding that "We must try to proceed with the analysis of ourselves as beings who are historically determined, to a certain extent, by the Enlightenment."[17]

Foucault's project is self-professedly genealogical, in quest of those ancestors who have made him who he is, down to this very desire, to read the past with intent of examining his own intellectual construction. In other words, it is entirely necessary that Foucault claim filiation with the very object of his study; he examines his own tradition with the recognition that his own project, that examination itself, is a product of that tradition.

He explains what can be learned from studying the history of how various fields of knowledge have been constructed, but also what must lie beyond the reach of any discovery. First, what cannot be deduced: "this critique will be genealogical in the sense that it will not deduce from the form of what we are what is possible for us to do and to know," since (according to Kant) the inherent human limitations on knowledge forbid us from knowing what it is we do not know. We cannot know which things we do not know. But here is what we can learn from this archeology of knowledge: "it will separate out, from the contingency that has made us what we are, the possibility of no longer being, doing, or thinking what we are, do, or think."[18] Even if we cannot know the precise limitations on our own knowledge—exactly how we might have turned out otherwise—we can find out which features of our knowledge might have turned out otherwise.

Then what about the scholar of China inspired by this article and seeking a version of modernity that applies to non-European nations? Where does she position herself in this version of historicism? One thing is clear: this version of historicism resists becoming a methodology; it does not allow for this style of study for traditions outside of this particular lineage, which cannot claim methodological descent from the object of study. Nor does it in some sense allow for conventional proof or disproof. For what is central to Foucault's style of analysis—born of the very tradition it studies—is that it cannot simply be moved to study texts from other traditions. On the one hand, Foucault acknowledges that the present is a contingent state, the result of many events each of which might have come out differently. Yet on the other hand, if the current state of affairs had come out differently, the past itself—history as Foucault writes it—could not be written in the same way.

In other words, those other possibilities—the alternative ways things could have turned out that would have led to other ways of looking at and representing the past—are central to his version of history, which rests on the belief that our current condition is a contingent one. As Anthony Pagden has shown with early modern thinkers accounting for Native American cultures, other cultures can often serve to suggest a counterhistory. In the minds of some observers, other cultures are a test case—as if the contingent and the essential could be separated to show how things might have turned out otherwise if different, somehow historically contingent events had come out in another way.

According to this way of thinking, other cultures appear to one as morphological counterparts, a necessary foil to one's own lineage, signifying the contingent nature of our own state, and how easily it might be otherwise. Foucault focuses his own work on the contingency of what we are now (which of course is a matter of belief rather than of proof); consequently, he assumes we might have turned out differently. But then he finds himself in the position of needing at least to imply how things might have turned out otherwise.

One's own situation can be special only by way of contrast; to put it in other words, what Foucault calls the Western tradition can be known and thought of as a discrete whole, only because others with separate trajectories are also known. Consequently, he can describe the Western tradition as a whole, contrasted against all others: "the singular historical destiny of Western societies (such a peculiar destiny, so different from the others in its trajectory and so universalizing, so dominant with respect to the others)."[19] Paradoxically, Foucault needs to assume both the contingency of his own tradition and the truth value of one of its central universalizing moves (one that I have already tried to place in a specific historical and cultural context): the reading of different cultural traditions as homologues.

Perhaps more importantly, though, he implies that enterprises crossing different traditions are external to the real working of culture. Diffusion, for example, cannot be central to any notion of cultural formation here if the independent development of cultures is precisely what makes them worthy of study. Homologies (though mostly unmentioned, and historicized when they are) actually have a central, implicit place here as well.

The problem we encountered with Cavell we face here as well, where the notion of a single tradition allows for historicist explanations that are really tautological, defying any efforts to prove or disprove. Once again, the sort of historical influence within the tradition in question is one impossible to demonstrate—and perhaps even irrelevant. From this perspective, histories of purportedly single traditions seem always to start looking like tautologies, creating by fiat the tradition they purport to explore. Foucault's sort of history looks like a methodology, but it isn't. It is instead genealogy as tautology, where no other texts and no other turn of events could have created the sort of historian he is. No other trajectory the past might have taken could have led to Foucault, and so there are no possible counterparts. It turns out to be a sort of contingent history that is actually universalistic, meaning that others cannot lay claim to it.

There is a methodological bent to his work, though. A student of mine, in a discussion of "What Is Enlightenment?" proposed that in looking to apply Foucault's ideas, scholars of China should simply search out the Chinese Kant, as if in trying to replicate Foucault's methods, one must first seek out a corresponding ancestor, whose ideas about knowledge have been central in the formation of (in this case) Chinese notions of scholarly pursuit. To expect such a counterpart is morphological reasoning gone mad, but some of the elements of Foucault's genealogical sort of history have penetrated other lines of transmission through diffusion. To name some obvious examples, in addressing questions of social control, Foucault mentions the rise of technologies: "elements of social transformation, types of political institution, forms of knowledge, projects of rationalization of knowledge and practices, technological mutations that are very difficult to sum up in a word."[20]

I started off wanting to compare the spider and the snake, and they in turn led me to examine the grounds for historicist discussions of single traditions and morphological interpretations of different cultures as homologues of each other. The spider and the snake pose questions difficult for Cavell, Greenblatt, and Foucault to answer (to choose a few scholars almost at random), showing different ways in which the historical and the theoretical are sometimes confused, other times conflated. In short, there are sticky historicist webs everywhere, even for scholars who work within what is putatively a single tradition. The possibility that similarity is the result of coincidence rather than a causal relationship confronts Europeanists just as much as it does comparatists or Asianists.

Many of us who work on two or more supposedly independent literary traditions avoid the central stickiness of this problem by working on the chronological beginnings or ends. One might choose to compare the beginnings of two traditions, as scholars like Pauline Yu and Zhang Longxi have.

And in such cases, one can begin, even in our historicist age, to approach some ontological questions. If one examines Greek poetry and Chinese poetry at their separate beginnings, one can—and this is presumably the motivation—approach a question like: what really is lyric poetry? Such an approach promises that by looking at literary traditions at their very beginnings, one might approach what is intrinsic about a genre—or about writing itself. The faith that there is something intrinsic about Chinese literature, or Chinese culture, itself invites examination, for there is no particular reason to think that beginnings are any purer than endings.

That hunt for the intrinsic further suggests what one might pare away as extrinsic: the parameters of any specific literary tradition, encrusted with the accretions of cultural contingencies and historical accidents. For these literary historians, history itself becomes something to be pared away, until only the privileged origin remains. Such a methodology manages to account for cultural difference while it gestures towards the promises of the social sciences, in its comparison of what we assume are entirely independently arising phenomena—say, the Greek tradition and the Chinese tradition.

Or instead, one might choose to focus one's attentions on the literature of the modern era, and in such a case, the viable approaches and questions are essentially those of a scholar who works within a single tradition. It is the rare scholar of the twentieth century who will profess any degree of faith in the existence of a purely national literature; in our day, all authors and readers experience some texts at least—if not most—in translation. And experience through translation has certainly characterized Chinese literature of the last century, where practically every major writer's canon of influence seems to have consisted mostly of non-Chinese texts. And so similarity might be addressed under the rubric of influence, with all the power relations implied by that (although again, as I have noted, determining the precise degree of historical relatedness will always present certain problems).

There is a messiness to thinking about the chronological middle. Returning to the contemporaneous spider and snake—for *The Winter's Tale* and *Mudan ting* were written, as I have mentioned, a few scant years apart—most of the time I choose to pretend that they are only coincidentally simultaneous, since I do not really believe in a universal history, by which I mean I lack faith in any single scale along which the different stages of development of any culture can be measured. In other words, I do not think similarities between *The Winter's Tale* and *Mudan ting* can be explained simply by calling both of the cultures out of which the two plays arose early modern, suggesting that seventeenth-century England and late Ming China had independently arrived at a comparable state of development, with a certain set of capitalist characteristics.

But there are more persuasive cases for homologies (also resembling the social sciences) that I have a much harder time rejecting, like the following example: *Mudan ting* and *The Winter's Tale* are similar on many levels, because both plays were produced in theatre cultures, where a fascination with disguise creeps into cultural expression of all sorts. And there are manifest links between a concern with disguise and certain models of epistemology (which returns us back to the spider and the snake). People who are interested in what knowledge does to a person—whether knowing something can in fact kill you—are at the same time expressing a concern with dissimulation, whether in fact knowledge can be hidden. This question of identity and knowledge at once suggests the theatre. Imagine sitting in the audience of these two plays, both of which so foreground the possibility of duplicity. How can someone onstage be at once a lowly entertainer and the high official Du Bao? Such a question immediately suggests the question on which the ending of *Mudan ting* itself hinges: how can someone look like Du Liniang, even be like her in every respect, and yet turn out to be someone else, whether ghost or actress? Or to turn to *The Winter's Tale*, how can a young boy actor decked out in finery really be the beautiful Perdita? (Or once again to pose a question internal to the play: how can a humble shepherdess indeed be the Princess destined to inherit the kingdom?)

And, of course, in certain cultures, this is an intrinsically political question, summoning up both the most important and the ugliest parts of certain polities: the question of whether knowledge can kill, or of whether people can hide what they know, surely has a particular resonance when torture is used to establish the true loyalty and obedience of a subject, something which really did take place with some frequency in seventeenth-century China and England. How is one to prove one's allegiance in a world filled with spies and double agents, where what appears to be treason can sometimes be the truest loyalty of all?

That explanation sounds good. But isn't the comparison again one that rests on a belief in homologies? Am I simply saying that the Chinese state is to *Mudan ting* as the English state is to *The Winter's Tale*? I prefer instead to think that I am mediating a kind of conversation between the two plays—since after all, they meet in me, and in my students—while remaining sensitive to the historical context of each.

One radical solution to the problem of convergence simply denies the possibility that similarity might arise independently and suggests instead that similarities always arise through cultural diffusion. This argument has some currency in the period in which I work. The notion that in the sixteenth and seventeenth centuries, China and some still more reified entity called the West represented two entirely separate traditions is something of a fiction (as it would have been at any point in history, as research on Inner Asia seems increasingly to show). By the period of *The Winter's Tale* and *Mudan ting*, though, complex ties are well documented; a telescope first appears in fiction anywhere in the world in a story by Li Yu, a mere two decades after its invention in Italy.

And yet at the same time that complex interactions (whose precise dimensions we will never be able fully to document) were taking place, the idea of separate traditions, arising and developing separately and in relative isolation, became important. In fact, the idea of cultural difference as homology has itself been enlisted in the service of a much more interesting reality, a complex dialogue and conversation of different concerns, spanning centuries and continents.

Both Chinese and Western art historians and critics of our century have praised late Ming landscape painters such as Dong Qichang as representing the apogee of a discrete tradition, with concerns grown ever more rarified and specialized and the paintings themselves increasingly inaccessible. Nineteenth- and twentieth-century European painters have admired and even imitated these paintings, seizing upon what is seen as an alternative tradition, not trapped by the theoretical limitations of verisimilitude. And yet James Cahill has quite conclusively shown that even these Ming painters—highly educated amateurs precisely unfettered by verisimilitude and quoting from other paintings—were in fact demonstrably (albeit negatively) influenced by engravings and drawings brought over by the Jesuits. Some of these exaggeratedly non-representational paintings, it turns out, developed in response to perspectival engravings.

Victor Mair and Nicola Di Cosmo, among many others, have drawn attention to the active traffic in technology and other cultural artifacts along the Silk Road; horse-drawn carts, for example, seem to have been invented in a single location somewhere in Central Asia and to have spread throughout the Eurasian continent. And even earlier, so thoroughly Chinese a literary artifact as regulated verse (*lüshi*) seems to have arisen from contact with South Asian literatures and languages. In other words, the notion of independently arising traditions producing cultural homologues that welcome comparison might well be something of a fiction.

In his book on the witches' sabbath, the historian Carlo Ginzburg grasps at this possibility in his efforts to explain the curious persistence of certain aesthetic and ritual patterns, and he is as uncomfortable as I am with falling back on the notion of independently arising homologies. Another scholar in his place might suggest that the persistence of certain shamanistic rituals in cultures spanning centuries and continents indicates a constant of human nature—or perhaps that such shamanistic rituals characterize a certain stage of development all cultures pass through. But Ginzburg resists falling back on such an explanation.

He suggests one explanation of why, for example, the motif of a flying horse, legs outstretched, belly hanging down, recurs in widely ranging periods, in decorative arts from areas as far apart as Siberia to Western Europe. Perhaps, he suggests, these motifs might find their origin in a shared neolithic past, a time when cultural difference had not yet come to mark all of human endeavor. Even their recurrence, in the absence of even the possibility of written evidence, might suggest the power of cultural diffusion. At the same time, Ginzburg maintains that tracing similarities to diffusion still does not explain the sheer prevalence of certain features (and the disappearance of others that were evidently transmitted at the same time).

I feel some affection for this explanation, both because it lets me off the hook as far as coincidence and convergence go—how to differentiate one from the other—but also because in its nostalgia for a prelapsarian moment, before Babel and before culture and language, it reminds me of Renaissance thinking, itself before the advent of the nation, attempting to explain cultural difference. Leibniz, for example, in his search for the original, universal language (one of his final candidates for the language of Adam and Eve was Chinese—a detail that delights me), would not find Ginzburg's thinking too alien.

Ginzburg, however, ultimately has to concede, if regretfully, that a world history entirely linked by elaborate chains of causation—where things do not arise twice by coincidence, but instead appear only once and then spread—is something that lies forever beyond the purview of proof. But if the possibility of that world can never be proven, then its alternative, the social scientist's world in which cultures have developed in isolation and in which repeated patterns of cultural expressions thus manifest certain principles, finds itself in an equally indefensible position. Ginzburg writes, "Unfortunately, the absence of any form of historical connection whatsoever between two cultures is, by definition, indemonstrable. We know and always will know too little about human history."[21] Ginzburg concludes that the real explanation for those unexplainable recurrences and repetitions must be some ultimately unknowable combination of causation and homological repetition. I quote again: "In the absence of proof to the contrary, we can only postulate, behind the phenomena of cultural convergence that we have investigated, an intermingling of morphology and history."[22]

To return to Foucault's work, even if we had hundreds of different traditions to compare, we still could not tell whether similarities between different cultures prove that something must have happened (as models of development argue, for instance, when they assert that all economies must pass through certain phases) or whether things might have turned out otherwise. The precise dimensions of our own contingency can never be known by examining the histories of our own tradition and then implicitly comparing them to others, since ultimately we can prove neither homology nor coincidence nor even, often enough, causation. And the spider and the snake, in *The Winter's Tale* and *Mudan ting*, figures for a kind of knowledge that kills, become, in their mysterious convergence, figures for what we cannot know.

Throughout this book, I have assumed the possibility of a very complicated kind of translation—that spider and snake (and the cultures in which each is embedded) can in effect converse. I presume that between different cultures there is a certain level of commensurateness, even though that sort of presumption seems in many anthropological circles to be bucking the trend. This book is grounded in what seems an unfashionable faith at the moment, which can be summarized like this: cultural difference—whether generated through diffusion or through the separate development of discrete cultures—can be mediated. Wittgenstein puts it this way:

> The nonsense here is that Frazer represents these people as if they had a completely false (even insane) idea of the course of nature, whereas they only possess a peculiar interpretation of the phenomena. That is, if they were to write it down, their knowledge of nature would not differ *fundamentally* from ours. Only their *magic* is different.[23]

I hope that I have begun, in a very provisional and limited way, to have facilitated a conversation between spider and snake, with the faith that there is some common ground, remaining sensitive to the context of each and their different magic.

In my case, that different magic is embedded not just in different cultures, but in different literary and performance histories and in different cultures where theatrical texts have a different place. And once again, even lifetimes of research on the spider and the snake would fail to uncover the precise quality of their relation. So another kind of relation must take the place of that precise historical one. Once again, I turn to Wittgenstein:

> The historical explanation, the explanation as an hypothesis of development, is only one way of assembling the data—of their synopsis. It is just as possible to see the data in their relation to one another and to embrace them in a general picture without putting it in the form of any hypothesis about temporal development.[24]

That, then, has been the project of this book, to take historical context seriously, in many cases foregrounding it, and yet at the same time to recognize other associations—such as that between the spider and the snake—making the job of the literary critic that of assembling (in another quotation of Wittgenstein's) "perspicuous representations." I will be the first to admit the imperfection of this position—and even its lack of aesthetic appeal—but then there is nothing better.

Notes

Prologue

1. *Mencius* 2.1.6.3. Unless otherwise noted, all translations are my own.
2. *Mencius* 2.1.6.4.
3. Chun-shu Chang and Shelley Hsueh-lun Chang, *Crisis and Transformation in Seventeenth-Century China* (Ann Arbor: University of Michigan Press, 1992), p. 148.
4. Pu Songling, *Liaozhai zhiyi*, v. 1, ed. Zhu Qikai (Beijing: Renmin wenxue chubanshe, 1992), p. 28.

Introduction to Mudan ting

1. Tang Xianzu, *Mudan ting*, edited and annotated by Xu Shuofang and Yang Xiaomei (Shanghai: Gudian wenxue chubanshe, 1958), p. 1. All further references are to this edition. In all cases where the original language is in Chinese, unless otherwise noted, translations are my own.
2. *Mudan ting*, p. 277. *Chuanqi* are written in three distinct languages: the songs of the arias, the prose of the dialogue, and the poetry that ends each act. In this book, I have chosen to render the arias as if they were English prose to differentiate them from the poems that have been punctuated as verse in English.
3. *Mudan ting*, p. 278.
4. Ibid., p. 275.
5. Northrop Frye, *Anatomy of Criticism* (Princeton, N.J.: Princeton University Press, 1971), p. 166.
6. *Mudan ting*, p. 277.

Chapter 1

1. In the story, after a hundred days, Zhenzhen responds to him, descends from the screen, and becomes his wife. Two years later, a friend suggests to the young man

that his wife is a demon and offers him a magical sword with which to behead her. When he enters with the sword, Zhenzhen reproaches him tearfully, snatches up their son, and disappears again into the screen. There are obviously many ways in which the story of Zhenzhen has resonances with *Mudan ting*, since the story also asks whether it is possible to marry someone without familial sanction, and what can be done when that spouse turns out subsequently not to have been human. Both play and story also explore how a kind of suspicion can be antithetical to marriage.

2. *Mudan ting*, p. 68.

3. Marc Shell, *Art and Money* (Chicago: University of Chicago Press, 1995), p. 96. Shell cites *Old Money: American Trompe l'œil Images of Currency*, pp. 94–97 (Catalog for an exhibition of paintings at the Berry-Hill Galleries in New York City, 11–17, November 1988. Essay by Bruce W. Chambers, New York, 1988). Shell also describes another of Kaye's works, *Rembrandt's Etching of Jan Lutma, the Elder, with Half Dollar and Penny* (ca. 1931), which displays painted coins held down by illusionist cellophane tape over the face of a print that includes a real silver dollar. Shell writes, "Kaye here takes the question *What is an original work?* into yet another dimension, transforming it into a double sided conundrum, painting an original copy on top of a copy of an original."

4. *Mudan ting*, p. 204.

5. Ibid., p. 68.

6. T. J. Clark, "Gross David with Swoln Cheek: An Essay on Self-Portraiture" in *Rediscovering History: Culture, Politics, and the Psyche*, ed. Michael S. Roth (Stanford, Calif.: Stanford University Press, 1994), p. 266.

7. *Mudan ting*, p. 171.

8. Ibid., p. 151. In case the reader does not catch the pun on *zhen*, it comes around again with *rongna*, quite literally "countenance" in both its senses in English, jokingly suggesting again the possibility of an imperfect facial match, as if there is a chance that Liu Mengmei will not accept the substitution.

9. *Mudan ting*, p. 69.

10. *Jinshu*, "Biography of Gu Kaizhi," *juan* 92, *Liezhuan* 62, "Wenyuan": When Gu Kaizhi finished a portrait, sometimes he would go several years without painting in the eyeballs. When people asked him why, he replied: "The beauty of the body might originally not be lacking in virtues; but in terms of transmitting the spirit and capturing a likeness, it's right in this place."

11. *Mudan ting*, p. 68.

12. Ibid., p. 69.

13. This effort (to find out what the bride or groom really looks like) is central to a vast number of late imperial narratives, whether story or play: examples, one of vernacular short stories in Li Yu's *Shier lou* (*Twelve Towers*) features a young man who acquires a telescope so that he can choose a pretty bride. See Patrick Hanan's translation in *A Tower for the Summer Heat* (New York: Columbia University Press, 1998). Another *chuanqi* drama, *Wanghu ting* by Shen Zijin, has a picky father-in-law

who insists on inspecting prospective grooms for both talent and good looks; an ugly boor who aspires to his daughter's hand manages to bring a handsome, talented acquaintance for the inspection instead.

14. *Mudan ting*, p. 184. *Youzi*, or "beautiful visage," can have sepulchral connotations.

15. Richard Vinograd, *Boundaries of the Self: Chinese Portraits, 1600–1900* (Cambridge, U.K.: Cambridge University Press, 1992), p. 11.

16. Sometimes through stage directions for role types (for example, indicating that the speaker is the ghostly spirit of Du Liniang) and sometimes otherwise, it is of course my contention that the play is quite clear about pulling apart notions of unitary identity. The perceptive reader will by now have noticed that I have sometimes been less scrupulous. In the interest of clarity, I have chosen sometimes to subsume the ghostly spirit, the girl in the portrait, the girl who paints the portrait, the sacred tablet, and the corpse all under the name Du Liniang. I treat Liu Mengmei similarly, although as I shall discuss later, there it is even more clear that a person can be quite divorced from his name, and it is even more difficult to be as specific as one would like.

17. Derek Parfit, *Reasons and Persons* (Oxford: Clarendon Press, 1984), p. 200.

18. I am thinking of Socrates' question to Cratylus about a hypothetical double (*Cratylus*). Parfit, of course, is well-known for setting up hypothetical situations involving brain transplants and teletransportation to shed light on philosophical issues (see Parfit, *Reasons and Persons*). John Locke, too, seemingly cannot stay away from this form: "if the same Socrates waking and sleeping do not partake of the same consciousness . . . ," "Of Identity and Diversity" in *Personal Identity*, ed. John Perry (Berkeley: University of California Press, 1975), p. 46. The selection is Chapter 27 of *Essay Concerning Human Understanding*. Some recent work on the philosophy of identity has in fact centered on the use of these stories. Perhaps the most important critic is Kathleen Wilkes in *Real People* (Oxford, 1988), who both remarks on the generic continuity of these stories told by philosophers and challenges their outlandishness.

19. Amélie Oksenberg Rorty writes about this strategy in "Persons and Personae," in *Mind in Action: Essays in the Philosophy of Mind* (Boston: Beacon Press, 1988).

20. Locke, in *Personal Identity*, p. 40.

21. *Mudan ting*, p. 3.

22. Ibid., p. 138.

23. Tang Xianzu, *The Peony Pavilion*, trans. Cyril Birch (Bloomington: Indiana University Press, 1980), p. 145.

24. *Mudan ting*, p. 139.

25. Ibid., p. 70.

26. The vulnerability of the painting and the notable invulnerability of its subject in *Mudan ting* reverses perhaps the most common ekphrastic trope in Chinese literature, famous canonical examples of which are "Painted Hawk" and "Painted

Horse" by Du Fu. In these poems, only after time can one distinguish between a representation and what it represents because the representation lives on, unchanging, while what it represents ages and passes away.

27. *Mudan ting*, p. 149.
28. Ibid., p. 69.
29. Ibid., p. 149.
30. Ibid., p. 139.
31. Ibid., p. 148.
32. Ibid., p. 133. Needless to say, "cloudy residue" refers to stains from a nocturnal emission.
33. Ibid., p. 162.
34. Ibid., p. 161.
35. Ibid., p. 162.
36. Cao Xueqin, *Honglou meng* (Beijing: Renmin wenxue chubanshe, 1998), p. 166. Many critics have noted congruencies between the two texts and observed many ways in which the novel seems to have been influenced by *Mudan ting*.
37. *Mudan ting*, p. 139.
38. The jade-leaning reed refers to something mean and coarse against an object of beauty and refinement—here the girl in the portrait. *Mudan ting*, p. 149.
39. As in Rousseau's "livres qu'on ne lit que d'une main," discussed in Robert Darnton, *The Forbidden Best-Sellers of Pre-Revolutionary France* (New York: W. W. Norton, 1995). Many late Ming writers also thought of reading both as a private and as an addictive pleasure. Of course, this was an age fascinated by addictions (especially if they were pursued to the point of insanity and even fatality). Dorothy Ko writes of such a perception of reading in *Teachers of the Inner Chambers: Women and Culture in Seventeenth-Century China* (Stanford, Calif.: Stanford University Press, 1994).
40. In their focus on dream and on "enchantment and disenchantment," both *Mudan ting* and *Honglou meng* might at first glance seem reminiscent of the Tang tales "Nanke taishou zhuan"("Biography of the Governor of South Bough") and "Zhenzhong Ji" ("The Record of Inside the Pillow"). In fact, I would argue, this is only superficially true. In the Tang tales, there is only one perspective with which to identify, that of the protagonist; while the two late imperial works barrage the reader with outside perspectives, contrasting it with the unseeable inside, going so far as to surround Jia Rui's deathbed with pitiless observers. In contrast, no Tang tale tells us how the dreamers looked when asleep, nor makes it ambiguous which frame we should really believe.
41. Jianjian jushi, "Xiao Qing" in *Qingshi*, comp. Feng Menglong, ed. Zhou Fang and Hu Huibin (Yangzhou: Jiangsu guji chubanshe, 1993), p. 501.
42. "For the influence of the perspective paradigm over western thought, from Descartes and Pascal to Nietzsche and Wittgenstein (we might even trace it back to Plato, necessitating a new approach to the problem of 'ancient' perspective), has

been remarkably powerful." Hubert Damisch, *The Origin of Perspective*, trans. John Goodman (Cambridge, Mass.: MIT Press, 1994), p. 52. Damisch goes on to discuss at length some of the philosophical implications of scientific perspective.

43. In *Richard II*, Bushy's speech on perceiving grief draws extensively on anamorphosis as a metaphor: "For sorrow's eyes, glazed with blinding tears,/Divides one thing entire to many objects,/Like perspectives, which rightly ga'd upon/Show nothing but confusion; ey'd awry/Distinguish form . . ." (II.ii.16–19). I will discuss the close connection between certain political ideas and perspective in the second half of this book.

44. Damisch, p. 17. Damisch cites Leonardo: "Ma questo tale invencione costrignie il veditore a stare coll'ochio a uno spiracolo e allora da tale spiracolo si dimostrerà bene; Ma perchè molti occhi s'abbattono a vedere a un medisimo rempo una medesima opera fatta con tale arte e solo un di quelli vede bene l'ufitio ti tal prospective e li altri tutti restano confusi."

45. In *The Ambassadors*, the portraits of two opulently dressed men viewed head-on are juxtaposed against a *momento mori*, seen from the front as just a blur across the bottom of the painting, and visible only from an extreme angle on the side as a skull. Since the subjects of the painting can only be properly viewed from the front and the skull only from an extreme sideways angle, no single viewer can at one glance see everything there is to be seen in the painting. The men are shown with every conceivable instrument of human knowledge—a lute, mathematical instruments, a globe—all of which are inadequate compared to the invisible, looming skull.

46. James Cahill, *The Distant Mountains* (New York: John Weatherhill, 1982), p. 213.

47. James Cahill, *The Compelling Image: Nature and Style in Seventeenth-Century Chinese Painting* (Cambridge, Mass.: Harvard University Press, 1982), p. 70ff.

48. Cahill, *The Distant Mountains*, p. 213. I should note here that in a very cursory search I could not find earlier critics praising the likeness of portraits by comparing them to mirror images.

49. Of course, that shot—the camera into the mirror showing what the viewer sees—is a lie, since a shot from the same angle as the viewer would reveal exactly what must stay hidden, the circumstances of filmic production, a camera, a cameraman, and a grossly made-up subject. Instead, the camera must choose a subtly different angle from which it is invisible.

50. *Mudan ting*, p. 237.

51. From the poem "Yinghushang chuqing houyu" (Drinking on the River After the Rain Clears).

52. *Mudan ting*, p. 74.

53. Ibid., p. 69.

54. Birch, p. 69.

55. *Mudan ting*, p. 187.

324   NOTES TO CHAPTER 2

56. T. J. Clark, p. 266. Clark writes this specifically in relation to the painter Jacques-Louis David, who had a gruesome facial deformity, which varies tremendously in conspicuousness from portrait to portrait.
57. *Mudan ting*, p. 68.
58. Jianjian jushi, p. 498.
59. Huineng, *Tanjing jiaoshi* (Beijing: Zhonghua Shuju, 1983, p. 12. I have used the translation from *Sources of Chinese Tradition*, v.1, compiled by Wm. Theodore de Bary, Wing-tsit Chan, and Burton Watson (New York: Columbia University Press, 1960), p. 351. There are other alternative versions of these *gathas*.
60. Ibid., p. 16; de Bary, p. 351
61. *Mudan ting*, p. 275.
62. Ibid., p. 275.

Chapter 2

1. Blurring the distinction between dream and memory is hardly exclusive to the late Ming and the early Qing. Dream stands in for memory much earlier as well. *Dongjing meng hualu* is very much to the Song dynasty what Zhang Dai's work is to the Ming, a detailed recreation of a never-to-return past.
2. *Mudan ting yanjiu ziliao kaoshi*, ed. Xu Fuming (Shanghai: Shanghai guji chubanshe, 1987), p. 115.
3. Wai-yee Li, *Enchantment and Disenchantment: Love and Illusion in Chinese Literature* (Princeton, N.J.: Princeton University Press, 1993), p. 53.
4. *Mudan ting*, p. 277.
5. Ibid., p. 122.
6. But then according to this logic, Du Bao and Du Liniang share elements of the same legal identity as well. Another exculpatory factor invoked in Du Liniang's trial is Du Bao's history of service and good deeds, which accrues to the credit not just of the human Du Liniang, but also the spirit Du Liniang as well. As his only child, her descendants are the sum total of his. If she is punished, then his bloodline ends.
7. *Mudan ting*, p. 3.
8. "Car d'où sait-on que les pensées qui viennent en songe sont plutôt fausses que les autres, vu que souvent elles ne sont pas moins vives et expresses?" René Descartes, *Discourse on the Method: A Bilingual Edition*, ed. and trans. George Heffernan (Notre Dame, Ind.: University of Notre Dame Press, 1994), p. 57. Or as Du Liniang asks in Act 32: "Whether a dream or not, how can one say?"
9. *Mudan ting yanjiu ziliao kaoshi*, p. 125.
10. *Mudan ting*, p. 149. This aside provides yet another explanation for Du Liniang's ghostly emergence, one that conflicts with what we know from Act 23. There, the judge of the underworld grants Du Liniang a pass because her union with Liu Mengmei is already recorded in the Register of Marriages.

11. *Mudan ting*, p. 144.
12. Ibid., p. 187.
13. Ibid., p. 199.
14. Ibid., p. 46.
15. Ibid., p. 47.
16. Hume writes on the subject: "The true idea of the human mind is to consider it as a system of different perceptions or different existences, which are link'd together by the relation of cause and effect, and mutually produce, destroy, influence, and modify each other."
17. *Mudan ting*, p. 256.
18. *Honglou meng*, p. 166–67.
19. Greg Dening, *Performances* (Chicago: University of Chicago Press, 1996), p. 19.
20. Patrick Hanan, *The Invention of Li Yu* (Cambridge, Mass.: Harvard University Press, 1988), p. 27. Hanan cites the essay "Li Liweng lungu."
21. *Mudan ting yanjiu ziliao kaoshi*, p. 21.
22. Ji Yun, *Yuewei caotang biji* (Shanghai: Shanghai guji chubanshe, 1980), p. 65.
23. Lorraine Daston, "Marvelous Facts and Miraculous Evidence in Early Modern Europe" in *Questions of Evidence: Proof, Practice, and Persuasion Across the Disciplines*, ed. James Chandler, Arnold I. Davidson, and Harry Harootunian (Chicago: University of Chicago Press, 1994), p. 270. Daston traces the discussion of miracles from the seventeenth to the eighteenth centuries, the period coinciding with the beginnings of Western science. She writes, "In seventeenth-century evidentiary theology, miracles began as 'the principal external Proof and Confirmation of the Divinity of a Doctrine'; they ended as themselves requiring 'Proof and Confirmation' from doctrine."
24. Ji Yun, pp. 98–99.
25. Daston, p. 261.
26. Arthur C. Danto, *The Transfiguration of the Commonplace: A Philosophy of Art* (Cambridge, Mass.: Harvard University Press, 1981), p. 28.
27. Danto, p. 23.
28. *Mudan ting*, p. 178.
29. Ibid., p. 178. It is revealed earlier that the inscription on Du Liniang's sacred tablet remains incomplete: the character *zhu* lacks a dot and awaits completion by a distinguished personage.
30. Ibid., p. 178.
31. Ibid., p. 178.
32. Ibid., p. 184.
33. Ibid., p. 239.
34. Where Shen Bin lived, there was a great tree, and he often said, "When I die, I want to be buried there." At his burial, they dug open a cave, where there was already an ancient tomb. Inside was an old lamp stand, with a single lacquered lamp.

A bronze tablet at the head of the vault read: "Now the beautiful city is opened,/Though opened, it is not buried./The lacquered lamp has not yet been lit,/Waiting for Shen Bin's arrival." Ibid., p. 241.

35. Ibid., p. 238.
36. Ibid., p. 238.
37. Ibid., p. 238.
38. Ibid., p. 238.
39. Ibid., p. 239.
40. René Descartes, *Selected Philosophical Writings*, trans. John Cottingham, Robert Stoothoff, Dugald Murdoch (Cambridge, U.K.: Cambridge University Press, 1988), p. 79. From *Meditations on First Philosophy*.
41. *Mudan ting*, p. 239.
42. Ibid., p. 274.
43. "According to the Great Ming Code, opening up a coffin to examine the corpse is a capital offense, whether one is the ringleader or an accessory. As a Song Dynasty student, you cannot have seen these imperial laws. But it is not like an ordinary task, like going through a hedge or digging up a wall." *Mudan ting*, p. 178.
44. Caroline Walker Bynum, *The Resurrection of the Body in Western Christianity 200–1336* (New York: Columbia University Press, 1995), p. 16.
45. Some of the problems implicit in comparison lie even at the level of translation. For example, mentions of ghosts in European languages cannot fail to evoke the most famous ghost of all—the Holy Ghost (the closeness of the connection is even closer in German, say, than English). This is by no means to imply that Chinese is a blank slate, however, and I am well aware that my discussion of subjectivity and the spirit conflates many distinct terms in Chinese, each with its own history and philosophical echoes, among them *hun, xin, ling*, and many others.
46. Yü Ying-shih, "'Oh Soul, Come Back': A Study in the Changing Conceptions of the Soul and Afterlife in Pre-Buddhist China," *Harvard Journal of Asiatic Studies* 47:2 (1987) 363–95.
47. Ibid., p. 376–77.
48. Ibid., p. 363.
49. *Tianzhujiao dongchuan wenxian xubian*, v.1, ed. Wu Xiangxiang (Taipei: Xuesheng Shuju, 1966), pp. 473–77. Giulio Aleni, *Sanshan lun xueji*.
50. Ibid.

Chapter 3

1. *Mudan ting*, p. 277.
2. Necrophilia and grave robbery are frequently related crimes, and it is entirely appropriate for us to regard Liu Mengmei as accused of both. They might be related by design or by accident. In one *huaben*, a thief breaks into a grave to steal the goods

inside. Encountering the corpse of a beautiful young girl, he cannot resist and violates her.

3. *Mudan ting*, p. 189.
4. Ibid., p. 172. Waiyee Li suggests a pun here with "return" (also *gui*).
5. Ibid., p. 178.
6. Arthur P. Wolf, "Gods, Ghosts, and Ancestors" in *Religion and Ritual in Chinese Society*, ed. Arthur P. Wolf (Stanford, Calif.: Stanford University Press, 1974), p. 176.
7. *Mudan ting*, p. 261.
8. Valerie Hansen, *Negotiating Daily Life in Traditional China: How Ordinary People Used Contracts, 600–1400* (New Haven, Conn.: Yale University Press, 1995), p. 37.
9. Terry Kleeman, "Land Contracts and Related Documents." *Chugoku no shukyo: shiso to kagaku (Religion, Thought, and Science in China: A Festschrift in Honor of Professor Ryokai Makio on his Seventieth Birthday)*. (Tokyo: Kokusho kankokai, 1984), p. 12.
10. *Mudan ting*, p. 269. Chunxiang is on to something; marking a moment of lost virginity turns out to be a literary problem in this period. A generation later, the great literary critic Jin Shengtan will attempt to make the argument that Yingying, the heroine of *Xixiang ji*, did not (contrary to all indication) actually surrender herself to her lover, instead merely promising herself, withholding the actual sexual act until marriage.
11. Ibid., p. 269.
12. Ibid., p. 275.
13. Confucius, *Analects*, trans. D. C. Lau (New York: Penguin, 1979), 11:11.
14. *Mudan ting*, p. 277. Of course, it might also be the case that what Du Liniang has redeemed is not Liu Mengmei's crime, but her own elopement (although if that is the case, it is not exactly clear what she did to make up for that crime).
15. Ibid., p. 118.
16. Or in other words, as an indication of a weight goes, a symbolic one—more like a pound sterling than like an actual pound of metal.
17. Tseun-hsuin Tsien, *Science and Civilisation in China*, 5:1, *Chemistry and Chemical Technology: Paper and Printing* (Cambridge, U.K.: Cambridge University Press, 1985), p. 102.
18. *Mudan ting*, p. 184.
19. Ibid., p. 184.
20. Ibid., p. 244.
21. Marc Shell, *Art and Money*, p. 7.
22. Hong Sheng, *Changsheng dian* (Beijing: Renmin wenxue chubanshe, 1991), p. 193.
23. *Mudan ting*, p. 184.
24. Ibid., p. 184.

25. I thank Matthew Sommer for drawing my attention to this symbolic use of silver, comparing its use in *Jinping mei* to its presence in this act.

26. *Mudan ting*, p. 181.

27. Ibid., p. 184.

28. Ibid., p. 170.

29. Ibid., p. 187.

30. Wolfram Eberhard, "Oracle and Theater in China," in his *Studies in Chinese Folklore and Related Essays* (Bloomington: Indiana University Press, 1970), 191–99. Wang Qiugui's work on ritual and theatre also touches on these themes. Or Tanaka Issei, "The Social and Historical Context of Ming-Ch'ing Local Drama" in *Popular Culture in Late Imperial China*, ed. David Johnson, Andrew Nathan, and Evelyn Rawski (Berkeley: University of California Press, 1985). Also see Victor Turner's anthropological work on the relationship between ritual and theatre, Nietzsche on the birth of tragedy, and Stephen Greenblatt on intersections between Roman Catholic practices and the Elizabethan theatre.

31. *Mudan ting yanjiu ziliao kaoshi*, p. 217.

32. *Mudan ting*, p. 184.

33. There are other doors leading out of the central area of the tomb as well: the Heavenly Gate (*tianmen*), the Human Gate (*renmen*), and the Earthly Door (*dihu*). Hansen, p. 176.

34. Li Yu poses a similar question in the story *Wusheng xi* (*Silent Operas*): there, a young actress and her lover flirt onstage, in the middle of a performance express their mutual love, and finally die in such a way that all watching are uncertain as to whether the characters or the actors have died.

35. *Mudan ting yanjiu ziliao kaoshi*, p. 217.

36. *Mudan ting*, p. 173.

37. Ibid., p. 187.

38. Stephen Owen, *Readings in Chinese Literary Thought* (Cambridge, Mass.: Harvard University Press, 1992), pp. 6–7.

39. As is written in the *Liji*: "To treat as family those who are family, to treat with respect those who are owed respect, to treat the elder as the elder, to respect the differences between men and women—these are the important parts of the way of humanity." And in the *Shiji*: "The divisions between husband and wife are the most important in the way of humanity."

40. Hua-yuan Li Mowry, *Chinese Love Stories from Ch'ing-shih* (Hamden, Conn.: Archon, 1983), p. 6.

41. *Mudan ting*, p. 171.

42. *The Great Qing Code*, trans. William C. Jones (Oxford: Clarendon Press, 1994), p. 172. A statute rather than part of the code.

43. *Mudan ting*, p. 263.

44. Ibid., p. 263.

45. Wang Xiuchu, *Yangzhou shiriji*, trans. Stephen Owen, *An Anthology of Chi-*

nese Literature, ed. and trans. Stephen Owen (New York: W. W. Norton, 1996), p. 831.

46. Ann Waltner, *Getting an Heir: Adoption and the Construction of Kinship in Late Imperial China* (Honolulu: University of Hawaii Press, 1990), p. 2.

47. *Mudan ting*, p. 78.

48. Ibid., p. 137.

49. Ibid., p. 137.

50. Alan Cole, *Mothers and Sons in Chinese Buddhism* (Stanford, Calif.: Stanford University Press, 1988), p. 97.

51. *Mudan ting*, p. 239.

52. Ibid., p. 184.

53. Ibid., p. 199.

54. Ibid., p. 199. All of these passages present significant problems in translation. To provide a sense of the difficulties, Birch's translation here differs significantly from my own: "I listen in amazement; yet my own passion brought me to believe in your living presence" and "to bring you from the grave" (p. 221). For example, no reader could conceivably see *chutu chengren* and not immediately mark off *chengren* as the common binome, usually meaning adult, but also that full manifestation of human potential of the *Analects* and elsewhere (*chengren* can also refer to the deflowering of a prostitute, which may also have its echoes in this particular situation). But such a reading would be a misapprehension or, at the very least, the insertion of an unnecessary layer of metaphor, since this passage makes perfectly good sense read literally—yet *chengren* and all of its complex Confucian implications still stands in the phrase.

55. *Mudan ting*, p. 277.

56. Ibid., p. 78.

57. *Book of Rites*, 7.2.19.

58. John Milton, "The Doctrine and Discipline of Divorce" in *Complete Poems and Major Prose*, ed. Merritt Y. Hughes (New York: Macmillan, 1957), p. 711.

Introduction to Taohua shan

1. The Ming ruled for almost three centuries, but the dynasty was rocked by one controversial succession after another. In other words, the problem of legitimacy cast a pall over the Ming from its beginnings to the end—and was used by the Qing to justify its own usurpation. In obvious ways, *Taohua shan*'s depiction of political culture picks up on some of these concerns. Perhaps the most famous of these battles over the succession occurred near the beginning of the Ming dynasty. The founder passed on the throne to his grandson, who was overthrown by his own uncle. For decades afterwards, rumors persisted that the Yongle Emperor had survived (perhaps by fleeing through the sewage system of the palace) and was living either as a hermit or as a monk.

2. For readers interested in the play's accuracy in reporting events, refer to Lynn Struve's article in *Renditions*, Autumn 1977, "'The Peach Blossom Fan' as Historical Drama." Struve shows that for the most part, the play is quite accurate, but that some historical events have been dressed up for literary purposes; i.e., Shi Kefa has his suicide witnessed by one of the characters instead of being dragged off by the Manchus before his eventual execution.

3. Ostensibly the play is set in the Song dynasty; for example, Liu Mengmei makes reference to Song law. However, most readers agree that the reference comes off more as a joke than anything else, and that it hardly makes sense to try to place an exact date on a play that delights in foiling such exactitude.

4. Kong Shangren, *Taohua shan*, edited and annotated by Wang Jisi, Su Huanzhong, and Yang Deping (Beijing: Renmin wenxue chubanshe, 1993), p. 214. All further references are to this text.

5. Ibid., p. 215.
6. Ibid., p. 58.
7. Ibid., p. 25.
8. Ibid., p. 26.
9. Tao Qian, *Jingjie xiansheng ji* (Taipei: Huazheng shuju, 1987), *juan* 6, 1.
10. *Taohua shan*, p. 258.
11. Ibid., pp. 201–2.
12. Ibid., p. 202.
13. Ibid., p. 220.
14. Ibid., p. 221.
15. Ibid., p. 240.

Chapter 4

1. The influence of *Mudan ting* on plays written after it can hardly be overestimated. Playwright after playwright is compared to Tang Xianzu; and play after play, to *Mudan ting*. For comments by traditional critics on Tang Xianzu's influence on *Taohua shan*, see *Mudan ting yanjiu*, pp. 244–45, and *Tang Xianzu yanjiu ziliao huibian*, v.2, p. 887.

2. *Taohua shan*, p. 259.
3. Ibid., p. 154.
4. Ibid., p. 249.
5. Ibid., p. 47.
6. As the words *wujia* and "priceless" suggest, the fan treads a fine line: it is at once beyond any value (any appraisal can only be considered an insult) and yet in real terms worthless, at least in the ways that the market considers worth.

7. *Taohua shan*, p. 154.
8. In practice the distinction is often blurred. Metaphorical portraits are often

praised for being synecdochical, as if by being like, object and image come to share the same substance.

9. In *The Complete Essays of Montaigne* (Stanford University Press, 1965), Donald Frame translates: "I have no more made my book than my book has made me—a book consubstantial with its author, concerned with my own self, an integral part of my life; not concerned with some third-hand, extraneous purpose, like all other books" (p. 504).

10. Frame translates: "Painting myself for others, I have painted my inward self with colors clearer than my original ones" (p. 504).

11. *Taohua shan*, p. 149.

12. In *Yanzi jian*, a prostitute and the daughter of the Minister of Rites look enough like each other—despite the difference in their births—that they can substitute for each other. First, the official's daughter mistakes the prostitute's portrait for her own; later, the Minister of Rites and his wife (having lost track of their daughter in the course of a war) adopt the prostitute, partly because she so resembles their own lost child. In other words, the play lingers long and playfully over the possibility that doubles allow one person to substitute for another.

13. Richard Brilliant, *Portraiture* (Cambridge, Mass.: Harvard University Press, 1991), p. 109.

14. Professor C. T. Hsia brought this question up after a talk I gave at Columbia University.

15. *Taohua shan*, p. 154.

16. Ibid., p. 179.

17. Ibid., p. 180.

18. Ibid., p. 180.

19. Gail Hershatter, *Dangerous Pleasures: Prostitution and Modernity in Twentieth-Century Shanghai* (Berkeley: University of California Press, 1997), p. 84–85.

20. *Taohua shan*, p. 160.

21. Marc Shell, "Portia's Portrait: Representation as Exchange," *Common Knowledge* 7 (spring 1998): 94–144.

22. Hershatter, p. 83.

23. Zhang Dai, *Tao'an mengyi Xihu mengxun* (Shanghai: Shanghai guji chubanshe, 1982), p. 51. Zhang Dai writes about the trade in young women in a short essay called "*Yangzhou shouma*," "The Skinny Horses of Yangzhou."

24. Even those from the Song dynasty do not look too dissimilar, though a greater variety of poses seemed to be permitted, and the robes worn by the Emperor tended to be far simpler.

25. In *Soulstealers* (Harvard University Press, 1990), Kuhn describes a widespread panic in the Qianlong period, that men's souls were being stolen by having their queues surreptitiously cut. Kuhn discusses the ways in which by the eighteenth-century queues and properly shaved pates had become highly symbolic. In "The Death of the Xiaoxian Empress" (*Journal of Asian Studies*, August 1997), Kutcher fo-

cuses on one event, the Qianlong Emperor's mourning for his Empress, and the way in which the Emperor regarded failure to follow precise prescriptions for mourning (specifically the prohibition against shaving) as treasonous.

26. *Qingdai dihou xiang*, 4 vols. (Beiping: Guoli Beiping gugong bowuyuan wenxian guan, 1934), III.iii.

27. Evelyn Rawski, *The Last Emperors: A Social History of Qing Imperial Institutions* (Berkeley: University of California Press, 1998), p. 5. Throughout the Qing, Rawski argues, imperial institutions were set up precisely so that the Emperor would not be bound by a single culture's ideology of legitimacy.

28. Likewise, there is a famous photograph of a bitter-faced, seventy-year-old Empress Dowager Cixi dressed as Guanyin, surrounded by attendants costumed as fairies. Despite flattery that she was truly the Goddess of Mercy, the whole scene is transparently staged, down to giant lotus pads for her and her attendants to stand on.

29. *Taohua shan*, p. 235.

30. *Taohua shan*, "*Taohua shan* xiaoshi," p. 3.

31. *Taohua shan*, p. 180.

32. James L. Watson, "Transactions in People: The Chinese Market in Slaves, Servants, and Heirs" in *Asian and African Systems of Slavery*, ed. James Watso (Berkeley: University of California Press, 1980), pp. 240–45.

33. Matthew Sommer has pointed out to me that dowry served as a status symbol; a generous dowry was a statement that a rich family, unlike a poor one, did not need to sell its daughters.

34. Zhang Dai, p. 51.

35. *Taohua shan*, p. 53.

36. Ibid., p. 55.

37. *Jiangnan tongzhi*, reprint of the mid-Qing gazetteer of the entire Jiangnan province (Taibei: Jinghua shuju, 1967), p. 3189.

38. Frederic E. Wakeman, *The Great Enterprise: the Manchu Reconstruction of Imperial Order in Seventeenth-Century China* (Berkeley: University of California Press, 1985), p. 564.

39. *Taohua shan*, p. 193.

40. Ibid., p. 149.

41. Ibid., p. 180.

42. Ibid., p. 257.

43. Ibid., p. 38.

44. Ibid., p. 38.

45. Ibid., p. 39.

46. Ibid., p. 39.

47. *Shijing*, Guofeng 68.

48. Yang Lien-sheng, "The Concept of *Pao* as a Basis for Social Relations in China" in *Excursions in Sinology* (Cambridge, Mass.: Harvard University Press, 1969), p. 308. "The mere position of a ruler or a parent guaranteed his privilege to

receive respect and service from his subject or son. In extreme cases, when a loyal official was punished for no reason, he might still say to his emperor, 'Your minister deserves his punishment. Your majesty is sagacious and just.' To justify the absolute piety required from a son, Confucianists invented the sweeping generalization, 'There are no wrongdoing parents in the world.'"

49. Qu zhougrong, ed., *Jiaozheng jinwen xiaojing ershisi xiaokao* (Taibei: Guangwen shuju, reprint 1981), p. 4.

50. *Analects*, trans. D. C. Lau (New York: Penguin, 1979), XVII.xxi.

51. *Taohua shan*, p. 209.

Chapter 5

1. *Taohua shan*, p. 169.
2. Ibid., p. 169.
3. Ibid., p. 16.
4. Ibid., p. 23.
5. Ji Liuqi, *Mingji nanlue* (Taibei: Taiwan yinhang, 1963), p. 81. Struve dates the text to the early 1670s. Ji Liuqi was in his early twenties at the time of the dynasty's fall, and the *Mingji nanlue* and its companion history *Mingji beilue* (about events before the Manchus) are both products of written and oral accounts as well as personal experience.
6. *Taohua shan*, p. 1.
7. Ibid., p. 1.
8. All people are obligated to sacrifice for their parents; but it is one of the preconditions for becoming Emperor that one's father has died. To be Emperor then is to be an orphan, as the royal first person *gu* and *guaren* both imply, without the obligation to obey anyone else (except his mother, if she still survives, which perhaps explains the peculiar relationship that Qing monarchs like Qianlong, Kangxi, and the unfortunate Guangxu seemed to have with their grandmothers and mothers both biological and adoptive).
9. *Taohua shan*, p. 241.
10. Ibid., p. 96.
11. *Hongguang shilu chao* (Taibei: Taiwan yinhang, 1968), p. 1. According to Struve, authorship of this text is unclear, although clearly the author was a Revival Society supporter.
12. *Taohua shan*, p. 15.
13. Ibid., p. 5.
14. Ibid., p. 17.
15. Ibid., p. 17.
16. Ibid., p. 17.
17. While an Emperor is alive, he needs no proper name, for there ought to be only one Emperor, and he can be referred to as His Imperial Majesty (*shengshang* or

huangshang) or other such appellations. This is in contrast to the personal name borne by the young prince and serving the function of differentiating himself from his equals, his brothers and cousins. Once laid to rest with all of his fellow Emperors, his posthumous name serves the same purpose. The form of these two sets of names reflects these functions: as with most Chinese personal names, that of the young prince differs from those of his brothers and cousins by only one character. Similarly, one can interpret the choice and conferral of the posthumous name— again differing only in one character from the other Emperors—as departure from singularity and entrance into another brotherhood, those of his dead imperial ancestors. Before crowned, he is simply a prince; once dead, the Emperor is no longer *the* Emperor, but *an* Emperor, and this is a different proposition altogether.

18. Richard E. Strassberg, *The World of K'ung Shang-jen: A Man of Letters in Early Ch'ing China* (New York: Columbia University Press, 1983), p. 73.

19. *Taohua shan*, p. 115.

20. Ibid., p. 111.

21. Ibid., p. 111.

22. Constantin Stanislavski, *Creating a Role*, trans. Elizabeth Reynolds Hapgood, ed. Hermine I. Hopper (New York: Theatre Arts Books, 1961), p. 241.

23. Pu Songling, *Liaozhai zhiyi*, v. 3, p. 1542.

24. Dorothy Ko, *Teachers of the Inner Chambers: Women and Culture in Seventeenth-Century China* (Stanford, Calif.: Stanford University Press, 1994), pp. 166–68 and passim.

25. *Taohua shan*, p. 17.

26. Ibid., p. 17.

27. Ibid., p. 17.

28. Ibid., p. 18.

29. Ibid., p. 18.

30. Ibid., p. 18.

31. Ibid., p. 18.

32. Ibid., p. 17.

33. Ibid., p. 206.

34. Ibid., p. 10.

35. Ibid., p. 71.

36. Ibid., p. 72.

37. Ibid., p. 72.

38. Ibid., p. 73.

39. Ibid., p. 70.

40. Zhang Dai, *Tao'an mengyi*, p. 102. Zhang Dai describes Liu's repertoire in "*Liu Jingting shuoshu*," "Liu Jingting Tells Stories."

41. *Taohua shan*, p. 161.

42. Ibid., p. 161.

43. Ibid., pp. 161–62.

44. Ibid., p. 162.
45. Ibid., p. 162.
46. Ibid., p. 162.
47. *The Great Qing Code*, p. 180.
48. *Taohua shan*, p. 102.
49. Ibid., p. 102.
50. Ibid., p. 158.
51. Ibid., p. 168.
52. Ibid., p. 25. Zhou and Wei refer to Zhou Chaorui and Wei Dazhong, two censors who were persecuted and eventually put to death for their opposition to Lady Ke and Wei Zhongxian.
53. Caroline Walker Bynum, *The Resurrection of the Body in Western Christianity, 200–1336* (New York: Columbia University Press, 1995).
54. *Taohua shan*, p. 256.
55. Ibid., p. 256.
56. *Taohua shan*, "*Taohua shan* fanli," p. 12.

Chapter 6

1. For a guide to these sources in general, Lynn Struve's *The Ming-Qing Conflict 1619–1683* (Ann Arbor, Mich.: Association for Asian Studies, 1998) is an invaluable monument of scholarship. Struve first provides a survey of all the accounts, ranging from contemporary witnesses to historical scholarship of the twentieth century. In the second half of her book, she catalogues the most important sources, roughly dating each and explaining textual provenance.
2. *Taohua shan*, p. 208.
3. Donald Frame translates: "Tortures are a dangerous invention and seem to be a test of endurance rather than of truth. Both the man who can endure them and the man who cannot endure them conceal the truth. For why shall pain rather make me confess what is, than force me to say what is not?" p. 266.
4. Page Dubois, *Torture and Truth* (New York: Routledge, 1990), p. 59.
5. Cecil Roth, *The Spanish Inquisition* (New York: W. W. Norton, 1964), p. 132.
6. Ji Liuqi, *Mingji nanlue*, p. 158.
7. Gu Yanwu attributed, *Shengan benji*, p. 153. According to Struve, the text is really *Jiayi shian* by Wen Bing but was later attributed to the much more famous Gu Yanwu.
8. *Hongguang shilu chao*, p. 1.
9. Ibid., pp. 78–79.
10. René Descartes, *Meditations on First Philosophy*, in *Selected Philosophical Writings*, trans. John Cottingham, Robert Stoothoff, and Dugald Murdoch (Cambridge, U.K.: Cambridge University Press, 1988), p. 79.
11. *Taohua shan*, p. 83.

12. Ibid., p. 83.
13. Ibid., p. 83.
14. Ibid., p. 84.
15. Ibid., p. 84.
16. Ibid., p. 65.
17. Ibid., p. 162.
18. Ibid., p. 25.
19. Ibid., p. 255.
20. Ibid., p. 230.

21. The Old Ceremonial Assistant happens to recognize Shi Kefa from his days in Nanjing, a coincidence that frees Shi Kefa from having to introduce himself and explain his reasons for suicide. Here, as elsewhere, the play (in marked contradistinction to *Mudan ting*, for example), scrupulously provides witnesses and evidence for every event it relates. In case we might not believe the Old Ceremonial Assistant's account later on of Shi Kefa's last moments—a single witness might be suspected of unreliability, as we know—the general has even considerately stripped himself of his uniform before drowning, providing the Old Ceremonial Assistant with hard evidence supporting his story.

22. Thomas Hobbes, *Leviathan*, (London: Everyman's Library, 1987), p. 270.
23. Ibid., p. 270.
24. Ibid., p. 270.
25. Ibid., p. 270.
26. *Taohua shan*, p. 239.

27. But his concern solely with behavior makes it hard for him to grasp why he should be more concerned with matters offstage than onstage. Ruan Dacheng asks his sovereign why he is so unhappy, citing all sorts of political and military reasons. But Hongguang frets because he fears he will not be able properly to stage *Yanzi jian* before the Lantern Festival. Hongguang's priorities naturally indicate his incompetence; as a monarch whose investiture was staged, whose ministers simply pose as loyal, what is onstage and offstage might not differ so much.

28. Strassberg, p. 103.

29. In Zhang Wei's vision, Shi Kefa ceases to be a playactor. His words are no longer directed towards an audience. Similarly in Zhang Wei's dream (which forms an important part of the interstitial act between the two halves of the play), Chongzhen appears onstage, but to no detriment of his legitimacy, since he is clearly on another plane.

30. *Mingji nanlue*, p. 168.

31. Lin Shidui, *Hezha congtan* (Taibei: Taiwan yinhang, 1962), pp. 126–27. Lin includes this account with two other identity disputes: the case of the putative Crown Prince (Lin is inclined to disbelieve him), and that of Lady Tong. Since all the cases involve the same group of people, they are implicitly intertwined. Lin Shidui was a mid-level official in the Southern Ming court; after the Qing consoli-

dation of power, he returned to his home in Zhejiang County and did not pursue a public career under the Qing.

32. *Hezha congtan*, p. 127.
33. *Taohua shan*, pp. 180–81.
34. Ibid., p. 241.
35. The most famous marriage between a prostitute and a young man of good family in Chinese literature, Li Wa's marriage to a profligate turned high official in *Liwa zhuan*, can only take place because the young man's father not only blesses, but actually forces the match, overriding the modesty and refusal of the woman (who not only saved the young man's life, but supported him until his success in the examinations). Matthew Sommer points out that a relationship contracted by individuals approaches very closely how a jurist might categorize *jian*, or fornication.
36. Mi Chu Wiens, "Masters and Bondservants: Peasant Rage in the Seventeenth Century," *Ming Studies* 8:57–64 (spring 1979), p. 59.
37. *Taohua shan*, p. 98.
38. Ibid., p. 107.
39. Ma Shiying asks, "Who else is willing to go with us?" Xu Hongji is the first name Ruan Dacheng mentions. *Taohua shan*, p. 101.
40. *Analects*, 12.11. The translation is my own.
41. *Yizi* looks like it might mean "righteous son" or some such, but instead it is a shortened version of *jieyi zi*, "sworn child." Similarly *jiazi* seems like it could mean something relatively innocuous, where *jia* might substitute for *jie* as so often happens with the two words. *Jiazi* might then mean something like "assumed child"—but there is no term *jiezi*—and consequently no possible alternative meaning for *jiazi* but "false child."
42. *Taohua shan*, p. 54.
43. Two famous *huaben* (or vernacular short stories), for example, feature heroines who purchase themselves: "Du Tenth Sinks the Jewel Box in Anger" from *Jingshi tongyan* and "The Oilseller Monopolizes the Queen of the Flowers" from *Xingshi henyan*. And, of course, there is Li Wa, the Tang heroine who buys her own freedom so that she can nurse her lover back to health.
44. James Watson, p. 229.
45. *Taohua shan*, p. 98.
46. Ibid., p. 235.

Epilogue

1. Stephen Greenblatt, *Renaissance Self-Fashioning*. (Chicago: University of Chicago Press, 1984), p. 1.
2. Among Western scholars, Catherine Swatek especially has worked extensively on the history of the performance of *Mudan ting*. See her article in *Asia Major*,

"Plum and Portrait: Feng Meng-lung's Revision of *The Peony Pavilion*" (6:1993, 127–60) and works forthcoming.

3. *Mudan ting*, p. 269.

4. From Kant's Review of Herder's *Ideas on the Philosophy of the History of Mankind*, Part Two (1785) in *Race and the Enlightenment*, ed. Emmanuel Chukwudi Eze (Cambridge, Mass.: Blackwell, 1997), p. 70.

5. Ludwig Wittgenstein, *Philosophical Occasions 1912–1951*, ed. and trans. James Klagge and Alfred Nordmann (Indianapolis: Hackett, 1993), p. 131.

6. John Boswell, *Same-sex Unions in Premodern Europe* (New York: Vintage, 1994), p. 38.

7. Ibid., xxii.

8. Marshall Sahlins, *How "Natives" Think: About Captain Cook, For Example* (Chicago: University of Chicago Press, 1995). Gananath Obeyesekere, *The Apotheosis of Captain Cook: European Mythmaking in the Pacific* (Princeton, N.J.: Princeton University Press, 1992).

9. Stanley Cavell, *Pursuits of Happiness: The Hollywood Comedy of Remarriage* (Cambridge, Mass.: Harvard University Press, 1981), p. 9.

10. *The Great Qing Code: A New Translation with Introduction by William C. Jones*, trans. William C. Jones (Oxford: Clarendon Press, 1994), p. 134.

11. Stanley Cavell, *Pursuits of Happiness*, p. 99.

12. Stanley Cavell, *Disowning Knowledge in Six Plays of Shakespeare* (Cambridge, U.K.: Cambridge University Press, 1987), p. 3.

13. Wittgenstein, p. 153.

14. Introduction, *Body, Subject, and Power in China*, ed. Angela Zito and Tani E. Barlow (Chicago: University of Chicago Press, 1994), p. 6.

15. Roger Chartier, "The Chimera of the Origin: Archeology of Knowledge, Cultural History, and the French Revolution" in *On the Edge of the Cliff: History, Language, and Practices*, trans. Lydia G. Cochrane (Baltimore: Johns Hopkins University Press, 1997), p. 52.

16. "What Is Enlightenment?" translated by Catherine Porter from *The Foucault Reader*, ed. Paul Rabinow (New York: Pantheon, 1984), p. 40.

17. Ibid., p. 43.

18. Ibid., p. 46.

19. Ibid., p. 47.

20. Ibid., p. 43.

21. Carlo Ginzburg, *Ecstasies: Deciphering the Witches' Sabbath*, trans. Raymond Rosenthal (New York: Penguin, 1991), p. 267.

22. Ibid., p. 267.

23. Wittgenstein, p. 141.

24. Ibid., p. 131.

Selected Bibliography

Primary Texts

Cao Xueqin 曹雪芹. *Honglou meng* 紅樓夢. Beijing: Renmin wenxue chubanshe, 1998.

Feng Menglong, ed., *Qingshi*, comp. Jianjian jushi, "Xiao Qing." Zhou Fang and Hu Huibin, comp. and ed. Yangzhou: Jiangsu guji chubanshe, 1993.

The Great Qing Code. Trans. William C. Jones, with the assistance of Tianquan Cheng and Yongling Jiang. New York: Oxford University Press, 1994.

Gu Yanwu 顧炎武, attributed. *Sheng'an benji* 聖安本紀. Taibei: Taiwan yinhang, 1964. Wen Bing 文秉, *Jiayi shian* 甲乙事案.

Hong Sheng 洪昇, *Changsheng dian* 長生殿. Beijing: Renmin wenxue chubanshe, 1980.

Hongguang shilu chao 弘光實錄鈔. Taibei: Taiwan yinhang, 1968.

Ji Liuqi 計六奇. *Mingji nanlüe* 明季南略. Taibei: Taiwan yinhang, 1963.

Ji Yun 紀昀, *Yuewei caotang biji* 閱微草堂筆記. Shanghai: Shanghai guji chubanshe, 1980.

Jiangnan tongzhi 江南通志. Reprint of the mid-Qing gazetteer of the entire Jiangnan province. Taibei: Jinghua shuju, 1967.

Kong Shangren 孔尚任. *Taohua shan* 桃花扇. Ed. and annotated by Wang Jisi, Su Huanzhong, Yang Deping. Beijing: Renmin wenxue chubanshe, 1993.

Lin Shidui 林時對. *Hezha congtan* 荷牐叢談. Taibei: Taiwan yinhang, 1962.

Owen, Stephen, ed. and trans. *An Anthology of Chinese Literature*. New York: W. W. Norton, 1996.

Pu Songling 蒲松齡. *Liaozhai zhiyi* 聊齋志異. 3 vols. Ed. Zhu Qikai. Beijing: Renmin wenxue chubanshe, 1992.

Qingdai dihou xiang 清代帝后像, 4 vols. Beiping: Guoli beiping gugong bowuyuan wenxian guan, 1934.

Qu Zhongru 瞿中溶, ed. *Jiaozheng jinwen xiaojing ershisi xiao kao* 校正今文孝經二十四孝. Taibei: Guangwen shuju, reprint 1981.

Tang Xianzu 湯顯祖. *Mudan ting* 牡丹亭. Ed. Xu Shuofang, Yang Xiaomei. Shanghai: Gudian wenxue, 1958.

Tang Xianzu. *Mudan ting.* Trans. Cyril Birch. Boston: Cheng & Tsui, 1994.
Tianzhujiao dongchuan wenxian xubian 天主教東傳文獻續編, vol 1. Ed. Wu Xiangxiang. Taipei: Xuesheng Shuju, 1966.
Xu Fuming 徐拂明, ed. *Mudan ting yanjiu ziliao kaoshi* 牡丹亭研究資料考釋. Shanghai: Shanghai guji chubanshe, 1987.
Zhang Dai 張岱. *Tao'an mengyi xihu mengxun* 陶庵夢憶西湖夢尋. Shanghai: Shanghai guji chubanshe, 1982.

Secondary Texts

Boswell, John. *Same-Sex Unions in Premodern Europe.* New York: Vintage, 1994.
Brilliant, Richard. *Portraiture.* Cambridge, Mass.: Harvard University Press, 1991.
Bynum, Caroline Walker. *The Resurrection of the Body in Western Christianity 200–1336.* New York: Columbia University Press, 1995.
Cahill, James. *The Compelling Image: Nature and Style in Seventeenth-Century Chinese Painting.* Cambridge, Mass.: Harvard University Press, 1982.
———. *The Distant Mountains.* New York: John Weatherhill, 1982.
———. *The Painter's Practice: How Artists Lived and Worked in Traditional China.* New York: Columbia University Press, 1994.
Cavell, Stanley. *Pursuits of Happiness: The Hollywood Comedy of Remarriage.* Cambridge, Mass.: Harvard University Press, 1981.
———. *Disowning Knowledge in Six Plays of Shakespeare.* Cambridge, U.K.: Cambridge University Press, 1987.
Chang, Chun-shu, and Shelley Hsueh-lun Chang. *Crisis and Transformation in Seventeenth-Century China.* Ann Arbor: University of Michigan Press, 1992.
Chartier, Roger. "The Chimera of the Origin: Archeology of Knowledge, Cultural History, and the French Revolution." In *On the Edge of the Cliff: History, Language, and Practices.* Trans. Lydia G. Cochrane. Baltimore: Johns Hopkins University Press, 1997.
Clark, T. J. "Gross David with Swoln Cheek: An Essay on Self-Portraiture." In *Rediscovering History: Culture, Politics, and the Psyche.* Ed. Michael S. Roth, 243–307. Stanford, Calif.: Stanford University Press, 1994.
Damisch, Hubert. *The Origin of Perspective.* Trans. John Goodman. Cambridge, Mass.: MIT Press, 1994.
Danto, Arthur C. *The Transfiguration of the Commonplace: A Philosophy of Art.* Cambridge, Mass.: Harvard University Press, 1981.
Darnton, Robert. *The Forbidden Best-Sellers of Pre-Revolutionary France.* New York: W. W. Norton, 1995.
Daston, Lorraine. "Marvelous Facts and Miraculous Evidence in Early Modern Europe." In *Questions of Evidence: Proof, Practice, and Persuasion Across the Disciplines.* Ed. James Chandler, Arnold I. Davidson, and Harry Harootunian. Chicago: University of Chicago Press, 1994.

Dening, Greg. *Performances.* Chicago: University of Chicago Press. 1996.
Descartes, René. *Discourse on the Method: A Bilingual Edition.* Ed. and trans. George Heffernan. Notre Dame, Ind.: University of Notre Dame Press, 1994.
———. *Meditations on First Philosophy.* In *Selected Philosophical Writings.* Trans. John Cottingham, Robert Stoothoff, and Dugald Murdoch. Cambridge, U.K.: Cambridge University Press, 1988.
Eberhard, Wolfram. "Oracle and Theater in China." In *Studies in Chinese Folklore and Related Essays.* Bloomington: Indiana University Press, 1970.
Foucault, Michel. "What is Enlightenment?" Trans. Catherine Porter. In *The Foucault Reader.* Ed. Paul Rabinow. New York: Pantheon, 1984.
Frye, Northrop. *Anatomy of Criticism.* Princeton, N.J.: Princeton University Press, 1971.
Gernet, Jacques. *China and the Christian Impact: A Conflict of Cultures.* Trans. Janet Lloyd. Cambridge, U.K.: Cambridge University, 1985.
Ginzburg, Carlo. *Ecstasies: Deciphering the Witches' Sabbath.* Trans. Raymond Rosenthal. New York: Penguin, 1991.
The Great Qing Code: A New Translation with Introduction by William C. Jones. Trans. William C. Jones. Oxford: Clarendon Press, 1994.
Greenblatt, Stephen. *Renaissance Self-Fashioning.* Chicago: University of Chicago Press, 1984.
Hansen, Valerie. *Negotiating Daily Life in Traditional China: How Ordinary People Used Contracts, 600–1400.* New Haven, Conn.: Yale University Press, 1995.
Hershatter, Gail. *Dangerous Pleasures: Prostitution and Modernity in Twentieth-Century Shanghai.* Berkeley: University of California Press, 1997.
Hobbes, Thomas. *Leviathan.* London: Everyman's Library, 1987.
Huang, Ray. *1587: A Year of No Significance.* New Haven, Conn.: Yale University Press, 1981.
Hunt, Lynn. *The Family Romance of the French Revolution.* Berkeley: University of California Press, 1992.
Janson, H. W. *History of Art,* 4th ed., rev. Anthony F. Janson. New York: Harry N. Abrams, 1991.
Kant, Immanuel. Review of Herder's *Ideas on the Philosophy of the History of Mankind,* Part Two (1785). In *Race and the Enlightenment.* Ed. Emmanuel Chukwudi Eze. Cambridge, Mass.: Blackwell, 1997.
Kleeman, Terry. "Land Contracts and Related Documents." *Chugoku no shukyo: shiso to kagaku (Religion, Thought, and Science in China: A Festschrift in Honor of Professor Ryokai Makio on his Seventieth Birthday).* Tokyo: Kokusho kankokai, 1984.
Ko, Dorothy. *Teachers of the Inner Chambers: Women and Culture in Seventeenth-Century China.* Stanford, Calif.: Stanford University Press, 1994.
Kuhn, Philip. *Soulstealers: The Chinese Sorcery Scare of 1768.* Cambridge, Mass.: Harvard University Press, 1990.
Kutcher, Norman. "The Death of the Xiaoxian Empress: Bureaucratic Betrayals

and the Crises of Eighteenth-Century Chinese Rule." *The Journal of Asian Studies* 56:3, Aug. 1997, 708–27.

Lejeune, Philippe. *On Autobiography*. Trans. Katherine Leary. Minneapolis: University of Minnesota Press, 1989.

Li, Wai-yee. *Enchantment and Disenchantment: Love and Illusion in Chinese Literature*. Princeton, N.J.: Princeton University Press, 1993.

Locke, John. "Of Identity and Diversity" (extract from chapter 27 of *Essay Concerning Human Understanding*). In *Personal Identity*. Ed. John Perry. Berkeley: University of California Press, 1975.

Mann, Susan. *Precious Records: Women in China's Long Eighteenth Century*. Stanford, Calif.: Stanford University Press, 1997.

Mauss, Marcel. "Une Catégorie de l'Esprit Humain: La Notion de Personne, Celle de 'Moi'." In *The Category of the Person: Anthropology, Philosophy, and History*. Trans. W. D. Halls. Ed. Michael Carrithers, Steven Collins, and Steven Lukes. Cambridge, U.K.: Cambridge University Press, 1985.

——— . *The Gift: Forms and Functions of Exchange in Archaic Societies*. Trans. Ian Cunnison. New York: W. W. Norton, 1967.

Mowry, Hua-yuan Li. *Chinese Love Stories from Ch'ing-shih*. Hamden, Conn.: Archon, 1983.

Obeyesekere, Gananath. *The Apotheosis of Captain Cook: European Mythmaking in the Pacific*. Princeton, N.J.: Princeton University Press, 1992.

Owen, Stephen. *Readings in Chinese Literary Thought*. Cambridge, Mass.: Harvard University Press, 1992.

Pagden, Anthony. *The Fall of Natural Man: The American Indian and the Origins of Comparative Ethnology*. Cambridge, U.K.: Cambridge University Press, 1982.

Parfit, Derek. *Reasons and Persons*. Oxford: Clarendon Press, 1984.

Rorty, Amélie Oksenberg. "Persons and Personae." In *Mind in Action: Essays in the Philosophy of Mind*. Boston: Beacon Press, 1988.

Roth, Cecil. *The Spanish Inquisition*. New York: W. W. Norton, 1964.

Sahlins, Marshall. *How "Natives" Think: About Captain Cook, For Example*. Chicago: University of Chicago Press, 1995.

Shell, Marc. *Art and Money*. Chicago: University of Chicago Press, 1995.

Stanislavski, Constantin. *Creating a Role*. Ed. Hermine I. Hopper. Trans. Elizabeth Reynolds Hapgood. New York: Theatre Arts, 1961.

Strassberg, Richard E. *The World of K'ung Shang-jen: A Man of Letters in Early Ch'ing China*. New York: Columbia University Press, 1983.

Struve, Lynn. "'The Peach Blossom Fan' as Historical Drama." *Renditions* 8, Autumn 1977, 99–114.

——— . *The Ming-Qing Conflict 1619–1683: A Historiography and Source Guide*. Ann Arbor, Mich.: Association for Asian Studies, 1998.

Tanaka Issei. "The Social and Historical Context of Ming-Ch'ing Local Drama." In *Popular Culture in Late Imperial China*. Ed. David Johnson, Andrew Nathan, and Evelyn Rawski. Berkeley: University of California Press, 1985.

Tsien Tseun-hsuin. *Science and Civilisation in China*, 5:1, *Chemistry and Chemical Technology: Paper and Printing*. Cambridge, U.K.: Cambridge University Press, 1985.
Vinograd, Richard. *Boundaries of the Self: Chinese Portraits, 1600–1900*. Cambridge, U.K.: Cambridge University Press, 1992.
Wakeman, Frederic E. *The Great Enterprise: the Manchu Reconstruction of Imperial Order in Seventeenth-Century China*. Berkeley: University of California Press, 1985.
Waltner, Ann Beth. *Getting an Heir: Adoption and the Construction of Kinship in Late Imperial China*. Honolulu: University of Hawaii Press, 1990.
Watson, James L. "Transactions in People: The Chinese Market in Slaves, Servants, and Heirs." In *Asian and African Systems of Slavery*. Berkeley: University of California Press, 1980.
Wiens, Mi Chu. "Masters and Bondservants: Peasant Rage in the Seventeenth Century." *Ming Studies* 8:57–64: Spring 1979.
Wilkes, Kathleen. *Real People*. Oxford: Clarendon Press, 1988.
Wittgenstein, Ludwig. *Philosophical Occasions 1912–1951*. Ed. and trans. James Klagge and Alfred Nordmann. Indianapolis: Hackett, 1993.
Wolf, Arthur P., "Gods, Ghosts, and Ancestors." In *Religion and Ritual in Chinese Society*. Ed. Arthur P. Wolf. Stanford, Calif.: Stanford University Press, 1974.
Wolf, Arthur P., and Huang Chieh-shan. *Marriage and Adoption in China, 1845–1945*. Stanford, Calif.: Stanford University Press, 1980.
Yang Lien-sheng. "The Concept of *Pao* as a Basis for Social Relations in China." In *Excursions in Sinology*. Cambridge, Mass.: Harvard University Press, 1969.
Yü Ying-shih. "'Oh Soul, Come Back' A Study in the Changing Conceptions of the Soul and Afterlife in Pre-Buddhist China." *Harvard Journal of Asiatic Studies* 47:2 (1987), 363–95.
Zeitlin, Judith. *Historian of the Strange: Pu Songling and the Chinese Classical Tale*. Stanford, Calif.: Stanford University Press, 1993.
Zito, Angela, and Tani E. Barlow. "Introduction." In *Body, Subject, and Power in China*. Chicago: University of Chicago Press, 1994.

Index

Actors: and actions, 230, 245; and ancestor worship, 119; and burial rituals, 121; competition between, 229; and Confucianism, 203; and farmers, 218–19; and ghosts, 118; identity of, 217, 226, 228, 231, 290; as impersonators, 205, 215, 216, 228–29, 232; and the sovereign, 282; in *zaju*, 12–13
Adoption, 137, 283, 285
Aisin Gioro, 183, 270
Aleni, Giulio, 94–95
The Ambassadors (painting; Holbein), 50, 323n45
Anamorphosis, 50–51, 323n43
Ancestor worship, 15, 101–2, 119, 299
Anderson, Anna, 170–71
Anhao (password, secret signal), 257, 258
Aquinas, Thomas, 91
Arias, verse, 12, 20, 54, 319n2b
Art and Money (Shell), 30
Audience, 48, 49, 53
Authenticity, 14–15, 33, 260; and Du Liniang's self-portrait, 28, 29–30, 32; philosophy of, 14–15. See also *Zhen*

Bao (reciprocity), 191, 193–97, 263, 264, 282, 284
Bao, Lord. *See* Di, Lord
Barbarian Prince (*Mudan ting*), 53–54, 131
Barlow, Tani, 308, 309
Baudelaire, Charles, 309
Beijing: fall of, 146, 147, 148, 150, 152, 153, 207, 250; Forbidden City in, 146, 148, 207
Benye (vocation), 223, 225

Berlin, Isaiah, 297
Bian He, jade disk of, 164
Bian Yujing (*Taohua shan*), 163
Binbai (prose dialogue), 12, 20
Birch, Cyril, 43, 54, 76, 86, 87, 329n54
Bo Ya, 221
Body, Subject, and Power in China (Barlow and Zito), 308, 309
Body and soul, 36, 115; separation of, 34, 39–40, 94–95, 114
The Book of Rites, 141, 184
Boswell, John, 300, 301
Brilliant, Richard, 169
Buddhism, 10, 29, 59, 181, 182; and family, 138–39; introduction of, 92–93
Bynum, Caroline Walker, 91, 236

Cahill, James, 14, 51, 54, 315
Cai Yisuo (*Taohua shan*), 154, 156, 191
Cannibalism, 91, 296
Cao Cao, 227
Capra, Frank, 303, 305, 306, 307–8
Catholicism, 94, 95, 243; *vs.* Protestantism, 244, 299
Cavell, Stanley, 24, 303–8, 311, 312
Certeau, Michel de, 301
Ceyin (compassion), 3
Chang, Chu-shu, 7
Chang, Shelley Hsueh-lun, 7
Chang E, 44, 166, 168, 170
Changsheng dian (*The Palace of Eternal Life*), 40, 114, 120, 204
Chartier, Roger, 309

345

Chastity, 189, 197, 263; and dreams, 34, 78; of Du Liniang, 34, 40, 78, 115, 135; and identity, 281; and self-mutilation, 190; in *Taohua shan*, 163, 190, 327n10; in *A Winter's Tale*, 294
Chen Hongshou, 14
Chen Zuiliang (*Mudan ting*), 19, 22, 33, 47, 76, 85, 137; and contents of Du Liniang's grave, 112, 116; and false deaths, 43, 134
Cheng (sincerity), 14, 173, 269, 304
Chengqin (to marry, form one family), 26, 98, 99
Chongzhen Emperor (*Taohua shan*), 154, 198, 261, 283; death of, 146, 148, 152, 157, 186, 268, 279, 280; and identity, 176, 201, 205, 267; legitimacy of, 205, 272, 336n29; sons of, 150, 197, 240, 250
Chou (clown), 231, 234, 259
Chou (enmity, requital), 187
Chou (match, cipher), 229
Christianity, 91–92, 94, 113
Chuanqi (classical short stories), 42
Chuanqi drama, 12, 84, 114, 120, 234, 320n13; complexity of, 20, 42; early Qing, 40; endings in, 23, 245; language of, 5, 11, 85, 319n2b; second acts of, 43
Chuci (*The Songs of the South*), 34
Chunxiang (*Mudan ting*), 19, 22, 32, 71, 137, 291; and death of Shang Xiaoling, 122–23; and Du Liniang's self-portrait, 29, 36, 37, 45, 57, 58; and Du Liniang's story, 20, 60, 61; on Du Liniang's virginity, 105, 327n10; escape of, 42–43; and ghost of Du Liniang, 86, 88–89, 123; identity of, 134; and identity of Du Liniang, 38, 87
Cixi, Empress Dowager, 332n28
Clark, T. J., 32, 57, 59
Clunas, Craig, 7
Coffins, 114–15, 116, 121, 160, 326n43
Cole, Alan, 138
Colonialism, 296, 297
Comedy: Greek Middle, 22; and lawsuits, 26; marriage in, 22–23, 294, 299; in *Mudan ting*, 84–85, 92, 101, 115, 151; Shakespearean, 25–26; in *Taohua shan*, 258, 286; and tragedy, 24–26

Comedy of Errors (Shakespeare), 169
Commentary of the Three Wives, 64, 65, 68, 78
Compassion, 2–4, 9
The Compelling Image (Cahill), 14, 51
Confucianism, 2, 163, 204; in dream and waking, 97–98; and family relationships, 69, 136, 283, 328n39, 332n48; and friendship, 245; and identity, 126, 135, 170, 212, 223; and marriage, 301, 303; recognition in, 128; redemption in, 193; and theatre, 201, 203, 222; view of supernatural in, 107; virtues of, 124, 271–72
Confucius, 6, 195–96, 222, 281; and Kong Shangren, 149, 212–13, 272
Crown Prince (*Taohua shan*), 230, 259; claims of, 246, 250, 252, 253, 255, 267, 268, 269, 271, 336n31; costume of, 272; and Hongguang Emperor, 150–51, 197, 247, 248, 249, 354; identity of, 175, 176, 244, 247–48, 253, 266, 267, 275; imprisonment of, 202, 240, 249, 260; investiture of, 204; recognition of, 286; release of, 202; torture of, 241–43, 244, 249, 267; trials of, 150, 239–41, 246–47, 267; and Zuo Liangyu, 261
Cultural differences, 7, 295–98, 301, 302, 305, 311–17

Dan (female lead), 12, 200, 220, 231, 234, 235, 259
Danto, Arthur C., 84
Daoism, 119, 149, 154, 156, 287; and portraits of Qianlong Emperor, 181, 182
Daoist Shi (*Mudan ting*), 5, 30, 49, 89, 139; and Du Liniang's coffin, 115, 121; and Du Liniang's disinterment, 39, 86, 121; and Du Liniang's identity, 37, 38, 86–87, 88; and Du Liniang's memorial service, 71–72; and Du Liniang's self-portrait, 53; and Du Liniang's tomb, 19, 120; and Liu Mengmei, 47, 85, 90, 101, 128; and sacred tablet, 61
Daston, Lorraine, 83, 325n23
David, Jacques-Louis, 32, 57, 324n56
Dechang, Prince (Hongguang Emperor), 208, 211–12, 249, 260, 275, 276

"De la Conscience" (Montaigne), 242
Dening, Greg, 75–76
Descartes, René, 253, 255, 266, 291, 322n42; and cross-cultural communication, 93, 302, 303; on dreams, 67, 76, 89, 94, 324n8; and Shakespeare, 237, 307; skepticism of, 254, 259
Di, Lord (Judge), 65, 109, 118, 242
Dialogue, prose (*binbai*), 12, 20
Di Cosmo, Nicola, 315
Dili xinshu (*Earth Patterns*), 121
Ding (ingot), 110–11, 113
Discourse on the Method (Descartes), 67, 94, 324n8
Disguise, 11–12, 13–14, 181
Dong Qichang, 14, 51, 315
Dong Yue, 13, 14
Dorgon, Regent, 147
A Double Life (film), 216
Doubles, 169, 175–77, 178, 331n12
Dowager Empress, 275–76
Dowries, 184–86, 332n33; of Li Xiangjun, 184, 187, 188, 189, 193, 284, 287
Doyle, Sir Arthur Conan, 109
Dreams: and cross-cultural parallels, 298, 302; Descartes on, 67, 76, 89, 94, 324n8; of Du Liniang, 34, 39–40, 63, 64, 66, 67, 69–75, 78, 94, 124, 135, 200, 324n8; and Du Liniang's self-portrait, 43–44, 46, 55, 57; and identity, 66, 71; and knowledge, 76, 95; and legal issues, 64–65, 74, 76, 95, 96; and memory, 324n1; and subjectivity, 52, 64, 67, 78, 95; and theatre, 74–76, 84; and trials, 65, 80; and waking, 65–67, 78, 91, 95, 97–98, 99, 253, 266, 322n40
Du Bao (*Mudan ting*), 76, 163, 293; and Chen Zuiliang, 137; doubts of, 20–27, 28, 60, 80, 82, 91, 131, 140, 177, 241, 285; and Du Liniang, 19, 108, 117, 120, 126, 140–41, 146, 190, 196, 324n6; and Du Liniang's description of the underworld, 100; and Du Liniang's identity, 33, 35, 36, 40, 69, 126–27, 129, 134, 170; and Du Liniang's self-portrait, 58; and Emperor, 140, 146, 278; and human emotions, 141; identity of, 314; and Liu Mengmei, 99, 108–9, 120, 130, 135, 136, 146; and living *vs.* dead, 98, 101; punishment of, 108, 158; recognition of Du Liniang by, 21–22, 27; and resurrection of wife, 43, 135, 140, 141; and supernatural, 83, 88, 89, 106–7
Du Liniang (*Mudan ting*): chastity of, 34, 40, 78, 105, 106, 115, 135, 162, 163, 327n10; coffin of, 114–15, 121; and competing testimonies, 81–82; corpse of, 39, 61, 111, 114, 129, 160; death of, 97, 98, 105, 108, 122, 136–37; disinterment of, 85, 86, 90, 145, 162; dream of, 34, 39–40, 63, 64, 66, 67, 69–75, 78, 94, 124, 135, 200, 324n8; and Du Bao, 19, 108, 117, 120, 126, 140–41, 146, 324n6; Emperor's promise to, 98, 125, 128, 139, 285, 287; ghost of, 19–23, 30–34, 36, 37, 45–47, 56, 60–62, 71, 74, 77, 87–89, 105, 106, 111, 119, 160, 171, 286, 294, 321n16, 324n10; as ghost *vs.* human, 123, 129, 134, 139, 140; as human, 23, 40, 42, 59–60, 88–89, 91, 96, 97, 99, 100, 123, 140, 141; identification with, 217, 219, 222; identity of, 26, 27, 31–34, 39, 40, 43, 45, 65, 69, 72, 73, 89, 96, 99, 100, 104, 106, 150, 157, 160, 162, 241, 275, 280, 314, 321n16; identity of, and self-portrait, 166, 167, 168, 170, 171, 172, 177; and knowledge, 76, 91; Liu Mengmei praised by, 135–36; Liu Mengmei searched for by, 67–68, 71; Liu Mengmei's meetings with, 78, 140; and Liu Mengmei's name, 70, 71, 73, 74; and Liu Mengmei's redemption, 107, 327n14; Liu Mengmei's relationship with, 80, 92, 98, 101, 103, 116, 128; Liu Mengmei's reunions with, 163; and marriage, 116–17, 134, 136, 158, 160, 278, 294, 295, 300, 324n10; and mirrors, 52, 55, 57, 59–60, 61, 62; mortality of, 29; and mother, 275; multiple versions of, 34–38, 39, 55, 60, 61, 62; painting of self-portrait by, 35–36, 49, 61, 62, 66, 75, 129, 130, 190; personal history of, 60–61; poem of, 80; resurrected version of, 36, 66, 99, 102, 106, 111–16, 123–28, 135–36, 138, 140, 145; resurrection of, 20, 21, 37–38, 39, 44, 56, 61, 62, 69, 70, 78, 81, 85, 86, 90, 92, 97–101, 105, 113, 121, 151, 191, 291, 293, 294;

Du Liniang (*Mudan ting*) (*continued*)
  role of, 217; sacred tablet of, 35, 39, 61, 102, 129, 160, 325n29; self-portrait of, 14, 19, 28–62, 71, 160–68, 170–72, 177, 299; self-portrait of, described, 53, 54–55; and Shang Xiaoling, 215; specific identity of, 24, 177; tomb of, 111–12, 116, 120; trial of, 47, 66

Eberhard, Wolfram, 117–18
Elizabeth I, 282
Emerson, Ralph Waldo, 303, 305, 307–8
Emperor (*Mudan ting*), 85; and Du Bao, 140, 146, 278; and Du Liniang, 60, 63, 99, 278, 294; and identity, 170, 254; identity of, 135, 145–47, 184, 196, 207; and Lady Zhen, 134; onstage, 146; power of, 246; recognition by, 21, 23, 128, 139, 140, 160–61; tests of, 23, 61, 62, 90, 91, 98; twofold promise of, 98, 125, 128, 139, 285, 287; and underworld, 107; verdict of, 20, 26, 27, 40, 42, 96, 98, 99, 105, 106, 121, 126, 135, 145, 150
Emperor (*Taohua shan*), 157, 158, 159; identity of, 146, 205, 230–31, 267, 268–69; legitimacy of, 199, 206, 260; playing role of, 203–4, 205, 214; portraits of, 233; singularity of, 232. *See also* Hongguang Emperor
Emperors, 15; and hierarchy, 279–81; names of, 212, 333n17; as orphans, 333n8; portraits of, 179–83; specific identity of, 181–83, 208; in *zaju*, 145–46
the Enlightenment, 93, 296, 308, 309–10
Essais (Montaigne), 167
Essai sur le Don (The Gift; Mauss), 186

Family reunions, 22–23, 151, 163, 276–77, 285, 293
Filial piety, 138, 189, 262, 268, 272; and identity, 277, 281; and parents, 281, 286; and reciprocity, 194–96, 263; and self-mutilation, 263–64. *See also* Confucianism
Film, 24–25, 52, 175, 216, 303, 305, 323n49
Foucault, Michel, 308–9, 310–12, 317
The Four Masterworks of the Ming Novel, 6
Frame, Donald, 331nn9,10, 335n3
Frazer, James, 308, 317

French Revolution, 133
Friendship, 4, 8, 10, 195, 245
Frye, Northrop, 26, 292, 293, 299
Fu (husband), 101
Fu, Prince (*Taohua shan*), 148, 176, 183, 211, 249, 270, 274–76; and Ma Shiying, 208, 255; and Ruan Dacheng, 208, 280, 286; and Shi Kefa, 279
Fumo (supporting male role), 205–6, 234

Gao Jie, 261
Gao Ming, 299
Gaslight (film), 303, 305
Gernet, Jacques, 302–3
Ghosts: and actors, 118; and ancestors, 8, 101–2; definitions of, 102; and identity, 8–11, 15, 102; and legal issues, 83, 103, 108; in *Liaozhai zhiyi*, 1–2, 4; and Liu Mengmei, 24, 47, 49, 55, 96, 100, 103, 119–20; and marriage, 102, 103–4, 116, 125; recognition of, 22; and sexual intercourse, 125; terms for, 99, 100, 119, 121, 326n45; tests for, 23, 59–60, 87, 88, 89–90; *vs.* humans, 5, 88, 89, 93, 96, 99, 103–4, 123–24, 126. *See also* Du Liniang: ghost of
Gifts, exchanges of, 185–87, 193
Ginzburg, Carlo, 315–17
Goethe, Johann Wolfgang von, 297
The Golden Bough (Frazer), 308
Gongan literature, 65, 109, 242
Greenblatt, Stephen, 289, 305–6, 308, 312
Gu Bingqian, 229
Gu Kaizhi, 320n10
Guan Yu, General, 118
Guangxu Emperor, 333n8
Guanyin, 35, 44, 166, 168, 170, 332n28
Gui (ghost), 99, 100, 119
Gui (soul), 92, 93
Guihua (ghost talk, nonsense), 100
Guimen (ghost gate), 121
Guo Tuo (*Mudan ting*), 30–31, 74, 76, 129, 130, 131
Guomen (bride's entrance to the house), 99

Han dynasty, 93, 104, 227
Han people, 7

Han Yu, 138
Han Zicai, 69
Handan Ji (*The Record of Handan*; Tang Xianzu), 63, 78
Hansen, Valerie, 104, 108, 121
Hao, 211
Hegel, Georg Wilhelm, 292
Henry VIII, 133, 299
Herder, Johann Gottfried, 295–96, 297
Hermione (*The Winter's Tale*), 290, 294, 295, 299
Hershatter, Gail, 174, 177
Hobbes, Thomas, 264–66, 268, 271, 282
Holbein, Hans, 50
Holmes, Sherlock, 65, 109
Homer, 305
Hongguang Emperor (*Taohua Shan*), 134, 146, 147, 148, 255; capture of, 149; claims to throne of, 150–51; compared with Kangxi Emperor, 272; and Crown Prince, 150–51, 197, 247, 248, 249, 254; and Dowager Empress, 276; and Huang Degong, 149, 159, 207, 269, 277, 279; and identity, 151, 159, 183, 184, 198, 204, 206, 208, 213, 263, 267, 269, 270, 274; identity of, 174–76, 177, 275, 276, 282; investiture of, 232; legitimacy of, 205, 268, 274, 275; and Liu Liangzuo, 273, 278; and Li Xiangjun, 161, 199, 200, 206, 207, 214, 235, 259, 270–71; and Mandate of Heaven, 197; and Ma Shiying, 152, 197, 232, 233, 280, 281, 282, 283; names of, 211–12; personal identity of, 178, 182, 224; portrait of, 179; as Prince Dechang, 208, 211–12, 249, 260, 275, 276; as refugee, 269, 277; and Richard II, 282–83; and Ruan Dacheng, 152, 197, 205, 207, 214, 232–33, 281; and subjects, 284; and theatre, 169, 214, 215, 227, 234, 246, 260, 270; transfer of loyalty to, 201; value of, 207; and Zhang Wei's vision, 263, 267
Hongguang shilu chao, 208, 249–55, 261, 333n11
Honglou meng (*Dream of the Red Chamber*), 39, 47–49, 75, 322nn36,40
Hongyan boming (rosy-faced beauty's unlucky fate), 165

Hongzhi Emperor, 133
Hou Fangyu (*Taohua shan*): and actors, 229; and Emperor, 183, 249; and fall of Nanjing, 157, 223, 276; flight of, 147–48; friends of, 153, 154, 246, 255, 276; in hiding, 149, 154, 155; identity of, 209; letter to Zuo Liangyu, 223–24, 255, 256, 257, 258; and Li Xiangjun, 167, 176, 177, 184, 187, 188, 190, 191, 213, 214, 231, 235, 272, 274, 276, 278, 283, 284; Li Xiangjun's first meeting with, 192–94; and Li Xiangjun's identity, 176, 177, 184, 190; Li Xiangjun's love for, 167, 191; Li Xiangjun's reunion with, 163; and Liu Jingting, 222–23, 224, 225, 237; and peach blossom fan, 163–66, 172–73, 178, 184, 188, 191–93, 263, 284; and Peach Blossom Spring, 156, 158, 159; and Prince Dechang, 267; and Prince Fu, 286; in prison, 250, 255; and punishment, 250; return to family, 151, 276–77; and Ruan Dacheng, 186, 187, 250, 255–56; and Zhu Yousong, 274
Hou Xun, 268
Huaben stories, 127, 326n2, 337n43
Huang Degong, General, 240, 247, 261, 267, 278, 280; and Hongguang Emperor, 149, 159, 207, 269, 277, 279
Huanhun ji (*The Record of the Soul's Return*), 93. See also *Mudan ting*
Human beings *vs.* ghosts, 5, 88, 89, 93, 96, 99, 103–4, 123–24, 126
Human nature, 2–4, 6, 7, 8, 216; of Du Liniang, 23, 40, 42, 59–60, 88–89, 91, 96, 97, 99, 100, 123, 140, 141. See also *ren*
Hume, David, 42, 91, 170, 291, 325n16
Hun (soul), 92, 93
Hunt, Lynn, 133

Identity: of actors, 119, 121, 217, 226, 228, 231, 290; adjudication on, 65, 72, 86, 96, 123, 132, 145, 247, 268; and appearance, 36, 55–56, 61, 62, 259; of brothers, 277–78; and bureaucracy, 157–58; and causal integrity, 72; and chastity, 281; and complexity, 92; and Confucianism, 126, 135, 170, 212, 223; continuity of, 9; culpability and, 66;

Identity (*continued*)
different types of, 34–38, 174, 183–84, 290; and dreams, 66, 71; economy of, 34, 45; of Emperor, 145–47, 183, 206; and filial piety, 277, 281; fragmented, 50, 57, 62, 71, 73; and ghosts, 8–11, 15, 102; and hierarchy, 6–7; human, 30, 159; and kinship, 138; and knowledge, 314; and legal issues, 41–42, 324n6; and loyalty, 234–35, 277, 281; as matter of choice, 126, 273, 285; and mirrors, 32–33, 55, 57, 98; in *Mudan ting*, 20, 34, 65, 119, 149; mutual creation of, 280–81, 287; and names, 69, 72, 73, 74; and narrative, 41–42, 60–61, 321n18; paradoxes of, 93; and patriarchy, 119, 272, 273, 277; and politics, 6–7, 157; and portraiture, 167, 168–71, 174–78, 179–80, 236; and prostitution, 167–68, 170, 174, 176, 207, 216–17; and responsibility, 137; and resurrection, 91; in *Taohua shan*, 149, 159, 213–14, 245, 275; tests of, 77, 205, 254; and theatre, 75, 237–38, 246; and torture, 241–42; unitary, 67, 72, 73, 130, 321n16; in Western traditions, 26, 40–42, 67, 91, 321n18. *See also* Personal identity; Specific identity; *and under particular characters*
It Happened One Night (film), 305

Jesuits, 301–2, 315
Ji Liuqi, 204–5, 246, 333n5
Ji Yun, 82, 96
Jia (false), 28, 99
Jia Rui (*Honglou meng*), 47–49, 75
Jiajing Emperor, 133
Jian (licentiousness), 80
Jiang Shaoshu, 51
Jianmin (hereditary chattel), 118
Jiayi shian (Wen Bing), 247
Jiazi (*jianü*, foster child), 283
Jing (singing clown character), 13, 220
Jinqian di (source of money, ground for wealth), 218, 223
Jinshu (*History of the Jin*), 291
Jiufang Gao, 237

Judaism, 243–45

Kagemusha (film; Kurasawa), 175
Kangxi Emperor, 33n8, 203, 205, 268; and Kong Shangren, 272, 273; portraits of, 170, 171, 180
Kant, Immanuel, 296, 303, 305, 306, 307, 309, 310, 312
Kaye, Otis, 30, 31, 320n3
Kleeman, Terry, 104–5, 111, 120
Ko, Dorothy, 49, 304
Kong Shangren, 4, 8, 191, 225, 245, 263, 285; and Confucius, 149, 212–13, 272; and Crown Prince, 266, 271; family of, 212–13, 276; on identity, 159, 162, 273; and legitimacy of emperors, 268, 272, 275; and peach blossom fan, 184, 190; politics of, 152, 153; on role-playing, 237, 242–43, 259
Kuhn, Philip, 179, 331n25
Kurasawa, Akira, 175
Kutcher, Norman, 179, 331n25

Laitou Yuan (*Mudan ting*), 30–31, 33, 39, 47, 61; and disinterment of Du Liniang, 86, 112, 121
Landscape painting, 53–54, 315
Language: in *chuanqi* drama, 5, 11, 85, 319n2b; in *Mudan ting*, 5, 54, 76, 85, 87, 100, 101
Lantern Festival, 234, 336n27
Lan Ying, 152, 154, 210
Legal issues, 26, 47, 65, 80; in dreams, 74, 76; and ghosts, 83, 103, 108; and identity, 41–42, 324n6
Leibniz, Gottfried, 316
Lei Yingzuo (*Taohua shan*), 157–58
Leonardo da Vinci, 50
Leontes (*The Winter's Tale*), 25–26, 290, 291, 293, 295, 299
Leviathan (Hobbes), 264
Li, Lady, 189
Li, Wai-yee, 20, 64, 67
Li Wa, 337nn35,43
Li Xiangjun (*Taohua shan*), 147; chastity of, 148, 176, 190; doubles of, 176–77; dowry of, 184, 187, 188, 189, 193, 284, 287; and Du

Liniang, 161, 200, 203, 211, 219; in hiding, 149, 154, 155; and Hongguang Emperor, 161, 199, 200, 206, 207, 214, 235, 259, 270–71; and Hou Fangyu, 167, 176, 177, 184, 187, 188, 190, 191–94, 213, 214, 231, 235, 272, 274, 276, 278, 283, 284; Hou Fangyu's first meeting with, 192–94; Hou Fangyu's reunion with, 163; and identity, 206–7, 213, 226, 260; identity of, 174, 175, 176, 177, 178, 184, 187, 190, 208–11; and Li Zhenli, 176, 187, 208, 209, 210, 211, 217, 222, 223, 231, 276, 283, 284, 286–87; and marriage, 158, 159, 186–89, 197, 231, 272–73, 274, 278, 283, 287; and Ma Shiying, 227, 228, 229, 230; and Mi Heng, 228; naming of, 209–11; and peach blossom fan, 162–64, 166–74, 177, 178, 183, 184, 188, 189, 190, 199, 233, 263, 330n8; as performer, 203, 206, 208, 215, 226–28, 230, 259, 262; price of, 207; as prostitute, 151, 152, 176, 183, 186, 192, 193, 211, 214, 273, 276; role-playing of, 226–28, 231, 234, 237; and Ruan Dacheng, 184, 186, 187, 188, 227, 228, 230, 231, 235, 255, 284; and Su Kunsheng, 161, 217, 220; wedding of, 186; as Yang Jisheng, 228; and Yang Wencong, 191, 192, 201, 211, 217–18, 231, 235, 284, 286–87

Li Yu, 77–78, 315, 320n13, 328n34

Li Zhenli (*Taohua shan*), 147, 149, 186, 187, 188, 192, 245; and acting, 218, 226; in hiding, 154; and Li Xiangjun, 217, 222, 223, 231, 283, 284, 286–87; and Li Xiangjun's identity, 175, 176, 187, 208, 209, 210, 211; as mother, 273–74; name of, 174; and peach blossom fan, 164, 165, 172, 173; on singing, 218, 219; and Su Kunsheng, 276; and Tian Yang, 283–84, 287

Li Zhi (*Taohua shan*), 14–15, 125–26, 278, 304

Li Zicheng, 146, 148, 250, 268

Liangmin (commoners), 118, 223

Liaozhai zhiyi (Pu Songling), 1–2, 11, 103, 216

Liezi, 237

Lin Daiyu (*Honglou meng*), 49

Lin Shidui, 275, 276, 336n31

Ling (soul), 92

Literature: coincidence in, 307–8, 312, 316, 317; comparative, 6, 291, 312–13; *gongan*, 65, 109, 242; historicism in, 293–94, 296, 303, 306, 307, 308, 310, 312–13; and language, 85; loyalist, 152; Ming-Qing, 284, 289; national, 33, 313; of supernatural, 42, 102; vernacular, 65; Western, 22, 24, 50

Liu Cui (*Yu chanshi*), 13

Liu Jingting (*Taohua shan*), 156, 192, 193, 220, 257; flight of, 273; and Hou Fangyu, 222–23, 224, 225, 237; identity of, 203, 213, 260; in prison, 250, 255; and role-playing, 237, 245, 262; as storyteller, 222–23, 224–26; and Su Kunsheng, 246

Liu Liangzuo, 205, 207, 273, 277, 278, 280

Liu Mengmei (*Mudan ting*), 19, 330n3; and Daoist Shi, 47, 85, 90, 101, 128; and dreams, 63, 64, 66–67, 69–71, 72, 77, 94; and Du Bao, 99, 108–9, 120, 130, 135, 136, 146; and Du Liniang's ghost, 33–34, 47, 49, 55, 86, 96, 119–20; and Du Liniang's grave, 82, 85, 86, 112, 114, 116, 120; and Du Liniang's identity, 177, 190, 280; Du Liniang's meetings with, 78, 140; and Du Liniang's name, 70, 127; Du Liniang's relationship with, 80, 123, 140; and Du Liniang's resurrection, 37–38, 98, 121; Du Liniang's reunions with, 163; and Du Liniang's self-portrait, 28, 30, 32, 37, 39, 44–45, 67, 68, 69, 72, 87, 160, 165–66, 172, 320n8; as examination candidate, 129, 130, 131, 132; as ghost, 24, 100; and ghosts, 24, 47, 49, 55, 96, 100, 103, 119–20; as grave robber, 20, 23, 31, 38, 90, 99, 108, 129, 132, 326n2; and human nature, 30, 141; identity of, 24, 30, 31, 34, 38, 43, 73, 129, 131, 157, 321n16; and language, 100; and marriage, 102, 103, 117, 126–28, 136, 140, 158, 160, 162, 278, 295, 300; name of, 43, 69, 70, 71, 73, 74, 130; punishment of, 108; recognition by, 21, 128; sexuality of, 46–49, 96, 125; and supernatural, 83, 85, 87, 90

Liu Zeqing, 207

Locke, John, 41–42, 43, 60, 291, 321n18
Loyalty (*zhong*), 269; to Emperor, 198, 201; and identity, 234–35, 277, 281; to Ming, 12, 222, 245, 249, 252, 262, 265; and obedience, 263, 264, 265, 314; in Qing, 232, 245, 265, 267; and reciprocity, 264; of Shi Kefa, 203, 249, 252, 261, 264; and torture, 314; of Zuo Liangyu, 198, 263, 267
Lü Zhongyu, 79, 80–81, 83
Lugui bu (*Record of the Ghosts*; Zhong Sicheng), 119
Lushi (exposure to the elements), 103
Lüshi (regulated verse), 315
Luther, Martin, 299

Ma Shiying (*Taohua shan*), 148, 151–52, 153, 158, 265; and Crown Prince, 249; and fall of Ming dynasty, 157, 222, 240; and Hongguang Emperor, 152, 197, 232, 233, 280, 281, 282, 283; and Hou Fangyu, 256, 257, 258; and identity, 159, 236; and Lady Tong, 274–75; and Li Xiangjun, 227, 228, 229, 230; political enemies of, 156; and Prince Fu, 208, 255; and punishment, 261–62, 267; and Revival Society, 191; and Ruan Dacheng, 230, 249, 250, 274; and Shi Kefa, 249, 251–53, 254, 262; and Su Kunsheng, 220; on theatre, 230, 231, 260, 285; and Yang Jisheng, 231; and Yang Wencong, 214, 230; as Yan Song, 228, 231
Macbeth (Shakespeare), 79
Mair, Victor, 315
Manchus, 146, 150, 152, 159, 202, 277; and fashion, 12, 232; fear of, 251; and Ming monarch, 268; and Shi Kefa, 249, 251, 262, 330n2; surrender to, 207; women and, 132, 133, 189. *See also* Qing dynasty
Mao Zedong, 248
Marie Antoinette, Queen, 133, 156
Marriage, 15, 98–99, 194; and ancestor worship, 299; and authenticity, 28; and choice, 301, 304; in comedy, 22–23, 294, 299; companionate, 304; and Confucianism, 301, 303; and dowries, 184–87, 332n33; and Du Liniang, 116–17, 134, 136, 158, 160, 278, 294, 295, 300, 324n10; in film, 24–25;
ghosts and, 102, 103–4, 116, 125, 139, 324n10; and Jesuits in China, 301–2; and Liu Mengmei, 102, 103, 117, 126–28, 136, 140, 158, 160, 162, 278, 295, 300; between living and dead, 101, 104; and Li Xiangjun, 158, 159, 186–89, 197, 231, 272–73, 274, 278, 283, 287; Mencius on, 117; and money, 184–87, 189; in *Mudan ting*, 22, 26–27, 104, 106, 116, 127, 128, 134, 136, 140, 141, 278, 294–95, 297, 298, 299, 300, 303; and prostitution, 196–97, 337n35; and remarriage, 277–78; same-sex, 300, 301; in seventeenth-century England, 298–99; in *Taohua shan*, 154–55, 184–90, 278, 283–84, 287, 294–95; in *The Winter's Tale*, 294, 297
Mauss, Marcel, 186
Meditations (Descartes), 94, 253–54, 306, 307
Mencius, 9, 10, 117, 195, 304; on human nature, 2–4, 6, 8
Mi Heng, 227
Miao Shunbin (*Mudan ting*), 24, 30, 130, 131–32
A Midsummer Night's Dream (Shakespeare), 25
Ming (name), 69, 211
Ming dynasty: actors in, 118, 245; court entertainment in, 145–46; culture of, 7, 11–12; dreams in, 64, 84; fall of, 4, 5–6, 117, 146, 147, 149, 156, 157, 183, 191, 206, 222, 239, 240, 261, 294; fashion in, 11–12, 232; and grave robbing, 90; histories of, 5, 132, 149, 156, 206, 239, 240; landscape paintings in, 54, 315; late, 204, 273; legal codes of, 103, 326n43; literature of, 284, 289; loyalty to, 12, 222, 245, 249, 252, 262, 265; marriage in, 125, 304; portraiture in, 51; problem of legitimacy in, 248, 329n1; Southern, 134, 254; sovereign's family life in, 133; theatre in, 11–12, 84, 118; transition to Qing from, 232, 244, 245, 279
Mingfeng ji ("The Record of the Calling Phoenix"), 227, 229, 231
Mingji nanlue (Ji Liuqi), 202, 204, 205, 246, 274, 333n5
Mirrors: and Du Liniang, 35, 52, 55, 57, 59–

60, 61, 62; in film, 52, 323n49; in *Honglou meng*, 47–48, 75; and identity, 32–33, 55, 57, 98; and portraiture, 51, 323n48
Mo (lead male character), 12
Mohists, 196
Money: and marriage, 184–87, 189; in the underworld, 109–11, 113, 115
Monkey King (*Xiyou ji*), 13–14
Montaigne, Michel de, 166, 167, 168, 169, 242, 243, 244
Mothers and Sons in Chinese Buddhism (Cole), 138
Moye (branch occupations), 223
Mu Lian, 138
Mu Mocai, 79, 80
Mu of Qin, Duke, 237
Mudan ting (*Peony Pavilion*; Tang Xianzu), 4, 19–141, 200, 274, 275, 305; characters in, 85, 190; and Christian theology, 91–92, 95; and comedy, 84–85, 92, 101, 115, 151; competing testimonies in, 81; connection between family and nation in, 132, 133, 134, 135, 158; dreams in, 65, 67, 75, 78, 91, 95, 97, 99, 253, 266, 322n40; ending of, 245–46, 285, 299, 314; event that inspired, 79; family relations in, 126, 128, 285, 287; garden in, 39, 43; identity in, 20, 24, 34, 65, 119, 149; influence of, 330n1; interpretations of, 79–82; language of, 5, 54, 76, 85, 87, 100, 101; as legal case, 80; as literary text, 290; marriage in, 22, 26–27, 104, 106, 116, 127, 128, 134, 136, 140, 141, 278, 294–95, 297, 298, 299, 300, 303; performance of, 5, 84; plots of, 5, 19–20, 42–43; realism in, 76; recognition in, 21–22, 23, 27, 128, 139, 140, 160–61, 285; retellings of, 71; reunions in, 163, 285; role of Emperor in, 145–46, 241, 278; and socioeconomic conditions, 7; subjectivity in, 67, 80, 92, 94, 124; and *Taohua shan*, 117, 146, 151, 158–59, 161, 162–63, 203, 219, 261, 272, 278, 280–81, 283, 285; and theatre, 75, 118; and the underworld, 107–9; and *The Winter's Tale*, 291–94, 297, 299–300, 302, 303, 313–15, 317. See also particular characters
"Mugua" (*Shijing*), 193, 194, 196, 197

Multiple Personality Disorder (MPD), 41, 215

Nanjing, 146, 193, 202, 276; fall of, 147, 149, 150, 152, 159, 206; government of, 148, 240, 241, 249, 255; politics of, 248, 252, 253, 255, 257, 261, 271; and refugees, 154, 155, 158, 274, 287
Nanke ji (*The Record of Southern Bough*; Tang Xianzu), 63, 64
Naoshang ("Mourning the Dead"; *Mudan ting*), 122
Narrative, 41–42, 60–61
Neo-Confucianism, 124
New Historicism, 306
Nietzsche, Friedrich, 309, 322n42

Obeyesekere, Gananath, 302
Old Ceremonial Assistant (*Taohua shan*), 150, 262, 268, 272, 273, 336n21; in epilogue, 245; as *fumo*, 205–6, 234; in prologue, 149, 203, 205–6, 213, 271; and Ruan Dacheng, 153, 201, 261
Othello (Shakespeare), 25
Owen, Stephen, 124

Pagden, Anthony, 297, 311
Parfit, Derek, 41, 291, 321n18
Parmagianino, 57
Pascal, Blaise, 322n42
Patriarchy, 27, 119, 135, 277
Peach Blossom Fan. See *Taohua shan*
Peach blossom fan (*taohua shan*): and dowry, 189; as portrait of Li Xiangjun, 166–74, 177, 178, 184, 188, 189, 190, 199, 228, 233, 263, 330n8; second, 199–200, 271; value of, 164–65, 330n6
Peach Blossom Spring, 152–54; society in, 158, 278–79, 287; staging of, 155–56; yearning for, 155, 156–57, 158, 159
Perdita (*The Winter's Tale*), 294, 314
Personal identity, 4–8; and compromise, 150; and consumerism, 7; continuity of, 10; and ghosts, 8–11; of Hongguang Emperor, 178, 182, 224; of Li Xiangjun, 174, 175; and names, 69; and paternity, 135; and peach blossom fan, 165–74; and portraiture,

Personal identity (*continued*)
174–78; and reincarnation, 9, 10, 13; and science fiction, 215; and specific identity, 6–7, 8; and theatre, 146; uncertainty about, 134
Perspective, scientific, 50–52, 53, 322n42
Petrarch, 305
Phèdre (Racine), 25
Photographs, 168–69, 171, 177
Pingduo (gauge), 35–36
Pipa ji (*The Story of the Lute*; Gao Ming), 299
Plaks, Andrew, 6
Platform Sutra, 59
Plato, 41, 76, 322n42
Po (soul), 92
Poetry, 43, 59, 80, 135, 321n26
Politics, 12, 27, 179; and identity, 6–7, 157; in Nanjing, 248, 252, 253, 255, 257, 261, 271; of Su Kunsheng, 221, 222; in *Taohua shan*, 4, 153–54, 215, 229–30, 248, 258, 329n1; and theatre, 201, 202, 215, 248, 263, 269, 273
Portraiture, 38–39, 45–46, 54, 298; and identity, 167, 168–71, 174–78; and individuality, 179–80, 182; and mirrors, 51, 323n48; and prostitution, 177–78, 180
The Postman Always Rings Twice (film), 24–25
Privacy, 48, 49–50, 52, 59, 78, 322n39
Prostitution: and acting, 202–3, 216, 218; and foster mothers, 283, 284–85; and identity, 167–68, 170, 174, 176, 207, 216–17; and Li Xiangjun, 151, 152, 176, 183, 186, 192, 193, 211, 214, 273, 276; and marriage, 196–97, 337n35; and portraiture, 177–78, 180; in *Taohua shan*, 151, 152, 163, 164, 219
Pu Songling, 1, 3–4, 11, 103
The Pure Land Ghost Festival Sutra, 138

Qianlong Emperor, 76, 183, 331n25, 333n8; portraits of, 180–83
Qiannü lihun (*Qiannü Leaves Her Spirit*), 39–40, 114
Qianzi wen (*Thousand Word Classic*), 5
Qideng (tomb lamp, lacquered lamp), 87, 325n34
Qin (emotional intimacy, consanguinity), 69

Qin dynasty, 154, 156, 157
Qin Gui, 106
Qin Shihuang, 158, 270
Qing (passion), 19, 285
Qing dynasty, 80, 114, 216, 329n1, 332n27, 333n8; consolidation of power by, 151; dreams in, 64; early, 239, 304; fashion in, 12; filial piety in, 272; identity in, 271; legal codes of, 103, 127–28, 304; literature in, 284, 289; loyalty in, 232, 245, 265, 267; transition to, 232, 244, 245, 279. *See also* Manchus
Qiqing (natural desires), 159

Racine, Jean, 25
Rawski, Evelyn, 181, 332n27
Reciprocity (*bao*), 191, 193–97, 263, 264, 282, 284
Recognition (*ren*): and marriage, 26–27; in *Mudan ting*, 21–22, 23, 27, 128, 139, 140, 160–61, 285; in Shakespeare, 25–26; in *Taohua shan*, 27, 260, 269–70, 277, 281, 285–86, 287
"The Record of Inside the Pillow," 78, 322n40
Reincarnation, 1–2, 71; and personal identity, 9, 10, 13
Religion: popular, 108, 117–18. *See also* Buddhism; Catholicism; Christianity; Daoism; Judaism
Ren (benevolence), 304
Ren (human, personhood), 3, 99, 100, 304
Ren (lover), 101
Ren (status), 270
Renaissance, European, 50, 299, 305, 316
Renaissance Self-Fashioning (Greenblatt), 289
Rendao jiaogan (human union), 125
Renfu (workmen), 101
Renqin (ceremony of recognition), 27
Renren (person of fellow-feeling), 2, 9
Renshi zhuan (Tang dynasty tale), 125
Revival Society (*Taohua shan*), 147–49, 152–54, 156, 157, 260–61, 333n11; and Li Xiangjun, 177; and Ma and Ruan clique, 191, 234–35, 255; and Su Kunsheng, 221; and Wei Zhongxian, 283

Ricci, Matteo, 51, 94, 301
Richard II (Shakespeare), 50, 282–83, 323n43
Rongna (countenance), 320
Rorty, Amèlie Oksenberg, 291
Ruan Dacheng (*Taohua shan*), 147, 148, 151–52, 158, 169, 200, 201; as actor, 232, 233–34, 236, 259, 260; and allegiance, 265; beating of, 153–54; costuming of, 232–33, 236; and fall of Ming dynasty, 157, 222, 240, 279; and Hao Fangyu, 186, 187, 250, 256, 257, 258; and Hongguang Emperor, 197, 205, 207, 214, 232–33, 281, 336n27; and identity, 159, 236; identity of, 260; and Liu Jingting, 222; and Li Xiangjun, 184, 186, 187, 188, 227, 230, 231, 235, 255, 284; and Ma Shiying, 230, 249, 250, 274; political enemies of, 156; and Prince Fu, 208, 280, 286; and punishment, 261–62, 267; and Revival Society, 191, 234–35; on role-playing, 231, 234; and self-understanding, 237; and Shi Kefa, 252, 253, 255, 256, 263, 279–80, 286; and Su Kunsheng, 220, 221, 226, 267; and Wei Zhongxian, 147, 220, 222, 232, 234, 235, 268, 283; as Zhao Wenhua, 228
Rugu (as before), 113
Runbi ("moistening of the pen"), 110

Sahlins, Marshall, 302
Sexuality, 46–49, 66, 96, 125
Shakespeare, William, 169, 236–37, 282–83, 323n43; comedy and tragedy in, 24, 25–26; and perspective, 50, 79; skepticism in, 306, 307. *See also particular plays and characters*
Shang Xiaoling: acting theories of, 219; death of, 121, 122, 161, 215, 217; identity of, 118–19, 121–22
She (snake), 291
Shell, Marc, 30, 113, 177
Shen (soul), 92
Shen qi cheng (embodying sincerity), 173
Shenwei (sacred tablet), 35, 39, 61, 102, 129, 160, 325n29
Shi (individual), 270
Shi (scholars), 223
Shi (solid), 124

Shi (to know, recognize), 260, 269, 270
Shi Kefa, 148, 151–52, 185, 274; and Crown Prince; and Emperor, 205, 267; and fall of Yangzhou, 133, 262; and Lady Li, 189; as loyalist, 203, 249, 252, 261, 264; and Ma Shiying, 249, 251–53, 254, 262; and northern claimant to throne, 250–52, 253, 255; and Prince Fu, 279; punishment of, 249–50; and Ruan Dacheng, 252, 253, 255, 256, 263, 279–80, 286; seal of office, 280; "Seven Reasons Against" (memo), 249, 254–55; suicide of, 149, 256–57, 262, 267, 330n2, 336n21; and theatre, 262; and Zhang Wei's vision, 263, 336n29
Shiding (ten ingots), 110
Shiguan chao (money string), 110
Shijing, 135, 193, 194, 196, 197
Shili (to effect propriety), 124
Shoemaker, Sydney, 40–41
Shuangkuai (refreshing, pleasant), 153
Shuiyin (liquid silver, mercury), 112–13, 115
Shun Emperor, 203
Shunzhi Emperor, 146–47
Sima Qian, 263
Sincerity (*cheng*), 14, 173, 269, 304
Six Dynasties, 152, 201
Socrates, 321n18
Sommer, Matthew, 332n33, 337n35
Song dynasty, 85, 106, 326n43, 330n3, 331n24
Song Qi, 279, 280
Spanish Inquisition, 243, 244
Specific identity, 184, 203, 206, 243; and compassion, 9; and doubles, 178; of Du Liniang, 24, 177; of Emperors, 181–83, 208; and ghosts, 15; of Hongguang Emperor, 174–76, 177; of Liu Mengmei, 24, 30; of Li Xiangjun, 208–9; in *Mudan ting*, 24; and personal identity, 6–7, 8; and portraiture, 170, 171, 174–78; and relationships, 15, 128–29; of Wang Liulang, 8–9
The Spring and Autumn Annals, 149
Stanislavski, Constantin, 216, 219
Strassberg, Richard, 212
Struve, Lynn, 330n2, 333nn5,11, 335n1
Su Kunsheng (*Taohua shan*): and acting, 203, 209, 220, 222, 226, 229, 237, 241, 242–43,

Su Kunsheng (*Taohua shan*) (*continued*) 245; and Du Liniang, 220; flight of, 273; and Hou Fangyu, 239, 267; and identity, 260; and Li Xiangjun, 161, 217, 220; and Li Zhenli, 276; and Liu Jingting, 246; and peach blossom fan, 164–65, 172–73, 184, 191; political beliefs of, 221, 222; and Ruan Dacheng, 220, 221, 226, 267; on singing, 219, 220, 224, 225; and Zuo Liangyu, 149, 150, 157, 197, 258, 262, 267

Su Shi, 53

Subjectivity: and dreams, 52, 64, 67, 78, 95; and mirrors, 52, 59; in *Mudan ting*, 67, 80, 92, 94, 124

Suicide, 190, 263; of Shi Kefa, 149, 256–57, 262, 267, 330n2, 336n21

Sumptuary laws, 232

Supernatural: and Du Bao, 83, 88, 89, 106–7; literature of, 42, 102; and Liu Mengmei, 83, 85, 87, 90; proof of, 87, 90–91; and theatre, 84, 118, 119; *vs.* natural, 82, 83–84, 86, 91, 92, 95, 163

Swatek, Catherine, 337n2

Taizhou School, 14, 304

Tang dynasty, 78, 93, 104, 114, 120, 125, 322n40

Tang Xianzu, 4, 8, 71, 93, 125, 141, 282; allusions of, 291; and Descartes, 302; dream plays of, 63–64, 78; and identity, 72; influence of, 330n1; preface to *Mudan ting* of, 19, 63, 126, 234; and supernatural, 83, 100

Tao Qian, 152, 154, 155, 156, 287

Taohua shan (*Peach Blossom Fan*; Kong Shangren), 145–287; appearance in, 55; belief and behavior in, 270; characters in, 103, 206, 209; chastity in, 163, 190, 327n10; coercion of belief in, 26, 264–65; comedy in, 258, 286; disparities of knowledge in, 79; and Emperor, 121, 134, 146, 202–4, 259; ending of, 246, 260, 285; and entertainers, 118, 259–60; exchanges in, 191, 193, 196; and fall of Ming, 5–6, 147; family in, 132, 273, 276–77; framing of, 42; historical accuracy of, 330n2; identity in, 149, 159, 213–14, 245, 259, 275, 285; as literary text, 290; as loyalist literature, 152; loyalty in, 198, 201; marriage in, 154–55, 184–90, 278, 283–84, 287, 294–95; and *Mudan ting*, 117, 146, 151, 158–59, 161, 162–63, 203, 219, 261, 272, 278, 280–81, 283, 285; performance of, 5, 155; plot of, 5, 149; politics in, 4, 153–54, 215, 229–30, 248, 258, 329n1; prostitution in, 151, 152, 163, 164, 219; punishment for the dead in, 107; recognition in, 27, 260, 269–70, 277, 281, 285–86, 287; relationship between lord and vassal in, 197; reunions in, 163; simultaneity in, 120; skepticism in, 89, 253; and socioeconomic conditions, 7; and theatre, 76, 199–238, 215, 260, 290; as work of history, 149, 293–94; and *Yanzi jian*, 203. *See also particular characters*

Taohua yuan ji ("The Record of Peach Blossom Spring"; Tao Qian), 152, 153, 154, 155, 159

Theatre: and Confucianism, 201, 203, 222; culture of, 314; and dreams, 74–76, 84; and Hongguang Emperor, 169, 214, 215, 227, 234, 246, 260, 270; and identity, 75, 146, 237–38, 246; Ma Shiying on, 230, 231, 260, 285; in Ming, 11–12, 84, 118; and *Mudan ting*, 75, 118; and obedience, 264; and politics, 201, 202, 215, 248, 263, 269, 273; role *vs.* person in, 215, 290; and Shi Kefa, 262; and supernatural, 84, 117, 118, 119; in *Taohua shan*, 76, 199–238, 260, 290; and tombs, 120–21

"Three Crimes and Five Reasons Against His Elevation" (Hou Fangyu), 249

Three Wives (critics), 20, 65, 68, 78

Ti (devotion between brothers), 277

Tian Yang, 187, 188, 191, 209, 214; and Li Zhenli, 283–84, 287

Tong, Lady (*Taohua shan*), 248, 274, 275, 336n31

Torture, 241–45, 249, 255, 298, 314, 335n3

Tripitaka (*Xiyou ji*), 13

Tsien, Tseun-hsuin, 111

Tu Wei-ming, 296

Tuanyuan (grand reunion), 22–23
Twelfth Night (Shakespeare), 169
Twenty-four Paragons of Filial Piety (*Ershisi xiao*), 195

Ukiyo-e (Japanese prints), 177
Underworld Magistrate (*Mudan ting*), 30, 102, 104, 106, 114, 119; and identity, 157; and money, 109–11, 113, 115

Vico, Giambattista, 297
Vinograd, Richard, 38–39, 45

Wakeman, Frederic, 189
Wang Liulang (*Liaozhai zhiyi*), 1–4, 5, 8–11, 13, 15
Wang Xifeng (*Honglou meng*), 47–48, 75
Wang Xiuchu, 132, 133, 189
Wang Zhaojun, 168
Wang Zhiming, 241, 267
Wanli Emperor, 133–34, 208, 270
Watson, James, 184, 285
Wei, kingdom of, 227
Wei Zhongxian, 221; and Ruan Dacheng, 147, 220, 222, 232, 234, 235, 268, 279, 283
Wen Bing, 247
Wen Tianxiang, 264
Western thought, 67, 82, 91–94, 315; and literature, 22, 24; visual perspective in, 50–52
West Lake (Hangzhou), 53–54, 64
"What Is Enlightenment?" (Foucault), 308, 309–10, 312
Wilkes, Kathleen, 321n18
The Winter's Tale (Shakespeare), 25–26, 290; compared with *Mudan ting*, 291–94, 297, 299–300, 302, 303, 313–15, 317
Wittgenstein, Ludwig, 298, 303, 308, 317, 318, 322n42
Wobei (one of us, our sort), 225, 237
Woderen (*anderen*, my beloved), 100
Wolf, Arthur, 8, 101
Women: and ancestor worship, 15; filial piety of, 189; identity of, 170; and Manchus, 132, 133, 189; names of, 174; self-portraits by, 14

Wu Song, 226
Wu Yingji (*Taohua shan*), 153, 157, 261

Xi Shi (beauty), 53
Xia Yunyi, 210
Xiang (think, looks like), 271
Xiaoqing cult, 49–50, 58, 217
Xiezhao, 165
Xiezhen ("Inscribing a Likeness;" Act 14 of *Mudan ting*), 29, 165
Xihu mengxun (*Dream Seekings of West Lake*; Zhang Dai), 64
Xin (trustworthiness), 269
Xing (punishment, torture), 242
Xiyou bu (*Supplement to the Western Journey*; Dong Yue), 13, 14
Xiyou ji (*Journey to the West*), 13–14
Xu (empty, plastic), 124
Xu Hongji (Duke of Wei), 269, 270, 277, 281
Xu Shuofang, 54, 76
Xu Wei, 13
Xuanzong, Emperor, 114, 120
Xunmeng ("Seeking the Dream"; *Mudan ting*), 122, 227
Xuqing (to be careless about passion), 124

Yan Song, 227, 229
Yang Jisheng, 227, 231
Yang Liensheng, 195
Yang Wencong (*Taohua shan*), 147, 187, 208, 209; and Hou Fangyu's forged letter, 255–56, 257, 258; and Liu Jingting, 224; and Li Xiangjun, 191, 192, 201, 211, 217–18, 231, 235, 284, 286–87; and Ma Shiying, 214, 230; and officials, 214–15; paintings of, 210; and peach blossom fan, 148, 162, 163–64, 172, 173, 210; and Ruan Dacheng, 186, 214, 230
Yang Xiaomei, 54, 76
Yangzhou, 132–33; massacre at, 149, 262
Yangzhou shiri ji (Wang Xiuchu), 189
Yanzi jian (*The Swallow Letter*; Ruan Dacheng), 214, 336n27; casting of, 148, 169, 200, 205, 227, 234; doubles in, 331n12; plot of, 169

Yao Emperor, 203
Ye Xianggao, 94, 95
Ye Xiaoluan, 217
Yeshi (unofficial histories), 133, 252, 257; and Crown Prince case, 239, 240, 246, 255, 267; of Hongguang's reign, 248, 274, 275
Yizi (foster son, sworn son), 283, 337n41
Yongle Emperor, 329n1
Yongzheng Emperor, 80, 180
Youqu (marvelous, entertaining), 173
Youshi (sepulchral chamber), 87
Youzi (beautiful visage), 321n14
Yu, Pauline, 312
Yu chanshi (Zen Master Yu, Xu Wei), 13
Yü Ying-shih, 92–93
Yuan brothers (philosophers), 14
Yuan dynasty, 114, 119, 146
Yuewei caotang biji, 82–83, 90, 96
Yuji (extra skill), 224, 225

Za (bit part), 200
Zaju (Northern drama), 12–13, 65, 77, 114, 282; Emperor in, 145–46
Zhang Dai, 64, 178, 186, 226, 324n1
Zhang Longxi, 312
Zhang Pu, 210
Zhang Wei (*Taohua shan*), 152, 155, 156, 158, 159; and Emperor, 277, 278, 279; on marriage, 287; and peach blossom fan, 154, 161, 165; vision of, 236, 261, 262–63, 267, 336n29
Zhao Wenhua, 227, 228
Zhaoshi guer (*The Orphan of Zhao*; Li Yu), 77
Zhen (likeness), 29, 30, 31, 33, 43, 111, 320n8
Zhen (real, authentic), 28–29, 31, 33, 43, 64, 99, 111, 283
Zhen, Lady (*Mudan ting*), 19, 27, 71, 91, 96, 98; and Du Bao, 136; and Du Liniang, 129, 134, 137, 138, 139, 140, 209, 276; and Du Liniang's identity, 36, 40, 86–89, 170, 291; and Du Liniang's story, 61; and human nature, 141; identity of, 174, 178; and Li Zhenli, 187; and motherhood, 101, 137, 139; recognition by, 21; resurrection of, 22, 42–43, 135, 140, 141
Zheng, Lady (Wanli Emperor's concubine), 133
Zheng Tuoniang, 183, 186, 202, 218, 226, 234, 259
Zheng Xuan, 92
Zhengming (rectify names), 128, 136
Zhenzhen gushi ("The Story of Zhenzhen"), 28, 47, 319n1
Zhiguai (short accounts of marvelous happenings), 42
Zhiyin (knower of the tone), 221
Zhong Sicheng, 119
Zhong Ziqi, 221
Zhongli Emperor, 205
Zhou Lu (*Taohua shan*), 157–58
Zhu family, 183
Zhu Xi, 124
Zhu Yousong, 148, 157, 211, 270, 274. *See also* Hongguang Emperor; Dechang, Prince
Zhuangtun (storehouses of grain), 218, 223
Zhuangzi, 37, 66, 291
Zi (style), 69, 73, 211, 257
Zichai ji (*The Record of the Purple Hairpin*; Tang Xianzu), 63–64
Zito, Angela, 308, 309
Zuo Chongxi, 104, 105
Zuo Liangyu, General (*Taohua shan*), 148, 152; Hou Fangyu's letter to, 223–24, 255, 256, 257, 258; loyalty of, 198, 261, 263, 267; move on Nanjing by, 147, 149, 197, 221–22, 240, 255, 256, 258, 261, 262; and Su Kunsheng, 149, 150, 157, 197, 258, 262, 267
Zuozhuan, 65, 210

The authorized representative in the EU for product safety and compliance is:
Mare Nostrum Group
B.V Doelen 72
4831 GR Breda
The Netherlands